POLITICS AND THE AMERICAN
TELEVISION COMEDY

ALSO BY DOYLE GREENE
AND FROM McFARLAND

*The Mexican Cinema of Darkness:
A Critical Study of Six Landmark Horror and
Exploitation Films, 1969–1988* (2007)

*Mexploitation Cinema:
A Critical History of Mexican Vampire, Wrestler,
Ape-Man and Similar Films, 1957–1977* (2005)

POLITICS AND THE AMERICAN TELEVISION COMEDY

A Critical Survey from
I Love Lucy through *South Park*

DOYLE GREENE

McFarland & Company, Inc., Publishers
Jefferson, North Carolina, and London

LIBRARY OF CONGRESS CATALOGUING-IN-PUBLICATION DATA

Greene, Doyle, 1962–
    Politics and the American television comedy : a critical survey from I love Lucy through South Park / Doyle Greene.
        p.   cm.
    Includes bibliographical references and index.

    ISBN-13: 978-0-7864-3235-6
    softcover : 50# alkaline paper ∞

    1. Television comedies — United States — History and criticism. 2. Television and politics — United States.   I. Title.
PN1992.8.C66G74 2008
791.45'6170973 — dc22
                                          2007035530

British Library cataloguing data are available

©2008 Doyle Greene. All rights reserved

No part of this book may be reproduced or transmitted in any form or by any means, electronic or mechanical, including photocopying or recording, or by any information storage and retrieval system, without permission in writing from the publisher.

Cover illustration ©2008 Photodisc

Manufactured in the United States of America

McFarland & Company, Inc., Publishers
   Box 611, Jefferson, North Carolina 28640
      www.mcfarlandpub.com

Table of Contents

Acknowledgments   vi
Preface   1
Introduction: Subverting the Medium   3

PART ONE. Is Avant-Garde Television Comedy Possible?

1. American Comedy and the European Avant-Garde   9
   Dada and Distraction: The Origins of Avant-Garde Comedy   9
   "Nightmare Farces": Surrealism and Silent Film Comedy   13
   The Other Marxism: Artaud and the Marx Brothers   19
   Waiting for Buster: Theater of the Absurd and American Film Comedy   22

2. The Culture Industry and American Television Comedy   29
   Camera, Cinema, Revolution: Benjamin, Artaud, and Adorno   29
   Adorno: The Culture Industry and Television   31
   The Dual-Character of Comedy and Drama in Early American Television   34
   From "Comedy-Variety" to "Situation-Comedy"   36
   Clash of the Titans: Lucy Ricardo versus Ralph Kramden   42

PART TWO. Deconstructing Television: American Television Comedy, 1951–1966

3. The Humor of Anomaly: Ernie Kovacs   49
   Ernie in Kovacsland   49
   The Cockeyed World: Kovacs and Benjamin   52
   Surrealism and Sight-Gags   56
   "The Intimate Vacuum"   58
   Poetry in Motion: Music, Montage, and "Sound to Sight"   62

Fanfare for the Modern Man: "Eugene," The Ernie Kovacs Show
(ABC, 1961)   65

4. Say "Dada": *The Soupy Sales Show*   78
    A Brief History of Children's Television   78
    Soupy Sales: The WNEW Years   84
    When Worlds Collide: On-Screen and Off-Screen Space   88

PART THREE. From Bumpkins to Bigots: American Television Comedy, 1962–1971

5. The Idiocy of Rural Life: *Green Acres*   99
    Barnyard Comedy   99
    Class Struggle: The Beverly Hillbillies   101
    Absurdist America: Green Acres   103
    The Life of the (Capital L) Law: Oliver Wendell Douglas   108
    Contradiction and Overdetermination: The Hooterville Order   112

6. Archie Bunker for President! The Crisis of American Television Comedy in the Counterculture Era   117
    Monkee Business   117
    The March on CBS: The Smothers Brothers Comedy Hour   120
    Culture Industry Counterculture: Rowan and Martin's Laugh-In   125
    The Great CBS Purge and the Rise of the Political Sitcom: All in the Family   133

PART FOUR. Anti-Television: American Television Comedy, 1975–1983

7. Game Shows of Cruelty: Chuck Barris and *The Gong Show*   141
    Disasters Waiting to Happen: The Dating Game *and* The Newlywed Game   141
    Two Minutes of Fame: The Gong Show   144
    The Process of Elimination   149
    "The King of Schlock"   150

8. Situationist Comedy: Andy Kaufman   156
    That's Entertainment: The World of Andy Kaufman   156
    "I Don't Know if You're Laughing with Me or Laughing at Me": Saturday Night Live, 1975   158
    "Maybe I Went Too Far": Pushing the Boundaries of Television   161
    "I Was Just Teasing in Fun": Taking on the Talk Show   171

"Andy Kaufman Is Not Funny Anymore!": Revenge of the
  Culture Industry 177
Requiem for a Comedian: "The Andy Kaufman Show,"
  Soundstage *(PBS, 1983)* 181
"A Sum of Spectacles": The Legacy of Andy Kaufman 190

PART FIVE. Is Avant-Garde Television Comedy Still Possible?

9. Damage Control: Comedy-Variety and Situation-Comedy
   After 1974 195
   Now Ready for Prime-Time Players: Saturday Night Live 195
   Happy Days *Are Here Again* 198
10. Fair and Balanced Satire: Against *The Simpsons* 200
    A Franchise Is Born 200
    Simpsons, Meet the Simpsons... 201
    Biting the FOX That Feeds It? 204
    Parody, Pastiche, Politics 206
11. Comedy Is Not Pretty: In Praise of *South Park* 212
    A Sore Sight for Eyes 212
    "Friendly Faces Everywhere..." 215
    Democracy Happens 219

Notes 225
Bibliography 249
Index 255

Preface

This book is a critical investigation of the politics and possibilities of "avant-garde" American television comedy, emphasizing the era from approximately 1951 to 1983. In terms of specific artists and shows, I have focused on the work of Ernie Kovacs, Soupy Sales, and Andy Kaufman, as well as producers Paul Henning (*The Beverly Hillbillies, Green Acres*) and Chuck Barris (*The Dating Game, The Newlywed Game, The Gong Show*). From a historical standpoint, I discuss the crisis in American television comedy during the cultural and political unrest of the late 1960s: variously represented by *The Monkees, The Smothers Brothers Comedy Hour, Rowan and Martin's Laugh-In*, and *All in the Family*. By way of a conclusion, and to provide a contemporary perspective on the arguments presented here, I will offer an assessment of the current state of avant-garde and political TV comedy. However, rather than attempt to condense or summarize twenty-five years of recent TV comedy, this conclusion concentrates on a comparative analysis of two specific shows: the referential postmodernism and ostensibly liberal politics of *The Simpsons* versus the confrontational absurdism and ostensibly conservative politics of *South Park*.

It bears mentioning that certain omissions were unfortunately, but necessarily, made. Because I focus exclusively on American television comedy, British television programs, such as *Monty Python's Flying Circus* (BBC, 1969–74), arguably the most famous example of avant-garde television comedy, and *The Young Ones* (BBC, 1982, 1984), were excluded. My focus on American television also meant that I had to avoid international television, and possible studies ranging from the TV work of Jean-Luc Godard in the 1970s to Univision's flagship comedy-variety show *Sábado gigante* (*Giant Saturday*, 1986–). Because I use 1983 as an approximate endpoint (excepting *The Simpsons* and *South Park*), many recent examples of possible avant-garde comedy since the 1980s are conspicuous by their absence, especially given the proliferation of numerous cable TV networks (HBO, Cartoon Network, Comedy Central, MTV, etc.), and local public access channels, as prospective sites for comedic experimentation. The performers and shows I have ultimately chosen best reflect, in my view, a TV comedy sharing the artistic and ideologi-

1

cal mission of Dada, Surrealism, Absurdism, Brecht, or the Situationist movement. Conversely, others have been given attention because they exemplify the artistic and ideological problems of postmodernism or provide overtly political comedy within conventional genres (sketch comedy, sitcoms, stand-up): approaches that have largely dominated television since the 1980s.

Nevertheless, I would not go so far as to say that any possibility of avant-garde TV comedy died with Andy Kaufman in 1984. In a more comprehensive setting, or a project focusing on recent TV comedy, numerous potential examples could have been addressed as case studies (with "potential" being the operative word): *It's Garry Shandling's Show* (Showtime, 1986–8; FOX, 1988–1990), *Married with Children* (FOX, 1987–97), *Mystery Science Theater 3000* (Comedy Central, 1988–1996; Sci-Fi Channel 1997–9), *Seinfeld* (NBC, 1990–8), *Get a Life* (FOX, 1990–1992), *The Jerry Springer Show* (syndicated, 1991–), *The Tom Green Show* (MTV, 1999–2000), and *Arrested Development* (FOX, 2003–6). Even within the focus on earlier TV, certain exclusions as potential case studies had to be made: *Your Show of Shows* (NBC, 1950–4); *Rocky and Bullwinkle* (ABC, 1959–61, 1964–73; NBC, 1961–4); *Gilligan's Island* (CBS, 1962–5); *The Wacky World of Jonathan Winters* (syndicated, 1972–4); *SCTV* (syndicated, 1976–80; NBC, 1981–3); the short-lived *Richard Pryor Show* (NBC, 1977); and Michael O'Donoghue's *Mr. Mike's Mondo Video* (a 1979 special NBC refused to broadcast, which was later released on home video). Admittedly, all could have eventually merited much greater consideration in a different scope or context. I do not claim to offer the last word on any debate with this project, but, perhaps, an opening salvo.

Ultimately, my argument is not only concerned with *what* might be classified as avant-garde and subversive TV comedy, but *in what ways* TV comedy can be read as avant-garde and subversive. I have adopted an interdisciplinary approach incorporating film studies, media studies, cultural studies, American history, art history, literary theory, and critical theory: specifically, the theories of Theodor W. Adorno, Antonin Artaud, Walter Benjamin, and Fredric Jameson. In addition to a close textual analysis of the performers and shows in question, I have emphasized contextualization of the various texts in the following areas: the specific historical context in which these shows were produced; the historical relationship of the avant-garde and comedy, dating back to the early twentieth century; the specificity of the medium of television to other forms of visual and mass media culture (cinema, painting, radio); and the nature of the television industry in a capitalist economy. Art, in whatever form, is not produced in a cultural or historical vacuum; it is both a product of, and a commentary on, the culture from which it emerged. It is from this perspective, and this framework, that the possibility of TV comedy as politically subversive and artistically avant-garde will be addressed.

Introduction: Subverting the Medium

This book is based on a contradiction. On the one hand, American television exemplifies the workings of the Culture Industry as defined by Theodor W. Adorno. Through systematic standardization, the "cognitive-value" of culture to provide, let alone *provoke*, any challenge to social conditions is neutralized; the Culture Industry supplies, and demands, predictable patterns of artistic production, consumer consumption, and ideological instruction.[1] In this context, American television comedy can not only be seen as a collection of highly uninspired, and uninspiring, situation-comedies and comedy-variety shows, but a history of cultural commodities disseminating dominant ideology.

Nevertheless, in certain instances, American television comedy has attained avant-garde and subversive moments (as absurd as it may initially appear to even use the words "avant-garde," "subversive," and "television" in the same sentence). In this respect, a central issue in discussing the possibility of avant-garde American television comedy is the politics of *form* and the politics of *content*. Shows such as *The Smothers Brothers* and *All in the Family* infused conventional genre forms (comedy-variety show, sitcom) with liberal political stances. In regard to political content, as Adorno suggested, "Artworks exercise a practical effect, if they do so at all, *not by haranguing but by the scarcely apprehensible transformations of consciousness.*"[2] For this reason, Adorno championed the literature of Kafka and Beckett over the plays of Brecht in capturing and criticizing the horrors of the modern world; he chastised Brecht's Marxist "didacticism" for ultimately overshadowing the confrontational power of his avant-garde formalism while arguing, "Kafka and Beckett arouse the fear that existentialism merely talks about."[3] The didactic approach to television comedy, politicizing content without challenging form, reached its full fruition and consequences in the sitcoms-as-morality plays of the 1970s, typified by *All in the Family* and *M*A*S*H*— shows which did not provide political criticism but proscribed idealistic, liberal-humanist political solutions well within genre and ideological boundaries.

Conversely, a show such as *Rowan and Martin's Laugh-In* adopted — or appropriated — current avant-garde styles and formal strategies while offering topical political comedy quite compatible with Establishment views. *Rowan and Martin's Laugh-In*'s rapid-fire, hodge-podge approach to the comedy-variety show manifested Fredric Jameson's assessment of the failure of postmodernism as the triumph of pastiche over parody: "Pastiche is, like parody, the imitation of a peculiar or unique, idiosyncratic style.... But it is a neutral practice of such mimicry, without any of parody's ulterior motives, amputated of the satiric impulse.... Pastiche is thus blank parody, a statue with blind eyeballs."[4] It is the postmodern approach to television comedy which also defines the ultimate failure of FOX's ostensibly subversive animated sitcoms (*The Simpsons* and especially *Family Guy* and *American Dad*), where cartoon surrealism and surface political commentary ultimately play second-fiddle to pastiche: a barrage of innocuous pop-culture references.

Ultimately, neither of these strategies is a satisfactory solution; form and content must be equally "politicized." In this way, performers such as Ernie Kovacs, Soupy Sales, and Andy Kaufman, along with shows such as *Green Acres* and *The Gong Show*, created a thoroughly political space with comedy. They did so with explicit, implicit, or even unintentional subversive messages; they produced difficult and demanding television that confronted as much as entertained the viewer; they tested the conventions and constraints of the medium and the Culture Industry itself: the deconstructions of television done by Ernie Kovacs's Surrealist sketch comedy and Soupy Sales's Dadaist children's shows; the TV-of-the-Absurd of *Green Acres*; the anti-art savagery of *The Gong Show*; Andy Kaufman's efforts to turn national television into a Situationist battleground. Jean-Luc Godard, one of the most artistically and politically radical film directors, once suggested, "The problem is not to make *political* films but make films *politically*."[5] It can also be said that "the problem is not to do *political comedy* but do *comedy politically*"—the essential difference between the "political comedy" of Norman Lear sitcoms and "doing comedy politically" in the case of Andy Kaufman's career. Ultimately, this book can be seen as an attempt not to analyze political TV comedy, but analyze TV comedy politically.

Not to be facetious, but this work does treat comedy quite seriously. In response to the idea that it is "just comedy," and that too much is read into comedy, I say that there is much more to comedy than making the public laugh, and perhaps not enough has been read into comedy as a cultural force. When Antonin Artaud formulated his conception of the "Theater of Cruelty" in *The Theater and Its Double*, he also championed the Marx Brothers:

> The poetic quality of a film like *Animal Crackers* might correspond to the *definition of humor*, if this word had not long since lost its meaning of total liberation, of *the total destruction of all reality in the mind....* If the Americans, to whom the spirit of this genre of film belongs, refuse to see these films as anything but humorous, and if insist on limiting themselves to the *comic and superficial connotations of the word "humor,"* so much the worse for them.[6]

This fundamental distinction between the *superficiality of comedy* and the *destructiveness of humor* Artaud posited is crucial in discussing the radical artistic and cultural possibilities that may, or may not, have occurred in American television comedy. If American television is the acme of a Culture Industry that homogenizes its cultural products to absolute triviality with ruthless efficiency, the cynic could easily suggest that television comedy already and continually accomplishes a "total destruction of the reality of the mind" in a way dialectically opposed to Artaud: not functioning as "total liberation" but absolute repression through mind-numbing consistency and conformity. The critical issue is whether, and to what degree, American television comedy has provided a space to not only *comically amuse* the intellect but *humorously assault* the viewer's perceptions and conceptions of reality, to confound audience expectations of entertainment, to shatter any confidence in a rational world, and to not only challenge *what* the viewer thought, but *how* the viewer thought — perhaps the most revolutionary prospect of all.

Part One. Is Avant-Garde Television Comedy Possible?

> The comic alone is able to give us strength to bear the tragedy of existence.
> — Eugène Ionesco, as quoted in
> *The Theater of the Absurd* (1962)

> There is nothing more painful than a tamed, disciplined public which feels obliged to applaud as one man, even things which are boring, things which it dislikes. Such a public is ready to goose-step.
> — René Clair, "Picabia, Satie, and the First Night of *Entr'acte*" (1967)

Chapter 1

American Comedy and the European Avant-Garde

> This session will be something definitive. These lunacies ... are not lunacies at all but what I would call new poetry. Surrealism in the cinema is only to be found in these films. Much more genuine Surrealism than in the films of Man Ray.[1]
> — Luis Buñuel, notes for a 1929 Madrid film festival featuring Charlie Chaplin, Buster Keaton, Harold Lloyd, and Harry Langdon

Dada and Distraction: The Origins of Avant-Garde Comedy

If avant-garde comedy had a patron saint, the title would belong to Alfred Jarry, author of the *Ubu* play cycle: *Ubu roi* (*King Ubu*), *Ubu cocu* (*Ubu Cuckolded*), and *Ubu enchaîné* (*Ubu Enchained*).[2] Without hyperbole, *Ubu roi* revolutionized modern theater overnight by provoking a near-riot and becoming the center of controversy for weeks after its Paris premiere in 1896 and immortal opening lines:

Pere Ubu: Shit!
Mere Ubu: Oh, that's pretty! Pere Ubu, You're a great big oaf!
Pere Ubu: Why don't I bash your skull in, Mere Ubu!

Originally conceived by Jarry in his teens as a puppet show mocking a particularly unpopular teacher, *Ubu roi* evolved into an intentionally crude and unintelligent parody of canonical Western theater, specifically Shakespeare's *Macbeth*. Replete with obscenity, sophomoric humor, nonsensical oratories, and violent slapstick, *Ubu roi* was specifically envisioned by Jarry to be "wretched and repugnant."[3] As with puppet shows, scenery was condensed into one painted backdrop, and the various acts designated by placards set on an easel describing the numerous scenes and locales. Reducing the actors to living marionettes, Jarry insisted they speak in robotic, affected voices and wear costumes of "little colour and historical accuracy as possible."[4] A vicious satire of war, greed, and human stupidity in general, *Ubu roi* chronicled the ambitions of the bloated, clownish Pere Ubu, a symbol of all things reprehensible in the modern world. Yet, as much as *Ubu roi* was a scandalous and highly unflattering denunciation of the bourgeois state and society, it was an equally scandalous and unflattering destruction of bourgeois theater. While they agreed on little else, much of the twentieth-century European avant-garde pointed to Jarry as inspiration: Dada, Surrealism, Antonin Artaud, and the Theater of the Absurd.

Dada was born in 1916 at a Zurich tavern christened "Cabaret Voltaire." The brainchild of poet Hugo Ball and dancer Emmy Hennings, the Dada movement attracted a number of artists from across Europe, including Jean Arp, Richard Huselbeck, and Tristan Tzara, who soon supplanted Ball as Dada's chief spokesman and, for lack of a better term, theoretician. Cabaret Voltaire featured performances defining Dada "anti-art" contempt for Western bourgeois conventions of beauty, taste, and relevance — concepts Dadaists felt were irrevocably destroyed in the ongoing carnage of World War I. As Marcel Janco proclaimed:

> We had lost confidence in our culture. Everything had to be demolished. We would begin again after the *tabula rasa*. At the Cabaret Voltaire we began by shocking the bourgeois, demolishing his idea of art, attacking common sense, public opinion, education, institutions, museums, good taste, in short, the whole prevailing order.[5]

The performances at the Cabaret Voltaire and later Dada revues included cacophonous music, thrashing dancers, elaborate and often misshapen costumes, absurd vignettes (such as excerpts from *Ubu roi*), polemical monologues, and, perhaps most famously, the notorious Dada "poetry-readings." Hugo Ball performed "sound-poems" made up of rhyming, meaningless phonetics recited somewhere between an automaton and a Catholic priest delivering a liturgy; his cardboard costume resembled a mechanical Pope. Other readings featured several performers shouting one or several poems in different meters, sometimes in a variety of languages both real and invented by the poet(s).[6] Performances were minimally rehearsed and frequently improvised; this allowed for a great deal of spontaneity, the opportunity for chance events to direct the performances, and a large measure of audience interaction — preferably hostile. Jean Arp described a typical evening:

Total pandemonium. The people around us are shouting, laughing, gesticulating. Our replies are sighs of love, volleys of hiccups, poems, moos, and miaowing of medieval *Bruitists* Tzara is wiggling his behind like the body of a belly dancer. Janco is playing an invisible violin and bowing and scraping. Madame Hennings, with a Madonna mask, is doing the splits. Huselbeck is banging away nonstop on the great drum, with Ball accompanying him on the piano, pale as a chalky ghost. We were given the honorary title of Nihilists.[7]

An evening at the Cabaret Voltaire usually concluded in stunned silence, mass participation, or a riot prematurely ending the performance. At the "Greatest-Ever-DADA-Show" in the spring of 1919, the final Dada performance in Zurich before Tzara relocated to Paris, the show was almost cut short twice due to the intense audience opposition, which the performers did their best to fuel. Delighted with the result, Tzara simply proclaimed the evening, "Final victory for DADA."[8]

As Walter Benjamin observed in his seminal essay "The Work of Art in the Age of Mechanical Reproduction" (1936), the Dada mission was not merely destroying the *commercial value* of art (profitability), but any *contemplation value* that art could create for its audience (profundity):

> The Dadaists attached much less importance to the sales value of their work than to its uselessness for contemplative immersion.... What they intended and achieved was a relentless destruction of the aura of their creations.... *In the decline of middle-class society, contemplation became a school for asocial behavior; it was countered by distraction as a variant of social conduct.* Dadaistic activities actually assured a rather vehement distraction by making works of art a center of scandal. One requirement was foremost: to outrage the public.[9]

Contemplation of art in "the decline of middle-class society" could become a form of ideological complicity; complacent contemplation with a book in a study, a painting in a museum, or a symphony in a concert hall — followed by the requisite appreciative sigh or polite applause — was the unconditional acceptance, appreciation, and approval of the culture that produced the artwork, and the culture the artwork represented.[10] *Distraction* entails a different mode of reception. While paradoxical, it can be said that the difference between contemplation and distraction is that distraction demands less attention while requiring more participation from the audience. Thus, distraction is explicitly not *diversion* in the sense of passive enjoyment, such as Georges Duhamel's condemnation of cinema as a "pastime for helots ... a spectacle that requires no concentration and presupposes no intelligence."[11] Rather, distraction encompasses both a sense of *dispassion* and *disruption*. In the sense of dispassion, distraction denies the sanctity and overpowering "aura" of the art-object (its "cult-value") by constructing a more casual relationship between the art-object and the audience; it allows for objective criticism, collective concentration, and even healthy skepticism (its "exhibition-value") — the estrangement effect of Brecht's theater, the audience response as part of a Dada performance, and the advent of cinema. "The film makes the cult-value recede into the background not only by putting the public in the position of the critic, but also by the fact that at the movies this position requires no attention. *The public is an examiner, but an absent-minded one.*"[12]

In the sense of disruption, distraction entails jarring the audience from "contemplative immersion" by generating a "shock effect." For Benjamin, the shock effect posited by Dada again found an inherently compatible site in cinema:

> Dadaism attempted to create by pictorial — or literary — means the effects which the public today seeks in the films.... The work of art of the Dadaists became an instrument of ballistics. It hit the spectator like a bullet, it happened to him, thus acquiring a tactile quality. It prompted a demand for the film, the distracting element which is also primarily tactile, being based on changes in place and focus which periodically assail the spectator.... The spectator's process of association in view of those images is indeed interrupted by their constant, sudden change. This constitutes the shock effect of the film, which like all shocks, should be cushioned by heightened presence of mind. By means of its technical structure, the film has taken the *physical shock effect* out of the wrappers in which Dadaism, as it were, kept it inside the *moral shock effect*.[13]

However, rather than Dada and Surrealist films of the 1920s (to be discussed shortly), Benjamin pointed to the work of Charlie Chaplin: "Before the rise of the movie the Dadaists' performances tried to create an audience reaction which Chaplin later evoked in a more natural way."[14] Nevertheless, it was Buster Keaton's aptly-titled *The Cameraman* (1928) which directly essayed the inherent power of cinema to "assail the spectator." As a young photographer named Buster, his bulky movie camera perpetually in tow, Keaton seeks a job in the MGM Newsreel Department as he attempts to record the everyday excitement of the world around him and, more importantly, impress the girl at the MGM office (of course, *The Cameraman* is an MGM film). Buster's first attempt at a newsreel is considered an unmitigated disaster due to his inability to "correctly" use the camera. By running the film in reverse, divers bounce out of the water and back onto the diving board. Through double exposures, a battleship appears to be sailing down the streets of Los Angeles, and traffic becomes a baffling scene where cars careen in every possible direction across the screen. Buster's first attempt at making a documentary newsreel is tantamount to making a Dada film *á la* René Clair or May Ray — the creation of a disordered and disorderly film universe. For his second assignment, Buster films a parade in Chinatown, which erupts into a Tong war. With his trademark ironic detachment — what could be seen as the embodiment of the receptive mode of *distraction*— Keaton stands in the middle of the chaos cranking his camera before seeking cover in a machine-gun nest, mounting his camera next to the machine-gun. However, instead of cranking the camera, he mistakenly cranks the machine-gun, issuing a hail of bullets instead of recording the action on film. Indeed, the "shooting" of the crowd with the camera is equated with "shooting" into the crowd with a gun, echoing Benjamin's assessment of the inherent power of Dada, which reached its full fruition in film: "*It hit the spectator like a bullet.*" In *The Cameraman*, violent social upheaval is no longer the domain of the gun, but the camera as well, the two literally working side by side.

"Nightmare Farces": Surrealism and Silent Film Comedy

After relocating to Paris, Tzara's Dada movement contentiously evolved into Surrealism in the early 1920s under the autocratic guidance of André Breton, who infused the Dada artistic project with a more systematic approach, highly influenced by Freudian psychoanalysis (the unconscious and especially the dream) and eventually Marxist ideology (world socialist revolution). However, Breton disdained self-conscious art films in favor of popular films such as Louis Feuillade's action-filled crime serials: "It's in *Les Vampires* [1915–6] that one should reach for the great reality of this century ... *Beyond fashion. Beyond taste.*"[15] American silent comedians were also hailed by the Surrealists. Salvador Dalí remarked, "Modernity ... does not mean ... Fritz Lang's *Metropolis* ... it also means comedy film, of the silly, nonsense type."[16] Surrealist Robert Desnos was a vocal champion of Mack Sennett and Hollywood serials. Sennett, who began his career as an actor and assistant to D.W. Griffith before forming his own Keystone Studios in 1912, made hundreds of his two-reel comedies, some featuring his most famous creation, the Keystone Cops. The surrealistic power of Sennett entailed excising the melodramatic narratives, bourgeois sentimentality, and transcendent morality steeped in Griffith's films by distilling cinema into pure motion and chaos: a series of illogical, comic situations; dangerous, suspense-filled predicaments; and the eventual anarchic, climactic chase that mocked rather than affirmed the establishment of social order.[17]

Considered an early and seminal "Surrealist" film (a problematic categorization that will be addressed shortly), René Clair's *Entr'acte* (*Intermission*, 1924; written by Francis Picabia) is constructed as a series of bizarre slapstick events. Picabia wrote in the film's program notes, "*Entr'acte* ... respects nothing except the desire to *burst out laughing, for laughing, thinking, and working are of equal value and indispensable to each other.*"[18] One of *Entr'acte*'s highlights are Man Ray and Marcel Duchamp playing chess on a rooftop, with the board superimposed with long shots of the Parisian cityscape; when rain is superimposed over the shots, they are doused with water from off-camera. Another scene has a ballerina pirouetting on a glass stage so the camera can look up her tutu; "she" is revealed to be a bearded Picabia. The extended "chase" finale suggests a merger of the frantic chaos of a Sennett two-reeler, the disorientating Dada motion studies of Fernand Léger's *Ballet mécanique* (*Mechanical Ballet*, 1924) and Man Ray's *Emak Bakia* (1926–7), and the startling imagery of Buñuel and Dali's subsequent *Un Chien andalou* (*An Andalusan Dog*, 1928).[19] A funeral procession winds through the streets of Paris, the carriage with the casket being pulled by a camel, and the mourners follow — skipping in slow-motion. When the carriage breaks loose and starts careening down the streets, the bereaved frantically pursue it in a lengthy, bewildering array of shots and techniques, including fast-motion, high-speed tracking shots, movement in all directions across the screen, double-exposures (one featuring the mourners running away from *and* running towards the camera), and inserts of point-of-view shots from a rollercoaster car careening on the winding tracks. Abrupt jump-cuts alternating with long dissolves turn the chase into a thoroughly disorientating whole that indeed attains a physical shock effect, even by virtue of its ability to induce motion sickness in the unsuspecting viewer. Eventually, the coffin flies off the carriage and lands in a field. As a small crowd gathers, the corpse flings open the casket, broadly grinning and dressed as a magician. He points his wand at each person, who, one by one, disappears via Mèliés-like jump-cuts, and then he disappears himself in a long dissolve. To end *Entr'acte*, a man leaps through a sheet of paper with the word *Fin* in slow-motion. After waving a finger at the audience as a gesture that the film is not over, the magician walks into the shot and slaps him. As the man lies prone, the magician kicks him in the temple; the shot of the man leaping through the paper is shown again *backwards*, repairing the rupture in the ending by ironically concluding the film with a violation of reality — and a blow to the head.

While Breton viewed literature as Surrealism's preferred vehicle for its strident attacks on bourgeois society, the visual arts (painting and cinema) became its primary weapon: Clair, Buñuel, Dalí, Max Ernst, and René Magritte, among others. However, what are often considered early Surrealist films were not made by Surrealists proper. *Entr'acte* was made in the conflict-ridden transitional period between Dada and Surrealism. Despite the participation of key Surrealists, *Entr'acte* is often considered a Dadaist film, or reflective of the evolution of Dada's avowed anti-art aesthetic into what Rose-Lee Goldberg succulently termed Surrealism's world of "nightmare farces."[20] *Ballet mécanique* was a wry juxtaposition of humans and machines in motion, including such images as gears churning with copulating fury, heavily made-up eyes and lips impassively blinking and smiling like a gaudy machine, a two-second loop of a woman climbing stairs copiously used throughout the film, and even a Cubist stop-motion animation of Charlie Chaplin. Using an array of cinematic techniques, ranging from montage, jump-cuts, pulsating zooms, and kaleidoscopic lenses, *Ballet mécanique* was an extension of the exploration of the "man-machine" relationship central to the early twentieth century avant-garde (Constructivism, Cubism, Futurism, and Dada). Rather than the stationary painting, cinema — the "motion picture" — served as a highly appropriate medium for chronicling and critiquing the modern age: an issue addressed by Benjamin in the 1930s, and a crucial element of the TV comedy of Ernie Kovacs.[21]

However, beyond the peripheral involvement of Man Ray, *Ballet mécanique* was not part of the Surrealist project, and is often classified as a Dada film. Man Ray himself made experimental films in the 1920s. His collaboration with Marcel Duchamp, *Anémic Cinema* (*Anemic Cinema*, 1924–6), was a minimalist motion study of "rotoreliefs": circular paintings of words and asymmetrical spirals spun on a wheel and filmed. Ray's own version of *Ballet mécanique*, *Emak Bakia*, was a motion study ranging from such images as a woman's legs as she frantically jitterbugged to cavorting geomantic shapes (flickering light patterns, spinning abstract sculptures, and stop-motion animation of variously shaped blocks). His final film, *Le Mystère du château de dé* (*The Mystery in the House of Dice*, 1929), was a sort of experimental home movie, described by John Baxter as "something between a travelogue, a Surrealist exploration of chance, and a spoof mystery story."[22] Man Ray was part of the Dada movement that evolved into Surrealism, and *Anémic Cinema*, *Emak Bakia*, and even *Le Mystère du château de dé* have also been considered more in keeping with Dada than Surrealism (the reaction to *Emak Bakia* from Ray's fellow Surrealists was decidedly unenthusiastic).[23] Another famous surrealist film, Jean Cocteau's *La Sang d'un poète* (*Blood of a Poet*, 1930), was roundly denounced by Breton and the Surrealist orthodoxy, with Cocteau long before deemed *persona non gratis* in the Surrealist movement by Breton.

In this context, the Surrealist interest in early cinema was initially and largely confined to critical curiosity and occasional enthusiasm. As Baxter noted:

> It was one thing to relish the vigor of Pearl White serials and Mack Sennett two-reelers or the naïve poetry of Feuillade, but quite another to use film to convey a Surrealist idea. To spend a year raising money and painstakingly create a film would be to sell out to the very establishment they were sworn to subvert. A few filmmakers compromised by exploiting cinematic tricks to achieve an effort consistent with Dada.... Slowing the camera down or running

it backwards, as René Clair did in *Entr'acte* and *Paris qui dort* (*Paris Sleeps*), and Cocteau in all his films, *interfered amusingly with reality* as Tzara had done with his cut-up texts ... but until 1928 the Surrealist interest in cinema ended there.[24]

Even after 1928, very few films came from the Surrealist movement proper, and Breton eventually viewed Surrealism's lack of engagement with the medium of cinema as one of the movement's major failures.[25] Man Ray's collaboration with Robert Desnos, *L'Etoile de la mer* (*Star of the Sea*, 1928) epitomized the Surrealist film as a strange, unsettling, dream-like journey replete with multiple and even conflicting symbols. Germaine Dulac and Antonin Artaud's *La Coquille et le clergyman* (*The Seashell and the Clergyman*, 1928) also emerged from the Surrealist movement. However, by the film's completion, Artaud publicly criticized Dulac for reducing the extremity of what he wanted to capture as the dream-experience *in toto* to mere dream-imagery; he had also rancorously parted ways with the Surrealist movement after Breton made Marxism its official political stance (to be returned to shortly). Not surprisingly, the film's premiere ended in a near-riot.

Rather, Buñuel's collaborations with Dalí, *Un Chien andalou* and *L'Âge d'or* (*The Age of Gold*, 1930), became the most famous Surrealist films; *Un Chien andalou* arguably became the *objet d'art* synonymous with Surrealism. However, Buñuel and Dalí were only dubbed official Surrealists by Breton *after* making the film, their appointment stemming from Breton's desire to capitalize on the film's obvious potential for controversy and rejuvenate a movement wracked by ongoing defections and Breton's arbitrary dismissals (René Clair was never officially made a Surrealist).[26] Moreover, Buñuel's own relationship with Surrealist cinema was, at best, ambivalent. Recalling his comments beginning this chapter, Buñuel endorsed the surrealism of American silent film comedy over the official Surrealist cinema of his colleagues, and it is not surprising that Buñuel preferred Keaton, Chaplin, and even *Entr'acte* over Man Ray.[27] Ray's films, while highly compelling in their own way, chronicled events more ethereal than comical, more mechanical than madcap (simply put, *Ballet mécanique* is much funnier than *Emak Bakia*). From its notorious opening sequence when the Man (Pierre Batcheff) slices the Woman's eye with a straight razor in grisly close-up (the Woman was played by Simone Mareuil; a dead sheep was used as a stand-in), *Un Chien andalou* can be seen as a two-reeler slapstick comedy where slapstick is magnified into the drives of lust, violence, and moral transgression; the comedy is exploded into a sadistic destruction of reality.[28] A brutal and macabre satire of the melodrama, silent film conventions, and bourgeois conduct, *Un Chien andalou* is the "nightmare farce" *par excellence*.[29] In a typical sequence, the Man looks out the window and watches a woman run over by a car, with obvious sexual arousal, and then rushes to grope the Woman with comical,

1. American Comedy and the European Avant-Garde   17

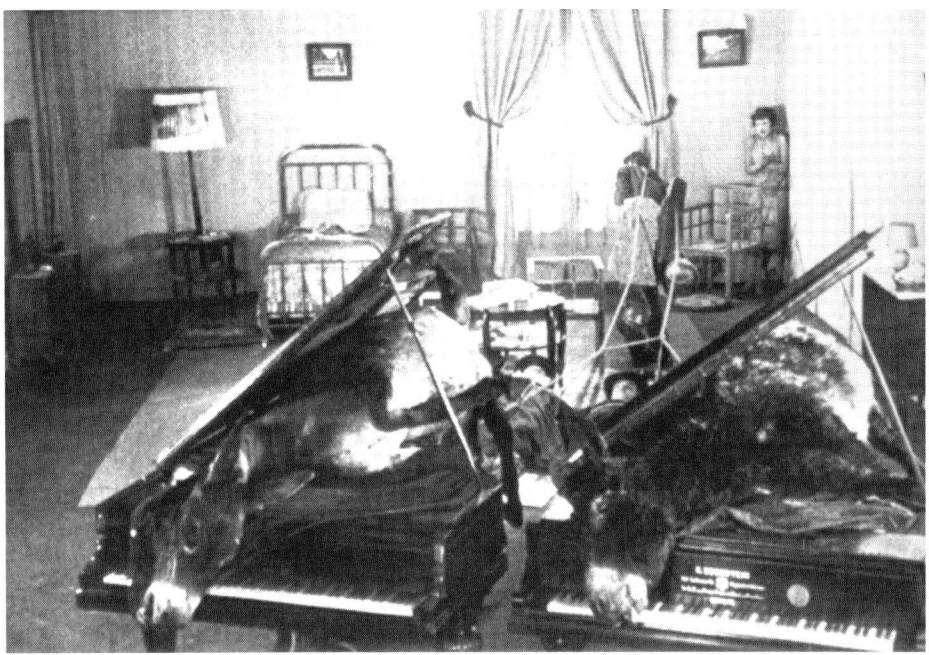

Slapstick Surrealism: Buñuel and Dalí's 1928 *Un Chien andalou* (Photofest).

exaggerated expressions of sexual pleasure; the Woman responds by briefly glancing at the camera with bored disdain. After chasing her around the room, he ponders the situation and then inexplicably attempts to pull two pianos toward her, each adorned with a dead, decomposing donkey and two lethargic priests tied between the ropes. The scene not only embodied Surrealism's provocative attack on the rational, but the Man's overstated straining and pratfalls exhibit a sense of pure physical comedy, much like Chaplin or Keaton (minus, of course, the dead donkey and priests). Meaningless subtitles and title cards discourage rather than provide any connections between events, and Buñuel adamantly (if perhaps a bit disingenuously) stated: "*Nothing*, in the film, *Symbolizes Anything!*"[30] Yet while the images may mean nothing, they do not discourage interpretation, but rather allow and invite *multiple* interpretations. For instance, from a symbolic standpoint, the donkey-priest-piano scene represents the Man's carnal desire and/or homicidal urges literally constrained by material manifestations of bourgeois morality.

    In the transition from Dada to Surrealist cinema, Rudolf E. Kuenzli suggested that one distinction that can be made is between

> *their different strategies of defamiliarizing social reality*.... The incoherent, non-narrative, illogical nature of Dada, which constantly defamiliarize the world

through cinematic manipulations, never lets the viewer enter the world of the film.... The cinematic apparatus is used by Surrealist filmmakers as a powerful means to realistically portray the symbolic order, which they then disrupt with shocking, terrifying images.[31]

With *Entr'acte*'s climactic chase, the frequent "cinematic manipulations" with the camera (slow- and fast-motion, double-exposures, non-diagetic footage) are what push the film towards Dada. Had the illogical finale been presented more "realistically," *Entr'acte* could be considered Surrealist: a camel pulling a coffin through the streets of Paris turning into a slapstick chase would not be out of place in any of Buñuel's film.

To make another distinction, Gilles Deleuze contended the cinematic transition from Dada to Surrealism can be seen in how the comedy of Keaton and Chaplin respectively embodied the ideological world-views that separated the two movements:

> Keaton's biographers and commentators have emphasized his *liking* for machines, and his affinity in this respect with Dadaism rather than Surrealism.... [T]his is the first important aspect of his difference with Chaplin, who advanced by means of tools and is *opposed* to the machine.... [T]here are two very different socialist visions, the communist-humanist in Chaplin, the other anarchistic-mechanistic in Keaton.[32]

In Deleuze's formulation, Keaton represented the anarchism of Dada, and the confounding and hilarious *interaction* of man and machine, captured in his precarious encounters with out-of-control machinery, such as the mystifying technological wonders in *The Electric House* (1922); the gigantic, adrift yacht and its oversized modern machinery in *The Navigator* (1926); and the individual's relationship to the cinematic apparatus in *Sherlock, Jr.* (1924) and *The Cameraman* (1928). Conversely, Chaplin embodied the Surrealist mission of world revolution and the dehumanization of humanity in a confounding and hilarious *struggle* of man against the machine, captured most overtly in *Modern Times* (1936) — which itself owed a considerable debt to René Clair's surreal comedy about mechanized modern life, *A Nous la liberté* (*Freedom for Us,* 1931).[33] While Deleuze's implicit construction of a "Keaton-Dada-anarchism-machine affection" versus a "Chaplin-Surrealism-Marxism-machine opposition" binary is ultimately too limited and limiting (as will be addressed in Chapter Three concerning Ernie Kovacs), Deleuze does point out that a central difference between Dada, Surrealism, and, by extension, Futurism was not so much *artistic* as *ideological*.[34] Dada embraced anarchy and nihilism as a reaction to the modern disaster of World War I. Choosing sides as World War II became all but certain, Futurism, under F.T Marinetti, aligned itself to Fascism, whereas Surrealism, under Breton, adopted Marxism as its official ideology. Beyond expressing cultural outrage at the bourgeoisie, each movement represented, and endorsed, a political solution to the modern world's crisis.

The Other Marxism: Artaud and the Marx Brothers

The problematic issues of the avant-garde, politics, and comedy emerging in the 1930s were best represented by Antonin Artaud. A poet, actor, playwright, and theatrical director, Artaud's lone contribution to Surrealist cinema was his screenplay for *La Coquille et le clergyman*.[35] Discussing the film in his essay "Cinema and Reality" (1927), he opposed two emerging strains of cinema: avant-garde abstract cinema (Man Ray) and dramatic narrative cinema (D.W. Griffith). Instead, Artaud contended:

> [C]inema creates situations that arise from the mere collision of objects, forms, repulsions, attractions. It does not detach itself from life but discovers the original order of things. The films that are most successful in this respect are those dominated by a certain kind of humor, *like the early Buster Keatons or the less human Chaplins....* A certain excitement of objects, forms, and expressions can only be translated into *the convulsions and surprises of a reality that seems to destroy itself with an irony in which you can hear a scream from the extremities of the mind.*[36]

In *The Theater and Its Double* (1936), Artaud's manifesto on the obsolescence of Western theater, he postulated a new, revolutionary form of theater: "the Theater of Cruelty." Decrying the failure of Western theater, Artaud wrote, "[I]t has broken with gravity, with efficacy that is immediate and pernicious — in short with Danger.... It has also lost the sense of true humor and of the physical and anarchistic, *dissociative power of comedy* ... that spirit of profound anarchy that is all poetry."[37] This concept of "dissociative power" in the work of Artaud becomes pivotal in Deleuze's assessment of thought and cinema, specifically in relation to Sergei Eisenstein and Artaud. In Eisenstein's films, the construction of shots complimented, contrasted, and even contradicted each other to generate the shock of *intellectual* or *associative montage*. The collision of images produced metaphorical meanings as well as a narrative teleology; said images were not "horizontal linkages" that merely told stories, but an escalating collision of shots that were "vertically stacked" one on top of another to provoke ideas.[38] For instance, in Eisenstein's *Potemkin* (1925), an account of a mutiny on a Russian battleship serving as a metaphor for the Russian Revolution, a shot of the captain of the ship cuts to a close-up of the maggots crawling on the spoiled meat that he insists the crewmen eat, signifying that the captain (the bourgeoisie) is a parasite preying on the body-politic of his crew (the proletariat). Or, to use a less sophisticated, but nonetheless quite effective, example of "intellectual" montage from a film comedy, in the Farrelly Brothers' *Me, Myself, and Irene* (2000), Jim Carrey walks onto his neighbor's front lawn, drops his pants, and squats; as he is about to defecate on their property, the shot cuts to a shot of soft-serve chocolate ice cream being dispensed from a machine.

To admittedly strain the comedic metaphor, if Eisenstein's associative shock produces the proverbial light bulb over the viewer's head, Artaud's dissociative shock was Moe Howard cracking said light bulb over the viewer's head while bellowing "Knucklehead!" For Artaud, who eventually abandoned cinema in the early 1930s, the power of film did not reside in its ability to shock the viewer into *thought*, but to provide the shock of *thought's limitations*. Delueze suggested:

> There is an absolute opposition between Artaud's project and conception such as Eisenstein's.... It might be said that Artaud turns around Eisenstein's argument: if it is true that thought depends on a shock to give birth to it ... it can only think one thing, *the fact that we are not yet thinking*, the powerlessness to think the whole and to think oneself, thought which always fossilized, decomposed, collapsed.[39]

For Eisenstein, the shock effect of cinema was one that changed consciousness by producing "thought," sparking a *revolutionary consciousness* and how one thinks of the world *ideologically*. For Artaud, the shock effect that revealed "we are not yet thinking" sparked a *revolution of consciousness itself*.[40] It is vital that Deleuze defines the difference between Eisenstein and Artaud as shock producing "thought" versus the shock of "not *yet* thinking"—and *yet* cannot be overemphasized. The dissociative shock exposed that existing modes of thinking were obsolete and useless, but also revealed that a new way of thinking and articulating the world was necessary: that *we now must think differently*. As Susan Sontag noted:

> At least in his intention (Artaud's practice in the nineteen-twenties and thirties is another matter), his theater has little in common with the anti-theater of playful, sadistic assault conceived by Marinetti and the Dada artists.... [T]he aggressiveness that Artaud proposes is controlled and intricately orchestrated, for he assumes that sensory violence can be a source of embodied intelligence.... [T]heater resembles consciousness, and therefore lends itself to being turned into a theater-laboratory in which to conduct research on changing consciousness.[41]

After his acrimonious break with the Surrealist movement, recounted in his essay "In Total Darkness, or, the Surrealist Bluff" (1927), Artaud denounced their collectivist mentality and, in particular, Breton's insistence that all Surrealists join the French Communist Party.[42] Artaud was not at all a supporter of the bourgeoisie or its culture, but realized the contradiction of a Surrealist movement that reveled in the illogical coexisting with a political

1. American Comedy and the European Avant-Garde

"Seething anarchy": The Marx Brothers in *Animal Crackers* (1930) — Antonin Artaud's favorite movie (Paramount Pictures/Photofest).

philosophy that demanded ideological rigor.[43] The Marxist-Surrealist revolution to Artaud was "'revolution' [in] its utilitarian and practical meaning, the social meaning that is alleged to be the only valid one ... incapable of imaging, of conceiving a Revolution which did not evolve within the hopeless limitations of matter."[44] Rather than the Marxism of Soviet cinema or Surrealism, Artaud championed the Marxism of the Marx Brothers' *Animal Crackers* (1930) and, to a lesser degree, *Monkey Business* (1931). Everything corrupted by staid Western theater, and abandoned by Surrealism's growing artistic and ideological rigidity, Artaud found in the Marx Brothers: a *dissociative* power that elevated comedy beyond superficial jokes and into a realm of

> seething anarchy, a total breakdown of reality by poetry.... If there is a characteristic state, a distinct poetic level of mind that can be called *Surrealism*, *Animal Crackers* belongs to it ... something which could only be compared to certain successful Surrealist poems, if any such existed ... *the destruction of all reality in the mind.*[45]

The Marx Brothers' barrage of *non sequiturs,* puns, and asides rendered the Symbolic Order into a ridiculous parody of itself. Gestures and action combined the primal and poetic, exemplified by Harpo Marx's arsenal of lyrical and grotesque facial expressions and random bursts of illogical action. In the Marx Brothers' assault on logic and language, respectability and rationality was laid waste in the process, be it sophisticated high society in *Animal Crackers,* the ivory tower of academia in *Horsefeathers* (1932), or the machinations of the State as it careens towards war in *Duck Soup* (1933) — with *Duck Soup* being nothing short of the *Ubu roi* for the twentieth century.

Waiting for Buster: Theater of the Absurd and American Film Comedy

Clair, Buñuel, and Artaud found kindred spirits in the Hollywood comedians rather than fellow Surrealists; and the post–WWII "Theater of the Absurd," specifically Samuel Beckett and Eugène Ionesco, were similarly influenced as much by American film comedy as the Continental avant-garde. Originated in Martin Esslin's book *The Theater of the Absurd* (1962), the term situates Beckett, Ionesco, Jean Genêt, Arthur Adamov, Harold Pinter, Edward Albee, Fernando Arrabal, and otherwise highly divergent playwrights in similar theatrical terrain: repetitions of limited events or non-events; uncomfortable monotony; black comedy; baffling dialogue. Moreover, Absurdism also expressed another way of "defamiliarizing social reality." If Dada depicted an illogical world as manifestly illogical, and Surrealism depicted an ostensibly normal world disturbingly irrational, Absurdism depicted an insular, illogical world that becomes relentlessly "reasonable" within its own confines — the distinction that could be made between Clair, Buñuel, and Beckett and their respective TV comedy counterparts, Soupy Sales, Ernie Kovacs, and *Green Acres.*

While Ionesco cited the Surrealists as his formative inspiration, he insisted that the Marx Brothers were the primary influence on his work (conversely, *Monty Python's Flying Circus* was highly influenced by Ionesco).[46] Much like the Marx Brothers, Ionesco's plays radically but "non-politically" questioned and subverted rationality and social order through an assault on the order of logic and especially *language* (as opposed to Brecht's theater of estrangement and explicit political sloganeering). Ionesco claimed, "[Art] is nothing if it does not go beyond the temporary truths and obsessions of history."[47] Ionesco's first play, *La Cantratrice chauve* (*The Bald Soprano,* 1950), with its appropriate subtitle of "Anti-play," chronicles a dinner with two bourgeois couples, the Smiths and their guests, the Martins. The banter begins with a fair amount of intentionally banal small-talk and random clichés; many of these lines were lifted verbatim from an instructional book on conversational English. Arguments follow that parody Platonic dialogues and Aristotle's principles of logic and rhetoric, and the "anti-play" climaxes in a barrage of haranguing voices shouting useless nonsense, even after the stage lights go dark — a parody of the vaudeville "blackout" sketch. (The term "blackout" is the theatrical practice of ending a comedy sketch, which often contained numerous running jokes, with the climactic punchline accompanied by the stage lights being abruptly shut down, a direct signal to the audience that the sketch had concluded and a new and unrelated sketch was beginning.) After the voices abruptly stop, the stage lights are slowly rekindled; the Martins now assume the positions of the Smiths and repeat the opening lines of their dialogue, awaiting their own guest couple to repeat the cycle *ad infinitum*.[48]

Similarly, in Ionesco's *La Leçon* (*The Lesson*, 1951), a simple tutoring session simultaneously builds and frustrates dramatic tension through the seemingly endless seminar. The Pupil's steadfast refusal to comprehend the difference between addition and subtraction (doing simple equations with her hands results in her inevitable conclusion that she has "ten fingers"), and the Professor's ridiculous exegesis on "the linguistic and comparative philology of the neo–Spanish languages," finally culminate with the Professor stabbing the young Pupil to death: the conclusion to *every* lesson with *every* pupil. The play ends with the Maid disposing of the body and a new pupil awaiting her lesson, and the Maid states the absurd maxim, "Arithmetic leads to philology, and philology leads to crime." In this way, *La Leçon* suggests a convergence of the black comedy of Buñuel with the dazzling and bewildering semiotics of Abbott and Costello, where torrents of misplaced signifiers rendered language into a mystifying web of misunderstanding, exemplified by the seminal "Who's on First" routine.[49] Indeed, the fairly independent sketches in Abbott and Costello's debut film *Buck Privates* (1941) become various convoluted exercises in "anti-math," achieving a level of baffling absurdity akin to the Professor and the Pupil's extended battle over addition and subtraction in *La Leçon*. Monetary exchanges are impenetrable negotiations in order to make a "buck" through "private" enterprise (selling ties, playing craps, arranging loans). Sexual morality is circumvented by Bud Abbott's perverse analysis of the appropriate age of consent by deducing a 40-year-old man can marry a 10-year-old girl because in five years the man will only be *three* times her age, and in fifteen more years only *twice* her age, so therefore eventually their ages will correspond. To this extent, *Buck Privates* is "absurdist" in its construction of a world where two plus two may or may not equal four, and where the stability of language is constantly jeopardized. From the perspective of Lacanian psychoanalysis, *La Leçon* depicts the Professor as the despotic Symbolic Father who must destroy the Pupil who will not adapt to the Symbolic Order. With Abbott and Costello, Bud Abbott, as the Symbolic Father (the castrating, tyrannical arbitrator of the signifier), constantly changes the rules of signification over his unfortunate victim, Lou Costello, as subject of the Symbolic Order.[50]

While Ionesco perhaps best exemplified the connection between Hollywood comedy and the avant-garde, Samuel Beckett's *Waiting for Godot* not only emerged as the defining text of the Theater of the Absurd, but arguably the most important play in twentieth-century Western theater. As grim, monotonous, and oppressive as Kafka's literature or the cinematic "antidramas" of Michelangelo Antonioni, *Waiting for Godot* becomes a torturous hell of helpless characters and narrative inertia, frequently described as "a play where nothing happens, twice."[51] Two characters, Vladimir and Estragon, aimlessly wander a desolate setting, engage in pointless conversations and debates that gives new meaning to the word "small talk," encounter another comedy team (Pozzo and his slave-pet Lucky), and continually await the arrival of Godot, who, of course, never shows up. Any possibility of breaking the cycle of meaningless monotony is utterly impossible from the outset, as succulently noted in Estragon's opening line: "Nothing to be done." While certainly not "comical" in the conventional sense, *Waiting for Godot* is structured and performed more as an endless series of strange vaudeville routines than portentous drama — a depiction of the horror of existence through the puns, *non sequiturs,* and double-talk of the Marx Brothers or Abbott and Costello.

Ultimately, the relationship between the avant-garde and early film comedy reached full fruition in 1965 when Beckett wrote the experimental short film *Film* (1965, dir. Alan Schneider). Both Zero Mostel and Irish actor Jack McGowran were initially approached for *Film;* each appeared in well-received, respective productions of *Waiting for Godot* and were successful comedic actors. However, neither was available, and Beckett, reportedly none too seriously, suggested Buster Keaton, whose work Beckett had long admired. Much to their surprise, Keaton accepted the invitation. *Film* is a twenty-minute essay on human perception devoid of any sound (dialogue, music, sound effects) — in effect, a silent two-reeler. Keaton, his face obscured throughout and his back to the camera for much of the film, is continually placed in positions where he tries to avoid being seen — by other people, by the animals in his apartment, by the camera (and thus the film audience), and, ultimately, himself. In this way, *Film* is not a story but more a series of morbid "sight-gags." Early in *Film,* a well-dressed couple encounters Keaton wandering through a world composed of urban ruins; they react in revulsion, and then stare directly at the camera, only to react with even *more* revulsion at the viewer. When the man tries to express his horror with a scream, his wife

Buster Keaton in Samuel Beckett's 1965 *Film*, directed by Alan Schneider (Video Specialists International/Photofest).

places a finger over her pursed lips, the gesture comically exaggerated. Similarly, Keaton is both amusing and unnerving as he stealthily yet unsteadily maneuvers about his barren apartment, pulling a tattered shade down over a window and covering the birdcage, fishbowl, and mirror in his room with black sheets — all the while trying to prevent the camera seeing his face. In a hilarious routine highly reminiscent of his early work, Keaton tries to lock his small dog and cat out of the apartment in order to not be perceived by them, resulting in several instances where the dog or cat darts back into the room when he ties to evict the other from his presence.

As a series of repeating situations that are at once horrific and humorous (typical of Beckett's work), *Film* concludes with both a philosophical statement and a chilling "punchline." Throughout *Film* there is a strict, discernable distinction of the point-of-view shots: the first-person subjective shots from the perspective of Keaton are distorted, blurred, perhaps even *flawed*; the third-person objective shots from the perspective of the camera are clear and pristine. The final shots of *Film* depict Keaton from behind, seated in a rocking chair looking at a set of photographs representing his life, many of which are magazine advertisements or other generic sources. Finally, the last photo reveals a portrait of Keaton in his trademark straw hat, a baggy black suit, and an eye patch — the outfit he wears in *Film*. The first time the viewer sees a frontal shot of Keaton, it is as a photograph, the product of a camera. Slumping in the chair, the camera pans and circles the room, and eventually returns to Keaton sleeping in the chair, finally shown from the front. Awakened by the interruption, Keaton silently screams, looking directly at the camera; the shot cuts to a blurred point-of-view shot of Keaton seeing Keaton staring back at him. Covering his eye(s) with the palms of his hands as he wearily bows his head, the camera lingers on Keaton before fading out, seemingly forever pondering the horrid moment of seeing oneself both as *a self* and *someone else*. To interpret from a psychoanalytic standpoint (which is not to say the intended meaning or only possible reading), *Film* becomes the perpetual trauma of Lacan's mirror-stage, with the camera replacing the mirror, manifesting "the deflection of the specular *I* into the social *I*."[52]

Besides some of the more overtly Keatonesque contributions to *Film*, one can also compare Beckett's *Film* to Keaton's own *Sherlock, Jr.* from four decades earlier. Keaton plays a young man working as a movie projectionist who aspires to be a famous detective and is despondent that a romantic rival has framed him for stealing a watch from his girlfriend's father. Falling asleep on the job, his dream consists of physically entering the movie he is screening, an action-mystery melodrama called "Hearts and Pearls" (a parody of D.W. Griffith's Biograph-era work). Yet the entry into the world of cinema is hardly a smooth one. When Keaton initially tries to enter the film by climbing through the orchestra pit of the theater and onto the screen, he is physically thrown off the screen by one of the actors. In his second attempt, Keaton is able to enter the screen. However, while a long shot depicts the film screen within its theater surroundings (the orchestra pit, the rows of seats), the projectionist must adjust and acclimate himself to a bewildering number of abrupt background changes: dodging cars on a city street, balancing on the edge of a cliff, standing in the jungle with two hungry lions. *Sherlock, Jr.* then shifts to the viewer watching the film-within-a-film "Hearts and Pearls," from the discovery of the theft of the pearls, the arrival of Keaton as famed detective "Sherlock, Jr." and the resolution of the mystery (including the requisite slapstick chase finale). As "Hearts and Pearls" concludes, Keaton awakens from the dream — his entry into cinema — and reconciles with his girlfriend in the projection room, their reunion shown in the frame of the projection booth window, an internal film frame within the film frame. As "Hearts and Pearls" ends with the unification of the couple, Keaton professes his love for his girlfriend by imitating the gestures of the actor on the screen: *himself.* The happy ending is achieved only through the final conversion of reality into a romance, a melodrama, and a comedy. In this sense, *Sherlock, Jr.* and *Film* were not altogether different in their depictions of *how* one perceives the self in the world. *Film* becomes a disturbing and disorientating cinematic essay on alienation and misrecognition obliterating the distinction between the seer (the camera) and the seen (Keaton) into a moment of unbearable self-realization. *Sherlock, Jr.* is an irreverent deconstruction of the cinematic apparatus where illusion and reality are no longer defined: to see and mimic one's own image-ideal on the sliver screen makes existence briefly more bearable.

In summary, Peter Bürger noted in *Theory of the Avant-Garde* that the avant-garde forces viewers to consciously and constantly struggle with the text, demanding that the audience unearth, or even manufacture, meaning out of works that make interpretation difficult, if not determinedly impossible:

> If recipients will not simply give up or be contented with an arbitrary meaning from just a part of the work, they must attempt to understand this enigmatic quality of the avant-gardiste work. They then move to another level of interpretation.... Between the shocklike experience ... of the mode of reception and the effort to grasp the principles of construction, there is a break: *The interpretation of meaning is renounced.* One of the decisive changes in the development art that the historical avant-garde brought work consists of this new type of reception.... *The recipient's attention no longer turns to a meaning of the work that might be grasped by a reading of its constituent elements, but to the principle of construction.*[53]

The historical avant-garde is not a monolithic construct but contains a variety of artistic movements, such as Dada, Surrealism, and Absurdism. The differences between Dada, Surrealism, and Absurdism can also be addressed by how they differ philosophically and politically as much as aesthetically and artistically. Moreover, while these movements can be defined by certain shared tendencies, there is not a uniform Dada, Surrealist or Absurdist formula (Breton's approach to leading the Surrealist movement to the contrary). The surrealism of Buñuel is distinct to the surrealism of Cocteau, and the absurdism of Ionesco distinct to the absurdism of Arrabal. On the one hand, an obsession with situating the avant-garde into what it *is* and purely aesthetic categories minimizes the importance of what the avant-garde *does* in a social-cultural context. On the other hand, discussing the avant-garde through a kind of all-purpose, critical jargon — without providing evidence underneath the claim — renders it ineffective and irrelevant, such as *The New Yorker* hailing *Family Guy* as subversive TV by simply proclaiming it "a Dadaesque vaudeville turn."[54] In the course of this study, it will be argued that *The Soupy Sales Show* and the much-vilified *Gong Show* were far closer to any "Dadaesque vaudeville turns" in the history of American TV comedy. Once beyond the rhetorical flourish, and the notion that "Dadaesque" has more intellectual panache than the clichéd "edgy," *Family Guy*— both stylistically and ideologically — ultimately merits a much different appellation: postmodern burlesque.

One crucial tendency in the historical European avant-garde in the twentieth century was the influence of American film comedy, and the function of comedy as a "dissociative force" which not only disrupted the *status quo* but ruptured the viewer's sense of the rational and reality. The artists and shows I contend constitute "avant-garde TV comedy" are not only comparable artistically, but provided comedy that violated TV industry and viewer expectations and conventions, comedy the audience had to work at to "get," and comedy that must be assessed by the "principles of construction" (form) as much as the "constituent elements" (content). However, it is necessary to first consider the context in which these avant-garde performers and shows operated — specifically, the conquest of the revolutionary impetus of comedy by American television in the Culture Industry.

Chapter 2

The Culture Industry and American Television Comedy

It is not enough to teach; sometimes you have to punish.
— Peter Sellers in *The Magic Christian*

Camera, Cinema, Revolution: Benjamin, Artaud, and Adorno

From 1919 to 1939 the world was buffeted by the aftermath of the Russian Revolution and World War I, the Jazz Age, the rise of the early twentieth century avant-garde (Dada, Surrealism, Artaud, Brecht), the Worldwide Economic Collapse of the 1930s, the advent of Fascism and Stalinism, and further disasters of modernity: World War II, the Atomic Bomb, and the Holocaust. Between the wars, the fledgling medium of cinema became the perceived site where avant-garde aesthetics and revolutionary struggle converged, exemplified by the Soviets and the Surrealists (although, as noted in the last chapter, the relationship between Surrealist films and the Surrealist movement proper was highly problematic). This optimism of cinema was nowhere more evident than in Walter Benjamin's "The Work of Art in the Age of Mechanical Reproduction":

> Process reproduction can bring out those aspects of the original that are unattainable to the naked eye yet accessible to the lens, which is adjustable and chooses its angle at will. And photographic reproduction, with the aid of certain processes, such as enlargement or slow-motion, can capture images which escape natural vision.... As compared to painting, filmed behavior lends itself more readily to analysis because of its incomparably more precise statements of the situation. In comparison to the stage set, the filmed behavior item

... can be isolated more easily. This circumstance derives from its tendency to promote the mutual penetration of art and science.... To demonstrate the identity of *the artistic and scientific uses of photography which heretofore were usually separated will be one of the revolutionary functions of film.*[1]

In this sense, Benjamin, writing in 1936, can be read as an extension and elaboration on the Left's overall vision of film as a vehicle for revolutionary change in the 1920s.[2] Benjamin's view suggests a strong affinity with Eisenstein, who proclaimed the revolutionary aspects of montage as Soviet cinema as "a purely intellectual film, freed from traditional limitations, achieving direct forms for ideas, systems, and concepts, without the need for transitions and paraphrases. We may yet have *a synthesis of art and science.*"[3] While Benjamin did not explicitly claim cinema rendered all previous forms of art obsolete, motion pictures represented a new and implicitly superior possibility of unifying the domains of art and science, separated by modernity: art the province where the world can be creatively depicted but not analytically described (literature, visual arts, music); science the regime were the world can be objectively explained without mimetic representation (mathematics, physics).[4] Benjamin viewed cinema as *both* an artistic and a scientific project capable of changing consciousness by representing and reconfiguring the modern world in a previously impossible, illuminating, and, above all, liberating way: "The film, on the one hand, *extends our comprehension of the necessities that rule our lives*; on the other hand, *it manages to assure us of an immense and unexpected field of action.*"[5]

In this respect, it is tempting to situate Benjamin with Artaud, in that both posited a revolution of perception and consciousness through art. However, the comparison is highly problematic. Benjamin lionized Brecht, defended Surrealism's allegiance to Marxism, positioned Chaplin as the heir to Dada, and viewed cinema's role in mass culture with revolutionary optimism.[6] With the rise of Hitler, the need for art to provide political instruction as part of changing consciousness became a growing imperative for Benjamin.[7] In contrast, Artaud acrimoniously split with Surrealism over adopting an ideological stance, hailed the Marx Brothers for their "seething anarchy" and the only true "Surrealist poetry," and eventually lost faith in film with his essay "The Premature Old Age of Cinema" (1933). One factor was certainly the advent of sound and the domination of cinema by Artaud's arch-enemy, verbal language: "The so-called mechanical magic of a constant drone of images has not survived the onslaught of speech."[8] Another issue was the evolution of cinema into the dominant strains of documentary film and narrative film, both of which demanded that the film record and replicate reality (or at least manifest a pseudo-realism) versus cinema that broke apart reality (as discussed last chapter, exemplified for Artaud by the Marx

Brothers' *Animal Crackers* and "early Buster Keatons or the less human Chaplins"). Ultimately, Artaud concluded that the revolutionary power of cinema was negated by the camera's inherent reification of the object: "[C]inema is a closed world.... By the time it collides with the mind, its dissociative force is broken. There has been poetry around the lens, to be sure, *but before the filtering by the lens, the recording on film.*"[9]

Artaud's reasons for abandoning cinema better compare to Benjamin's friend and frequent intellectual sparring partner, Theodor W. Adorno, who found little, if any, revolutionary value in cinema, especially in terms of potentially and radically redefining perception and consciousness. For Adorno, as Miriam Hansen suggested, "A major source of cinema's ideological complicity [is] because it allows the film image to function as an advertisement for the world 'as is.'"[10] Adorno, perhaps in reference to Benjamin's claim that cinema could "burst our prison-world asunder," described the individual's relationship to mass culture as one which "corresponds to the behavior of the prisoner who loves his cell because he has left nothing else to love."[11] The pseudo-realistic settings, characters, and narratives of bourgeois literature and theater, combined with the inherent nature of the camera to reify rather than reconfigure perceptions of the world, attained a dangerous synthesis in classical Hollywood cinema, which Adorno termed a "misalliance between the novel and photography."[12]

Adorno: The Culture Industry and Television

In this context, the crucial issue becomes if and how motion pictures and comedy can retain dissociative power: if they can undermine the hold of dominant ideology, the constraints of the rational mind, and the confidence in social reality within the medium of television — and the Culture Industry. In this respect, it is first necessary to consider the implications of the terms "culture" and "industry," as defined by Adorno:

> Culture, in the true sense, did not accommodate itself to human beings; but it always raised a protest against the petrified relations under which they lived, thereby honoring them. In so far as *culture becomes wholly assimilated to and integrated into those petrified relations, human beings are once more debased....* The expression "industry" is not to be taken too literally. It refers to *the standardization of the thing itself*— such as the Western, familiar to every moviegoer — and to the rationalization of distribution techniques, but not strictly to the production process.... It is industrial more in a sociological sense.[13]

The Culture Industry is a systematic process of standardizing culture while purging it of any critical capabilities; creating immediately recognizable cultural commodities to maximize their consumption by audiences; and conditioning audiences to expect and even desire more of the same, as any consumer demands a reliable product for their money.[14] The refusal of true culture to accommodate itself to conditions, and to protest against them, is negated in mass culture, which cynically acclimates its participants to its products and debases the consumers by forcing them into the realm of "pseudo-activity," epitomized by the Jazz Age "jitterbugs" despised by Adorno, whose flailing on the dance floor did not signify liberation but a desperate attempt to insert a semblance of cultural relevance and resistance into a hollow mass culture foisted upon them: "Their ecstasy is without content.... It has the convulsive aspects reminiscent of St. Vitus Dance or the reflexes of mutilated animals.... [T]he feet are unable to fulfill what the ears pretend."[15] Mass culture does not promote a dignified sense of individual non-conformity, but undignified "pseudo-individuals" who react to its vacuous nature by participating in their own domination with aimless pseudo-activity in conjunction with the mass culture product: the pseudo-activity of television as "ecstasy without content" effectively captured in an episode of *Everybody Loves Raymond* (CBS, 1996–2005). In it, grizzled Frank Barone (Peter Boyle), thrilled that his domineering wife Marie (Doris Roberts) has briefly left him after one of their many rows, can now finally enjoy TV the way it was meant to be enjoyed — sitting on the couch in his underwear and eating junk food, with the remote control's channel changer taped down to continuously cycle through the programs in order to "save time."

The Culture Industry permeates all facets of mass culture: popular fiction (romance novels, detective novels, or science fiction), popular music (from Tin Pan Alley to Alternative), and Adorno's primary target — Hollywood cinema ("The central sector of the culture industry"[16]). From the creation of fetish-commodity stars, the frequent reliance on technological innovation over artistic creativity, the specialization and division of labor, the "studio system" of production control through investment capital and creative interference to maximize box-office potential, and the standardization of the products into easily produced and consumed cultural commodities, Hollywood is the Culture Industry incarnate. However, more than the popular fiction, hit songs, and especially the Hollywood films Adorno decried, American television, or, as it came to be known in America (with equal parts affection and derision), "the Idiot Box" and "the Boob Tube," made Adorno's acerbic and pessimistic ruminations on the Culture Industry nothing short of prophetic.

Television was not mentioned in Horkheimer and Adorno's initial description and denouncement of the Culture Industry in *Dialectic of Enlightenment*, which was written in 1944, just prior to television's pervasive impact on post–World War II American popular culture. As Adorno made the totalizing and totalitarian aspects of mass culture and the Culture Industry a primary focus of his philosophical project, he eventually confronted the then-nascent medium in his essay "How to Look at Television" (1954). Not surprisingly, Adorno found little to embrace:

> Rigid institutionalization transforms mass media into a medium of undreamed of psychological control. The repetitiveness, the selfsameness, and the ubiquity of mass culture tend to make for automatized reactions and to weaken the forces of individual resistance.... The ideas of conformity and conventionalism were inherent in popular novels from the very beginning. Now, however, these ideals have been translated into rather clear-cut prescriptions of what to do and what not to do. The outcome of conflicts is pre-established, and all conflicts are mere sham. Society is the winner.[17]

The drive towards standardization and conformity that television instills in both its shows and its audience is manifest by what Adorno described as constructing "overt and hidden messages" through a reliance on "presuppositions and stereotypes." The overt messages appeared explicitly in the text, with the hidden messages ascertained through closer inspection and analysis of the text, insidiously complimenting the text with an ideological component, or even opposing and overriding any overt "oppositional" message (as will be discussed shortly with Rod Serling's problematic teleplay "Patterns," and becomes pivotal in reading *The Simpsons*). In describing an episode of *Our Miss Brooks* (CBS, 1952–56), Adorno noted:

> The script does not try to "sell" any idea. Rather, the "hidden meaning" emerges simply from the way the story looks at human beings. The audience is invited to look at the characters in the same way without being made aware that indoctrination is present.... *[T]he script is a shrewd method of promoting adjustment to humiliating conditions by presenting them as objectively comical* and by giving a picture of a person who experiences even her own inadequate position as an object of fun apparently free of any resentment.[18]

These messages become housed in TV shows structured around the recognizable genres and stock characters which provide immediate reference points and expected events for the audience, creating identifiable and inevitably predictable situations and characters as "slices of life" for the audience — a *pseudo-realistic* television world not fundamentally different from their own experience: "[P]seudo-realism allows for the direct and extremely primitive identification achieved by popular culture ... a façade of trivial buildings, rooms, dresses, and faces as through they were the promise of something thrilling and exciting taking place at any moment."[19]

The Dual-Character of Comedy and Drama in Early American Television

American television experienced an almost immediate separation of comedy and drama into two mutually excusive forms with mutually exclusive cultural functions. Television comedy became the domain of undemanding amusement, which is certainly not to say that television comedy did not contain its fair share of overt and hidden meanings. In contrast, television drama became the exclusive site of serious culture and social commentary. However, with the exception of *Dragnet* (NBC, 1951–9; 1967–70), the seminal weekly dramatic shows using a genre format, recurring characters, and already known narrative outcomes (the criminal apprehended, the guilty convicted, the patient saved) to house overt and hidden messages did not emerge until the later 1950s, with the Western (*Gunsmoke*, CBS, 1955–75; *Bonanza*, NBC, 1959–73), the legal drama (*Perry Mason*, CBS, 1957–66), the action-based detective show (*The Untouchables*, CBS, 1959–63), science-fiction (*The Twilight Zone*, CBS, 1959–64), and the medical drama (*Dr. Kildare*, NBC, 1961–6; *Ben Casey*, ABC, 1961–66).

Rather, the responsibility for manufacturing socially-relevant and thought-provoking television, and providing the necessary social and political education for its audiences, was assumed by the portentous TV dramas of the 1950s, now hailed as part of the "Golden Age of Television."[20] Fred Coe, producer of *NBC Television Playhouse* (1948–55), simply stated, "It was our mission to bring Broadway to America via television."[21] While this "Golden Age" was hailed as the acme of quality television, particularly as TV plummeted to an intellectual and cultural nadir in the eyes of critics in the 1960s and beyond, these teleplays proved problematic. Despite their artistic pretensions, teleplays were designed to sell products as much as provide a serious, thought-provoking cultural experience for America. As Anna Everett observed, "'Golden Age' dramas quickly became the ideal market vehicle for major U.S. corporations seeking to display their products favorably before a national audience."[22] Many of the teleplays appeared on shows sporting the names of their sponsors: *Kraft Television Theater* (NBC, 1947–1958; concurrent on ABC, 1953–5), *Ford Television Theater* (CBS, 1948–52; NBC, 1952–6; ABC 1956–7), *Philco Television Playhouse* (NBC, 1948–55), *Goodyear Playhouse* (NBC, 1948–1955), *The U.S. Steel Hour* (ABC, 1953–5; CBS, 1955–63); *General Electric Playhouse* (CBS, 1953–62). First and foremost, network television's cultural mission has not been to "sell ideas" but to sell advertising space, with efforts to entertain and provide socially-relevant programming running, respectively, second and a distant third. To this extent, the corporate sponsorship and control over teleplays generated a strong pattern of self-censorship.[23] As Everett noted:

Only those dramas that supported and reflected positive middle-class values, *which likewise reflected favorably the image of its advertisers*, were broadcast.... [S]cripts exploring problems at the societal level (i.e. racial discrimination, structural poverty, and other social ills) were systematically ignored.... [M]any "golden age" dramas were little more than simplistic morality plays focusing on the everyday problems and conflicts of weak individuals confronted by personal shortcomings such as alcoholism, greed, impotence, and divorce.[24]

"Patterns," written by Rod Serling, aired live on *Kraft Television Theater* (ABC, January 16, 1955 — henceforth referred to as *Patterns*). An indictment of "office politics," *Patterns* examined the daily deceit and domination of a typical American white-collar workplace. A young executive, Fred Staples (Richard Kiley), balancing idealism with ambition, is recruited by ruthless CEO Mr. Ramsey (Everett Sloane) as eventual replacement for Ramsey's current assistant, Andy Sloane (Ed Begley), who has become a detriment to the company (not only due to his declining heath, but his compassionate approach to the workings of big business). Staples becomes increasingly disgusted as he watches Ramsey abuse his underling Sloane, forcing him to endure ever-increasing difficulties and indignities. In effect, Ramsey and Sloane act out the Hegelian "Master-Slave" relationship where the dialectic resolution is suspended: the slave's realization a slave can exist without a master but a master cannot exist without a slave. Because Sloane is unwilling to quit or challenge Ramsey, he can be exploited until he literally outlives his usefulness: Sloane dies of a heart attack while at the office. Deciding the situation is intolerable, Staples resigns his position and confronts Ramsey, who responds with an intriguing proposition: if Staples stays and keeps the business profitable, he can begin to implement his own visions of corporate management, perhaps one day dethroning Ramsey himself. Staples accepts the offer — and challenge.

Certainly, the *overt* message of *Patterns* is the importance of maintaining humanity, integrity, and dignity in inhumane, dishonest, and debasing environments, especially through Serling's favored stereotype, "the last angry man" (a public image Serling himself adopted). However, Serling's critique in *Patterns* is very much rooted in the conventions of modern bourgeois (televised) theater: a pseudo-realistic study of a complicated character and individual ethics and morality in the workplace (versus attacking the system of capitalism itself through avant-garde formalism, as in the case of Brecht). The central conflict becomes the crisis of principles for Staples, torn between advancing his career and maintaining a clear conscience, and ultimately the possibility to do *both*. It is here the *hidden* messages of *Patterns* emerge. Initially tempted with profit and prestige, Staples ultimately chooses principle. However, Ramsey, impressed with Staples' conviction, views Staples as a worthy adversary (unlike the milquetoast Sloane) and envisions a partnership, however contentious it might be, that might produce profit, principles, *and* public good. Staples is not so much rewarded for demonstrating a "corporate conscience," but rather for having the temerity to stand up to his brow-beating boss — for having backbone as well as moral fiber. Likewise, the conclusion of *Patterns* depicts a subtle but important character shift in the tyrannical Ramsey, who is not a two-dimensional character (let alone the *one*-dimensional caricatures of capitalists in Brecht), but a nuanced character as complex and interesting as the forthright Staples or the pathetic Sloane. In his review the day after *Pattern*'s initial broadcast in 1955, *New York Times* television critic Jack Gould hailed actor Everett Sloane's portrayal of Ramsey as one which "made a part that easily might have been a stereotype 'menace' a figure of dimension, *a man of stature*."[25] Yet by making the vindictive CEO "a man of stature," *Patterns* does not only make Ramsey multi-dimensional and even sympathetic, but *noble*. While not directly referring to *Patterns*, but certainly applicable to it, Adorno noted that in television drama, "It would be more commendable to show how the life of ordinary people is affected by terror and impotence than to cope with the phony psychology of the big-shots, whose *heroic role is silently endorsed by such a treatment even if they are pictured as villains*."[26] The pathetic Sloane, feebly living and literally dying in a state of "terror and impotence" under the yoke of Ramsey, becomes the ultimate "villain" of *Patterns*: a weak-kneed man whose inability or unwillingness to challenge his boss perpetuated a climate of intimidation and obedience in the workplace that can now be changed by Staples. To battle corporate ambition, competition and ruthlessness to create a better workplace and society, Staples learns that he must become *more* ambitious, competitive and ruthless.

By using *Patterns* as a representative text, the teleplays that constituted the Golden Age of American television may have attempted to offer serious social criticisms of the injustices in American society (the overt message). However, they also offered the American television viewer lessons in how to be an ethical and productive member of American society (the hidden message). As Adorno remarked, "The vast majority of television shows aim at producing, or at least reproducing, the very smugness, intellectual passivity, and gullibility that seems to fit in with totalitarian creeds, even if the explicit surface messages of the shows may be anti-totalitarian."[27]

From "Comedy-Variety" to "Situation-Comedy"

In television comedy's infancy, the comedy-variety show was its primary vehicle, and among the era's most famous stars were Milton Berle, Jackie Gleason, Sid Caesar, and Red Skelton. Two other variety shows also began long TV runs during the era. *The Ed Sullivan Show* (CBS, 1948–71; titled *Toast of the Town*, 1948–55) featured comedic acts, usually stand-up comedians or teams, as one part of a variety program including music, dance, drama, and specialty variety acts (Sullivan's famous and frequent inclusion of acrobats, circus acts, and animal acts drawn from numerous nations). *The Lawrence Welk Show* (ABC, 1955–71; syndicated 1971–82) focused almost exclusively on light musical performances.

While derived from various forms of lower- and middle-class popular theater — burlesque, night clubs, music halls, even circus and carnivals — the comedy-variety show most directly owed its structure to *vaudeville*. As Mary Desjardi noted, variety shows

> presented a series of *unrelated* acts, featured stars or "headlines," in addition to supporting acts.... [E]ntertainment emphasized presentational or performative aspects — immediacy, spontaneity and spectacle — over storyline and character development....Performers might develop a "persona," but this character mask would usually represent a well-known stereotype...rather than embody a fleshed-out character growing within the context of dramatic situations.[28]

Many early stars of the comedy-variety show achieved their success prior to television on stage, radio, and even in cinema, and often transplanted their established routines verbatim to television, performing the material on a soundstage in front of a live audience and static television camera. As well as the featured performer, the star of a given comedy-variety show functioned as an unofficial master of ceremonies, allowing direct interaction with the live studio audience and the television viewer. The star could also serve as a pitchman, promoting products at any point during the show, rather than the program relying on designated commercial breaks (Milton Berle's shows became particularly notorious for the inordinate amount of time devoted to advertising). As well as the star, a typical comedy-variety show included a stable of regular performers (a number of whom could go on to become stars in their own right), high-profile guest stars, and lesser-known acts. While offering musical performances and specialty acts, the comedy-variety show, of course, focused on an array of stand-up and sketch comedy, usually vaudeville-style "blackout" sketches. Thus, the structure of the comedy-variety shows was theatrical but *non-narrative*. Each performance was self-contained. Sketch comedy could range from slapstick to tragicomedy, which might be followed by a moving musician or adroit acrobats. Or, in the case of *The Gong Show* (as a Dadaistic "anti-variety show"), a pointless and usually puerile sketch between Chuck Barris and the Unknown Comic could be followed by a man's random bashing on a drum kit or men dressed as cheerleaders doing calisthenics.

Despite its initial widespread popularity, by the late 1950s the comedy-variety show became an exhausted genre. *The Red Skelton Show* (NBC, 1951–3, 1970–1; CBS, 1953–70), with its innocuous vaudeville format featuring Skelton's kitsch personas, was the sole survivor by 1960. Sid Caesar was among the early casualties; the idiosyncratic and unpredictable *Your Show of Shows* (NBC, 1950–4) gave way to the revamped *Caesar's Hour* (NBC, 1954–57) and finally *Sid Caesar Invites You*, a short-lived replacement show for ABC in 1958. However, the decline of the genre was no better demonstrated than by the rise and fall of "Mr. Television," Milton Berle (NBC: *Texaco Star Theater*, 1948–52; *The Buick-Berle Show*, 1952–3; *The Milton Berle Show*, 1953–9). Certainly the most popular performer on television when the 1950s began, Berle practiced a brand of loud, fast-paced, innuendo-laced burlesque comedy (the distinction between vaudeville and burlesque being not the style but the latter's reliance on more adult-orientated comedy). Berle's TV trademark, or "persona," became his cross-dressing skits. This is not to say that Berle and his eventual disfavor with the public stemmed from providing a problematic "gender-bending" subversion of sexual and gender stereotypes. To the contrary, Berle's hideous drag routines defined "difference" and a grotesque "Other" to the red-blooded American male that fundamentally reflected disgust for women, sexuality, and "femininity." However, Berle's burlesque became increasingly unpopular and controversial over the course of the 1950s for two reasons. One involved a moral climate in America focusing on post–World War II popular culture fostering an epidemic of immorality and anti-social behavior among young people: the congressional attack on the comic book industry, the public furor over rock and roll music, and even the controversy over children's show content (*Howdy Doody*, *The Pinky Lee Show*). Conversely, the advent of *Playboy* magazine in 1955 was part of an emerging Sexual Revolution promoting sexual liberty as socially healthy and productive, at least for men (as will be discussed further with *Rowan and Martin's Laugh-In*). Berle's burlesque approach to sexuality, equal parts puerile fascination and Puritan repugnance, was increasingly anachronistic as much as being deemed offensive in the context of the era. At the peak of Berle's popularity, NBC signed him to a six-million-dollar, 30-year guaranteed contract. After *The Milton Berle Show* was cancelled in 1959, NBC paid Berle $200,000 to host a season of *Jackpot Bowling*.

The rise of the sitcom represented a growing desire to standardize TV comedy production, regulate content, and effectively administer public taste. As David Marc observed, networks and sponsors

> became increasingly anxious to assert quality control over TV product. Spontaneity and uniqueness of occasion and performance — precisely those qualities that were potentially most satisfying in a comedy-variety show — came to be

2. *The Culture Industry and American Television Comedy*   39

"Mr." Television: Milton Berle (NBC/Photofest).

viewed as liabilities. Seed money was attracted by the rationalized system of film production. In terms of comedy, this meant the sitcom.[29]

I Love Lucy (CBS, 1951–57) pioneered the pre-taped, three-camera sitcom filmed in front of a studio audience. The show's long-time director of photography was Karl Freund, director of two classic horror films from the 1930s: *The Mummy* (1932) and *Mad Love* (1935). As far as a formal model, the sitcom could initially be seen as a descendent of the two-reeler format of American film comedy. Not only were two-reelers and the sitcom roughly equivalent in their duration (twenty minutes, with the sitcom's commercial break allotments padding a show to a convenient half-hour for broadcast scheduling), but both constructed a simple situation in which a series of comedic mishaps ensued. However, the crucial difference was that the sitcom stressed narrative development towards *conflict resolution*, whereas the two-reeler emphasized loosely-connected events and *pure conflict* (Mack Sennett, early Laurel and Hardy, and certainly the Three Stooges). Rather, the "screwball comedy" film genre and its emphasis on managing domestic, romantic, and social entanglements through rapid-fire verbal comedy can be seen as the primary cinematic style influencing the development of the sitcom.

Likewise, dialogue-driven radio comedy shows served as a key structural influence as much as film, manifest by the sitcom's overall reliance on verbal sketch-comedy over physical comedy and sight-gags. Early sitcoms starred performers who honed their craft on radio before moving to television (George Burns and Gracie Allen), or even originated as radio shows (*I Love Lucy* was based on Lucille Ball's 1940s radio show *My Favorite Husband*). Moreover, TV, despite being considered a visual medium, is one where sound is as important as sight, as noted by John Ellis:

> Broadcast TV has areas which tend toward the cinematic, especially the eras of serious drama or of various kinds of TV film. But many of TV's characteristic broadcast forms rely on sound as the major carrier of information and the major means of ensuring continuity of attention. The news broadcast, the documentary with voice-over commentary, *the bulk of TV comedy shows* ... sound tends to anchor meaning on TV, where the image tends to anchor cinema.[30]

As a medium that emphasizes sound (the voice) as much as vision (physical performance), and is enjoyed in the private space of the home rather than the public space of performance, TV becomes analogous to *radio* as much as *cinema*. A comedy-variety show emphasized spectacle and the visual aspects of television, requiring the audience to sit and watch the show. The sitcom's emphasis on narrative development and verbal comedy meant that a show could essentially be listened to as well as watched — a radio show with visuals optional — and ultimately allowed the viewer to engage in other activities around the home while enjoying TV in the background.

By constructing a fairly inoffensive and audience-friendly genre, the potential dangers inherent in the comedy-variety show were neutralized by television. Sitcoms centered on the narrative, pseudo-realistic comic foibles of stock characters set in a variety of everyday locations: school, work, and, most often, the home, focusing on relationships between married couples and, in most cases, their children: *I Love Lucy*; *The George Burns and Gracie Allen Show* (CBS, 1950–8); *The Adventures of Ozzie and Harriet* (ABC, 1952–66); *The Life of Riley* (NBC, 1953–8); Danny Thomas's *Make Room for Daddy* (ABC, 1953–57) and *The Danny Thomas Show* (CBS, 1957–64); *Father*

Knows Best (CBS, 1955–56, 1958–63; NBC, 1955–58); *Leave It to Beaver* (CBS, 1957–8; ABC, 1958–63); *The Donna Reed Show* (ABC, 1958–66); and the most problematic and challenging of the early domestic sitcoms, *The Honeymooners* (CBS, 1955–6).[31]

However, many of the early domestic sitcoms problematized pseudo-realism as well. Many were semi-autobiographical depictions of show-business personalities playing themselves, or thinly-veiled fictional characters modeled on themselves to the point of transparency.[32] *I Love Lucy* and *The Danny Thomas Show* both featured male heads of households who worked as nightclub entertainers: Desi Arnez as "Ricky Ricardo," and Danny Thomas as "Danny Williams." On *Ozzie and Harriet*, popular musician and radio performer Ozzie Nelson and his actual family played themselves dealing with the daily problems of a typical American family. *Burns and Allen* allowed for an extraordinary degree of self-reflexive comedy. George Burns and Gracie Allen portrayed themselves: a married couple and comedy team working in television. Moreover, while Burns did not technically "break character," he frequently "broke the fourth wall" by directly addressing the audience and the camera, functioning as an *intermediary* between the show and audience, a *commentator* as well as *performer* (a technique also used by Garry Shandling on *It's Garry Shandling's Show*).[33]

However, by the late–1950s and early–1960s, the sitcom world was primarily defined by fictional but entirely self-contained, pseudo-realistic worlds where the sitcom family could easily be the family next door, if not the viewer's *own* family.[34] Any self-reflexivity, yet alone direct interaction between the performers and viewer, was non-existent; the viewer watched the narrative comedy unfold while absorbing the ethical (read: ideological) message over the course of a half-hour, messages, as Adorno noted, hidden in the shows through the very interactions of the characters themselves rather than explicit polemics. The father was the unquestioned head of the household (as the title *Father Knows Best* prescribed with a Freudian ruthlessness), and also a white-collar professional. *Leave It to Beaver*'s Ward Cleaver (Hugh Beaumont) was an office-bound businessman; *Father Knows Best*'s Jim Anderson (Robert Young) was an insurance agent, and *The Donna Reed Show*'s Alex Stone (Carl Betz) was a doctor whose very name, "Stone," described him as the "rock of the family." They may occasionally become irritated by their jobs — and kids — but for the most part were content with middle-class life. The wife-mother was generally a fairly benign character providing love and support, even when she received top billing. Donna Reed, famous for starring opposite Jimmy Stewart in Frank Capra's *It's a Wonderful Life* (1946), essentially recreated that role to provide a stereotype, and even a cultural role model, of the devoted housewife whose goal was the maintenance of the family structure as "Donna

Stone" on *The Donna Reed Show* (she also achieved every American girl's dream of marrying a handsome doctor). Children usually numbered between two and three (2.3 children being the mean for American families in America at the time), and they demonstrated a youthful but harmless insolence, as well as a precocious power of observation and commentary far beyond their years. With the exception of *The Honeymooners*, the early domestic sitcom world was primarily an idyllic petit-bourgeois, suburban, patriarchal utopia, with *Father Knows Best* epitomizing, as Marc succulently put it, "the sum and substance of these benevolent Aryan melodramas."[35]

Clash of the Titans: Lucy Ricardo versus Ralph Kramden

As an opening salvo to their debate over the revolutionary potential of cinema in mass culture, an early draft of Benjamin's "The Work of Art in the Age of Mechanical Reproduction" provoked a stern rebuke from Adorno. Miriam Hansen pointed out that a primary source of contention between Adorno and Benjamin stemmed from an unlikely figure: Mickey Mouse. Benjamin marveled at the possibilities of cartoon animation to construct an anamorphic world where humans, animals, and machines take on attributes of each other, resulting in a world combining Charles Fourier's phantasmal utopian vision of a synthesis of nature and machines with a nightmare scenario of modern progress run amok (as theorized by Max Weber's "Iron Cage" of modern administration, and cinematically articulated by Chaplin's *Modern Times*). It was through laughing *with* Mickey Mouse's manic, frantic struggles in a surrealistic cartoon world of modernity gone mad that Benjamin argued the audience engaged in a "collective laughter ... and *therapeutic eruption of mass psychosis.*"[36] For Adorno, the production and response of laughter was far different, with the viewer laughing *at* Mickey Mouse's frenetic struggle in the modern world: "The laughter of the cinema is ... anything but good and revolutionary, instead, *it is full of the worst bourgeois sadism.*"[37] The "collective laughter" of cinema audiences becomes a ritual of organized derision, and, in a none-too-subtle allusion to Walter Benjamin's fascination with cartoons from *Dialectic of Enlightenment*, "With the audience in pursuit, the protagonist becomes the worthless object of general violence.... Donald Duck in the cartoons and the unfortunate in real life get their thrashing so the audience can learn to take their own punishment."[38]

Arguably the show that defined early television comedy, *I Love Lucy*, if not actually creating the genre, firmly established the domestic sitcom as TV comedy's primary genre. While Lucille Ball was already a film and radio star, the great contradiction of *I Love Lucy* was that she did not portray Lucille Ball, a popular entertainer (Burns and Allen, the Nelson family), but played Lucy Ricardo, a suburban *housewife* who desperately and pathetically *wanted* to be a star. One of the show's running plot devices was Lucy continually trying to become a successful entertainer alongside her husband, singer-musician Ricky Ricardo (Ball's husband at the time, singer-musician Desi Arnez).[39] The subplot became an essential "hidden message" to *I Love Lucy*, as David Marc perceptively observed:

> The nightclub is territory verboten to Lucy by her bandleader husband Ricky. She plots and schemes to find a way out of her drab domestic existence and into one of Ricky's "shows." ... Even though she is funny — both to the on-screen audience and the television viewer — her attempt to cross over from neighborhood (urban provincial) life into the cosmopolitan world of show business is revealed to be both ridiculous and futile.... Incompetence is the source of her humor. The audience, which watches television and knows professional television when it sees it, *laughs at Lucy Ricardo, not with her*.... As the episode ends, she is, in quick order, reminded of her rightful place, forgiven by her exasperated but loving husband, and sent back home to Little Ricky and the roast.[40]

By depicting Lucy Ricardo as an object of audience scorn, someone whose desperate attempt to transcend the barriers of her living conditions are both mockingly amusing and shamelessly wretched, the "hidden message" that the "woman's place is in the home" was none-too-hidden at all: *any* attempt by Lucy to transcend her domestic role was not only unsuccessful, but a dismal disaster of slapstick comedy. In "Job Switching" (1952), the famous episode where she and friend Ethel Mertz (Vivian Vance) find jobs in a candy factory, employment turns into an assembly-line fiasco of *Modern Times* proportions. However, the key difference is that in *Modern Times* the villain is industrial order attempting to reign in the Little Tramp; in "Job Switching" the villains are displaced housewives Lucy Ricardo and Ethel Mertz, who are too incompetent to meet the standards set by the factory.

As noted, Adorno's assessment of *Our Miss Brooks* argued that the show's ideological function was "promoting adjustment to humiliating conditions by presenting them as objectively comical." While Lucy Ricardo's struggle has sometimes been interpreted as a Chaplinesque suburban suffragette valiantly attempting to transcend her domestic confinement, Marc's assessment of *I Love Lucy* is quite consistent with Adorno. If less overt and grotesque than Milton Berle's drag routines, Lucy Ricardo's more nefarious purpose in mass culture was to function as "an other" who is not unique due to any exceptionality or merit, but simply there to be designated and dismissed as different, a freakish and reprehensible signifier of what does *not* constitute "the mean" in modern society. Therefore, they can be punished with ridicule, coerced into conformity, or entirely eliminated from society (an issue that becomes crucial in reading *The Gong Show* and Andy Kaufman's use of "personas"): "The mere existence of an other is a provocation. Every 'other' person who 'doesn't know their place' must be forced back within his [or her] proper confines — those of unrestricted terror."[41] Lucy Ricardo's efforts to break out of domestic dullness is not a noble and dignified struggle but a pathetic and foolish display providing laughs for the audience at her expense, as well as thoroughly demonstrating what was her place (the suburban home) and *not* her place (the workplace, urban nightlife).

With the sitcom becoming the preferred mode of television comedy with both networks and audiences, Jackie Gleason temporarily abandoned the highly successful comedy-variety show format of *The Jackie Gleason Show* (CBS, 1952–5, 1956–9) to briefly explore the sitcom.[42] Drastically restructuring *The Jackie Gleason Show* for the 1955–6 season, Gleason divided it into two sections: a half-hour, pre-taped, three-camera sitcom performed in front of a live audience, followed by a half-hour devoted exclusively to jazz music, featuring big-band stars the Dorsey Brothers. For the sitcom section, popular sketches starring his Ralph Kramden character from *The Jackie Gleason Show* were recycled and reworked, along with new scripts, into *The Honeymooners*.[43]

In many respects, *The Honeymooners* turned the domestic sitcom on its head to present a bleak study of the American Dream: a pseudo-realistic world at times almost *too* grimly pseudo-realistic. While parents and children could both relate to Beaver Cleaver's dilemmas and their resolution by Ward Cleaver, it was quite another matter when Ralph Kramden led a rent-strike, culminating in his eviction in the middle of winter and a humiliating victory for the landlord ("Please Leave the Premises," 1956). Unlike his contented white-collar contemporaries, Ralph Kramden was a resentful and raging blue-collar bus driver who despised his class position. If the sitcom father could be stubborn and testy, Ralph Kramden was pathologically hard-headed and volatile, with his potential for explosive violence magnified by Gleason's imposing physical size. The desire for success was not simply rooted in financial security, but the possibility that one day he could push people around in the same way he was now being pushed around. His wife Alice (Audrey Meadows) was more of a sparring partner than spouse — the antithesis of Donna Stone or June Cleaver. Most arguments ended with Ralph's famous punch in the air and some variation of "One of these days... Bang! Zoom! To the Moon!"— an unrequited gesture of spousal abuse. Unlike middle-class suburbia, *The Honeymooners* was set in a claustrophobic, urban *noir* apartment where Ralph and Alice ritually acted out their highly contentious relationship.

Adding fuel to the fire of Kramden's latent but never fully expressed wrath was neighbor and best friend Ed Norton (Art Carney), a lanky and lackadaisical counterpoint to the rotund and raging Kramden, the two functioning as an urban proletariat version of Laurel and Hardy.[44] However, Norton shared little of Kramden's grandiose dreams of bourgeois life, and happily toiled as a sewer worker: a man who cheerily made a living by literally shoveling the shit of other people and whose occasional successes, often at the expense of the ambitious Ralph, came about by sheer accident. In "The Man from Space" (1955), Ralph Kramden becomes obsessed with winning the grand prize at his lodge's yearly masquerade ball — not only to receive a much-needed monetary reward, but public recognition for being proclaimed, however briefly, "a winner" by his peers. Constructing a hideous costume out of kitchen utensils and junked appliances, Kramden is convinced that his cunning has produced a costume destined for victory, the "Man from Space" (although Alice strongly suspects otherwise and is quick to repeatedly offer that opinion). At the ball, Ralph's costume impresses the judges, although they believe he has entered as the "Human Pinball Machine"—a mistake that insults Ralph but which he'll overlook if it secures him first prize. Unfortunately, as Ralph is about to be crowned the winner, Ed Norton arrives at the last minute, having been detained by a work emergency in the sewers. Bursting into the party still in his work gear — a gas mask hanging around his neck and protective rubber overalls — Norton inquires if he's "too late," referring to the free food. The judges deem Norton not "too late" at all, and promptly award him the first prize in the costume competition for *his* costume: "Man from Space." With clenched teeth, Kramden congratulates Norton, scarcely able to contain his anger in enduring yet another last-minute defeat.

In this respect, Ralph Kramden becomes a particularly problematic figure in television comedy. In some respects, he is a working-class buffoon whose attempts to break out of his living conditions are noble only to him, provoking consternation and contempt from those around him (specifically his wife), and becoming a constant source of pleasure for the television audience who laugh *at* Kramden's ill-conceived plots and feeble attempts to better his life. However, Ralph Kramden's plight is not simply an ignoble source of amusement. Kramden does not at all "experience [his] inadequate position as an object of fun," but sees it as a demeaning and merciless joke by a society that has made him the perennial punchline. While he may be ironically resigned at the end of "The Man from Space," or humiliated but haughty at the end of "Please Leave the Premises," Ralph Kramden is *never* "apparently free of any resentment" at the conclusion of the show — or from the moment the show begins. Many of Kramden's struggles begin with grandiose arrogance and end with disturbing mortification. In "The $99,000 Answer" (1955), Ralph is scheduled to appear on a game show where a contestant wins increasing sums of money through identifying increasingly obscure popular songs. Alice repeatedly pleads with Ralph to be satisfied with winning *any* money to ease the financial burdens. Of course, Ralph is determined to answer the $99,000 question. As with "The Man from Space," the public recognition of success is as important as, or even moreso than, the money. Fortunately, Ed Norton plays piano and is enlisted into grueling hours of running through obscure songs that Ralph correctly answers with increasing overconfidence. In the running joke foreshadowing the episode's tragicomic punchline, Norton's habit of playing the opening bars of "Swanee River" before every song to warm up his fingers eventually produces a violent outburst from Ralph. On the game show, Ralph Kramden answers the pre-contest interview questions with unabashed self-importance, yet the inevitable disaster strikes when the host asks the first question for $100: "Who wrote this song?" The opening bars of "Swanee River" are heard on piano. His mouth agape, the panicking Kramden stammers and nervously surveys his surroundings before sheepishly answering, "Ed Norton?" As the TV camera slowly zooms in to a close-up of Ralph Kramden, lips trembling, he stares in abject horror, the objective camera assuming the point-of-view shot of the game show camera. He has not been merely defeated in front of his peers at the lodge ("The Man from Space"), but publicly humiliated on television. His "inadequate position" is not an "object of fun," but a moment of Kafkaesque horror where a blank stare is the only possible gesture. It is a moment where television — and at this very moment Ralph Kramden is indeed seen "on television" — encapsulates the fact that "the life of ordinary people is affected by terror and impotence."

In this context, to view television as a set of uniform cultural commodities providing ideological indoctrination, as exemplified by Adorno, also excludes *a proiri* any possibility that television comedy, including non-political comedy, can potentially be read "against the grain." It can contain oppositional hidden messages, and it can even become a space of open cultural and political conflict (as will be discussed with *The Smothers Brothers Comedy Hour*). While *I Love Lucy* and *The Honeymooners* provided vastly different versions and visions of American life (one affirmative and one pessimistic), what they had in common was the reliance on the conventional sitcom format. In this respect, two notable and even radical exceptions in American television comedy emerged: Ernie Kovacs and Soupy Sales. Their importance stems from how they challenged the growing standardization of television comedy, provided subversive yet non-pedantic social commentary, and, above all, used comedy to depict the breakdown of reality rather than replicate it.

Part Two. Deconstructing Television: American Television Comedy, 1951–1966

Surrealism has never meant anything to me but a new kind of magic.... The whole of concrete reality changes its garb or shell and ceases to correspond to the same mental gestures. The beyond, the invisible replaces reality. The world no longer holds.
  — Antonin Artaud, "In Total Darkness, or, the
    Surrealist Bluff" (1927)

Our taverns and our metropolitan streets, our offices and our furnished rooms, our railroad stations and our factories appeared to have us locked up hopelessly. Then came the film and burst this prison-world asunder by the dynamite of a tenth of a second, so that now, in the midst of its far-flung ruins and debris, we calmly and adventurously go traveling.
  — Walter Benjamin, "The Work of Art in the
    Age of Mechanical Reproduction" (1936)

Chapter 3

The Humor of Anomaly: Ernie Kovacs

> This is not a comedy show, this is more or less an experiment I'm doing.[1]
> —Ernie Kovacs on his ABC specials (1961)

Ernie in Kovacsland

For Ernie Kovacs, comedy became an exploration of the medium of television that largely abandoned *verbal* comedy in favor of *audio-visual* comedy influenced by the silent comedians (Chaplin, Keaton), cartoon animation (*Fritz the Cat*, Tex Avery, Chuck Jones), and early experimental films (Dada, Soviet, and Surrealist cinema). While Kovacs began his comedy career on radio in the 1940s, by 1951 he was working in TV at Philadelphia's NBC-affiliate WTPZ in a variety of formats: game shows, talk shows, and a comedy-variety show, *Ernie in Kovacsland*, which briefly ran nationally on NBC as a summer replacement show (July-August 1951). In April of 1952, Kovacs began a long-running, weekday comedy show for WCBS titled *Kovacs Unlimited* (1952–4). Its success in the New York City market encouraged CBS to offer Kovacs a network primetime slot for *The Ernie Kovacs Show*, although the invitation was motivated by a pressing need to fill the dreaded "Black Tuesday" programming slot opposite Milton Berle (at the time, *The Buick-Berle Show*). With a limited budget and almost no pre-production, the show was viewed as haphazard and unprofessional, although critics admired it in principle. *Variety* stated, "Kovacs' exaggerated informality, uniquely fresh type of humor, and new use of special effect, while to be commended, just weren't good enough to meet nighttime standards."[2] Pummeled in the ratings, *The Ernie Kovacs Show* ran from December 1952 to April 1953.

In December of 1955, Kovacs began a stint on NBC with another *Ernie Kovacs Show*. Faring slightly better than his ill-fated CBS show, it nevertheless ran less than one year: a weekday show from December 1955 to July 1956, which was converted to a weekly primetime show as a summer replacement for *Caesar's Hour* that aired from July to September 1956.[3] Producer Perry Cross later described it as "antiform":

> Guests were treated in a way that was different, like when Boris Karloff, who was very popular as the Frankenstein Monster, came on and read the alphabet dramatically.... [I]f we were going to do a dance ... we'd do the top halves of bodies on the bottom halves of other bodies, or on parts of a horse. It was really lunacy.[4]

Likewise, instead of featuring popular singers recycling or promoting hit songs, guest musical acts included mainstream piano duo Ferrante and Teicher performing on prepared pianos — an invention of John Cage where various objects (wood, screws, rubber) are inserted between the piano strings to provide an array of strange, percussive effects. Yma Sumac appeared with her brand of musical "exotica," a genre combining lounge music, avant-garde formalism, and Third World music (Latin American and Pacific Islands music being the more common sources).[5]

Although NBC did not renew *The Ernie Kovacs Show* for the 1956–7 season, Kovacs was still under contract to the network, and, somewhat reluctantly, he became the temporary host of *The Tonight Show* from October 1956 to January 1957 after Steve Allen moved to primetime to compete against *The Ed Sullivan Show*. Kovacs used his brief tenure on *Tonight* to further pursue his idiosyncratic comedy experiments, and *Tonight* routines such as the "tilted table" and the "library bit" served as basis for his legendary NBC special, often referred to as "The Silent Show," that aired on January 19, 1957 (to be discussed further in relation to the "Eugene" episode for ABC's *The Ernie Kovacs Show* that aired in November 1961).[6] "The Silent Show" not only garnered Kovacs critical acclaim, but a rarity in his career: a ratings coup. However, Kovacs's triumph was tempered by mounting personal financial problems and weariness with years of battling network executives and sponsors. Forgoing television, he accepted a lucrative contract with Columbia Pictures, where he planned to write and direct comedy films, although much of his Hollywood career consisted of supporting, comic-relief roles in genre films such as *Our Man from Havana* and *North to Alaska*.

In 1959, Kovacs returned to television as host of ABC's *Take a Good Look*, a primetime game show where celebrity panelists tried to guess a mystery guest's identity by asking general questions and figuring out "filmed

3. *The Humor of Anomaly: Ernie Kovacs* 51

A world out of balance: Ernie Kovacs, as Eugene (center), performs the tilted table sketch on "The Silent Show" (1957) (Photofest).

clues" devised by Kovacs. Kovacs used *Take a Good Look* to perfect what became his specialty — sight-gags lasting only a few seconds each, usually involving a mundane premise and unsound conclusion. For example, Kovacs played a used-car salesman standing next to a car: he smiled at the camera, placed his hand on the fender, and sent the car crashing through the floor of the soundstage. Needless to say, a three-second sight-gag that cost $10,000 infuriated his sponsor, Dutch Masters Cigars, when they saw Kovacs (literally) throw money down a hole. However, Dutch Masters and its parent company, Consolidated Cigar Company, were also largely responsible for Kovacs's network TV survival. As part of his contract, Kovacs personally made the Dutch Masters Cigar commercials on *Take a Good Look*. Despite the show's overall poor ratings, Dutch Masters sales dramatically *increased*, an upsurge credited to Kovacs's commercials. Consolidated Cigar Company executive Jack Mogulescu recalled, "It was a struggle to keep the show on the air.... ABC never understood what he was trying to do ... it confused us sometimes, it confused the public, it confused the critics, *and unnecessarily so*."[7]

ABC cancelled *Take a Good Look* in the spring of 1961, and Consolidated Cigar quickly hired Kovacs for the replacement show(s) for *Take a Good Look*: *Silents Please* (ABC, March-October 1961), a half-hour anthology show featuring silent comedy two-reelers or abridged feature films hosted by Kovacs, and an *Ernie Kovacs Show* special airing once a month in place of *Silents Please*.[8] With the star focusing on writing and directing as much as being the on-air personality, these ABC specials effectively encapsulated Kovacs's brand of avant-garde, audio-visual humor.[9] Beginning in May 1961 (excepting July and August), the monthly specials ran until January 1962 (the final show aired posthumously). In the early morning hours of January 13, 1962, Kovacs was killed in a car accident. Known for his penchant for gambling, spending, hard-living, and black comedy, Kovacs's tombstone was embossed with the epitaph "Nothing in Moderation."

The Cockeyed World: Kovacs and Benjamin

In some respects, Kovacs performed a similar operation on television in its nascent stage consistent with Georges Mèliés's experiments with cinema in its embryonic period: combining the *theatrical* (specially-designed *mise en scène*) with the *photographic* (camera manipulations and special effects). The primary difference being that Mèliés specialized in creating *unreal, magical* worlds, while Kovacs specialized in creating *surreal, modern* worlds.

Kovacs utilized a vast array of specially-built props and set designs. He occasionally employed a transparent platform as the stage, allowing him to film the actors from underneath the stage (ballroom dancers, cowboys in a gunfight). He placed cameras in front of tanks of water, where a submerged Kovacs performed sight-gags, understandably lasting only a few seconds. For example, a shot of a sign on a door reading "School for Skin Divers" abruptly cut to an underwater Kovacs in a suit and tie typing at a desk with a blackboard of complex mathematical formulas behind him. Antecedents of these sight-gags can found in René Clair's *Entr'acte* (Francis Picabia dressed as a ballerina dancing on a transparent stage) and Man Ray's *Le Mystère du château de dé* (Parisian artist and socialite Marie-Laure de Noailles juggling oranges underwater in a swimming pool). Such images could have easily appeared as typical sight-gags on a Kovacs show.

Kovacs was well aware that the vast majority of the audience owned black-and-white television sets, and used the medium appropriately—he did his shows in black and white, and for one sight-gag put signs on all the props designating their actual color.[10] Thus, light and shadow were utilized extensively in shot composition, variously echoing German Expressionism, Neo-Realism, and *film noir*. For his "Street Scene" sketches, Kovacs combined silent cinema, modern dance, and classical music (usually Béla Bartók) to create highly-stylized, dramatic vignettes of urban life. As well as filming with a variety of lenses (wide-angle, depth-of-field), Kovacs frequently employed disorientating camera angles: extreme close-ups, long shots, high-angle and low-angle shots, and canted shots (tilted camera angles). The 180-degree rule was pushed to its limits: overhead shots, underfoot shots (courtesy of the transparent stage), and placing cameras at the outermost edges of the 180-degree stage axis. Perhaps most importantly, studio effects were used to augment or even manufacture sight-gags, including extensive use of fade-outs to a black screen (literally ending each sight-gag with a "blackout"), dissolves, double-exposures, superimposition, and rear-screen projection (filming in front of a "green screen" and inserting filmed backgrounds). One sight-gag simply exploited the process of reverse polarity — turning images into their negative form. A goateed character entered a room through a door marked "Dark Room," and after a rather inordinate amount of time with the camera focused on the sign, the off-camera sound of a flashbulb exploding was heard; the man then walked out of the Dark Room as an iridescent, photographic negative image (again recalling Ray's *Le Mystère du château de dé*, which also featured a section done in photographic negatives).

Moreover, sound was just as important as the visual components of the sight-gags — both in absence and excess. As Kovacs described his work, "Eighty percent of what I do is in the category of sight-gags, no pantomime. *I work on the incongruity of sight against sound.*"[11] Sight-gags were primarily visual and frequently devoid of dialogue (the one-liners and zingers of verbal sketch comedy), and sound effects were used to provide an exaggerated compliment to the visual, or an incongruous juxtaposition to the visual. One sketch involved a demonstration of how an oscilloscope responded to sound. First, Kovacs pounded on the floor with his palms and then rang a bell. The line at the bottom of the screen reacted accordingly. After a brief pause, Kovacs again shook the bell, only to produce the sound of a mammoth gong, sending the line into spasmodic waves and Kovacs issuing a double-take directly at the camera.

For his famous "tilted table" sequences, the set was built at a downward angle to the right, with the camera filming the table in a canted shot so the table appeared level on the TV screen. As Kovacs emptied a lunch pail and poured milk, the objects careened down the table, accompanied by various sound effects, in defiance of the basic laws of Newtonian physics. Producer

Roger Gimbel recounted that such routines worked tremendously well on the *Tonight* TV broadcast, but lacked that same comedic effectiveness on stage:

> He was trying things that didn't seem like big jokes, and they were funny in a totally new, different way. *Sort of avant-garde, experimental television....* The reaction in the theater was a bumpy one for us.... Heavier comedy, more stand-up, sketch material worked great. Ernie's sketches were entertaining and wildly imaginative, but they didn't always get big laughs.[12]

In this context, one can compare the effect of the tilted table sketch as it appears on television — a seemingly normal world rendered askew — with the live, theatrical stage, where the audience saw Kovacs aimlessly rolling objects off the table built on a tilted platform. Kovacs's shows were television comedy specifically designed to work *in*, *through* and even *against* the medium of television. Moreover, they were specifically intended for *television* audiences (as will be addressed further, Kovacs detested using studio audiences on his shows). In this respect, Walter Benjamin's assessment of acting and performance in "The Work of Art" provides an important comparison to how Kovacs approached television comedy:

> Guided by the cameraman, the camera continually changes its position with respect to the performance.... It comprises certain factors of movement which are in reality those of the camera, not to mention special camera angles, close-ups, etc. Hence, the performance is subjected to a series of *optical tests*.... Also, the film actor lacks the opportunity of the stage actor to adjust to the audience during his performance, since he does not present the performance to the audience in person. This permits the audience to take the position of a critic, without experiencing any personal contact with the actor. *The audience's identification with the actor is really an identification with the camera. Consequently, the audience takes the position of the camera; its approach is that of testing.*[13]

Kovacs consciously embarked on a form of comedy *only* effective as mediated by the camera and broadcast on television as *optical tests*; and *auditory tests* should also be added. In turn, Kovacs placed a television audience in the position of testing the comedy, the receptive mode of *distraction* combining objective critical awareness and the shock effect. Indeed, there was a sort of unification of art and science with Kovacs: the art of comedy merged with a scientific testing of the comedy with the camera, in the studio, and by the television audience — with the specific exclusion of any live, studio audience. Moreover, Benjamin championed film because of the camera's "incomparably more precise statements of the situation" than painting and the ability to "isolate" and study the event more effectively than theater. Similarly, Kovacs's humor lied in the possibilities of the camera and the medium of television to capture "filmed behavior" in a way painting and theater were unable to.

Whether by chance or design, a favorite target for Kovacs's sight-gags was canonical high culture: literature, theater, and especially paintings (to be discussed in reference to Benjamin in more detail regarding the ABC "Eugene" episode).

Kovacs's own interest was not elevating television to the ultimate form of comedy — yet alone art — but simply exploring and exploiting both its limits and possibilities: "My particular affinity for the medium is to make it an electronic one *and use this particular medium for its own intrinsic value and approach.* But I do not put it above — nor do I put it below — other forms of comedy. This happens to be mine."[14] Nevertheless, Kovacs understood that television was a potentially ideal medium to transmit the shock effect, even more so than cinema. As John Ellis noted:

> Broadcast TV has a particular regime of representation that stresses the immediacy and co-presence of the representation.... TV's regime of vision is less intense than cinema's: *it is a regime of the glance rather than the gaze.* The gaze implies a concentration of the spectator's activity into that of looking, the glance implies that no extraordinary effort is being invested into the activity of looking."[15]

If, as Benjamin claimed, the audience shifted from the appreciative engagement in books, plays, concerts, and static visual arts (painting, sculpture) to the status of "absent-minded examiner" with cinema, this shift from contemplation to distraction becomes even more pronounced with the transition from cinema to television. As Ellis suggested, the experience of the moviegoer and a captivated *gaze* at the silver screen is itself a form of concentration. With television, this is replaced by occasional *glances* at the TV screen, with *sound* a primary means of viewer identification (as discussed in Chapter Two). TV is frequently *listened* to as much as *watched*—often while the viewer is engaged in other activities (eating dinner, talking with other people, cleaning the home, balancing the checkbook, reading, or, in recent years, working on a computer). A sitcom and most sketch comedy can easily be listened to, and enjoyed, due to the reliance on narrative and verbal comedy. In contrast, listening to a typical Ernie Kovacs show entailed experiencing a mixture of musical snippets, sound effects, dead air, and occasional dry comments about the show or purposefully dull dialogue. The viewer, simply put, had to *watch* an *Ernie Kovacs Show* to fully grasp the juxtapositions and incongruities between image and sound.

Kovacs realized that the potential for the shock effect of television comedy was not only much *greater*, but had to be much more *immediate*. If the audience's attention was divided between watching TV and other activities, the potential for the shock effect was *heightened* due to their blasé attitude towards the television event; if the audience was only partially attentive to events on the TV screen — glancing rather than gazing — the shock effect had to be *abrupt* and *continuous* to keep the viewer in the state of distraction at all times. Thus, the short sight-gag became Kovacs's *modus operandi*. However, this is not to say that Kovacs's shows were fast-paced like *The Monkees* and, of course, *Rowan and Martin's Laugh-In*. In fact, they were quite the opposite — deliberate and almost leisurely in their tempo. While Kovacs demanded ongoing critical awareness from the TV viewer, he also encouraged, for lack of a better word, "relaxed" reception, which converted the TV audience into "absent-minded examiners." With Kovacs, the flow of sight-gags was closer to the loosely-connected and often unsettling dream-images that characterized Surrealist films than the highly disruptive and agitating formal nature of Dada films.

Surrealism and Sight-Gags

Admittedly, in terming Kovacs a "Surrealist," this is not to deny the Dada elements in his work. Numerous sight-gags, the famous Nairobi Trio sketches, his "sound to sight" pieces, and his overall "antiform" approach to television could be considered Dada from an artistic standpoint. Like Dada films, a great deal of Kovacs's work relied on "cinematic manipulations" to achieve the humorous shock effect. Where Kovacs becomes Surrealist is in his approach to *defamiliarizing social reality* (as discussed in Chapter One). Kovacs's TV world was not manifestly illogical; he established a normal, almost benign world, only to repeatedly pull the rug out from under the viewer with bizarre and frequently macabre actions. A sight-gag was simply an ordinary premise followed by any number of possible outcomes, regardless of rational cause-effect — what Kovacs termed "the humor of anomaly," and his colleagues simply referred to as "the switch." As *Ernie Kovacs Show* writer Mike Marmer recalled, "Ernie was the master of the switch ... he made you believe what he was doing ... *the more real it is, the more shocking the switch will be.*"[16]

Typical sight-gags could range from a finger suddenly protruding from the center of a phone to dial a number, to the camera slowly panning across a bathroom with a tub full of water and a hand desperately flailing in the drain, to a simple shot of a sink with the faucet spurting a superimposed jet of flame (followed by water running *upward* into the air). Sight-gags might be held together in a general sketch scenario (such as the tilted table or the library sequences in the ABC "Eugene" show). They might also be repeated with numerous variations over the course of a show. A recurring sight-gag of a woman simply entering a room through a door produced (among many outcomes): a standard burlesque joke (her skirt being pulled off when caught in the door closing behind her); a slapstick conclusion (the woman getting hit in the face with pie thrown from off-frame, *à la* Soupy Sales); a surreal effect (the woman tossing a long-stem rose on a nearby piano, causing it to collapse under the weight of the flower); or an absurd non-result (a shot of the door and a few seconds of dead air, with the woman never entering — perhaps the Beckett version of the sight-gag). Similar sight-gags could appear over the course of different shows, and sometimes the same sight-gags were simply recycled across shows (a number of *Take a Good Look* "filmed clues" later appeared on the ABC shows as sight-gags). This potential for "recycling" built into Kovacs's antiform sketch-comedy show ultimately became the chief formal influence on *Rowan and Martin's Laugh-In* (see Chapter Six).

Other sight-gags were built around choreographed sketches set to music, be it the violent musical numbers by the Nairobi Trio or the meticulous "sound to sight" pieces (to be discussed shortly). In what became a kind of trademark, Kovacs utilized a German recording of "Mack the Knife" from Weil-Brecht's *The Threepenny Opera*, accompanied by an oscillating electronic line pulsating wildly in response to the modulations of singer Wolfgang Neuss.[17] Used to bridge a series of disconnected blackout sight-gags, "Mack the Knife" and its accompanying oscilloscope image became as famous as many of the sight-gags themselves.

While certainly informed by the tradition of burlesque and slapstick, the burlesque sight-gags contained a subtle critique of the genre's sexism, while his slapstick sight-gags exhibited astonishing black comedy. Kovacs was not above a sight-gag where a vacuum cleaner salesman sucks a woman's dress off her body, leaving her in her undergarments — a visual perhaps more consistent with *The Benny Hill Show* than *The Ernie Kovacs Show*. Yet a woman nonchalantly relaxing in a bathtub might be shown in the tub with her legs impossibly extending out *through* the back of the tub, or scrubbing a foot in a physically impossible position — surreal parodies of pin-up photography as done by René Magritte. The first of two sight-gag commentaries on voyeurism saw a submarine periscope emerge out of the soapy water; in the other, it was a suds-covered television camera. Another blackout sketch mimicked a TV commercial for a new product geared to bored husbands: "The Invisible Girlfriend." A woman, her head *already* invisible (which reduced her to a "mindless" body), suggestively removed her dress and hat, leaving her completely naked and invisible, save for her gloves and high heels. Slinging the dress over her shoulder, the invisible woman walked out of the shot like a stripper leaving the stage. The erotic allure did not lie in seeing skin, but the thrill of a *dress* flying off an invisible body, articulating Roland Barthes's famous observation about striptease: "It is only the time taken in the shedding of clothing that makes the public voyeurs ... woman is desexualized at the very moment she is stripped naked."[18] In the "Invisible Girlfriend" sight-gag, a woman is not simply desexualized when she is naked, she is literally rendered into nothingness once she disrobes.

Like Buñuel, Kovacs extended slapstick into a realm of disturbing sadism (at least as far as 1960s network TV would permit). For instance, a man dressed as a boy with blond curls (show regular Bobby Lauher) donned a mask to pester Kovacs, dressed as a carpenter. The shot cut to a close-up of Kovacs smiling, and then slowly panned downward, revealing Kovacs cranking the hand-drill against the board and, below that, the boy's head rotating, still with the mask, impaled by the drill bit. In another, Kovacs, dressed as a painter, was sketching a portrait of a boy (again, Lauher); the camera panned to the canvas as Kovacs erased the boy's head, and then panned back to reveal the posing boy's head missing as well (an identically dressed, headless manikin now replacing Lauher). For another sight-gag, a shot of Kovacs as a barber shaving a man with a straight razor zoomed-in to a close-up of Kovacs, who suddenly sneezed. Responding to the sound of a loud thump, Kovacs looked off-frame at the chair and then directly at the camera with a revolted expression, having just inadvertently decapitated the customer. In yet another, a close-up of a woman lying on the ground with a golf ball on a tee in her mouth cut to a medium-full shot of Kovacs standing next to her about to drive the ball with a golf club. Again, the camera zoomed-in to Kovacs swinging the club, ending with a sickening thud and another appalled expression on Kovacs's face as he looked downward underneath the frame. Beyond their black comedy, these selected sight-gags manifest an underlying motif in Kovacs's work, where the joke does not "go over one's head," but was frequently and literally aimed *at* the head, or *mind*: a disruptive and destructive force directed at the intellectual center of its victims — the shock effect.

"The Intimate Vacuum"

As Frank J. Chorba noted, "While his contemporaries were treating television as an extension of the vaudeville stage, Kovacs was expanding the visible confines of the studio ... including dialogue with the camera crew, the audience, and forays into the studio corridor."[19] By radically experimenting with the medium, exploring its possibilities as well as demystifying its processes, Kovacs transformed the status of television audiences — both in the studio and the living room. Kovacs taped in front of a studio audience only when networks and sponsors insisted; he adamantly refused to add laugh tracks to the shows. The live audience simply became superfluous as Kovacs's shows became increasingly reliant on using the camera as much as the performers to tell the jokes. Beyond the *practical* reason of shunning a studio audience, Kovacs had a *political* reason as well:

> I don't have an audience for my shows, I don't believe in that. An audience with free tickets will laugh at the pauses, because, they've been told, nudgingly, and after long experience, you are now to laugh....This is wrong to me. It, first of all, destroys the timing of the show. My show is timed out to within, like three seconds, and if I find that something plays a little longer I will play it longer than re-time it. But I don't have it for laughs, I don't leave any space for laughs, and sometimes we don't get any.[20]

By refusing to structure his shows to allow for inserted laughter, they developed their own pacing, presentation, and, above all, reception. Kovacs was keenly aware of the role played by the internal TV comedy audience (live or a laugh track): providing guidance for the viewer to react accordingly and ultimately shaping a show to be a more easily-consumed comedy product. Occasionally on the ABC specials, Kovacs sat in the front row of an empty TV studio talking to the camera while a voice-over of Kovacs, completely out of synch with the movements of his mouth, discussed the show — and Kovacs himself— quite sardonically in the *third-person*. On one show, a young woman was superimposed climbing up Kovacs's back and then nonchalantly filing her nails, perched on his shoulder. The voice-over explained: "This is a show done purely for the people at home.... There is no studio audience for this show; there are no laughs on the soundtrack either. All in all, it's kind of like a ... *an intimate vacuum*. Incidentally, there is no little girl on his shoulder; there's something wrong with your set."

In constructing this "intimate vacuum," a locale Kovacs favored was the control room of the studio, surrounded by TV monitors, sometimes wearing a headset, and always puffing on a cigar. He simultaneously discussed the show with the technician sitting beside him and the television audience. One ABC show began with the camera trying to adjust its focus for a few seconds before the viewer could discern Kovacs sitting in the control booth rubbing his eyes: "There's nothing wrong with your set. I just have a slow focus." On camera, Kovacs assumed the roles of performer, director, and, above all, commentator directly engaging the television viewer and acting as an *intermediary* between the show and the audience — the relationship Brecht constructed between performer and audience in his plays ("The direct changeover from *representation to commentary*").[21] Moreover, Ellis suggested that the common use of direct address on television — a tactic virtually absent and implicitly forbidden in theater or cinema — stemmed from the nature of the medium itself. One again relates to the importance of sound in the medium of television, and that the constant stream of voices talking to the viewer, rather than the "glanced-at" images, becomes a primary source of identification. Also, the direct address provides a different type of identification in which a more informal relationship develops — one between "you and I" (the first and second person directly engaged with each other). This is opposed to the first person audience passively but intently observing third person characters — "me and them" — as with theater, cinema, and, of course, the sitcom's fictional characters, who are objects of contemplation as eminently "identifiable" stand-ins for the viewer's own relatives, friends, neighbors, or co-workers.[22]

In this respect, Kovacs's offhand comment labeling television "an intimate vacuum" becomes quite profound. Kovacs understood that the medium demanded "intimacy," simply by the fact that the audience was not making the effort to see the performer (going to a concert, movie, or play). Rather, the performer was being invited into the viewers' homes to entertain them; and they could easily change the channel if not entertained. Yet Kovacs understood that television was a sort of "vacuum," with the two disengaged parties (the show and the viewer) only connected in the performance by the TV broadcast transmission. This "intimate vacuum" allowed Kovacs to pursue TV as a medium that could potentially be developed "for its own intrinsic value and approach" — a neutral site of audio-visual *testing*.

In this context, numerous sketches were *about* television, going far beyond superficial and eclectic references to other TV shows and genres. Kovacs offered a clinical, critical, and often cynical study of television as an artistic medium and component of the Culture Industry. Kovacs devoted much of one ABC special to a lengthy deconstruction of the Western genre. Opening with a shot of Kovacs in his headphones in front of TV monitors in the control room, he directly addressed the camera and television viewer, sardonically expressing the logic of the Culture Industry: "There's a standard formula for success in the entertainment medium, and that is ... um, *beat it to death if it succeeds.*" A shot depicting the conventional Western gunfight was presented to the viewer as a point of reference (the control sequence of the experiment), followed by a demonstration of new ways camera angles and editing were utilized to reduce the predictability of the gunfight: an overhead shot, a shot from underneath the gunfighters on a transparent stage, an "art-film" montage of stylized close-ups depicting everything but the gunfight, and a slow-motion study of a bullet leaving the gun (parodying early scientific film applications). Kovacs followed with examples of updating the Western genre. The "Psychological Western" consisted of a cowboy talking to his psychiatrist. A take on the Western as done on *The Twilight Zone* depicted a cowboy battling vampire cowgirls with blinking light-bulbs on their hats in an Expressionistic background of cactus and cow skulls depicted in negative-image; his gun fired a bouquet of roses and then transformed into a handful of bananas (the entire sketch lasted fifteen seconds). B-Movie science-fiction Westerns featured the fifty-foot "Colossal Cowboy" crushing a town with his cowboy boots (a parody of *The Amazing Colossal Man*), and a six-inch cowboy trapped in a world of oversized Western props (a parody of *The Incredible Shrinking Man*). All these variations on the Western were accompanied by Kovacs's mordant commentary, either with voice-over or occasional inserts of Kovacs in the studio control room.

Straight parodies were occasionally employed to satirize conventional TV genres, such as a talk show parody in which Kovacs interviewed a guest (Joe Mikolas) who could not remember any details of his exciting life, with Kovacs becoming exasperated at having to be both the interviewer *and* the one filling in the details for the interviewee. Much of the humor lay in the sketch being thoroughly dull, overlong, talky, and depicted by a predictably static shot/reverse shot pattern — precisely like the talk show format itself. In a sketch parodying popular "arts shows," which appeared on the posthumous Kovacs show, Joe Mikolas appeared as a noted, and aptly-named, American poet, "Tension Breft." He endlessly explained his poems and read two particularly turgid and pretentious examples in a single long take while Kovacs played the role of the obsequious off-camera interviewer. Like the talk show parody, the satirical humor was ultimately rooted in the interminable nature of the segment itself.

Indeed, Kovacs famously provided his own sardonic take on the dreariness and pretentiousness of verbal poetry through his persona Percy Dovetonsils, a lisping, booze-swilling poet with fake bulging eyes painted on the lenses of his horn-rimmed glasses (his martini glass was garnished with a small daisy — although a "pansy" may have been more appropriate). Accompanied by lush orchestral music, he recited excruciating and execrable poetry to the camera and the television audience, his face filling the fame in a wide-angle close-up. Additionally, Dovetonsils provided self-amused witticisms and thinly-veiled homosexual innuendo that left *him* smirking through awkward pauses of deadening silence, with any "laugh track" provided by the off-camera crew caught off-guard by the ad-libs: "That bartender with all the mathscera tried to slip me a brown martini!" In one segment, Dovetonsils explained that the usual background painting — a parody of *Whistler's Mother*, with the matron seated on a motorbike instead of a rocking chair — was absent because he was replacing it with a copy of Gainsbourgh's *Blue Boy* (also a slang term for a homosexual), but first needed to have it re-colored because it "clasthed with the room." Certainly, Kovacs can be accused of constructing a homosexual stereotype with Dovetonsils, and, more specifically, the stereotype of the "artist as sissy."[23] Buñuel stated that silent comedians such as Chaplin,

Keaton, and Lloyd were more surrealist than the Surrealists (Man Ray), and termed their work a "new poetry." With Kovacs, comedy was the assemblage and engineering of image and sound as a form of modern *audio-visual poetry*, with the Percy Dovetonsils persona literally exemplifying his disdain for comedy as *verbal poetry*.

Poetry in Motion: Music, Montage, and "Sound to Sight"

In a 1961 interview, Kovacs explained, "I personally don't approve of the joke albums, and I don't listen to them.... I have about 6 to 7 thousand classical albums, and there are one... two... three — three complete stereo systems in the house ... and I see no television, really, at all."[24] Yet if Kovacs showed more reverence for the classical composers than his comedic peers and other "high culture" targets (literature, theater, and especially painting), he was not above using classical music for broad sight-gags bordering on Dada. One show, parodying a high culture segment from *The Ed Sullivan Show*, featured an excerpt from Tchaikovsky's ballet *Swan Lake*. After a long, hyperbolic introduction by Kovacs in order to set up "the switch," *Swan Lake* was performed quite adeptly and dramatically — except all the dancers wore gorilla costumes and tutus (to give the sketch a sort of punchline; at the end of the performance the lead ballerina-gorilla received a bunch of bananas instead of the customary bouquet of flowers).

In this regard, Kovacs's most famous musical creation also bears mention: the Nairobi Trio.[25] Three performers dressed in heavy black overcoats, bowler hats, and grotesque gorilla masks, they mechanistically acted in conjunction to Robert Maxwell's exotica song "Solfeggio."[26] In a typical Nairobi Trio routine, the Trio member on the right robotically pounded on a piano, treating it more like a percussion instrument than a melody instrument. The Trio member on the left held two tympani mallets. The one in the center calmly conducted the piece by waving a baton back and forth, a huge cigar protruding from his mouth (signifying Kovacs under the mask, although a stand-in could have been easily used). Midway through the performance a banana inexplicably replaced the baton, and the banana later became dislodged and flew off-frame, leaving the conductor holding only the peel (probably an accidental prop malfunction incorporated into the sketch). The Trio member on the left periodically and predictably turned 90 degrees at various points in the song to strike the conductor on the head with the mallets, matching a bongo fill in the music. Repeating this process twice more, the conductor demonstrated his increasing exasperation by staring at the camera in close-up and sucking the mask back to achieve an annoyed, scrunch-up expression. Finally, he turned to glare at the mallet-wielding Trio member about to drub him on the head yet again. The song continued as a long staring contest until the Trio member at the piano tapped the conductor's shoulder, distracting him long enough for the Trio member with the mallets to rap out another bongo fill on his head. His patience lost, the conductor deliberately walked behind the Trio member with the mallets, removed a vase from a stand, and shattered it over his head in time to the cymbal crash ending the song: a finale where mechanized motion, primal violence, and animal-machine hybrids converge in what Diane Rico cogently termed a "nihilistic operetta."[27]

For his ABC specials, Kovacs utilized a musical selection — a popular standard, a piece of contemporary hi-fi music, or an excerpt from a classical composition — as a basis to construct nothing less than experimental short subjects. Introducing his second ABC special, Kovacs explained, "The inherent love I have for music is the reason why I'm here. The money means nothing — the money *is* nothing, consequently it means nothing. But it is a desire to illustrate music, *sound to sight* more or less."[28] One sound to sight piece was his adaptation of Tchaikovsky's "1812 Overture" set to a montage of a row of toy monkeys banging drums, another toy monkey with a bugle careening across the frame, a rotund ballerina, a cow's head mounted on a wall swaying back and forth, a man dressed as a Catholic cardinal breaking stalks of celery, and eggs being smashed in a frying pan — all tightly edited and synchronized with the driving tempos, dramatic fanfares, and overall bombast of the overture. At a visual level, it is comparable to Dada motion studies, specifically *Ballet mécanique* and *Emak Bakia*; from the perspective of formalism, it could be discussed in terms of Eisenstein's theories of montage, especially given Eisenstein's predilection to discuss montage in terms of music (meter, rhythm, tone).[29] However, Alexander Kluge's theory of montage and *phantasie* offers the most productive means to "read" the "1812" sight to sound piece. *Phantasie* refers to the spectator's imagination and film as a means of harnessing the imagination, and Kluge opposed Eisenstein's method of film montage "directing [spectators] towards a *predetermined* series of associations."[30] Rather, Kluge theorized and made films utilizing, for lack of a better term, *disassociate montages* which juxtaposed incongruous sounds and images in order for the audience (reader) to become a critical participant in the text by manufacturing the meaning of the montages. For Eisenstein, it is the impact of two shots that produces the shock effect and the thought; for Kluge, it is the space between the shots that produces the shock, and the need for the viewer to fill that space with *phantasie* (imagination). As Kluge described it:

[E]very cut produces phantasy, a storm of phantasy.... It is exactly at this point that information is conveyed. *This is what Benjamin meant by the notion of shock.* It would be wrong to say that film should shock the viewers — this would restrict their independence and powers of perception.[31]

Indeed, to recall a passage in "The Work of Art...," Benjamin suggested, "The spectator's process of association in view of those images is indeed interrupted by their *constant, sudden change. This constitutes the shock effect of the film,* which like all shocks, *should be cushioned by heightened presence of mind*" (emphasis added). In this respect, and returning to Deleuze, Kluge's conception of montage produces thought *through* the shock of "not-*yet*-thinking" (Artaud), and that the viewer must now *think differently* to connect and read the disparate images; as Deleuze noted, "To read is to *relink* instead of link."[32] Kovacs's "1812" does not comfortably lend itself to clearly interpretable associations with colliding images of toy monkeys bashing drums and eggs shattering in a frying pan set to Tchaikovsky. However, this is not to say that the montages "mean nothing," but any reading (interpretation) becomes subjective and speculative — the product of the spectator's *phantasie* and the shock effect (for instance, possibly reading "1812" as a commentary on the status of Cold War politics between the U.S. and Soviet Union, and the end result of atomic warfare).

One of Kovacs's most memorable essays on inanimate objects in motion — and one of his most politically subversive — was a sound to sight piece done for his June 1961 ABC special depicting a work day at a typical and ostensibly normal office set to the exotica music of Juan Garcia Esquivel: his unorthodox medley arraignment of "Jalousie/Sentimental Journey." Over Esquivel's music — a kind of cross between cocktail-jazz, a Warner Brothers cartoon soundtrack, and Stockhausen — Kovacs used specially-designed props and extensive editing to depict office equipment in constant action under their own volition: file cabinets opening and closing, typewriters typing, a water cooler gurgling, a pen squirting ink, a telephone dialing by itself and numerous other office images. All were precisely timed and edited to match the rhythms and timbers of Esquivel's singular avant-garde muzak — the office switchboard lights blinking in series to piano flourishes, and the plug-in cords swaying to the wordless vocals; later, a close-up of the front of a pencil sharpener with its handle spinning away matched by a man whistling the melody line of "Sentimental Journey."

An immediate comparison is again *Ballet mécanique,* in that it constructs a world of inanimate object that become animate; machines do not simply move, but attain a humorous sense of life. However, another comparison is Vertov's *Man with a Camera* (1922), a frenetic assemblage of montages essaying modernity. *Man with a Camera* did not simply record the modern world in perpetual motion for the sake of rapid-fire imagery. Through its continuous montages of assembly lines, streetcars, and other staples of industrial modern life and labor, Vertov critiqued a modern world *at work*, and for the modern world *to work*, it must be *moving at all times*. Like *Man with a Camera*, what will be termed the "Day at the Office" sound to sight piece is not simply an essay on motion and modernity but capitalism: in order to "work," everything must constantly be in motion.[33] While Vertov focused on urban milieus, factories and industrial production, Kovacs depicted the dynamics of *corporate* America "at work" in the office, where big business functions through a tightly-choreographed flow of impersonal memos, phone calls, and contracts: Vertov meets Busby Berkeley. Conspicuously absent are human office-workers; and the only moment a human being appears in "Day at the Office" is in an Expressionistic, low-angle long shot where a seated office worker (Bobby Lauher) sees what is occurring and promptly flees the room, horrified he may be caught up in the automatic, mechanistic processes. The office becomes a self-perpetuating economic apparatus where the human factor is nullified and completely irrelevant in the definition of "industry" offered by Adorno: "Industrial forms of organization even when nothing is manufactured — as in the rationalization of office work."[34] Capitalism in Kovacs's visual essay is not one of dehumanization, and, as such, the antithesis of the character-driven drama of *Patterns*, but an anti-humanist study of "office politics." The workings of the office are depicted *only* by the automatic activities of the various pieces of office machinery and equipment, inanimate objects that became animated and strangely human: file cabinets slamming shut as if extremely exasperated; overworked phones and typewriters simply trying to keep up with the pace; the belching water cooler fighting a severe case of gastric distress or impending ulcer; or, conversely, a pencil sharpener happily "whistling while it works." Benjamin noted that one of the many places of modern life that "appeared to have us locked up hopelessly ... [was] the office." Kovacs both confirms that dire assessment yet "burst this prison-world asunder" with a large dose of surreal humor: a *Ballet office*.

Fanfare for the Modern Man: "Eugene," *The Ernie Kovacs Show* (ABC, 1961)

With the possible exception of Percy Dovetonsils, Kovacs's most famous TV persona was "Eugene," a bemused modern everyman reminiscent of Keaton and Chaplin tackling the world in ill-fitting plaid suits. On January 19, 1957, Kovacs played Eugene in a half-hour NBC special he informally titled "No Dialogue," but which became widely known as "The Silent Show." "The

Silent Show" was hastily produced to fill a vacant half-hour time slot left open by a highly-anticipated Jerry Lewis comedy special, his first television comedy show after his break with Dean Martin. NBC scheduled the special for its 90-minute time slot, *Saturday Color Carnival* (so named because it was one of the few TV shows broadcast in color at the time). However, Lewis had already signed a contract for a 60-minute special, and insisted on the first hour of the show so his special would begin and end at the top of the hour. Scrambling to fill the gap in *Saturday Color Carnival*, NBC approached Kovacs, still under contract with NBC and current interim host of *The Tonight Show*. Kovacs agreed to fill in the half-hour of airtime on the condition of complete creative control. NBC acquiesced, assuming the Lewis special would inevitably overshadow anything that followed it (and happy to find anyone willing to follow Lewis in the first place — and on short notice). With free reign, Kovacs constructed "The Silent Show" around routines recently developed on *Tonight* which featured Eugene (the tilted table and library routines), as well as his other comedic staples (the Nairobi Trio closed "The Silent Show"). Much to everyone's amazement, "The Silent Show" was the evening's hit with both the critics and the public. While the Lewis special was widely panned, *New York Herald Tribune* critic John Crosby described "The Silent Show" as "reasoned nonsense much like that like of *Alice and Wonderland* ... weird and wonderful and — while Kovacs won't approve of this appellation — avant-garde."[35]

In November of 1961, Kovacs re-performed a retooled version of "The Silent Show," titled "Eugene," as a half-hour episode for his monthly ABC specials (for the purposes of clarity, the ABC "Eugene" show will be referred to as *Eugene*). Kovacs essentially turned "The Silent Show" into a two-reel silent comedy — with "silent" meaning an absence of dialogue, but a wealth of sound effects or "sound-gags." Indeed, when Kovacs discussed his plans for a never-made *Eugene* feature film in 1961, Kovacs described the title character's situation as a man "who lives in a world of *amplifications of sight and sound, not of fantasy ... his world is over-amplified*."[36] Moreover, Eugene does not valiantly struggle against the forces of the modern world conspiring against him, like Chaplin's "Little Tramp." Eugene manages his way through the mysterious workings of the modern world with equal parts fascination and irritation, much more akin to Keaton's stoic and bemused characters who encounter modern life with an ironic confusion, curiosity, and objectivity — in short, the receptive mode of *distraction* (as alluded to with Keaton and *The Cameraman* in Chapter One). This ultimately raises the problem classifying *Eugene* in terms of Deleuze's "Keaton-Dada" versus "Chaplin-Surrealist" dichotomy. Whereas Benjamin aligned Chaplin to Dada, *Eugene* conversely presents a kind of "Keaton-Surrealist" scenario, with Eugene negotiating his way through a changing TV world of anomalies — what might be termed "Buster in Kovacsland."[37] Indeed, Eugene wears a straw hat, Keaton's favored hat, rather than Chaplin's trademark bowler — an homage to Keaton's work and influence (at the time, Kovacs and Keaton were collaborating on a sitcom pilot, *The Medicine Man*).[38] Another more contemporary influence was French film comedian Jacques Tati. Mike Marmer noted, "Tati used a lot of sound effects with visuals, that slow pace of comedy. I don't think Ernie got it from Tati; he just liked it because both were doing the same things. But I know he was one of his heroes."[39] Indeed, as Diana Rico observed, "Eugene and Monsieur Hulot might be cousins — the one bumpkinly American, the other solemnly Gallic."[40] However, while Rico describes the charm of the Eugene persona as being a "sweet" and "gentle" kind of comedy (e.g. Chaplin's "Little Tramp"), Kovacs's comedy contained an extraordinary violence, a macabre sense of humor and a relentless destruction of logic and reality. If *Eugene* is comparable to Chaplin's work, to borrow from Artaud, it is "the less human Chaplins."

Eugene begins with a shot of Kovacs standing in the background of a long enclosed corridor, a white line running horizontally down the middle of the halls and across the back. There is no door at the end of the hallway, suggesting from the very first moment the viewer sees Eugene that he is trapped in his environment. Dressed in a suit, bow tie, straw hat, and large tennis shoes, Eugene walks down the hallway towards the foreground, his sneakers emitting loud squeaking noises. Noticing the camera, Eugene looks directly at it, studying it with a perplexed expression as he walks forward until his face fills the screen in close-up. Then, apparently distracted by something off-frame, he abruptly turns to the left. A statuesque profile is created, as the title (and character's name) dissolves into the shot over Eugene, still posing "in profile," which is indeed the premise of *Eugene*—a "profile" of modern man and his surroundings.

Over this shot the opening strains of Shostakovich's "Polka (op. 30)" from the ballet *The Golden Age* begin, an effervescent yet eerie xylophone-driven piece. The close-up abruptly jump-cuts to a medium shot as Eugene, seemingly unnerved by the camera, attempts to turn around and promptly runs into the backdrop. Painted to replicate and match the dimensions of the original hallway, Eugene now stands in front of a solid wall depicting the hallway in forced perspective. His mobility reduced to a few inches rather than several feet, it further denies the possibility of escape from the suddenly, and inexplicably, confined and claustrophobic area he now occupies between the theatrical *mise en scène* and the TV camera. Nonplussed, Eugene produces a roll of black electrical tape from his pocket and begins taping a rectangular shape directly onto the TV screen (a prop transparent barrier between Kovacs and the camera). While he slowly applies the tape, the word "Eugene" floats diagonally upward across the screen from the lower right corner to the upper left, followed by a written disclaimer scrolling upward: "Everybody's been talking all day. Since the milkman said 'Good Morning,' there's been nothing but talk talk. For the next half-hour there won't be any talk at all." However, while "there won't be any talk at all," this is not to say that there is an *absence of sound*: there is an *excess and incongruity of sounds* throughout *Eugene*.

The shot briefly fades out and suddenly cuts back to Eugene, having now completed the taping of the TV screen by constructing a door suspended in mid-air (the brief blackout allowing the addition of the prop door in the shot). The door becomes a portal that frees Eugene from the entrapment between the backdrop and TV camera, allowing him to enter a new world through the door he initially manufactured on the TV screen — and, by extension, the camera lens. In this sense, the door permits Eugene to enter the *intimate vacuum* of television. With the Shostakovich "Polka" in the hallway now replaced by the brittle, manic, mechanical sound of a rambling harpsichord, Eugene investigates this intimate vacuum — a bare, unlit soundstage, a "dark room" where the ensuing sight-gags "develop." Eugene first attempts to illuminate the room, or "enlighten" himself in his new surroundings. Eugene lights a match, and waves it in a rectangular pattern, which cuts to a small circular shot within a black field that follows the movements of Eugene's hand — a point-of-view shot from the perspective of the match, an intimate object. Discarding the useless match, Eugene waves his arm, and part of the wall slowly moves toward him, juxtaposed by the sound of marching boots. Producing a magic marker, he draws a light switch on the wall; when he presses it, an overhead (off-frame) light partially illuminates the room. The wall then marches back to its original position. Still unsatisfied, Eugene draws a lamp and nightstand on the wall and pulls an invisible switch — to no avail. Realizing he forgot to include a power cord and socket in the drawing, he adds them, and a light bulb promptly goes on in the lamp.

Much more content, Eugene wanders to the other side of the room to decorate the wall with a painting (the first of several sight-gags involving paintings in *Eugene*). After sketching a painting, complete with a jagged, distorted frame, he turns around, the camera tracking him. Distracted by an off-camera noise, Eugene turns back and sees it is now a three-dimensional *objet d'art* crookedly hanging from the wall, gently swinging from side to side — a two-dimensional wall drawing transformed into a three-dimensional "moving picture" within the paradoxical confinement and possibilities of Eugene's TV world. He walks back to steady it on the wall, his first of many attempts to bring some stability to his strange new world. In this way, these initial sight-gags can be read as Eugene making "sketches" (a pun on the comedy sketch itself), which in turn become Kovacs's patented surreal sight-gags.[41] Moreover, Eugene converts the intimate vacuum of television—initially a dark, empty space—into the typical American living room. By entering the world of television through the "door" he made in the TV screen/camera lens, he also enters the living rooms of the television viewer.

Appropriately, the next sight-gag directly pertains to TV itself: a TV repairman (Joe Mikolas) fixes an invisible set in the room, which draws Eugene's attention. The repairman turns a switch, a superimposed square frame shows a scene from a generic Western; when he shuts off the invisible television, the Western image disappears, much to Eugene's surprise. Walking around the table, Eugene tentatively jiggles the invisible TV, as if it were some sort of volatile explosive device (recalling Benjamin's proclamation that motion pictures could "burst our prison-world asunder with the dynamite of a tenth of a second"). Another sight-gag depicts a woman (Maggi Brown) in a skimpy, pin-up style maid costume using an invisible vacuum cleaner to remove crumpled pieces of newspaper strewn on the floor—useless bits of *verbal* or *written* information removed by a vacuum in the intimate vacuum of television via the sight-gag. Still surveying the room, Eugene walks over to a sign which reads, "Beware of the Gnarf." The shot pans down from a leash attached to the wall to the other end, a spiked collar in mid-air, and a water dish bubbling as the sound of slurping noises are heard. The Gnarf is obviously some sort of invisible (and dangerous) animal, and, as the newspapers on the floor suggest, still in the process of being housebroken—verbal language (writing) being useful only as a receptacle for animal excrement. Suddenly, the Gnarf strains at its leash, causing it to become dislodged from its moorings and taking a square chunk of the wall along with it as it runs off-frame. Understandably concerned for his safety, Eugene hurries to a blank section of the wall, and in a reprise of the initial sight-gag "sketches," draws a door on the wall, only to realize a more direct method of escape is prudent: Eugene tears a vertical slit in the wall and forces his way through it, with this portion of *Eugene* ending by cutting to a commercial.[42]

Commercials generally are requisite moments during which sponsors blandly hawk their products and viewers can get a snack or relieve their bladders without missing parts of the show. As noted, the sponsorship agreement with Dutch Masters entailed Kovacs personally making the commercials. The first commercial during *Eugene* bears brief mention in that it became one of Kovacs's more famous sight-gags, while the second Dutch Masters commercial becomes integral as part of *Eugene*'s conclusion. The Western genre again becomes a source of parody as two cowboys, one in white (Kovacs) and one in black (Mikolas), square off for a gunfight. When his gun refuses to operate, Mikolas hits it with his palm and shakes it—the barrel pointing towards his face — while Kovacs blasts away with both six-guns for several seconds at point-blank range and with a seemingly endless supply of bullets. However, Mikolas does not fall dead, but deeply inhales his cigar: smoke begins to billow out of various holes in his torso (a sight-gag clearly borrowed from cartoon animation). The shot pans from the "smoking" Mikolas to the ground and an open box of Dutch Masters Cigars surrounded by a revolver and other Western genre accoutrements.

Returning from commercial, *Eugene* begins with a pervasive theme in Kovacs's work: the collision of high culture against the parameters and possibilities of television comedy and its technological capabilities — "the classics" as interpreted through surreal sight-gags. Now apparently in a museum, the scene shifts to a hallway lined with Grecian statues; a white horizontal line also appears on the wall, recalling the hallway that trapped Eugene before he escaped into the world of television. As Eugene passes each statue, the inanimate objects become living beings through their appearance on television, and specifically the use of *sound*. The first figure holding a wine goblet is matched by the sound of a sneeze. The second, two figures kissing (a parody of Rodin's *The Kiss*), is accompanied by heavy breathing and giggles, with the aural display of public affection providing some embarrassment for Eugene. The third, a stoic man sitting deep in thought with his hand under his chin, parodies Rodin's *The Thinker*, the canonical study of the man engaged in contemplation; he makes humming and throat-clearing sounds. The fourth statue is a woman with a Greek harp. As Eugene passes her, the statue (Jolene Brand) comes to life and strokes the nape of his neck. The inert visual arts attain the capacity for motion through the power of television. As he turns around, the shot cuts to a close-up of Eugene, deeply smitten after literally being "touched"— not only by unexpected contact with the opposite sex, but the power of art to "touch" someone, especially as empowered by movement in the television world. However, as the shot cuts back to Eugene and the statue, she is now a manikin and not a living woman, and the statue collapses into a pile of body parts when Eugene tries to kiss her on the cheek: she "shrinks to his touch." Great art must be admired from afar, rather than involve a tangible interaction, to maintain its power; it must have a quasi-mystical "aura" rather than the "tactile quality" Benjamin contended was manifest in Dada and cinema, which destroyed the "cult-value" of art.

After encountering the statutes, Eugene's next stop is a surreal hybrid of library, study, and men's club: ornate chairs, famous paintings, and bookshelves are juxtaposed with a pinball machine and sports trophies, such as a moose's *body* mounted in the wall and a large, *headless* fish over the door (suggesting the recurring motifs of decapitation and the headless body in Kovacs's comedy). It is in this space that Eugene attempts to contemplate the master-

3. The Humor of Anomaly: Ernie Kovacs 71

pieces of Western culture as they become objects of distraction on television. First, he notices Luetze's painting *Washington Crossing the Delaware*. After studying it for a moment, he turns to investigate other areas of the room. However, loud gurgling and bubbling noises erupt off-frame. As he turns back, the shot cuts to the painting as the boat full of men sinks into the waves — the American "ship of state" plummeting into the icy waters, with the captain going down with the ship, and the founding father George Washington becoming a "floundering father." A close-up of Eugene pondering the abrupt change cuts back to the painting, now depicting the Delaware River clogged with floating hats and oars. Proceeding to the bookshelves, Eugene finds the books categorized into "fiction," "non-fiction," and "dirty books." After he discretely looks around the room, he takes a "dirty book" from the shelf, running his finger across the top for dust to see if the book is indeed "dirty." When he tosses the book back on the shelf, the sound of a woman giggling is heard as it lands. One initially suspects that the dirty book emitted the risqué noise, but the source is far different. Eugene looks off-frame, and the shot cuts to da Vinci's *Mona Lisa* hanging on the wall. The shot pans downward to reveal human legs under a black dress jutting from underneath the painting's frame, while a cat licks Mona Lisa's bare feet.

In this sense, these sight-gags compare to Benjamin's critique of cinema's inherent power over painting:

> Let us compare the screen on which a film is shown with the canvas of a painting. The painting invites the spectator to contemplation; before it the spectator can abandon himself to his associations. Before the movie frame he can not do so. No sooner has his eye grasped a scene than it has already changed. It cannot be arrested.[43]

In *Eugene*, the painting which the viewer contemplates literally becomes the "moving picture" that distracts. The viewer (Eugene) is longer allowed to merely contemplate the painting, but rather experiences the shock effect of cinema at its most basic: the unexpected and fascinating change of a moving image. If Kovacs is implying an irreverent, potential superiority of motion pictures (TV) over painting, he does so with two canonical and immediately recognizable "masterpieces"— one a hallmark of American culture and the other perhaps the single most important painting in Western art history.[44]

Having encountered great Western painting, Eugene next tackles canonical Western literature, also brought to life through a series of concise, surreal interpretations and audio-visual puns. Opening Dumas's *Camille*, a woman's fragile and dainty coughing can be heard while Eugene reads — or, rather, *listens*— with his lips quavering as he fights back tears. He turns the page, and a hacking cough produces a volley of (invisible) spittle which hits

Eugene in the eye. Given that Dumas's heroine dies of tuberculosis in the novel, and salvia is a frequent means by which tuberculosis is spread, the dark comedy of the audio-visual sight-gag is that Eugene is "touched" by a great novel by being spit in the eye (with disease-ridden saliva, to boot). This motif of the assault on the eye also figures prominently in *Eugene*'s conclusion. Finding a mammoth copy of *War and Peace*, Eugene opens the book to the beginning, and is greeted by a volley of cannon fire; opening the book's back cover, Eugene is delighted when a live dove emerges from the confines of the book and flies out of the shot. To see if anything was missed between the "war" and the "peace," he opens the book one last time: the sound of a bugle blast is cut off when Eugene closes the book and replaces it on the shelf. Finally, his attention drawn to Hemmingway's *The Old Man and the Sea*, Eugene removes the book and is promptly greeted by torrents of water spraying out of the bookshelf; he hurriedly forces the book back in place. One can only imagine, and dread, what might have transpired had a book by Kafka or Sade been opened.

The third section of *Eugene* begins, focusing on incongruities of sight and sound. A harp is again heard, piquing Eugene's interest (perhaps hoping for a return of the Greek statue that "touched" him). However, the shot cuts to a phone on a stand, the sound of a harp unaccountably substituting for a telephone ringing. A maid (again Maggi Brown) answers the "ringing" phone, dressed in a far more demure and respectable maid's outfit than when she was seen vacuuming, one much more appropriate to the surroundings of the study. Covering the receiver with her hand, an utterly useless gesture in that no one speaks throughout the show, she glances over to an older man reading in a chair (yet another role for Joe Mikolas) and holds up the receiver. He shakes his head to decline the call, and the maid simply shakes her head as well into the receiver before hanging up. Intrigued, Eugene investigates the phone and begins dialing a number — the dialing matched by the sound of machine-gun fire. To muffle the noise, Eugene thrusts the phone under his jacket as the volley of gunfire continues — only to pull his hand out of his jacket and see his fingertip covered in blood.

Eugene apparently only suffered a flesh wound from the phone, and refreshes himself with a glass of water. With great effort, Eugene forces himself to swallow, apparently even suppressing the urge to vomit, accompanied by the sound of gurgling water going down a drain. Greatly annoyed, the man being played by Mikolas glares at Eugene, the first of many times his quiet solitude is interrupted — his *contemplative* reading *distracted* by Eugene's physical movements and over-amplified bodily noises as a metaphor of the struggle between what Benjamin claimed was the distracting potential of mass culture (Eugene) and the contemplative nature of bourgeois culture (Mikolas, who will be referred to as the "Serious Man"). Responding to the Serious Man's contemptuous stare, Eugene does a mocking hula dance and wildly swivels his lips, matched by the sound of an object rattling in a metallic container. The camera tracks Eugene as he sits in the chair next to the Serious Man, with the headless fish mounted above the door of the study noticeable in the background over Eugene's head. Eugene begins popping his knuckles: each time Eugene "pulls his finger" (the reference to the flatulence joke intended), an explosion of artillery fire is heard. Pulling his thumb produces nothing short of an A-bomb blast, and pulling his pinky produces another gunshot and ricocheting bullet sound, which causes Eugene to flinch and fearfully scan the room (the gunfire in this sequence also recalling Benjamin's comparison of the tactile quality of Dada and cinema to ballistics). Growing thoroughly bored in the stuffy confines of the study, Eugene produces a minuscule phonograph and record album from his pockets and places them on the table, then plugs the tiny record player into an electrical socket—located in Eugene's abdomen. A sped-up, high-pitched version of the Wolfgang Neuss rendition of "Mack the Knife" begins, a moment of self-referential humor as Eugene jubilantly snaps his fingers and wiggles in his chair. The Serious Man responds with another stern, offended stare, and Eugene ceases the impromptu concert. Now deciding on a snack, Eugene opens his lunch pail, the clamps producing loud metallic clangs. He begins to chew on a piece of celery, accompanied by the sound of dry leaves being raked; and his subsequent difficulty in swallowing is accompanied by the sound of a bowling ball rolling down an alley and finally striking a set of bowling pins, signifying successful digestion.

Through this series of sight-and-sound-gags, the synchronization of the workings of Eugene's body with mechanical sounds compares to the modern avant-garde's fascination with the figure of the "man-machine" (his gastrointestinal system producing the sounds of plumbing and a bowling alley; popping his knuckles emits explosions and gunfire). Above all, Eugene's body itself is a "power plant," a source of electrical energy and current sufficient to operate a mechanical object (a phonograph), replete with an extra orifice—the electrical socket in his belly. Far from being "opposed to the machine" (Chaplin), and not merely having "an affinity for machines" (Keaton), Eugene *is* a machine: a hybrid of the human body and modern mechanisms.[45] There is also the obvious influence of cartoon animation, specifically the classic *Duck Amuck* (Chuck Jones, 1956).[46] As Erwin Panofsky suggested, "The virtue of cartoon animation is to *animate ... to endow lifeless things with life, or living things with a different kind of life.*"[47] As much as the sight-and-sound-gags themselves, it is this aspect of cartoon animation that is integral to Kovacs's work. Lifeless objects become living things, such as the statues and paintings in *Eugene*, the office equipment in "Day at the Office," or toy monkeys bashing out Tchaikovsky's "1812 Overture." Similarly, living things take on a different kind of life, demonstrated by Eugene's man-machine bodily functions and the mechanistic concerts by the gorilla-robot combo Nairobi Trio. With *Eugene*, Kovacs's use of sound against sight distorts reality and forces a redefinition of perception, logic, reason, and the laws of science themselves — ultimately represented by the tilted table routine.

Having lost all patience with Eugene's "distractions" in the study, the Serious Man rises from his chair and walks off-frame. Undeterred, Eugene follows him off-frame, and the shot cuts to the Serious Man already seated at the right side of a table (in profile to the audience). Eugene nonchalantly walks to the center of the table from the right (with Kovacs doing a commendable job of concealing the fact that he is walking up a fairly steep incline). As briefly discussed, the tilted table routine simply consists of Eugene placing food objects on the table and watching them careen down the right side of the table (and onto the Serious Man's lap). Various percussion instruments accompany the food objects during their flight: handfuls of olives sprint down the table as snare drum brushes, ending with the sound of a bell, play on the soundtrack; three oranges are sent plummeting one by one, accompanied by louder snare drum rolls and ending with a woodblock; a sausage tumbles down the table to the rhythms of a tom-tom roll, ending with a cowbell. Both puzzled and intrigued, Eugene constructs a pendulum out of a string and an olive. Holding it in the air in front of the camera, it swings to the right and holds its position, matched by a tympani thump. Eugene intently studies his rudimentary scientific experiment, literally conducting an optical test with the viewer as a sight-gag. Then, as his solution to the predicament, Eugene responds by throwing more food at the problem, and in exasperation he empties his lunch pail on the table, the contents of which cascade down the table to a burst of percussion.

Turning his attention to experimenting with liquid instead of solid matter, Eugene produces a thermos. He slowly unscrews the cap and removes the top, confused that a popping sound does not result when he removes the plug. As Eugene peers into the open thermos, the delayed popping sound finally transpires, with Eugene literally again "popped in the eye." Twice he attempts to pour milk into the thermos cap, only to watch the milk arc to the right over the cap and flow down the table; but unlike with the food, the pouring is accompanied by silence rather than percussion. Producing a clear glass from his lunch pail, Eugene sets it in the place of the thermos cap, which he aligns slightly to the right. He then again pours the milk, which, despite some spillage, finds its target and fills the thermos cap. Eugene grins broadly at the camera. Switching the positions of the cups, his experiment is again a success, producing another gleeful reaction he shares with the viewer. However, Eugene's process of deductive logic and scientific experimentation demonstrated by his (optical) tests with the milk is resolved with an illogical conclusion: he takes the cup on the right and places it in the cup on the left, forcing the milk in the bottom cup to overflow and run down the table, and then proceeds to pour the remaining contents of the thermos past the stacked cups and where the now-absent cup was formally located. The camera pans right, following the flowing milk to the Serious Man's lap, which is already filled with oranges, olives, and a large sausage (the Freudian interpretation is obvious); it then pans upward to the Serious Man staring most disgustedly— not at Eugene, but directly at the camera and the television viewer. Contemplation finally succumbs to distraction.

As Diana Rico described the finale of the original "Silent Show" from 1957, "Frustrated, Eugene stands up. He pushes down mightily on one end of the table. The whole room appears to tilt sideways; his mouth opens in a silent, triumphant laugh. Eugene has finally found a way to beat the bizarre forces that rule his world."[48] However, the same ending of *Eugene* has a subtle but important difference. Eugene, in attempting to correct the table, does not realign it properly, but *overcorrects* the table; the canted shot shifts the angle so drastically that the table angles downward too far to the *left*. Initially satisfied with his readjustment of the table, Eugene turns and looks at the right side of the table, now angled steeply *upward*. Rather than a Chaplinesque moment of victory, Eugene reflects a Keatonesque moment of bemusement: not only is his world even more out of alignment, but the viewer's previously stable view of the world is now altered and jeopardized as well. Eugene's world is even more out of balance, and the television viewer's relationship to the world — formally perceived as *level*— is also now completely off-balance.

Indeed, the destabilization of reality and visual perception becomes the climactic punchline of *Eugene*. The word "Finis" appears over the shot, and the second "i" in the word promptly collapses on itself, accompanied by the sound of a deflating balloon (the *finis* being a nod to French cinema). This deflation of the "i" is also a collapse of the *eye*, leaving the word "fin_s" as a reference to the beheaded fish over the door where Eugene made his initial entrance into the world of contemplative culture disrupted by distractions, and Kovacs's own propensity for sight-gags literally aimed at the head. However, *Eugene* does not end with the "fin(i)s." Another Dutch Masters commercial follows in which Kovacs plays a colonial American settler about to be *decapitated* by an axe-wielding Native American chief. A young Native American woman rushes into the shot to light Kovacs's final cigar. As she steadily works to light a fire with a stick, Kovacs worriedly waits. Shots of clock hands rapidly spinning and pages flying off a calendar follow in quick dissolves before a geyser of (superimposed) flame erupts to light the cigar. The aroma delights the chief, who takes the cigar and walks away, happily puffing. Kovacs and the woman embrace and turn their backs to the camera to gaze at a full moon in the sky. As the stage lights darken, the moon becomes a spotlight which moves from the sky to focus on an open box of Dutch Masters cigars strapped to the small of the woman's back, just above her buttocks, "mooning" the camera (inspiring the brief thought that Kovacs might cop a feel as he reaches for another cigar).

The close-up of the cigar box illuminated by the moon-spotlight abruptly cuts to an extreme close-up of Kovacs's eye staring directly at the camera, his blinking synchronized with the opening percussion accents of the Tony deSimone Trio's "Oriental Blues," a Spike Jones–style ragtime song Kovacs used to begin and end all of his shows. A reverse-iris effect emanating from Kovacs' own iris slowly expands to create a black screen. The next shot quickly fades-in: a spinning circular saw (also the past tense of "see") with the words "Written and produced by" at the top of the screen. One can suggest that the montage connecting the full moon, the close-up of Kovacs's eye, and the show being "written and produced by" a spinning blade is a subtle homage to *Un Chien andalou* and its legendary moment where a cloud intersecting a full moon cuts to a shot of a woman's eye being sliced open with a straight razor. The shot pans downward diagonally to the right as a young woman (Jolene Brand) pleads for her life while a mustachioed man (Joe Mikolas) is about to shove the woman (head-first, of course) into the rotating saw — a parody of cliff hanger melodramas (*The Perils of Pauline*). This cuts to a long shot of the entire scene as the name "Ernie Kovacs" appears at the top of the screen, suggesting that Mikolas, the mustachioed villain, is a representation of Kovacs himself as he is about to apply yet another sight-gag to the head of his victim (the viewer), who is spared when the saw blade spins off its moorings and out of the frame. The remaining credits follow, accompanied by a variety of sight-gags parodying melodrama serial "cliffhanger" situations, culminating in the last shot: another extreme close-up of Kovacs's open eye, which jump-cuts to a shot of his closed eye, which suddenly blinks wide open in unison to the final tympani beat ending "Oriental Blues." The wide-open eye matched by the tympani references what is perhaps the most important sight-gag in *Eugene* — the optical test conducted at the tilted table, with the olive on a string matched by a tympani thump. Through a course of *Eugene*'s measured assaults on perception, *Eugene* ends by suggesting the eye is now wide open, and, with apologies to Aldous Huxley, the doors of perception are now wide open as well.

As discussed last chapter, Antonin Artaud and Walter Benjamin diverged greatly in how art could affect a revolutionary change in consciousness, particularly in the efficacy of cinema. Nevertheless, the work of Ernie Kovacs can be seen as a kind of negotiation between Artaud and Benjamin (as well as Soupy Sales, although with substantially different formal strategies). As Sontag suggested, Artaud envisioned the Theater of Cruelty as a realm of "sensory violence" and a "controlled and intricately orchestrated ... theater-laboratory in which to conduct research on changing consciousness." Kovacs did nothing short of constructing a controlled and intricately orchestrated *television*-laboratory in which to conduct research on changing consciousness through sensory violence. To also apply Artaud's succinct definition of Surrealism, Kovacs turned TV into a "world that no longer holds." Moreover, Kovacs explored the possibilities of television consistent with how Benjamin theorized the revolutionary potential of the camera and cinema: to study the modern world through the mode of distraction as "an immense and unexpected field of action ... and burst this prison-world asunder by the dynamite of a tenth of a second, so that now, in the midst of its far-flung ruins and derbies, we calmly and adventurously go traveling." Much like Eugene himself.

CHAPTER 4

Say "Dada": *The Soupy Sales Show*

> I kept quitting because of illness. They got sick of me.[1]
> — Soupy Sales, on his numerous career moves

A Brief History of Children's Television

With the exception of Ernie Kovacs, the more avant-garde moments in early American television came from children's programming and its eccentric world of weekday and Saturday morning comedy.[2] Running on NBC from 1947 through 1960 (as well as a short-lived, revamped, and abysmal syndicated 1976–7 version), *Howdy Doody* invented the children's show format: a cast of human and puppet performers; a "peanut gallery" consisting of an on-stage, on-camera studio audience of children who both watched and participated in the show; a comedy-variety show presentation. Set in the fantastic frontier world of "Doodyville," *Howdy Doody* drew not only from the Western genre but Wild West popular culture, such as the rodeo, the hoedown, and especially the "tall tale." Host Buffalo Bob Smith was a square-jawed yet gregarious frontiersman, while other regulars were Chief Thundercloud (Bill LeCornec) and Princess Summerfall Winterspring (originally a marionette, later transformed into a human and played by Judy Tyler). Beyond the Native American stereotypes, they supplied an idealized representation of the American West as one of "cowboys and Indians" living in social harmony. Propelling the show with mild slapstick mayhem, Clarabelle Hornblow (played by various actors throughout the show's run) immediately suggested the circus clown, yet could also be seen as a *rodeo* clown. However, *Howdy Doody* is best-remembered for its array of marionettes. A red-haired, freckle-faced, American Everyboy whose wooden face was perpetually cast in a broad grin, Howdy Doody was the embodiment of American curiosity, enthusiasm, and optimism. In contrast, Phineas T. Bluster, the mayor of Doodyville, was a rotund, rambling schemer in an old-fashioned suit and bowler hat — a combination big-city political boss and capitalist robber-baron. A parody of the hybrid animals of ancient mythology — and their American equivalent, the tall tale — the Flubadub was a talking animal made up of a seal's body, a giraffe's neck, droopy dog ears, whiskers, a beak, and a flower-pot skull. In this sense, *Howdy Doody* served an ideological function as a TV "tall tale" itself: the American West and Manifest Destiny as a fairy-tale world of wonders and possibilities long since reduced to idealized nostalgia in post–World War II America. However, in the context of A-bomb anxieties and Cold War paranoia, *Howdy Doody* also celebrated the potential wonders of modern gadgetry with such devices as the "Super-Talk-o-Scope" (a panoptic TV-phone that could see, hear, and allow communication anywhere in the world at anytime) or the "Electromindomizer" (a mind-reading machine). Not surprisingly, the issues of surveillance and brainwashing were avoided.[3]

Howdy Doody's weekday, late-afternoon time slot provided children a much-needed space between school and the dinner hour, resulting in phenomenal ratings; despite being a marionette, Howdy Doody became one of TV's first bona fide stars. By the mid–1950s, NBC realized Saturday morning was an obvious space for children's programming: *The Paul Winchell and Jerry Mahoney Show* premiered in 1954, a Saturday morning version of *The Pinky Lee Show* appeared in 1955, and *Howdy Doody* was moved to Saturday mornings in 1956. NBC also began to self-censor the content of children's television by adding overt messages of parental obedience and civics lessons in response to repeated criticisms from parental groups and the press, who claimed shows such as *Howdy Doody* and *The Pinky Lee Show* encouraged "anti-social" behavior in children due to the alleged glorification of rambunctious behavior (although, as suggested, the hidden messages of *Howdy Doody* were highly conservative). Moreover, both *The Paul Winchell and Jerry Mahoney Show* and *The Pinky Lee Show* were more than obviously sponsored by Tootsie Rolls, clearly demonstrating that the primary goal of early children's TV was not to entertainment or education, but to blatantly peddle highly attractive products to easily persuaded consumers. Virtually all the early children's TV shows were sponsored, in part or in whole, by candy manufacturers.

The Paul Winchell and Jerry Mahoney Show (NBC, 1954–6; ABC, 1957–60, as *The Paul Winchell Show*) starred popular ventriloquist Paul Winchell and

Paul Winchell and his dummy Jerry Mahoney in front of the peanut gallery on *The Paul Winchell and Jerry Mahoney Show*, sponsored by Tootsie Rolls (ABC/Photofest).

his dummies, the wisecracking Jerry Mahoney and his dimwitted counterpart, Knucklehead Smiff.[4] The show situated its performers, the peanut gallery, and house band (led by musician-comedian Milton DeLugg, who later became the bandleader on *The Gong Show*) in a vaguely Expressionist clubhouse setting adorned with a surplus of Tootsie Roll advertisements. Indeed, one regular on *Winchell-Mahoney* was "Freddie, the Tootsie Roll Man," whose purpose on the show was performing commercials, some disguised as skits with Winchell. Freddie's garish uniforms predominately featured the Tootsie Roll logo, and, for good measure, a giant prop Tootsie Roll was strapped around his neck. While the series included the necessary amounts of slapstick and music to drive the show, *Winchell-Mahoney* was notable for its reliance on the *talk show* format, not altogether surprising in that Winchell's ventriloquist act inherently stressed verbal over physical comedy. Winchell and Mahoney hosted much of the show seated behind a desk in the clubhouse;

other times, Mahoney and Smiff sat behind the desk, running the show themselves, like a marionette comedy team without Winchell. Mahoney always sat on the left side of the desk, the word "president" inscribed on the wall over his head — the privileged desk space designating Jerry Mahoney as the true star of the show (much like Johnny Carson's elevated desk signified he was "king of late night" on *The Tonight Show*). In fact, *Winchell-Mahoney*'s set bore an uncanny similarity to *The Tonight Show* set-up: the hosts (some combination of Mahoney, Smiff, or Winchell) seated behind the desk center stage, a chair for guests to the left of the desk, and the house band on the right side of the set (the peanut gallery was on the far left of the set and frequently off-camera during the show). Regulars occasionally performed sketches gathered around the desk; other times, one might sit in the guest chair and blithely chat with the hosts as if they were appearing on an actual talk show. Guest interview segments also occurred, such as an utterly surreal segment with Winchell, Mahoney, and a local Girl Scout troop leader fielding probing questions about civic responsibility while she accepted the show's monthly "Winchell-Mahoney Achievement Award" on behalf of her troop for their volunteer work at nursing homes. While fairly tame by early children's show standards, especially in its emphasis on conversation rather than action, *The Winchell-Mahoney Show* can be seen as the precursor to the disturbing talk show/children's show hybrid Andy Kaufman utilized in his specials *Andy's Funhouse* (ABC, produced 1977; aired as *The Andy Kaufman Special* in 1979) and the *Soundstage* "Andy Kaufman Show" (PBS, 1983).

The Pinky Lee Show (1954–6) eschewed puppetry altogether in favor of the agitated antics of Pinky Lee. A vaudeville comedian universally despised by critics and even other TV comedians of the era (Lee and Milton Berle had a well-publicized feud), Lee's trademark was energetic but uninspired physical comedy. Nonetheless, *The Pinky Lee Show* was highly successful in the ratings, at the very least due to being the daily lead-in show to *Howdy Doody*. Lee's popularity earned a Saturday morning slot in 1955, in addition to his weekday show. However, in late 1955 Lee collapsed on-camera in visible pain during one of his manic routines, and the show cut to commercial. While it was later explained that Lee was suffering from a severe infection, it was widely rumored, and commonly believed by the public, that Lee suffered a massive heart attack on national television due to his hyperactive comic style.[5] Regardless of the medical specifics, and the unintended "shock effect" it had on the public, the ratings plummeted until the show's cancellation in the summer of 1956. (Lee's condition was serious enough that it required a medical leave; substitute hosts filled for the remainder of the show's run.)

Pinky Lee's tenacious brand of uninhibited physical comedy was characterized by aimlessly running around in his ill-fitting plaid suits while screaming and flailing his limbs. Paul Reubens parodied and consciously exaggerated Lee's gaudy wardrobe, physical mannerisms, and vocal delivery (Lee spoke with a noticeable lisp) with his persona "Pee-Wee Herman." Set in a circus big top rather than *Winchell-Mahoney*'s clubhouse, *The Pinky Lee Show*'s Tootsie Roll product placement was taken to an overdetermined absurdity. Virtually every prop on *The Pinky Lee Show* bore a Tootsie Roll wrapper logo, and many of Pinky Lee's skits quickly digressed into Tootsie Roll commercials. Other sketches ranged from straight vaudeville to surreal sight-gags relying on studio effects. On one show, a slapstick sketch set in an apartment was followed by a flight in Lee's "Super supersonic, atomic, pocket rocket Tootsie Roll plane" (apparently the term "pocket rocket" slipped past network censors). Lee sat in a prop Tootsie Roll with a steering wheel which was superimposed over a constantly changing montage of stock footage backgrounds, with Lee redundantly commenting on the obvious: a shot of a raging river behind the Tootsie Roll Plane, accompanied by Lee yelling, "Oh, what am I doing in the rapids?" was followed by heaving ocean waves, with Lee exclaiming, "Oh my goodness, now I'm in the middle of the ocean!"[6]

Lee's approach to television posited that *any* motion in front of the television camera equaled captivating entertainment. As noted last chapter, John Ellis suggested the audience's relationship to the cinematic apparatus is a *gaze*, whereas with television it is a *glance*. However, children's TV performers understood that their target audience did quite intently *gaze* at TV, often planted on the floor mere inches from the screen. Thus, the bane of television — dead air — was avoided at all costs by Pinky Lee. At any possible moment the show might lag, Lee compensated with some sort of aural and visual stimulation by feverish pseudo-activity: loud singing, spastic dancing, physical pratfalls, earsplitting sketches, cloying interaction with the peanut gallery, and, of course, endlessly shilling Tootsie Rolls. Even the performers periodically featured on *The Pinky Lee Show* did not necessarily appear for their talent, but the amount of motion they generated; one segment featuring a blindfolded woman jumping rope on a trampoline seemed closer to *The Gong Show* than the exploits of professional acrobats on *The Ed Sullivan Show*. *The Pinky Lee Show* was abrasive, disorganized, loud, unsophisticated, and frequently quite aggravating in its unfunny material, cheap circus acts, and ceaseless sales pitches for Tootsie Rolls. Yet these very qualities made *The Pinky Lee Show* a kind of unintentional Dada spectacle. Whether one was genuinely amused or thoroughly annoyed, *The Pinky Lee Show* was impossible to ignore, or often fathom — a TV formula *The Gong Show* and Andy Kaufman relied on two decades later.

In contrast to the NBC shows, in 1955 CBS launched the weekday children's show *Captain Kangaroo*, the brainchild of Bob Keeshan, who played

4. Say "Dada": The Soupy Sales Show 83

Clarabelle on *Howdy Doody* from 1947 to 1952. Reflecting the CBS ethos famously stated by Edward R. Murrow — the idea that TV was "the world's biggest classroom"—*Captain Kangaroo* employed the children's show format of human and puppet characters, cartoons, comedy skits, and music. However, it also consciously eschewed the frantic vaudeville style and excessive product promotion that characterized the NBC children's shows of the era by stressing low-key educational segments.[7] In this respect, *Captain Kangaroo* can also be seen as the prototype for the PBS shows that redefined children's TV in the late 1960s —*Mr. Rogers' Neighborhood* (1968–2001) and *Sesame Street* (1969–). In fact, *Captain Kangaroo* was the lone early children's show that survived into the 1970s and even the 1980s, running on CBS until 1984 and moving to PBS for its final years (1987–93).

Moreover, it was not coincidental that *Mr. Rogers' Neighborhood* and *Sesame Street* premiered during the peak of the counterculture era and quickly emerged as the definitive models for children's TV, while the more Dadaistic-anarchistic children's shows, epitomized by *The Soupy Sales Show*, disappeared nationally in the latter part of the 1960s. Fred Rogers, who combined the function of kindly teacher, nurturing father, and doting grandfather, languidly provided daily educational lessons on a variety of subjects with mild and unapologetic affirmation in a Norman Rockwell setting. *Sesame Street* placed a cast of gentle muppets and human performers in an inner-city version of Doodyville, with sketches stressing functional arithmetic and language skills intertwined with liberal-humanist messages of tolerance and understanding. Another PBS show, *The Electric Company* (1970–7), combined educational programming with animated and live-action sketch comedy.[8] While *The Electric Company* was notable to the extent the comedy demanded a great deal of cognitive participation from the younger viewer, the approach was antithetical to absurdist comedy, be it Abbott and Costello or Ionesco. Instead of deconstructing language to represent the difficulty, if not impossibility, of meaning, *The Electric Company* specialized in sketches beginning with language in a state of disruption — misplaced signifiers, puns, or *non sequiturs*— and the performers and audience reworked the sentences to make them grammatically correct and assume a state of coherency. In short, rather than dismantling the Symbolic Order, *The Electric Company* provided daily lessons on managing and reconstituting it.

In 1986, the Dada-inclined, early children's show format briefly returned with a decidedly postmodern slant: *Pee-Wee's Playhouse* (CBS, 1986–91). If Paul Reuben's "Pee-Wee Herman" persona was referenced from Pinky Lee, the overall structure of *Pee-Wee's Playhouse* was *The Soupy Sales Show*'s suburban living room infused with hallucinatory camp, kitsch and punk aesthetics. The door at the back of the set as a key point of continual action owed particularly to Sales; on *Pee-Wee's Playhouse*, the door was a space where the various regular characters entered and exited the set, as well as periodic surprise visitors — such as a six-foot traveling salesman marionette or a one-legged sea monster with a giant eyeball. However, what prevented *Pee-Wee's Playhouse* from becoming a self-conscious pastiche of old children's shows was Reuben's knowledge that it was one of TVs most neglected yet potentially subversive genres that adults as well as children could appreciate.[9] Especially in its legendary first season, *Pee-Wee's Playhouse* was infused with a wealth of jaw-dropping gender and sexual subtext. In regard to sexuality, Pee-Wee Herman demonstrated *both* pre-pubescent apprehension and post-pubescent ribaldry (which, along with *Playhouse*'s sometimes unflattering depiction of women, could also be faulted as little more than a hip variation on burlesque).[10] The relationship between Herman and crusty Captain Carl (Phil Hartman) suggested the old salt had a homosexual fixation for the man-boy Herman. Jambi (John Paragon), the genie head in a box, provided broad, sarcastic comedy akin to Paul Lynde. Tito, the Lifeguard (Roland Rodriguez), a muscular Latino who wandered the playhouse in a swimsuit, was essentially a gay pin-up fantasy. Reba, the Mail Lady (S. Eptaha Merkenson), was a parody of *Sesame Street*'s "Molly, the Mail Lady" (with "Reba" also a reference to one of the characters on *The Soupy Sales Show*); arguably the most masculine character on the show, she could also be called "Reba, the 'Male Lady.'" The cab driver Dixie (Johann Carlo) suggested a butch lesbian stereotype. The "girl next door," Miss Yvonne (Marie Lynne Stewart), was a buxom bombshell who, at times, came across as a prowling divorcé; her date with Cowboy Curtis (Laurence Fishburne) was the first interracial romance in the history of children's TV. If there was "an other" on *Pee-Wee's Playhouse*, it was Pee-Wee's obese, nosy neighbor "Mrs. Steve" (Shirley Stoler), a monstrous send-up of normal America who was nonetheless always welcome in the world of the Playhouse. While *Sesame Street* was a children's show teaching lessons in tolerance of "others," *Pee-Wee's Playhouse* constructed an illogical, delirious world where minority cultures co-existed as the majority egalitarian order.

Soupy Sales: The WNEW Years

While Soupy Sales did not achieve the critical recognition or respectability of Ernie Kovacs as an innovator in TV comedy, he did attain national stardom as a children's show icon. A mainstay at Detroit's ABC affiliate WXYZ from 1953 to 1960, Sales dominated the local market with the first incarnation of his weekday children's show, *Lunch with Soupy*, a weeknight variety-talk show, *Soupy's On*, and a weekly comedy-variety show, *Soupy's Ranch*. At

4. Say "Dada": The Soupy Sales Show

Someone's in the kitchen with Dada: *Lunch with Soupy Sales!* (1959–1961) (ABC/Photofest).

his peak in 1955–6, Sales personally accounted for *eleven* hours of WXYZ television time per week. In 1955, Sales also made his network TV debut with *Soupy Sales!*, which briefly ran as a summer fill-in show for *Kukla, Fran, and Ollie* on ABC. Impressed by his popularity (and stamina), ABC eventually hired Sales for a nationally televised Saturday afternoon children's show: *Lunch with Soupy Sales!* (1959–61).[11] *Lunch with Soupy Sales!* brought the approach to children's television Sales developed at WXYZ to a national audience: a chaotic mélange of pie-throwing, physical pratfalls, peculiar puppets, exuberant performances, unfathomable sketches, impromptu digressions, on-air verbal retorts between him and the production crew, and pun-laden jokes laced with an arguable degree of sexual innuendo. Indeed, *Lunch with Soupy Sales!* became notorious for an alleged abundance of raunchy double-entendres, which Sales staunchly claimed was purely an invention of the public.[12]

In 1964, another incarnation of his children's show, titled *The Soupy Sales Show*, began as a live weekday children's show for WNEW (the New York

City flagship station of Metromedia).[13] *The Soupy Sales Show* ran concurrent with other WNEW "kidult" shows, *The Sandy Becker Show* and *The Chuck McCann Show* (with McCann's show recalling Ernie Kovacs as much as *Howdy Doody*).[14] From 1965 until Sales quit in 1966 after repeated clashes with WNEW management, *The Soupy Sales Show* was nationally syndicated by Screen Gems and enormously popular with both children and a cult–TV audience of young adults, particularly college students. Comedy ranged from his singular brand of children's show Dada (which will be analyzed at length shortly), straightforward genre parodies (the "Philo Kvetch" gangster film lampoons), and old-fashioned vaudeville (the "Chez Bippy" restaurant sketches).[15] Numerous guest stars and musical acts appeared on the show, ranging from Henny Youngman to the Supremes. Frank Sinatra (with Sammy Davis, Jr. and Trini Lopez in tow) appeared in 1965 for a Chez Bippy pie-throwing sketch.

Most of all, the WNEW run of *The Soupy Sales Show* cemented Sales's television legend as a controversial TV personality, with a legendary moment occurring on New Year's Day, 1965. Due to the holiday, the regular show could not be done with the limited crew or regular set. Sales, already annoyed that the show was not simply pre-empted for the day, simply ad-libbed with a hand-held mike on an empty soundstage. As the broadcast closed, Sales inched toward the camera and suggested kids sneak into their parents' bedroom, go through the purses and wallets, find the "pieces of paper with George Washington's picture," and mail them to "Soupy Sales, Channel 5, New York, NY — and I'll send you a postcard from Puerto Rico." Sales noted it was simply a bit he recalled from the WXYZ era on the spot, and used it to kill the final minutes of air time. Intentionally or not, Sales effectively satirized the function of the children's show host. Instead of playing middleman between the sponsor and audience by hard-selling the sponsor's products to the adolescent viewers (Pinky Lee), it was far simpler to have the audience send money directly to the host (Sales). Regardless of intent, the show produced a storm of controversy. Parents were incensed and flooded WNEW and the FCC with letters of complaint, and local newspapers called for his firing. WNEW suspended Sales without pay over the incident, and the dispute became a NYC *cause célèbre*. Sales's fan base of college students protested outside WNEW with the same resolve they might have protested Vietnam. After two weeks, WNEW relented and reinstated Sales.[16]

While Sales is often remembered as an outlandish, brash, occasionally irritating physical comedian for whom discretion was nonexistent, an examination of the WNEW *The Soupy Sales Show* suggests this view is exaggerated, if not erroneous. Certainly, Sales was very much in the vaudeville tradition of physical comedy, a combination of stand-up, slapstick, singing and dancing, and a frequent pie in the face. Many suggested, including Sales himself, that his television persona was essentially a "king-sized kid."[17] Nevertheless, Sales did not constantly storm about demanding every second of the viewer's attention by filling the void with aimless action like Pinky Lee. For the WNEW shows, Sales abandoned the oversize top hats and bow ties of the early years and appeared in a nondescript sweater and bow tie of reasonable proportions. The set of *The Soupy Sales Show* was essentially a suburban living room: a door in the back of the set, a large picture window, a bookshelf, paintings on the wall, even an old-fashioned pot-stove—which Sales occasionally opened to engage in conversations with "Hobart and Reba," an aged couple living inside the stove (or perhaps subletting the space). Rather than the *energetic child*, Sales often played the *mystified adult* and a parody of a sitcom stereotype—the befuddled suburban dad. Sales became a bewildered *reactor* to the continuous flurry of illogic erupting around him in his living room—often supplied by his cast of puppets.

One of Sales's more enduring, and endearing, puppet sidekicks was "Pookie," a hipster lion hand-puppet who often lip-synched and danced to novelty songs. Pookie appeared on the windowsill (a disguised puppet stage), with Sales sitting by the window watching Pookie's energetic if excruciating performances, not unlike a suburban father enduring a child's efforts at entertaining him through song and dance. Moreover, the window itself became a television screen *on* television, with Sales seemingly watching his own television show on his living-room window-as-TV screen. On one show, Pookie performed a long lip-synch and dance to a novelty rockabilly song with lyrics that consisted mostly of the singer laughing over the music. Sales sat by the window (TV screen) and watched—or glanced at—Pookie before noticing at one point the puppet had his back to the camera and was entertaining the audience by wiggling his butt back and forth to the music, with the puppet manifesting a surprisingly lascivious expression. Shocked, Sales provided a firm, parental swat of Pookie's posterior, who resumed dancing and singing in a more appropriate manner for national television. In another performance, Pookie appeared in a long blonde wig and lip-synched Mrs. Miller's atonal, vibrato-laden version of Petula Clark's "Downtown."[18] Sales reacted with a mixture of laughter, grimaces, and comic gestures, such as cleaning his ear with his index finger or an open palm to the forehead.

In this respect, and admittedly with some sociological speculation, Sales's popularity stemmed not only from the fact that children identified with him as one of them—"a king-sized kid"—but from American kids seeing him as a TV father image-ideal: the antithesis of the bland and sometimes strict TV sitcom fathers disseminating dry, practical lessons and lectures on daily civic life (a tactic Sales satirized in his "Words of Wisdom" segments, to be discussed shortly). Rather than a Ward Cleaver, as a TV father-figure Sales was more of a Buster Keaton; the dull, pseudo-realistic TV suburbia of the domestic sitcom became a world of pure possibility as well as odd implausibility, a world of unbridled energy and enthusiasm. Rather than being a king-sized kid, Sales represented a king-sized kid's *world-view*. The appeal, and danger, Sales posited as a TV comedian was not depicting the experience of children through the corny cliché of childhood innocence (Robin Williams's sentimental brand of wide-eyed whimsy), but the liberating and disruptive power of the unencumbered imagination — an essential component of Dada.

If Ward Cleaver taught Beaver weekly lessons in conformity on *Leave It to Beaver*, Soupy Sales created daily opportunities to exercise non-conformity on *The Soupy Sales Show* — be it dancing along with Sales in their homes as he performed novelty songs such as "the Mouse" or spurring protests for free speech outside WNEW. As noted, Sales and his brand of Dadaistic children's shows were largely "shut down" by the late–1960s amid the unrest of the counterculture era and replaced by *Sesame Street* and *Mr. Rogers' Neighborhood*.[19] While Sales never considered his show subversive, let alone political (although, even if unintentionally, it can be read as such), he quit the WNEW show in 1966 after repeated confrontations with station management over the format and content:

> [A] recurring theme in my career [is] I've often had trouble with management. It's not that I'm working against the establishment, its just that the establishment has branded me as undisciplined, which is pure bullshit.... [T]o do the kind of show I did, you had to be incredibly disciplined.... There comes a time when you have to make a stand for what you believe, and at the time I thought it was time to move on. I was tired of the constant struggle.[20]

When Worlds Collide: On-Screen and Off-Screen Space

D.W. Griffith is often considered the father of narrative cinema. Unlike with the scientific studies of bodies in motion (Eadweard Muybridge), documentary depictions of people and places in everyday life (the Lumière brothers), or constructions of phantasmal worlds (Georges Mèliés), Griffith's goal was to establish cinema's importance to bourgeois culture on the level of the novel or the play — precisely by turning cinema into a medium that adopted the methods and goals of the novel and the play (complex characters in narrative situations that provided moral, ethical, and political lessons). For Griffith, the function of montage was not an escalating collision of shots that were "vertically stacked" one on top of another to provoke revolutionary consciousness, as in Soviet cinema (Eisenstein or Vertov), but "horizontal linkage" that coherently told stories and constructed a pseudo-realistic universe juxtaposing historical events and personal melodramas, culminating in unified social order (*The Birth of a Nation*, *Intolerance*, *Orphans of the Storm*). As Eisenstein observed, "The structure that is reflected in the concept of Griffith's montage is the structure of bourgeois society."[21] Moreover, Rick Altman suggested Griffith preformed an ideological operation on film with the shot itself. Griffith consistently structured his shots so that the film frame depicted a *self-enclosed* world, exemplified by Griffith consistently placing doorways at the edge of the film frame: for a character to walk out of the room was to walk out of the shot itself. *Each shot* became a self-contained stage, or space, constructing its own inner logic and pseudo-reality.[22]

In contrast, Sales's use of montage, and especially the film frame, constructed continual social *dis*order. Many of the strange events occurring onscreen on *The Soupy Sales Show* were the direct result of the interference of off-screen space as "an immense and unexpected field of action." To the extent that *The Soupy Sales Show* might be categorized as "surreal," it is the surrealism of Artaud, where "The beyond, the invisible replaces reality. The world no longer holds." "The beyond, the invisible" of the *off*-frame event constantly encroached on and demolished the stability, and reality, of the *on*-screen event, the space where "the world no longer holds."

On *The Soupy Sales Show*, Sales wryly, but quite accurately, mused: "I played straight man to a pair of hands."[23] Most of Sales's regular cast members were hand puppets, quite literally in the case of "White Fang," a bipedal, anti-social pet "dog" whose paws were the only body parts the viewer saw as they extended from the edges of the frame and into the shot. In fact, White Fang seemed more of a puppet version of Bigfoot. The huge, clawed puppet hands implied that White Fang was as much monstrous beast as cuddly creature, an impression Sales enhanced by consistently speaking with his dog by looking off-camera with his neck craned upward, suggesting the unseen White Fang physically towered over Sales. White Fang spoke in a collection of unintelligible noises Sales alone understood, resulting in Sales both hilariously reacting to and translating White Fang's discourses for the viewer, often in question or reply form ("You're doing what?" "Is that so?"). Similarly, the humans on the show (excepting the straight parody and vaudeville sketches) were also only gesticulating hands.[24] The most famous recurring character was known as "the Nut at the Door." His frequent, frantic interruptions involved the sounds of knocking and pleading until Sales answered the door. Then he manically waved his hands in the doorway while an off-camera voice posed trite "My wife thinks she's a …" jokes enlivened with *non sequitur* punch-lines (e.g., the Nut yelling, "My wife thinks she's Cleopatra!"; Sales asking, "Why don't you take her to a psychiatrist?"; the Nut responding, "— And lose Egypt?!" followed by several seconds of strained, hysterical laughter from the Nut while Sales looked disgustedly at the camera).

Moreover, Sales's door became a gateway to an outside world entirely depicted by inserts of erratic yet generic stock footage—montage as a collision between Sales's living room world and the outside world to produce *anti*-realism rather than *pseudo*-realism. On one show, Sales opened the door and the shot cut to silent film-era footage of a child running up a dirt road towards the foreground of the shot, falling flat on his face, and then getting up to resume the journey to Sales's door. The shot cut back to Sales crouched in the doorway greeting "the child"—portrayed by a screechy falsetto and large, muscular hands extending into the doorway just above the floor. With Sales appropriately squatting down to talk with the child, he played straight-man to several dismal jokes. When asked if he was going to the local community theater play, Sales answered that he already had "two seats," prompting the child to ask, "Does Ripley's know about that?" (with Sales literally becoming the "butt" of the joke referring to his posterior). On another show, Sales was repeatedly harassed and hit by a large rubber ball being bounced and thrown at him from off-frame. A long "conversation" followed between Sales and White Fang over proper play etiquette in the house. White Fang grunted explanations while gesturing with his paws; Sales, playing the confounded suburban father-figure, nodded sincerely and responded deadpan with lines like, "Well, yes, I understand that, but...." Finally, Sales opened the door and tossed the ball backstage, informing White Fang that such rambunctious activity should always be taken outside (a general message for kids at home as well). The shot cut to very grainy stock footage of a woman soccer goalie catching a ball. The shot then cut back to Sales in the doorway, who was promptly hit in the face with the ball (so much for proper playtime procedures). To add insult to injury, a hand entered the shot within the doorway, pointing a scolding finger at Sales and yelling, "Butterfingers!"

While *The Soupy Sales Show* depicted suburbia as a world of constant, bizarre *possibility*, it also became one of continual, dangerous *hostility*, with an antagonistic outside world relentlessly intruding on the suburban living room. The various Nuts at the Doors became obtrusive neighbors; White Fang was both a parody of the family dog and disobedient child; the pies and other objects flying into the shot became arbitrary moments of disarray; the world beyond the suburban living room door was a seemingly random collection of chaotic but generic events; and the production crews' frequent asides became everyday neighborly ridicule. In this respect, these collisions take on a political dimension in the context of post–World War II suburban flight: the desire to escape the city with its unsavory elements (crime, minorities) in favor of the idyllic conformity, normalcy, and security of the suburbs — an ideological vision of American perpetuated, above all, by early television domestic sitcoms. Sales not only turned TV suburbia on its head, he (to reiterate Benjamin) "burst this prison-world asunder ... in the midst of its far-flung ruins and debris, we calmly and adventurously go traveling."

While the conscious use of off-frame space entailed both vast potential and inherent danger, it also served another important function: it consciously and continually reminded the viewer that Sales's TV world was, at all times, a television show in production. Sales did not utilize a studio audience, a laugh track, or the children's show peanut gallery; nonetheless, Sales did perform before a "live audience": his own production crew. They functioned as an audience, performers, and, most importantly, commentators on the show. (The actual verbal commentaries were supplied by head puppeteer Frank Nastasi; if the actual stagehands spoke any lines, they would have to be paid for guest speaking performances, which the show's limited budget prevented.)[25] On any given broadcast, Sales spent as much time talking to the crew behind the camera as he did talking to the television viewer through direct address to the camera. The crew frequently and audibly interrupted Sales's routines with laughter, groans, cheers, boos, and Nastasi's sardonic interjections. In turn, Sales responded with laughter, equally sarcastic comments, or a simple "Shut up!" Not so much a supporting cast, the stage crew functioned as a *sabotaging* cast.

Like Kovacs, Sales commented on and deconstructed the medium while he performed within it on the air. While Kovacs engaged in a distanced, Brechtian "changeover from representation to commentary," Sales's approach to TV can be seen as in keeping with Dada. As Thomas Elsaesser noted, "What was Dada in regard to cinema is not a specific film, but the performance, not a specific set of techniques or textual organization, but the spectacle."[26] An integral part of this spectacle was the interaction between a performer and audience: performance, provocation, and reaction (something Andy Kaufman fully understood, and exacerbated, throughout his career). Elsaesser suggested that a problem for any Dada film is the fact that the interactive relationship is constrained by the cinematic apparatus: the prerecorded film, the gazing spectator, and the environment of the movie theater (darkness, silence). Consequently, Surrealist films and their emphasis on shocking dream-like images become conducive to the experience of cinema.[27] Thus, the problem with categorizing Ernie Kovacs as Dada is that he consciously excluded direct audience interaction in favor of hermetic studio production and constructing the "intimate vacuum" between his shows and the TV viewer. Conversely, live TV or live-to-tape telecasts with studio audiences allowed for the unexpected in both performance and reaction, and a more favorable space for the Dada spectacle: the potential volatility and danger of TV comedy manifest with *The Soupy Sales Show*, later with *The Gong Show*, and, as mentioned, reaching its apex with Andy Kaufman's unpredictable late-night comedy and talk show appearances.[28] With Sales, the Dada condition of the hostile audience was supplied by a trash-talking production crew.

One of the staples of Soupy Sales's shows was the "Words of Wisdom" segments: Sales read a joke written on the blackboard and then interpreted it to provide an explanation and daily lesson for children. Sales's contention that the dirty jokes on the show were a public invention notwithstanding, the "Words of Wisdom" arguably contained a certain degree of sexual innuendo. On one show, the message was: "Soupy sez: 'Show me a midget king and I'll show you a twelve-inch ruler.'" Sales spent several uncomfortable minutes trying to manufacture an exit from the precarious situation, laughing hysterically while Nastasi provided audible asides ("Yeah, whadda you mean by that?"). Such interjections deepened the potential morass of Sales attempting to turn a joke that could be construed as being about an oversized penis into a socially-relevant message for children. By eventually explaining that the statement meant kids should treat everyone with respect, Sales provided the most standard and reliable of children's show messages. Conversely, the "Words of Wisdom" served to essay the very limitations of verbal language through comedy (as noted, the opposite goal of *The Electric Company*). "Words of Wisdom" offered a daily lesson in the deconstruction of language and the Symbolic Order into eye-rolling puns and strained arbitrary meanings where a potentially obscene joke could be transformed into a banal message on appropriate adolescent behavior — or *vice versa*.

As well as alternating his performances between the camera and the off-stage crew, *The Soupy Sales Show* engaged in self-referential criticism while the show was being performed. One of the several novelty-dance songs Sales recorded for his show, "the Mouse," became a hit record, and Sales frequently lip-synched and danced to the song on his show. (The accompanying dance, or "anti-dance," simply consisted of Sales holding his hands in the air and wiggling the outstretched fingers while he put his front teeth over his bottom lip.) On one show, Sales performed "the Mouse," and the mid-song instrumental break was accompanied by freeze-frame close-ups zooming in and out of Sales staring idiotically into the camera. These exaggerated visual techniques satirized current television and media effects used in televised performances by rock bands of the era and soon became standard on *The Monkees* and *Rowan and Martin's Laugh-In*. Moreover, the shots of Sales alternated with shots of a man in a cheap monster costume and make-up performing the Mouse — as if an extra from a low-budget 1950s horror-film had walked onto the set of *American Bandstand*.[29] The juxtaposition between the dancing monster and Sales's pulsating, frozen, and rather unappealing stare constructed an associative montage between Sales and the monster, suggesting Sales was not the giddy host of a children's show, but the frightening host of a horror show. "The Mouse" ended with Sales nearly careening into the camera, his face filling the screen before retreating back into a more comfortable camera range for the viewer. A loud, shrill, raspy voice from off-camera (Nastasi) began to berate Sales mercilessly while the camera focused on Sales standing motionless and looking around the set uneasily (and obviously trying to suppress his laughter): "You've got *some* nerve singing on this show! ... And the guys who hired you have the *audacity* to pay you ?!...What are you trying to do ... *fool* the public?!" After being publicly insulted, Sales donned a pair of glasses and looked off-camera, staring intently before exclaiming in open-mouth horror, "Mother!" The Freudian connotations of the joke aside, the internal criticism of Sales's performance not only mirrored the scorn heaped on Sales by mainstream TV critics, but served as a sardonic on-air critique of the show's thinly-veiled record promotion disguised as a performance.

If a certain moment encapsulated *The Soupy Sales Show*, it was a four-minute sketch from 1965. Beginning with a close-up of a sign reading "Fang's Talent Agency," the shot panned right to a sign imploring "Let Me Book You," and slowly zoomed-out as Sales burst onto the set through the door. A desk full of phones occupied the foreground of the stage, and White Fang's paws appeared on the left side of the frame. Silently, Sales circled the desk to read the signs and then stood in the center of the shot as White Fang answered the first phone. A recording of orchestral music swelled on the soundtrack, and Sales prepared to provide the vocal; however, his dissonant bellow was interrupted by the dulcet voice of Sammy Davis, Jr. For several seconds, Davis's song filled the air as White Fang's paws mock-conducted and Sales glanced about the room, upward at White Fang, and directly at the camera: Sales *reacting* to the peculiar event. The song abruptly stopped, and "My name is Sammy Davis, Jr." was heard on the audio track; like all the celebrity voices in the segment, their introductions were culled from dry public service announcements. Following White Fang's incomprehensible grunting over the phone, Sales responded excitedly, "You're booking Sammy Davis, Jr.?" A second and third phone call followed, the viewer hearing, respectively, "This is Elizabeth Taylor" and "This is Ed Sullivan" on the audio track, with Sales responding to White Fang's "discussion" with Ed Sullivan: "You can get him a job Sunday night at 8:00? He's been on for eighteen years!" When another phone on the table rang, Sales answered, only to be promptly sprayed in the face by a jet of water from the phone receiver. Following the Kovacs-style sight-gag, a Dean Martin song played, with Sales nodding, "That's Dean"— a thinly-veiled joke revolving around Martin's public persona as a lush (and, certainly, one wonders how many children in the audience actually understood the entertainment industry in-jokes in the sketch). Informed through White Fang's grunting that he was soliciting promising new acts to book as well, Sales walked to the door in the back of the set, opened it, and shouted, "Fang's ready to book you!" A furious montage of stock footage set to swirling classical music followed Sales's announcement: a test pilot ejecting from a jet plane; sprinters crossing a finishing line at a track meet; a bobsledder careening down a hill; a soldier dangling from a helicopter; a group of people walking their dogs down a city street; and, finally, a man running off a dock and falling headlong into a lake. This last image cut to Sales, still in the doorway, as a pair of arms gracelessly landed at his feet: the unseen figure literally "falling over himself" trying to get booked by White Fang. Taking the record album the hands offered him, Sales asked, "Who are you?" Another taped reply answered: "I'm Frank Sinatra." Turning back toward the camera, White Fang's business desk had suddenly disappeared from the set, leaving Sales standing in the now-vacant space on the soundstage, the absence of the desk providing a moment of disorientating non-continuity for the viewer as well. Thrusting Sinatra's record into White Fang's paws, Sales hurried out the door, went behind the set, and quickly returned with his own act to audition for White Fang: a large French Poodle. After learning Sales's act could not "sing ... dance ... or tell funny stories," White Fang impatiently grumbled and grunted. Sales responded, "Why'd I bring him in here? I have to — he's my manager!" By bringing in his dog-manager to monitor his contract negotiations with White Fang, the act that "can't sing, dance, or tell funny stories" could actually be Sales himself, a reference to the criticisms directed at Sales of being long on enthusiasm and short on talent. The punchline was immediately complimented by Sales being hit in the side of the face with a pie and a camera fade-out to end the sketch with a "blackout"— a camera fade-out, or everything going black, with Sales being whacked in the head.

As suggested by Rudolf E. Kuenzli in Chapter One, a distinction which can be made between Dada and Surrealist cinema is that the Dada film depicted an illogical world from the outset and exacerbated the effect through formal disruptions; the Surrealist film established a rational world only to subvert it with irrational images. For Ernie Kovacs, the sketch comedy show was dismantling the seeming logic of everyday events with mordant, macabre humor. Soupy Sales used the safest elements of television — the children's show genre and a sitcom suburban setting — to permeate them with inexplicable, irrational events which denied any plausibility, let alone any semblance of order. By way of analogy, if Kovacs was sketch comedy meets *Un Chien andalou*, Sales was the children's show meets *Entr'acte*. While a distinction has been offered between Sales's Dada and Kovacs's Surrealism, what is ultimately more important is how both performed radical deconstructions of TV and reality through comedy: *The world no longer hold*s. By the mid–1960s, the pseudo-realistic world of the sitcom itself became a space where "the world no longer holds" as well: *Green Acres*.

PART THREE. From Bumpkins to Bigots: American Television Comedy, 1962–1971

[W]hen the social contract with reality is abandoned, and literary works speak as they were no longer reporting fact, hairs start to bristle. Not the least of the weaknesses on the debate on [political] commitment is that it ignores the effect produced by works whose own formal laws pay no heed to coherent effects. As long as it fails to understand what the shock of the unintelligible can communicate, the whole dispute resembles shadow-boxing.
— Theodor W. Adorno, "Commitment" (1962)

CHAPTER 5

The Idiocy of Rural Life: *Green Acres*

> [America] will remain virtuous for many centuries ... and this will be as long as there are vacant lands.[1]
> — Thomas Jefferson, letter to James Madison, 1787

Barnyard Comedy

As television proliferated in Middle America throughout the 1950s and 1960s, networks, specifically CBS, responded with programming targeted to that audience. While *The Real McCoys* (ABC, 1957–62; CBS, 1962–3) was arguably the first "rural sitcom," the seminal example remains *The Andy Griffith Show* (CBS, 1960–8), which depicted small-town life in Mayberry as a community of good neighbors and simple folks anchored by the sensible pillar of the community, Sheriff Andy Taylor (Andy Griffith). Taylor's interactions with family, friends, and neighbors provided the show's more memorable moments, particularly the dialectic constructed between the leisurely, matter-of-fact Taylor (representing American pragmatism) and his hilariously high-strung, obsessively officious deputy Barney Fife (Don Knotts, the authoritarian personality *par excellance*). When community disruptions arose, they were inevitably exacerbated by Fife's rigorous adherence to the law and almost pathological obsession to maintain order, and ultimately solved by Taylor's wry, common sense approach to conflict resolution.

Nevertheless, Paul Henning was blamed for single-handedly turning American television into a ludicrous parade of ignorant yokels with his CBS rural sitcoms in the 1960s: *The Beverly Hillbillies* (1962–71), *Petticoat Junction* (1963–70), and *Green Acres* (1965–71). When *The Beverly Hillbillies* became an unprecedented ratings hit (the top-rated show in America from 1962 to 1964), the logic of television was, as Ernie Kovacs put it, "beat it to death." By the end of the decade, *The Beverly Hillbillies, Petticoat Junction, Green Acres,* and other non–Henning rural comedies were integral to the network's programming schedule. When *The Andy Griffith Show* completed its run, a spin-off of the show's secondary characters, *Mayberry RFD* (1968–71), also performed well in the ratings. While not a rural sitcom proper, another *Andy Griffith* spin-off enjoyed considerable success for CBS: *Gomer Pyle, USMC* (1964–9), featuring country bumpkin Gomer Pyle (Jim Nabors) leaving Mayberry to join the Marines (of course, the thorny issue of Vietnam was never addressed on the show).[2] With the exception of *Green Acres*, the strangest example of what critics pejoratively termed "barnyard comedy" was *Hee Haw* (CBS, 1969–71; syndicated 1971–93), inspired by, and a reaction to, the controversies and popularity surrounding the counterculture comedy-variety shows *The Smothers Brothers Comedy Hour* and *Rowan and Martin's Laugh-In* (discussed at greater length next chapter).

TV critics branded rural comedy, and particularly Henning's sitcoms, as moronic programming catering to the unsophisticated masses while nostalgically pining for the quality and relevance of the Golden Age teleplays and even the sitcoms of the 1950s. However, Marshall McLuhan's critique of American newspaper comic strips proves useful in this context, specifically his comparison of Chick Young's *Blondie* and Al Capp's *Li'l Abner*. McLuhan detested *Blondie*, describing it as "a pastoral world of primal innocence from which America had clearly graduated."[3] Conversely, McLuhan championed *Li'l Abner*:

> The sophisticated formula used with [Capp's] characters was that of a reversal used by the French novelist Stendhal, who said, "I simply involve my people in the consequences of their stupidity of their actions and then give them brains so they can suffer." Al Capp, in effect, said, "I simply involve my characters in the consequences of their stupidity and then take away their brains so they can do nothing about it." The inability to help themselves created a sort of parody of all the suspense comics. Al Capp *pushed suspense into absurdity*. But readers have long enjoyed the fact that the Dogpatch predicament was a paradigm for the human situation in general.[4]

This dichotomy between *Blondie* and *Li'l Abner* is most applicable in comparing the Golden Age sitcoms to the rural sitcoms of Paul Henning. The "pastoral world of primal innocence from which America had clearly graduated" presented in *Blondie* found its television equivalents in *Father Knows Best, The Donna Reed Show,* and *Leave It to Beaver*. In contrast, Paul

Henning was television's answer to Al Capp, where the rural sitcom became an absurdist mockery of itself and the ideological tenets it represented.

Class Struggle: *The Beverly Hillbillies*

In 1962, Henning created *The Beverly Hillbillies*, also acting as producer and head writer, as a parody of *The Grapes of Wrath* (especially John Ford's 1940 film adaptation).[5] In *The Grapes of Wrath*, the Joads forsake the Dust Bowl of Oklahoma in search of the American Dream in California, only to find the American Dream has been an unattainable myth all along. For Tom Joad (Henry Fonda), the arrival in California does not provide economic security or social mobility, but instead awakens a radicalized political consciousness. *The Beverly Hillbillies* turned *The Grapes of Wrath* on its head when Jed Clampett (Buddy Ebsen) "through epic fortuity and sheer ineptitude rather than the Protestant work ethic, falls into unfathomable wealth."[6] After selling his property to the oil company for "some kind of new dollars — not gold dollars or silver dollars — but *million* dollars," his cousin Pearl (Bea Benaderet) convinces Jed to relocate his family to Beverly Hills and take advantage of its many socioeconomic opportunities. Jed's miraculous leap from the depths of the proletariat (peasant farmer) to the upper echelon of the bourgeoisie (oil baron) did not reinforce but satirized the belief that if class structures of "haves" and "have-nots" do exist in America, they can be eliminated through hard work, social mobility, and cultural assimilation (as demonstrated on *The Jeffersons*). The dialectic between rural poverty (the Clampetts) and urban wealth (Beverly Hills) did not attain synthesis, but remained in a perpetual collision between two economic classes and two American cultures thrust together by chance. *The Beverly Hillbillies* literally parodied the "rags to riches" story. While the Clampetts acquired the *riches* and live in a Beverly Hills mansion, they still sport the *rags* as well, wearing the same ratty clothing each episode as they dumbfoundedly wander their Beverly Hills mansion, replete with the latest appliances, fancy décor, and ostentatious Greek sculptures. In the episode "The Clampetts Meet Mrs. Drysdale" (1964), Jed's sycophantic banker Mr. Drysdale (Raymond Bailey) is caught between these two worlds: on the one hand, incorporating his new and best customers into their modern, bourgeois milieu by instructing the Clampetts on the mysterious workings of a contraption known as the "telephone"; on the other hand, preventing his wife, "in whose aristocratic veins flows blood the color of blue ink," from learning white trash have not just crept into their upscale community, but are their new neighbors. On *The Beverly Hillbillies*, the adage "There goes the neighborhood" was framed around class instead of race.

Granny (Irene Ryan), occasionally armed with a double-barreled shotgun, battled the encroachment of Federal bureaucrats, IRS agents, shady businessmen, snooty neighbors, and cosmopolitanism in general with survivalist tenacity. Conversely, *nouveau-riche* Elly Mae (Donna Dixon) and Jethro (Max Baer, Jr.) pathetically attempted to renounce their boondocks origins and ingratiate themselves into their newfound ritzy world of "swimming pools and movie stars."[7] Jed Clampett adopted the privileged position on the show. Far from being the rural rube, Jed's practical honesty and common sense allowed him to assimilate into his new class status on his terms, in the process invariably besting both his backwoods kin and the upper crust of Beverly Hills. As Paul Cullum noted, "Despite his mystification at the newfangled trappings of luxury, and the craven depths to which almost everyone around him sinks, Jed remains a bastion of homespun wisdom — very much the Lincolnesque backwoods scholar."[8] In this respect, while *The Beverly Hillbillies* parodied *The Grapes of Wrath*, another John Ford film provided ideological inspiration: *Young Mr. Lincoln* (1940). *Young Mr. Lincoln* constructed a mythic image of Abraham Lincoln (Henry Fonda) as the conscientious, pragmatic, wise, even virtuous symbol of America whose politics were shaped by humble rural origins, hard work, and self-education — conditions which left him immune to the corrupting influence of Federalism, urban political machinery, industrial monopolies, and elitist universities. Ford's Lincoln was the ideal, or idealized, product and embodiment of Jeffersonian Democracy (although not without problematics, as will be discussed shortly regarding *Green Acres*).[9] Likewise, Jed Clampett is also a product of rural life (or, more correctly, abject poverty); but despite his lack of economic privilege — or *because* if it — he is a man of principle, integrity, and acute common sense: the rural sitcom's pragmatic pillar of a community who brings a semblance of order to the collisions of rural ignorance, capitalist avarice, and class conflict which otherwise defined *The Beverly Hillbillies*.

In this sense, an essential issue of *The Beverly Hillbillies* was how class struggle was framed in the pivotal question of "the city" versus "the country" in modernity. The valorization of urban life in all its cosmopolitan splendor and possibilities were not only valorized in capitalism but Marxism, exemplified by Marx and Engel's concession that, if nothing else, the rise of industrial capitalism and an urban bourgeoisie "rescued a considerable part of the population from the idiocy of rural life."[10] Yet modernity and its contempt for rural life received an unwelcome shock as the Clampetts continually proved to be unwilling or unable to acclimate themselves to their new surroundings, and instead thrust the bourgeois world around them into disarray. *The Beverly Hillbillies* embodied one of modernity's worst fears: the ignorance of the masses would not only prove immune to the possibilities afforded by modernity, but thoroughly contaminate it. Indeed, the very possibility of backward, backwoods hillbillies miraculously entering the world of the upper class became a mortifying political reality during the second season of *The Beverly Hillbillies* when, on November 23, 1963, a magic bullet allowed the uncouth Southerner Lyndon Baines Johnson to succeed the debonair Ivy Leaguer John F. Kennedy: "Instead of glamorous Brahmins dictating the national agenda, we had Texas crackers straight off the farm (whose political fortunes could be traced to Texas Tea of their own) ... *who entered popular culture as a national embarrassment.*"[11]

Absurdist Amercia: *Green Acres*

Following the extraordinary success of *The Beverly Hillbillies*, Henning's next sitcom was *Petticoat Junction*, premiering in 1963. Much closer to the traditional rural sitcoms like *The Andy Griffith Show*, *Petticoat Junction*, if nothing else, was notable for featuring a woman, Kate Bradley (Bea Benaderet), in the rural sitcom role of pragmatic pillar of the community as she struggled to maintain her hotel business and family stability. These became especially arduous tasks, since her brother Joe Carson (Edgar Buchanan) viewed the Protestant work ethic as a distasteful inconvenience, and her three teenage daughters were reaching adulthood amid growing feminist dissent and the myriad discourses of the Sexual Revolution. This is not to say that *Petticoat Junction* had a feminist slant; it was the most conventional, both formally and politically, of Henning's shows.[12] Conventional, either formally or politically, however, would *not* be the applicable term for *Petticoat Junction*'s unofficial spin-off: *Green Acres*.

While often remembered as a Paul Henning show due to his status as executive producer, the core creative team of *Green Acres* (as Henning often pointed out) was creator, producer, and head writer Jay Sommers; Sommer's co-writer, Dick Chevillat; and director Richard L. Bare. With *The Beverly Hillbillies* and *Petticoat Junction* among CBS's most successful shows, Henning became executive producer in name only so he could pitch the show to CBS personally (Sommers worked for Henning as a writer on both shows); *Green Acres* was bought and scheduled before a pilot episode had even been filmed.[13] *Green Acres* revolved around the foibles of Oliver Wendell Douglas (Eddie Albert), a Harvard-educated, New York City lawyer who abandons his legal career and life of urban luxury to pursue the dream of Jeffersonian agrarian democracy by purchasing a decrepit farm in Hooterville, USA— much to the displeasure of his cosmopolitan, European wife Lisa (Eva Gabor).[14] The opening credit sequence, with its legendary theme song, provided a ritual weekly prologue to each episode. Recounting the couple's contentious decision to move from urban affluence to America's heartland, it culminated with the clashing, dissonant voices of Albert and Gabor bellowing "Green Acres — we are there!" The final shot of the opening titles, Oliver Douglas standing proudly with pitchfork in hand and Lisa next to him in a glamorous blue pantsuit, was a parody of Grant Wood's own problematic ode to American rural life, his painting *American Gothic*. While often treated as Americana, *American Gothic*'s satirical, even troubling essay on American rural life is quite different from the kitsch sentimentality of Norman Rockwell and much more in keeping with *Green Acres*. In *American Gothic*, the stern, elderly farmer glares at the viewer with a wary, weary, even accusatory expression; the painting does not comfortably welcome contemplation, let alone ideological affirmation. In contrast, Oliver Douglas stands with poise, pride, and exaggerated confidence — setting the stage for his inevitable, weekly downfall.

Hooterville, the name a pun on "Hoovervilles" (the shanty towns that punctuated America during the Great Depression, named in dubious honor of Herbert Hoover), was a bizarre wasteland composed of ramshackle buildings, rusty jalopies (the exception being Oliver's sleek, purple convertible), and obviously artificial backdrops resembling the most generic of mass-produced landscape paintings — suggesting Hooterville could be "anywhere" and "the middle of nowhere" at the same time. The Douglas homestead was itself a disorientating combination of rural poverty and cosmopolitan interior design. The kitchen combined lurid green walls with visible bracing planks, golden candelabras, and modern appliances painted bright pink. The bedroom consisted of an elegant brass bed, moldering brick walls, and purple velvet furniture. Most of all, the bedroom closet door opened directly to the arid front yard strewn with dilapidated farm machinery — a denial of any separation of public and private space so vital in American political life. With the growing popularity and increased affordability of color TVs in America, by the mid–1960s the common practice of doing weekly shows in black and white was largely abandoned.[15] *Green Acres* did not simply take advantage of color, it was one of the most garish shows ever presented on television. In "Getting Even with Haney" (1967), Oliver has the opportunity to sue Mr. Haney at the request of the Ziffels. In the climactic court battle parodying the legal drama genre, the dominant brown and black tones in the courtroom are punctuated by two striking images of red, white, and blue: the American flag and Lisa Douglas's outfit, which resembles a cross between Jacqueline Kennedy's couture and the Statue of Liberty.

In most episodes, Oliver Douglas became immersed in a community conflict, more often than not by applying his rational and pragmatic world-

5. *The Idiocy of Rural Life:* Green Acres

Modern technology and rural life collide on *Green Acres*; note the television ended up destroyed. Left to right: Lisa Douglas (Eva Gabor), Oliver Douglas (Eddie Albert), Fred Ziffel (Hank Patterson), Doris Ziffel (Barbara Pepper) (CBS/Photofest).

view to the everyday absurdities of Hooterville life. The issue was quickly and hopelessly exacerbated by his interactions with the supporting cast through a string of convoluted comic exchanges strongly recalling the absurdist plays of Eugène Ionesco, who described his work as a "dislocation and disarticulation of language," and theater as "extreme exaggeration of feelings that disjoint *the real*."[16] In fact, Oliver becomes engulfed in the maddening discursive web of Lacan's Symbolic Order, as vividly described by Slavoj Žižek: "Language [is] a synchronic structure, a senseless autonomous mechanism which produces meaning as an effect ... when the human being is caught in the signifier's network, this network has a mortifying effect on him; *he becomes part of a strange automatic order.*"[17] Thus, the conflict *illogically* resolved itself around Oliver despite his efforts, and he had no choice but to accept the resolution, no matter how ridiculous. Not content with satirizing the rural sitcom genre and American politics, *Green Acres* became "a flat-out assault on Cartesian logic, Newtonian physics, and Harvard-centrist positivism."[18]

The first of many contradictions on *Green Acres* arises from the juxtaposition of Oliver and Lisa Douglas. While Henning's creative role in *Green Acres* is often overemphasized, as a long-time writer for *The George Burns and Gracie Allen Show* during its radio years (1942–50) and television incarnation (1950–58), Henning specialized in sly, confusing verbal comedy constructed around the sensible husband (straight-man) and addle-brained wife (comic focus) — a staple of the domestic sitcom and an arrangement ideologically ideal for representing a patriarchal order. Oliver and Lisa were Burns and Allen transformed into cultural and political caricatures, even dialectical oppositions: husband versus wife; rural life versus urbanity; Protestant work ethic versus leisure time; thrift versus consumer extravagance; common sense versus flights of fancy; and, above all, America versus Europe. As the embodiment of Europe in all of its aristocratic glory, Lisa represents the very culture that America explicitly saw itself as being reborn from in the frontiers of the New World, a land of individual opportunity based on social mobility and individual perseverance rather than class privilege. Yet it is Lisa Douglas — adamantly opposed to the move to Hooterville, and frequently wanting to return to modern, urban life and its consumerist advantages — who not only adjusts to Hooterville life, but thrives, while Oliver Douglas, along with his idealistically rigid Jeffersonian ideology, flounders miserably.[19] While his farm constantly hovered on the edge of bankruptcy, Lisa Douglas engaged in philanthropic work (turning the Douglas farm into the local Humane Society in "It's Human to be Humane," 1967), became a local patron of the arts (sponsoring a noted conductor to lead the Hooterville Volunteer Fire Department Marching Band in "Culture," 1966), and even ventured into entrepreneurial business ventures (opening a profitable beauty salon in Drucker's Store in "What Happened in Scranton," 1965). While the rampant absurdities in Hooterville are a complete affront to Oliver's positivism and rationalism, she accepts them as givens.[20] Most importantly, in the confines of Hooterville's Ionesco-like dislocated and disarticulated Symbolic Order, her Hungarian-accented English malapropisms became as perfectly sensible as Mr. Haney's shifty sale-pitches and Hank Kimball's impenetrable bureaucratic jargon. Indeed, when she once informed Oliver that he frequently misunderstands her because he "always jumps to *concussions*," her comment is perhaps the ultimate expression of Artaud's dissociative power of comedy as "total destruction of all reality in the mind."

Oliver's Hooterville nemesis was certainly local door-to-door salesman Mr. Haney (Pat Buttram), who made P. T. Barnum's maxim "Never give a sucker an even break" into a fundamental bylaw of social contract theory. Working through a mixture of huckster double-talk and anti-math to rival even Bud Abbott, Mr. Haney repeatedly and ruthlessly swindled the erudite man of the law Oliver Douglas in every conceivable business opportunity — from the initial sale of the rickety farm through a series of useless tractors and various other worthless products. In the episode "Furniture, Furniture, Who's Got the Furniture" (1966), the moving company inadvertently delivered the Douglas' furniture to Mr. Haney; in a good-neighbor gesture, he attempted to sell it back to Oliver at an extortionate profit margin.

If Mr. Haney served a function for rural TV audiences by allowing them to enjoy watching a country bumpkin effortlessly and repeatedly con a city slicker, dimwitted county agent Hank Kimball (Alvy Moore) satirized the frustrations of rural Americans interacting with Federal Government bureaucracy. The good-natured but rather dumb Kimball combined Max Weber's "Iron Cage" of modern bureaucratic administration with the relentless signifying mechanisms of Lacan's Symbolic Order. His explanations of simple regulatory statutes exponentially grew an elaborate maze of unfathomable guidelines and procedures expressed entirely through a baffling series of *non-sequiturs*, a process of negative dialectics ("That's *x* ... no, wait a minute, that's not *x* ... it's *y* ... well, not really *y*..."), continual loss of any reference point in the conversation, and a complete absence of logical cause and effect (as if Ionesco wrote Department of Agriculture manuals).

General-store owner Sam Drucker (Frank Cady) was arguably the one person Oliver could relate to in the community, in part because Drucker's General Store was a nexus for two sitcom worlds: the *Waiting for Godot* horrors of *Green Acres*, and *The Andy Griffith Show* charms of *Petticoat Junction*. Both shows were set in Hooterville, and existed as televised parallel universes presenting antithetical versions and ideological visions of America. Characters occasionally appeared on each others' shows (Edgar Buchanan frequently appeared on early episodes of *Green Acres*), and Sam Drucker was a regular on *both* shows. Drucker's Store was the frequent site of Oliver Douglas's wonderfully pedantic monologues about American politics. However, Sam Drucker's practices of mercantile capitalism also bewildered Oliver Douglas with a strange variety of consumer products like "dehydrated chickens" or nail polish that doubled as bathtub sealant. Moreover, Sam Drucker was also the local Postmaster as well as primary merchant, and Drucker's General Store was also the Hooterville Post Office. Consequently, not only did the store serve as the primary site where money was exchanged, but as the place where "letters" (signifiers) were distributed and circulated through the community's "circle of restricted economy."[21]

Eb Dawson (Tom Lester), while ostensibly the handyman on the Douglas farm, was for all intents and purposes Oliver and Lisa's adopted and troublesome son (he routinely referred to Oliver as "Dad," much to Oliver's chagrin). Eb's presence converted the Douglas bourgeois couple into the

Douglas holy family: "mommy-daddy-me," with Eb's emphasis certainly on the "me." Eb's contribution to family life was an endless supply of flippant criticism while Oliver Douglas struggled to hold his farm together. The variant of "couple logic" were the Monroe Brothers: Alf Monroe, a man, and Ralph Waldo Monroe, a woman (played by Sid Melton and Mary Grace Canfield). They were ambiguously presented as two brothers, brother and sister, business partners, and a married couple (Ralph's on-again, off-again relationship with Hank Kimball notwithstanding). Another version of the holy family was Fred, Doris, and Arnold Ziffel—except in the Ziffel "mommy-daddy-me" configuration, the "me" was a 200-pound pig, Arnold Ziffel. Certainly, the most absurd component of *Green Acres* was child-pig-prodigy Arnold Ziffel, who not only became the all-but-official star of *Green Acres*, but assumed the status of respected pillar of the community privileged in the rural sitcom genre (as will be discussed shortly, the status Oliver Douglas perceives and presents himself as having, but no one else in Hooterville bothers to acknowledge). Arnold religiously watched *The CBS Evening News with Walter Cronkite* to keep abreast of current affairs, and excelled in school, despite proud papa Fred Ziffel bemoaning, "All the other kids pick on him!" As a learned pig of the arts and sciences, Arnold's various achievements included diligently typing out what promised to be the next great American novel, painting modern art masterpieces like "Pig Descending a Staircase" (which stirred local controversy), and making important discoveries on his chemistry set. He also fluently grunted several languages, both human and animal (for instance, communicating in French with a French Poodle—and, of course, "Pig Latin"), while often commenting on the subtitles as they appeared on the screen.[22] In turn, the citizens of Hooterville fully understood Arnold, the lone exception being Oliver Douglas.

The Life of the (Capital L) Law: Oliver Wendell Douglas

One of the more important aspects of *Green Acres* was its complete subversion of the rural sitcom's chief device: the main character providing the pragmatic wisdom to hold the community's idiosyncratic characters together. Whereas Andy Taylor, a native of Mayberry, was its source of social order as town sheriff, Oliver Wendell Douglas is a transplanted big-city lawyer whose name is a parody of Oliver Wendell Holmes, Jr. (the Supreme Court Justice whose famous maxim was "The life of the law has not been logic, but experience"). Holmes's principle that interpretation of the law must be pragmatic, pliable, and amenable to changes in social context rather than rigid statutes became a vicious parody of itself on *Green Acres*. Any concept of "law" based on logic or experience was utterly useless in the illogical confines of Hooterville. "The life of *the law*" in the sense of jurisprudence was completely subsumed by the "the life of *the Law*" in terms of the totalizing effect of the Symbolic Order: the "strange autonomous mechanism" where the subject "becomes part of a strange automatic order." Indeed, as Žižek also suggested, "The dead, formal character of the Law becomes now the *sine qua non* of our freedom, and the real totalitarian danger arises only when the Law *no longer wants to stay dead.*"[23]

If Jed Clampett embodied the ideological myth of the Lincolnesque backwoods scholar established in John Ford's *Young Mr. Lincoln*, Oliver Wendell Douglas and his relationship to Lincoln can be read through a controversial 1969 essay on *Young Mr. Lincoln* by the editors of *Cahiers du cinema*.[24] Eschewing a reductive, superficial reading of the film's overt message, the *Cahiers* analysis of *Young Mr. Lincoln* favors a symptomatic textual reading exploring the film's contradictions "where notions like 'community' fracture under the pressure of a monstrous ideology Ford cannot contain."[25] In *Young Mr. Lincoln*, Lincoln, the law and language converge; as Lacan suggested: "[T]he law ... is revealed clearly enough to be identical with an order of language."[26] The opening credit inscriptions are followed by a poem extolling Lincoln from the perspective of his dead (absent) mother, which segues to the first scene: a campaign speech formally introducing Lincoln to the field of American politics. From reading law books to speaking the law in court during the film's climactic trial sequence, young Lincoln is not only transformed into the mythic figure destined to become president, but from an authority of the law to the force of the Law, which might be termed the "symbolic founding father": "It is in the *name of the father* that we must recognize the symbolic function, which from the dawn of history, has identified this person with the figure of the law."[27] Yet in the *Cahiers* study of *Young Mr. Lincoln*, this ideological image of Lincoln is fraught with textual problematics in all their ideological contradictions and implications:

> The overdetermination of this inscription of the Lincoln figure, as an agent of the Law, in Ford's fictions by all the idealized representations of Law and the effects produced by the bourgeoisie, far from having been erased by Ford, has been declared by his writing and emphasized by his comedy to show what a strange ideological balancing act the filmmaker has insisted on performing, and what strange scriptural incongruities he has insisted on exploiting.[28]

If Ford's Lincoln becomes a problematic "idealized representation of Law" as an ideological myth, Oliver Wendell Douglas (his last name derived from Lincoln's political arch-rival, Stephen Douglas) unproblematically views *himself* as Hooterville's "idealized representation of Law" (the symbolic founding father), only to have this self-proclaimed status negated in the course of a given episode by the Law of Hooterville. In "Lisa Bakes a Cake" (1965), Lisa lists Oliver's occupation as "lawyer" in the Hooterville phone directory, much to his displeasure, in that he is now a "farmer." His irritation becomes infuriation when no one in Hooterville solicits his services, while Hank Kimball, the primary spokesman of Hooterville's insular and idiosyncratic Law, is routinely sought out for legal advice. (In 1966's "The Beverly Hillbillies," the residents of Hooterville perform a self-referential parody of Henning's flagship show for a fund-raising event at the community theater. Oliver Douglas appears only as a last-minute stand-in when Eb is unable to play the idiot Jethro; Mr. Kimball stars as the community axis and Lincolnesque rural scholar Jed Clampett.) Oliver's predicament continued with the fittingly Lacanain title, "What's in a Name?" (1966). With Ralph Monroe's amorous designs on Hank Kimball thwarted due to Kimball's refusal to marry a woman named "Ralph," Douglas acts as her lawyer in court so she can legally change her name to "Sophia," only to discover his license to practice law is invalid in Hooterville. Meeting with the county legal clerk — whose office is adorned with a large painting of Abraham Lincoln — Douglas is ordered to retake the bar exam. After demonstrating a formal competency with the local legal system, Douglas can again provide legal service, which becomes moot when Ralph finds a new man — a swarthy mechanic named "Evelyn." In "The Deputy" (1966), Sam Drucker is unable to begin his vacation until someone temporarily assumed his responsibilities as deputy sheriff of Hooterville. Douglas reluctantly accepts the position. However, the title "deputy" is only "symbolic," in that the totalizing Law of Hooterville effectively perpetuates itself in preserving community order, and Oliver's efforts to enforce the particulars of the law are reduced to fits of Barney Fife–style incompetence. In "His Honor" (1967), Oliver learns the citizens of Hooterville want him to be a judge, and he is ecstatic when Lisa informs him, "Mr. Drewker swatched him to apples judge." Interpreting the message as "Mr. Drucker switched him to *appeals* judge" and appointed him the recognized judicial authority to overturn any and all legal decisions in Hooterville, Oliver's hopes are dashed when he learns his newfound status and power in the community was imaginary and the product of typical Hooterville miscommunication: he was promoted to "apples judge" at the county fair. With grudging acceptance, he performs his duties in the traditional barrister accoutrements of white wig and black robe, and the episode closes with a fittingly disconcerting image: a statue of the figure of justice, her blindfold making her unaware that a half-eaten apple is sitting on one of the plates on the scales of justice, throwing them considerably out of balance.

As Oliver moved from jurisprudence to politics proper, the effect was the same. With the episode "The Candidate," which originally aired the week before the 1968 presidential election, Oliver runs for the state assembly, only to be defeated when the incumbent simply bribes the Hooterville voters: cash money triumphing over campaign rhetoric. In one of *Green Acres'* last episodes, "King Oliver I" (1971), Oliver finally achieves his dream of becoming the pillar of the community: Hooterville succeeds from the U.S. in protest of unfair taxation and appoints Douglas *king* of Hooterville; as David Marc succinctly observed, "So much for Jeffersonian democracy and/or sixties idealism."[29] In "Lisa the Psychologist" (1971), the unofficial final episode of *Green Acres*, after taking some college courses in psychology Lisa is sought out for her advice, much to the exasperation of Oliver, suggesting the Law of Hooterville is ultimately better explained by Lisa's methods of psychoanalysis than Oliver's expertise in the law.[30]

In sum, any aspirations Douglas may have to affect "the law" of Hooterville (lawyer, deputy, judge, and legislator) are nurtured in the workings of the Hooterville Law: the Symbolic Order as an impenetrable series of *non sequiturs*, absurd aphorisms, and meaningless monologues. As he became increasingly overwhelmed by the arbitrary and automatic circulation of signifiers and the community order they construct, Oliver's responses veered between unfettered frustrations to long-winded lectures (accompanied by a shrill fife playing "Yankee Doodle" on the soundtrack). His vague platitudes variously echoed Jefferson, Lincoln, Henry David Thoreau, and, perhaps most importantly, William James. Indeed, among the many philosophical systems trounced in Hooterville, it is Jamesean pragmatism which became a chief casualty on *Green Acres*. Through its reliance on experience, utility, and directness, pragmatism is often described as a philosophy born of and perfectly suited to the American experience (or a philosophy derived from, and for, the ideological superstructure of capitalism). James hailed the pragmatic philosopher as someone who

> Turns away from abstraction and insufficiency, from verbal solutions, from bad a priori reasoning, from fixed principles, closed systems, and pretended absolutes and origins. He turns towards concreteness and adequacy, towards facts, towards action and towards power. That means the empiricist temper regnant and the rationalist temper sincerely given up. It means the open air and possibilities of nature, and against dogma, artificiality, and the pretense of finality in truth.[31]

The valorization of pragmatism versus philosophical and ideological rigidity was central to rural sitcoms, exemplified by *The Andy Griffith Show* (and even *The Beverly Hillbillies* and *Petticoat Junction*). In the America represented by Mayberry, Andy Taylor epitomized pragmatism as a *method* to embrace "facts, action, and power" in resolving the minor disturbances in the social fabric of Mayberry with a mixture of common sense, modesty, and wit.

In *Green Acres*, pragmatism was reduced to the very type of philosophy James abhorred. In Hooterville's confounding milieu, pragmatism was no longer a liberating philosophical method of "facts, action, and power" thriving in "the open air and possibilities of nature." Pragmatism, as practiced by Oliver Douglas, became an absurd self-parody: abstract and insufficient, predicated on its own presupposed verbal solutions, a fixed philosophical system defined by inapplicable idealism, constant inertia, and abject powerlessness. Unlike Andy Taylor's low-key efficacy, Oliver Douglas became a pompous windbag, a man who embodied rather than rejected "dogma, artificiality, and the pretense of the finality of truth." He situated himself as the spokesman for a community that had no interest in what he said, constantly and passionately lecturing the thoroughly uninterested, long-time residents of Hooterville about the idealized splendor of rural life in America: independence, self-sufficiency, the Protestant work ethic, common sense, communion with nature. In this respect, Oliver Wendell Douglas represented *ideology*.

Contradiction and Overdetermination: The Hooterville Order

Marx's political and economic theory lies in the concept of *determination*: the inherent contradictions of capitalism inevitably reveal themselves and necessarily result in its downfall. Louis Althusser, who is variously hailed and denounced for his interpretations of Marx, formulated a concept of determination functioning as *overdetermination*, a term Althusser admitted using for lack of a better one, and perhaps better defined by Raymond Williams as "determination by multiple factors."[32] Althusser did not deny Marxism's "base-superstructure" model: economic *base* (forces and relations of production) determining an ideological *superstructure* of "social processes," including government, law, religion, education, and culture. Rather, Althusser granted superstructure a degree of "relative autonomy" from the base, to the extent the superstructure assumes its own myriad ideological points of contradiction and conflict: "Marx has at least given us the 'two ends of the chain,' and has told us to find out what goes on in between them: on the one hand, *determination in the last instance by the (economic) mode of production*; on the other, *the relative autonomy of the superstructure and their specific effectivity*."[33] Rather than the overt political oppression of "Repressive State Apparatuses" (the State, police, prisons), Althusser posited that capitalism maintains itself through the *discursive* dissemination of *ideology* by "Ideological State Apparatuses" (church, school, culture, art) not only functioning as an ideological "superstructure" but an ideological "Symbolic Order," with *language* itself a

5. *The Idiocy of Rural Life:* Green Acres   113

fundamental (over)determining force. Althusser defined ideology as "a system (with its *own* logic and rigor) of representations (images, myths, ideas, or concepts), endowed with a historical existence and role within a given society."[34] As a system, ideology is not merely *thought* (ideas and concepts) but continually *lived* by the subject through "*structures* continually imposed on the vast majority of men, not via their 'consciousness'.... Ideology is a matter of the *lived* relationship between men and their world."[35]

The strongest and most frequent objection to Althusser by orthodox Marxism is that he simply rephrased arguments that already appear (or "always-already" appear) in Marx's work through the scope of Lacanian psychoanalysis, specifically Marx's concept of "false consciousness."[36] In Lacan's concept of the mirror-stage, the moment the subject recognizes oneself in the mirror is a moment of both narcissism and alienation where the subject embraces one's image-ideal, yet sees oneself within an order beyond their own existence — a moment not of recognition, but *misrecognition*.[37] In Althusser's synthesis of Marx and Lacan, ideology becomes a similar misrecognition between the narcissistic self-image of capitalist society, which is also alienated from that image by the real conditions of existence surrounding that image:

> Ideology ... is the expression of the relation between men and their "world," that is *the (overdetermined) unity of the real relation and the imaginary relation between them and their real conditions of existence*. In ideology, the real relation is invariably invested in the imaginary relation, a relation that expresses a will ... a hope or nostalgia, rather than describing a reality.[38]

On *Green Acres*, Oliver Wendell Douglas is trapped between the imaginary relationship to Jeffersonian democracy and the real conditions of existence in Hooterville. In short, Oliver Douglas is ideology as thought; Hooterville is Ideology as lived. Moving to the country in an attempt to reinvent his life according to his own ideological illusions (his "hope or nostalgia"), Douglas represents the belief the individual can indeed be "reborn" in the American frontier and its vacant lands. Yet, according to Althusser, the individual is *always-already* a subject of Ideology from the moment of birth.[39] Far from entering the world as a "clean slate" (*tabula rasa*) who can "write" one's own destiny within the social fabric, the subject is "always-already" thrown into the discursive and social structures of Ideology that thinks, speaks, and lives *itself* through the subject's daily discourses, actions, and experiences. In *Green Acres*, the subject either is "always-already" part of the overdetermined Hooterville order (Mr. Haney, Mr. Kimball, Eb Dawson, Sam Drucker, the Monroe "couple," the Ziffel "holy family"), effortlessly and naturally assumes a place in that order (Lisa Douglas), or becomes hopelessly ensnared and overwhelmed by that order (the hapless Oliver Douglas).

In "The Hooterville Image" (1967), Oliver's penchant for doing his chores in a business suit rather than overalls proves to be a source of controversy and consternation, resulting in all the men in Hooterville resentfully donning their Sunday Best for their everyday activities in protest until Oliver conforms. Defiantly proclaiming, "It's a man's inherent right to dress the way he chooses!" Oliver begins a feud with his neighbors until he bows to public pressure (hardly what Thoreau would have done in the same situation). The issue is exacerbated when Lisa, knowing he would eventually relent to public opinion, already commissioned a new farmer outfit from her personal designer, resulting in Oliver being forced to wear a lurid set of black silk overalls with mink straps, a white shirt with blue polka dots, and a cowboy hat: "I feel like a chorus boy from *Oklahoma!*" (A particular source of complaint is the zipper being in the back of his overalls — the outfit further feminatizing and emasculating Oliver.) The Hooterville men react with loud indignation, feeling Oliver has made a mockery of them, when the primary object of mockery, as usual, is Oliver himself. Still reviled as the town's individualist, he finally dons the proper attire of blue overalls and seeks acceptance at Drucker's General Store — precisely at the moment when the men in Hooterville, much to their displeasure, inform him that their wives have burned their overalls, and suits are now the "accepted uniform of the American farmer" in Hooterville. The episode closes with Mr. Ziffel snarling at Douglas: "*Conform* ... this is the *new* Hooterville image." Oliver's attempts to integrate himself with the common man, only to become what he "always-already" was (a suit-wearing farmer), are rendered into an absurd travesty in which Oliver is enveloped in the Hooterville Order, where clothes literally make the man — and model citizen.

In the context of "The Hooterville Image," overdetermination can be understood as the process by which capitalism's contradictions are constantly *concealed* and *revealed* through a continual chain of discourses and representations, as well as historical crises and resolutions, persistently working to resolve the contradictions. As Althusser wrote:

> A vast accumulation of "contradictions" come into play *in the same court* ... of different origins, different sense, different *levels* and *points* of application — but which nevertheless "merge" into a ruptural unity.... They reconstitute and complete their basic animating unity, but at the same time also bring out its nature: the "contradiction" is inseparable from the social structure ... it is radically affected by them, determining, but also determined in one and the same movement, and determined by the various *levels* and *instances* of the social formation it animates.[40]

Hooterville is an insular social system utterly impervious to alteration by constantly redefining its own ideology and logic through the breakdown

5. *The Idiocy of Rural Life: Green Acres*   115

and reformation of its superstructure through the Law. Contradictions are "inseparable from the social structure ... determining, but also determined"— at once ridiculously obvious and yet absolutely irresolvable as they "merge into a ruptural unity."

In his essay "Pragmatism and Humanism," William James contended the essential difference between pragmatism and rationalism was how each viewed the universe:

> On the pragmatist side we have only one edition of the universe, unfinished, growing all sorts of places, especially in places where thinking beings are at work. On the rationalist side we have a universe of many editions, one real one, the infinite folio, or *édition de luxe*, eternally complete; and then the various finite editions, full of false readings, distorted and mutilated each in its own way.[41]

On *Green Acres*, the pragmatist universe is rendered impossible. Hooterville is not "unfinished, growing ... where thinking beings are at work," but an overdetermined, stagnant, "always-already" absurd universe where *un*thinking beings are at work. If ideology is not *thought*, but *lived*, the residents of Hooterville do not *think* ideology — or much of anything else for that matter. They simply *live* ideology automatically, and act accordingly within its contradictory limits and pressures with increasingly absurd explanations and illogical lived solutions. Or, as Marx defined ideology in *Capital*, "They do not know it, but they are doing it."[42]

In this regard, Leonard Cabell Pronko suggested a key difference between Beckett and Ionesco: "Ionesco's humor is not a humor of human suffering, like Beckett's, for [Ionesco's] characters lost in mechanism are usually unable to appreciate the pain of their predicament."[43] Hooterville is essentially political life according to Ionesco; the characters are unaware of their own automatic, meaningless existence and incapable of comprehending their circumstances — much like the "Dogpatch predicament" that McLuhan posited as the basis for *Li'l Abner*, where characters endure the consequences of their folly and can do nothing about it because they fail to recognize the situation. The exception, of course, is Oliver Douglas, who becomes all *too* aware of being ensnared in the apparatus, and helpless in its operations. With Oliver as its central character — and victim — *Green Acres* becomes the absurdism of Beckett. In each episode Oliver can only react rationally to a rationalist conception of the universe which has been turned on its head and suffer in the mechanism: Hooterville as the *irrationalist universe* "full of false readings, distorted and mutilated" which *becomes* the "one real one, the infinite folio ... eternally complete."

Ultimately, *Green Acres* was nothing short of the bastard child of Jefferson and Beckett. Life in Hooterville, U.S.A., was a rural sitcom converted into a weekly, nationally-televised Theater of the Absurd, a preposterous version of America as horrifying as it was hilarious. Through its demolition of language, logic, and ideology, *Green Acres* transcended the superficiality of comedy and entered the realm of the destructiveness of humor. Indeed, *Green Acres* jeopardized television comedy at its core in the late 1960s. The sitcom — TV's primary means to safely regulate comedic form, content, and political implications — became profoundly avant-garde and subversive. New strategies soon emerged on network TV to specifically address political comedy.

CHAPTER 6

Archie Bunker for President! The Crisis of American Television Comedy in the Counterculture Era

> I didn't realize I was important until they shut me up.[1]
> — Tom Smothers

> You think it, but ole' Archie, he *says* it, by damn.[2]
> — Unidentified railroad worker on
> *All in the Family*

Monkee Business

"Counterculture" TV comedy began on NBC in 1966 with *The Monkees*, although the show originated as a blatant example of Culture Industry practices. With the Beatles at the height of their popularity, Bob Rafelson and Bert Schneider sold Columbia Pictures a sitcom project about the misadventures of a struggling rock band highly "influenced" by Richard Lester's Beatles films *A Hard Day's Night* (1964) and *Help!* (1965). After auditioning over 400 applicants, four relatively unknown performers were selected: Micky Dolenz, Davy Jones, Mike Nesmith, and Peter Tork. Nesmith and Tork came from the folk music circuit; Dolenz and Jones were primarily actor-singers.[3]

In tandem with the sitcom, Columbia Records began churning out Monkees records. Don Kirshner served as the musical supervisor, drawing from a pool of professional songwriters and session musicians, with the Monkees providing the vocals and public image. Over the course of *The Monkees*' two-season run, the Monkees had several hit songs (the Neil Diamond–penned "I'm a Believer" was the top-selling single in 1967), and they released *five* albums, the first four topping the charts. Indeed, the Monkees' popularity as recording artists quickly superseded the TV show, which generated mediocre ratings (although *The Monkees* won the Emmy for Outstanding Comedy Series in 1967). While the records were calculatedly commercial, the show was wildly experimental, combining the influence of Mack Sennett and the Marx Brothers with contemporary trends in experimental cinema: non-continuity editing, jump-cuts, camera zooms, montages, and various visual effects. The band occasionally addressed the camera or the crew, making improvised asides, and the show incorporated takes which included flubbed lines or inadvertent laughter as part of the finished product. In short, *The Monkees* could be seen as two-reelers for the Psychedelic Revolution.

The Monkees also quickly became a Frankenstein's Monster to the Culture Industry that created it. While records sold phenomenally, the Monkees were often subjected to critical disparagement, and particular controversy developed over the band's "authenticity," due to the extensive use of outside songwriters and musicians.[4] While the Beatles were hailed as the "Fab Four," the Monkees were dismissed as the "Prefab Four." After two albums, the band (specifically, Mike Nesmith) demanded more creative input on their records. Amid much rancor, culminating in Don Kirshner's departure to CBS Saturday morning to develop "the Archies," Columbia agreed to let the band contribute original songs and instrumentation to the albums.[5] Improved critical reception was offset by steadily decreasing sales. Moreover, in 1967 *The Smothers Brothers Comedy Hour* began infusing the political commentary into mainstream TV comedy. Montages of the Monkees running about in fast-motion intercut with a requisite performance of their latest single seemed less than revolutionary when *The Smothers Brothers* confronted drug use, race relations, and Vietnam. Furthermore, *Rowan and Martin's Laugh-In* premiered in January 1968, directly following *The Monkees* on Monday nights; *Laugh-In*'s style of "counterculture" comedy provided NBC unprecedented ratings that *The Monkees* failed to produce.

As the show neared the end of its second and final season, the band members, the show's creators, and NBC all seemed in tacit agreement that *The Monkees* had run its course.[6] In the final two episodes, *The Monkees* adopted a pronounced level of self-criticism. The second to last episode, "The Monkees Blow Their Minds" (1968), depicted the band falling under the control of a hack vaudeville hypnotist (Monty Landis) so they can be his mindless sidekicks while he headlines their gigs — a none-too-subtle commentary about the band's and the show's growing disenchantment with itself. Moreover, "The Monkees Blow Their Minds" began with a largely-improvised skit featuring Mike Nesmith and Frank Zappa portraying each other. Zappa wore one of Nesmith's trademark stocking caps and Monkees shirts; Nesmith wore a wig, moustache, and fake nose to play Zappa (the nose repeatedly fell off during the sketch). Discussing the current state of rock music, Nesmith-as-Zappa chastised Zappa-as-Nesmith for the Monkees' "banal and insipid" pop music. The conversation cut to Nesmith and Zappa playing themselves. Nesmith waved a conductor's wand while Zappa assaulted a car with a sledgehammer, accompanied by the Mothers of Invention song "Mother People" on the soundtrack. The final episode, "Mijacogeo" (1968), involved a wizard named Glick (Rip Taylor) practicing mind control on the public through television. It ended with a guest performance by avant-garde folk singer Tim Buckley, who sat on the car that Zappa smashed in the previous week's episode and performed a stunning acoustic version of his "Song of the Siren"— not only the first time a song about the allure and decimating effects of heroin addiction was featured on primetime television, but suggesting TV itself was ultimately a hypnotic and destructive "siren."[7]

What the final *Monkees* episodes touched on was exploded in the Monkees' feature film *Head* (1968). Bob Rafelson produced and directed the film, which he co-wrote with Jack Nicholson in a marathon weekend session (allegedly fueled by copious amounts of marijuana). A vicious self-criticism of the Monkees as a product of the Culture Industry, the film gave new meaning to the term "career suicide." *Head* began with the Monkees jumping off the Golden Gate Bridge, followed by an extended psychedelic underwater sequence; it ended with a reprise of the underwater sequence which dissolved to the band trapped in a tank of water on a flatbed truck being driven into the Columbia Pictures studio lot. A substantial amount of criticism of the Vietnam War was added for good measure: one particularly memorable montage juxtaposed the infamous, on-camera execution of Viet Cong member Nguyen Van Lem by South Vietnamese Army general Nguyen Ngoc Loan with reaction shots of screaming teenage girls culled from Monkees concerts. *Head* became *A Hard Day's Night* directed by Jean-Luc Godard rather than Richard Lester.

Of course, *Head* and the resulting soundtrack album were commercial disasters, and essentially destroyed the band's career. Schneider went on to co-produce *Easy Rider* (1969); Rafelson subsequently wrote and directed *Five Easy Pieces* (1970); and Nicholson starred in both films. The Monkees' first — and last — post–*Head* TV appearance was a dismally-received 1969 special for NBC, *33 and ⅓ Revolutions per Monkees*. A combination of science-fiction, fairy-tale, musical, and heavy-handed allegory, the Monkees play musicians grown in test-tubes who rebel against their creators and are eventually granted the freedom to pursue their individual creativity and identity. In fact, Tork had already left the Monkees by the time the special aired, and Nesmith followed shortly after. The Monkees disbanded in 1970.[8]

The March on CBS: *The Smothers Brothers Comedy Hour*

Achieving national popularity through their combination of traditional folk music duets and low-key comedy team repartee during the folk music revival of the late–1950s and early–1960s, the Smothers Brothers were initially among the *least* politically inclined folk musicians and comedians of the era; they made their national television debut in 1963 on the folk-orientated variety show *Hootenanny* (ABC, 1963–4), which several folk performers were boycotting for banning Pete Seeger.[9] After an unsuccessful CBS sitcom, *The Smothers Brothers Show* (1965–66), the network offered the Smothers Brothers their own comedy-variety show after Sunday night stalwart *The Ed Sullivan Show*—in the unenviable time slot opposite NBC's ratings juggernaut *Bonanza*, the top-rated show in America from 1964 to 1967. Premiering in February of 1967 as a midseason replacement, *The Smothers Brothers Comedy Hour* (1967–9) earned surprisingly strong ratings, and CBS added the show to its 1967–68 Sunday night schedule.

The political fireworks soon began, and, as Tom Smothers recounted, "We reflected the same consciousness that was occurring in the country at the time."[10] *The Smothers Brothers Comedy Hour*'s run on CBS coincided with three of the most volatile years in American political and cultural history, and inaugurated the war between the Smothers Brothers and CBS over the show's content—and here *content* need be emphasized. Aniko Bodroghkozy noted, "Considering how contentious *The Smothers Brothers Comedy Hour* became, it is worth noting, *in form and style, the show was quite traditional,* avoiding the kinds of experiments associated with variety-show rival, *Rowan and Martin's Laugh-In.*"[11] By negotiating the tension between the traditional comedy-variety format and left-wing content, *The Smothers Brothers Comedy Hour* featured an equally strange contrast between the Establishment and the counterculture as its Sunday night companion, *The Ed Sullivan Show*: both shows were a marriage of convenience for the growing cultural Generation Gap in Americans. For *The Ed Sullivan Show*, which offered everything from Shakespeare to jazz to animal acts, the inclusion of rock was a necessary evil to attract younger viewers. For *The Smothers Brothers*, the Establishment acts and conventional format functioned as a concession to CBS and its older viewers as it steadily pursued a counterculture agenda.

To this extent, Tony Hendra argued that *The Smothers Brothers* not only

6. *Archie Bunker for President! The Crisis ... in the Counterculture Era* 121

They don't *look* like hippies...: Tom and Dick Smothers; surprisingly, Tom is on the right (CBS/Photofest).

succeeded in subverting the traditional comedy-variety show, but frequently made its Establishment guest stars the target of the jokes: "The Smothers, instead of droning on about the generation gap, played with it. Seeing George Burns with Herman's Hermits or Kate Smith singing Sergeant Pepper ... let all the generation in on the joke."[12] While David Marc was less enthusiastic in his appraisal of *The Smothers Brothers* as a generally below-average comedy-variety show redeemed by its occasional provocative material, he nonetheless suggested, "If the *structure* ... was somewhat old-fashioned, the show's *content* was, in self-conscious relation to its primetime setting, nothing less than avant-garde."[13] For instance, in September of 1968, *The Smothers Brothers* parodied its NBC rival *Bonanza*. Parodying the Western genre was one thing. Parodying a cultural institution, another network's show, and its direct competition was quite another at the time — especially since singer "Mama" Cass Elliot played Hoss Cartwright, and Herculean African American pro-football player Rosey Grier played *Bonzana*'s deceased Ma Cartwright.

Whereas *Laugh-In* became famous for *how* it said things, *The Smothers Brothers Comedy Hour* became famous for *what* was said. In 1968, deadpan comic Pat Paulson began his not-entirely facetious run for the presidency, becoming a national pop-culture phenomenon in the process, by elevating meaningless political campaign rhetoric to its logical conclusion ("If elected, I promise I will win"). Leigh French's "Tea Time with Goldie" skits, a parody of the daytime talk shows featuring French as loopy, rambling hippie "Goldie O'Kief," were thinly-veiled celebrations of pot smoking. While Red Skelton continued to rely on a dated vaudeville character, "Sheriff Deadeye," *The Smothers Brothers* featured a more topical character in Bob Einstein's humorless policeman and authoritarian personality, "Officer Judy."[14] Corporations, organized religion, and race relations became the targets of satirical comedy, and opposition to U.S. involvement in Vietnam became the Smothers Brothers' *raison d'être*— provided the commentary did not end up on the cutting room floor.

The legendary censorship battles between CBS and *The Smothers Brothers Comedy Hour* began early on (ironically, the first dispute was an April 1967 skit satirizing movie censors). However, the most notorious cases of CBS censorship were not comedians taking shots at the Establishment or long-haired rock musicians extolling hallucinogenic drugs or free love. The Smothers Brothers emerged from the folk music scene in the 1950s, and folk music was a musical genre synonymous with the Left: Bob Dylan, Pete Seeger, Joan Baez, Phil Ochs, and even Peter, Paul, and Mary. Both Seeger and Baez made highly controversial (non-)appearances on the show. Tom Smothers invited Pete Seeger to perform on the season premiere of *The Smothers Brothers* in

September 1967. CBS censored Seeger's performance of "Waist Deep in the Big Muddy," a ballad of World War II soldiers needlessly sacrificed by a hot-headed officer — an obvious metaphor for LBJ and his policies in Vietnam. In the wake of negative widespread publicity, CBS relented and Seeger returned to *The Smothers Brothers* in February 1968 to perform "Big Muddy" unedited — a move that was less contrition and more of an attempt to generate additional ratings in the wake of the controversy, and present CBS in a more favorable light. However, a March 1969 episode was pulled from scheduled broadcast and replaced with a rerun of a previous show, largely due to Joan Baez's performance of the country standard "Green, Green Grass of Home." A song about a Death Row inmate dreaming of his hometown before his execution, Baez dedicated the song to her husband, recently sentenced to prison for draft evasion (the episode subsequently aired later in March, with Baez's dedication censored). In September of 1968, Harry Belafonte performed the calypso standard "Don't Stop the Carnival" against news footage of the recent chaos at the Democratic National Convention. As Hendra recounted, "CBS cut it *in toto* and sold five minutes of the resultant gap to the Nixon for President Committee."[15]

Inevitably, CBS became highly uncomfortable with *The Smothers Brothers Comedy Hour*'s growing stridency and its association with the New Left and Haight-Asbury youth counterculture. Tom Smothers later recounted how the events of 1968 — the Tet Offensive in Vietnam, the assassinations of Martin Luther King, Jr., and Robert F. Kennedy, the Democratic National Convention, the election of Nixon — had a profound impact on him, and strengthened his political commitment to the point of subsuming the comedy altogether: "I discovered later that I'd started acting like Jane Fonda."[16] CBS demanded completed shows be submitted to weekly network review for necessary approval before broadcast, and were routinely editing controversial material. By the third season (1968–9), the network escalated its censorship. The response was even more controversial segments, and Tom Smothers began withholding shows until the last minute, a strategy devised to make extensive cuts impossible: there would be no time to write and shoot new segments to fill the ever-increasing gouges made by the censors. In a June 1969 interview with *Look* magazine, Tom Smothers claimed, "Seventy-five percent of the twenty-six shows we've done this season were censored. And we're mild ... what will happen to someone who has something really important to say?"[17]

In fact, two months prior, Tom Smothers already found out exactly what would happen. Amid the Joan Baez controversy in March 1969, CBS renewed the show for the upcoming 1969–70 season, which Tom Smothers envisioned doing on location in San Francisco to incorporate more counterculture music and comedy acts—and possibly limit CBS interference. Less than two weeks later (April 4, 1969), CBS president Robert D. Wood summarily cancelled *The Smothers Brothers Comedy Hour*—the same man later canonized by television critics for his role in bringing social relevance to television in the early 1970s with *All in the Family* and other political sitcoms. In a press release, Wood charged that the Smothers Brothers failed to deliver the last show of the season before the appointed network review deadline—a show deemed unfit for broadcast because it was "irreverent and offensive"—and fired them for breach of contract. Tom Smothers vehemently denied Wood's accusations, stating that the episode was submitted the day before the deadline with cuts CBS demanded already made (specifically, CBS ordered a "sermonette" satirizing religion by guest comedian David Steinberg cut due to the show airing on Easter Sunday). Filing a countersuit against CBS, Tom Smothers launched a free-speech campaign, openly and quite angrily discussing this case in the media and lobbying Congress and the FCC for support. Public and press sympathy sided with the Smothers Brothers, viewed as heroic underdogs fighting for freedom of political expression, and increasingly popular causes, against a cold-blooded Establishment corporation.[18]

Yet despite the outpouring of public support, the Smothers Brothers' television career was effectively ended. (The courts eventually ruled CBS fired the Smothers Brothers illegally and awarded financial damages.) While tempting, it is erroneous to simply blame the Smothers Brothers' demise entirely on their political content or monolithic CBS censorship, let alone promote the mythic status *The Smothers Brothers* has since attained as single-handedly having brought down the Johnson Administration or being cancelled by CBS under orders from the Nixon Administration. While the Smothers Brothers were being routinely censored by CBS, on February 27, 1968, Walter Cronkite called for immediate negotiations to end the Vietnam War on *The CBS Evening News*: "We are mired in stalemate.... And with each escalation, the world comes closer to the brink of cosmic disaster." While Walter Cronkite was not thrown off the airwaves, it is unthinkable that Tom Smothers could have voiced such sentiments. In this context, it was not only politics that doomed the Smothers Brothers, but that TV *comedy*, and not journalism or drama, had become a popular site of political commentary and conflict. *The Smothers Brothers Comedy Hour* served as an example that television would only provide popular and economically profitable "counterculture" comedy and entertainment without the threat of cultural provocation and confrontation—something *Rowan and Martin's Laugh-In* accomplished far more successfully.

Culture Industry Counterculture: *Rowan and Martin's Laugh-In*

> The Smothers Brothers had an agenda. I frankly didn't give a fuck.[19]
> —*Laugh-In* creator George Schlatter

In early 1968, NBC launched its own counterculture comedy-variety show: *Rowan and Martin's Laugh-In*, which became the top-rated show in America in its first two seasons (1968–70).[20] Better-known simply as *Laugh-In*, the title itself was an obvious pun on the term "Love-In," hippie slang for an evening of getting high and making out fueled by the pretext the festivities were inherently subversive—aspects of emerging "social politics" *Laugh-In* fully embraced. However, while *Laugh-In* offered its share of commentary on Vietnam, racism, organized religion, and, above all, the Sexual Revolution, it is best remembered for *how* the political and social commentary was expressed through the comedy-variety show genre. Like *The Monkees*, *Laugh-In* made extensive use of experimental cinematic and video effects: non-continuity editing, jump-cuts, inserts, montage, and disorientating camera work with an emphasis on zoom-ins. The techniques were used to maintain a frenetic stream of fragmented jokes, sight-gags, catchphrases, and the occasional topical political commentary. Henry Jenkins suggested, "If *The Smothers Brothers* captured the political earnestness and moral conscience of the 1960s counterculture, *Laugh-In* snared its flamboyance, its anarchistic energy, and its pop aesthetic, combining the black-out comedy of the vaudeville tradition with a 1960s-style 'happening.'"[21] However, *Laugh-In*'s ideological vision of America had less in common with the growing, radicalized youth culture shaped by *Mad* magazine, Lenny Bruce, and the Beatles, and more in common with their Silent Majority parents informed by *Playboy*, Milton Berle, and Frank Sinatra. If the success of *The Smothers Brothers* was converting the standard comedy-variety show into a space for politically discontent young people, *Laugh-In* was very much designed to appeal to their parents as well, where exposure to counterculture frills through familiar and respected Establishment figures allowed older viewers to perceive themselves as being not so square after all, or else turn to *The Lawrence Welk Show* for cultural and political solace.[22]

Despite the visual discontinuity, *Laugh-In* was far from a disorganized or unpredictable show, as it was constructed around a series of recurring weekly segments. Structurally (if less so politically), *Laugh-In* was more comparable to an issue of *Mad* magazine than contemporary comedy-variety shows such as *The Dean Martin Show* (NBC, 1965–74) or *The Carol Burnett Show* (CBS, 1967–79).[23] Each *Laugh-In* episode opened with a Rowan and Martin routine. A "cocktail party" sequence followed where the various guests

...And they *sure* don't look like hippies: Dan Rowan and Dick Martin, Rowan on the left with the peace medallion (NBC/Photofest).

and regulars danced on a soundstage resembling a jet-set pad while shots frantically panned, jump-cut, and zoomed across the party as the performers fired off topical one-liners and risqué jokes at a blistering pace.[24] Near the midpoint of the show, the "*Laugh-In* Looks at the News" section occurred, introduced each week by the female regulars singing and dancing to the segment's theme in various, usually stereotypical, ethnic costumes. Encompassing "news of the past, present, and future," Dick Martin provided topical jokes pertaining to current events, followed by Dan Rowan supplying jokes about news twenty years in the future. "The Mod, Mod World," segment, usually near the end of the show, was a loose collection of jokes, sight-gags, and an occasional musical revue number focusing on a specific topic (the news media, advertising, the legal system). *Laugh-In* concluded each week at the multi-colored "joke wall," where the cast popped their heads in and out of small doors to shout more jokes over the closing credits.

To say *Laugh-In* "deconstructed" the variety show into a series of fragmentary sight-gags and sketches inevitably suggests a comparison to Ernie Kovacs. While Kovacs's deliberate timing was replaced by *Laugh-In*'s breakneck tempo, he was also a direct source of material. His "woman in the bathtub" sight-gags were borrowed on *Laugh-In*, with much lewder implications.[25] On *Laugh-In*, the woman might suddenly stand, revealing she was sitting in the tub in a strapless evening gown, the joke simply being the dashed if unrealistic expectation that the woman was going to be seen naked. In another sight-gag, while the woman sat in the tub, a plumber (Arte Johnson) emerged from the water, leaving the viewer to ponder whether he was working on the bathtub or the woman's "plumbing." Henry Gibson's most famous routine was appearing in mod fashions holding a large plastic daisy to effeminately recite turgid, truncated poetry: the counterculture Percy Dovetonsils — which is to say that the problematic "artist as sissy" stereotype Kovacs used as Dovetonsils for a satirical commentary on verbal poetry was simply converted into a "hippie as sissy" stereotype on *Laugh-In*. The famous sketches between Arte Johnson as a lecherous "dirty old man" and Ruth Buzzi as a sexually frustrated "old maid" consisted of Johnson harassing Buzzi on a park bench, making an off-color remark, being hit in the head with a purse by Buzzi, and repeating the process until unconsciousness: Kovacs's Nairobi Trio framed in traditional burlesque-slapstick versus surreal "nihilistic operetta."

Unlike the Draconian censorship CBS imposed on the Smothers Brothers, NBC adopted a *laissez-faire* approach because *Laugh-In* self-censored itself quite effectively in the editing room, where the show's unrelenting pace diluted and obscured controversial material as much as being any attempt to revolutionize television comedy along the lines of Kovacs's "antiform" experiments. Bodroghkozy noted, "The black-out, rapid-fire manner of delivery tended to blunt the political implications of much of the humor. By the time the viewer got the message behind the joke, two or three other non-political jokes or black-outs had already whizzed by."[26] Moreover, *Laugh-In* reduced jokes to concise one-liners, brief sight-gags, and, above all, meaningless catchphrases — ironically, the best-remembered being the least relevant. Dressed as a World War II German soldier, Arte Johnson peered into the camera and muttered, "Verrrry interesting ... but schtupid!" (or a minor variation on the line) as self-referential criticism about the previous or following joke. Judy Carne looked at the camera and exclaimed, "Sock it to me!" only to be hit with a bucket of water, fall through a trap door, or experience some similar slapstick indignity. Simply through their constant circulation and repetition on every episode of every show, *Laugh-In*'s stock characters and catchphrases became ingrained in the pop-culture vocabulary of the era, even though they had little if any substantive impact or value ("You bet your sweet bippy!" somehow paled next to "Burn, baby, burn!"). Functioning more as pop-culture jargon rather than cultural critique, such moments on *Laugh-In* are remembered far more than any specific political content, let alone controversies, and, as will be discussed shortly, suggests *Laugh-In*'s overall affinity for postmodernism.

While one or two guest stars usually appeared alongside the regulars and participated in the show proper, *Laugh-In*'s abundance of guest-star appearances were brief, pre-filmed inserts of numerous Hollywood and television icons, as well as current celebrities. Their observations ranged from burlesque one-liners (Johnny Carson: "Happiness is bumping into Raquel Welch — very slowly!"), comments about the show (John Wayne: "I'm very surprised at NBC!"), *non sequiturs* (Milton Berle: "Lewis and Clark: 1875!"), and the ubiquitous *Laugh-In* catchphrases (1968 presidential candidate Richard Nixon's infamous "Sock it to *me?*"). Inserts were edited into an episode throughout its duration, and often recycled in several episodes of *Laugh-In*. They seemingly appeared at random, with any connection to what was actually occurring on the show being purely coincidental. Because they were such vague commentaries, they could not only be incorporated at any point in the show, but in *any* show and at *any* time. Even the cast inserts continually interrupting the show to provide self-referential commentary were quite general; as a result, they were also eminently reusable from one show to the next. Jo Anne Worley took the direct approach, shouting derogatory comments such as "Dumb!" or "Bored!" or "Is that a chicken joke?" at the camera; Goldie Hawn looked at the camera with a perplexed expression and coyly muttered her catchphrase, "I don't get it" (which also had obvious *double-entendre* value). In fairness, the inserts could be quite witty comments about the medium of television: Henry Gibson, looking forlorn at the camera, asking, "Marshall McLuhan — Whatcha doin'?" or B-movie Hollywood star Van Johnson telling viewers, "Quit drinking! I'm not on this show; I'm in a war movie on Channel 13!"

Moreover, jokes could, and would, appear in numerous forms anywhere at anytime. Derived from the news bulletin, jokes ran across the bottom of the screen as printed "crawls" during the show. Some were pointed political commentaries: "It's KKK week ... take a bigot to punch" or "Pope Paul does not lead a rhythm band." Others were Hollywood in-jokes: "Dean Martin is closed on Election Day" or "Cary Grant ... call your travel agent" (referring to Grant's reported use of LSD). Still others typified *Laugh-In*'s burlesque mindset: "Raquel Welch — your cup runneth over" or "For a real fun evening ... make a fruit cordial." The women regulars (excepting Jo Anne Worley) occasionally appeared in grainy home-movie film stock as they go-go danced in bikinis. Shot from a multitude of angles, distances, zooms, and edited together with jump-cuts, they parodied both experimental underground cinema and stag films. Lines ranging from an innocuous "Peek-a-boo!" to the more charged "Mann Act" were written on a dancer's body. Jokes also appeared written on a bathroom wall, like men's room graffiti, occasionally by Johnson's dirty old man persona. In one early 1968 episode, he was caught writing the meaningless question, "Is Spiro Agnew really Howard Hughes?" In fact, the much more important joke appeared directly over it: "Senator McCarthy is a party pooper," a commentary on 1968 presidential hopeful McCarthy and his strident anti–Vietnam stance factionalizing the Democratic party mixed with some scatological comedy as well. Indeed, jokes appearing as restroom graffiti, written on "blue" tiles no less, implied *Laugh-In*'s comedy was ultimately not rooted in newspaper headlines, but the men's room wall. While *Laugh-In* relied on working as "blue" as network television allowed, one could say that *Laugh-In*'s humor was "red, white, and blue," given that the vast majority of jokes revolved around Vietnam, race relations, and the Sexual Revolution — often with fairly conservative stances.

While *Laugh-In* appeared more "experimental" than *The Smothers Brothers Comedy Hour*, it sought a much more peaceful co-existence with the Establishment, despite George Schlatter's claim, "We were obviously anti-establishment."[27] Among *Laugh-In*'s many guest stars were conservative icons John Wayne, William F. Buckley, and Richard Nixon himself, appearing on *Laugh-In* mere weeks before the 1968 election to awkwardly ask America, "Sock it to *me*?" *Laugh-In*'s original head writer, Paul Keyes, was a close friend and campaign worker for Nixon, and *Laugh-In* premiered during the height of the contentious 1968 presidential campaign, running from January to June 1968 as a midseason replacement show. These shows and the first full first season (1968–9) reflected *Laugh-In*'s mixture of experimental television techniques and sizable amount of comedy attacking both the Left and the Right, provided all the targets were *Democrats*: LBJ, Robert F. Kennedy, Hubert H. Humphrey, Eugene McCarthy, and George Wallace. In an April 1968 episode of *Laugh-In*, comedian John Byner impersonated RFK throughout the show; all the jokes focused on Robert and Ethel Kennedy's reproductive habits and prodigious production of children rather than RFK's "positions" on Civil Rights or Vietnam. Nor surprisingly, criticism of Nixon on *Laugh-In* was virtually non-existent prior to the 1968 election.[28]

While opposition to military involvement in Vietnam was the central political issue for the Smothers Brothers, *Laugh-In* initially took a decidedly different take on the war. Early in the show's run, many of the jokes were directed at North Vietnam's leader, Ho Chi Mihn. An insert of actor James

Garner proclaimed, "As far as I'm concerned, Ho Chi Mihn is a pain in the East!" During a weekly "Laugh-In Looks at the News" segment, Dan Rowan, reading "The News of the Future," included a joke with the punchline: "— and the Governor of Hawaii, Canada, and California: Ho Chi Mihn." When criticism of U.S. military policy occurred in these early years of *Laugh-In*, it was directed at the LBJ Administration for waging a militarily ineffectual war against Communism. In one opening party segment, Jo Anne Worley remarked, "Boris says that General Westmoreland should have been replaced by Genghis Kahn; after all, he's the only general who ever won a war in Asia! Isn't Boris smart?!" Similarly, race relations were also part of *Laugh-In*'s comedy. In one blackout-skit, Chelsea Brown interrupted a Ku Klux Klan meeting in the suburbs and asked, "Is this Stokely Carmichael's house?" (The response: "No, this is the B'nai Brith!"). George Wallace — segregationist Alabama governor and 1968 third-party presidential candidate — was the specific target of many jokes, such as guest star Flip Wilson musing, "I don't agree with the people who say that Wallace better calm down or we'll have a madman in the White House — or a white man in the madhouse." However, *Laugh-In*'s attacks on Wallace as a bigot were not necessarily rooted in outrage against segregation, but, like the anti–LBJ commentaries about Vietnam, thinly-disguised campaign work on Nixon's behalf.[29]

To this extent, one can question Bodroghkozy's contention that *Laugh-In* "emphatically took a left-liberal stance."[30] Rather, as Jenkins suggested, "The humor was sometimes topical, sometimes nonsensical, sometimes 'right on,' and sometimes right of center."[31] Only *after* Nixon became president, and his policies came under attack, did *Laugh-In* demonstrate any "emphatically left-liberal politics"— resulting in Keyes acrimoniously leaving the show to become a speech writer for Nixon. By September of 1969, with the majority of Americans opposed to military involvement in Vietnam, and the Smothers Brothers unceremoniously booted from network television, Dan Rowan introduced the recurring character of "General Bullright," a pathological military officer. While George Carlin and Richard Pryor were conspicuous by their absence, by 1972, *Laugh-In* had indeed moved enough to the left that Mort Sahl appeared as a guest.

Ultimately, the majority of *Laugh-In*'s comedy centered on the changing landscape of sexual politics in America, highly reliant on the vision of a sexually-liberated and sophisticated America offered in the world of *Playboy*: cocktails, consumerism, cosmopolitanism, and copulation (not surprisingly, Hugh Hefner appeared on *Laugh-In*). While *Laugh-In*'s take on the Sexual Revolution was its most "liberal" stance, it defined "sexual liberation" through an unwavering belief in what Michel Foucault termed the "Repressive Hypothesis": the myth that sex in modern society is a binary battle between monolithic forces of sexual expression versus sexual repression, rather than sexuality being a topic of multiple competing discourses that shape and reshape conceptions of sex itself.[32] *Laugh-In* was one of these discourses on sexuality during the Sexual Revolution, and thoroughly consistent with *Playboy*—extolling the rights of men to express their sexual freedom and the rights of women to have men's sexual freedom expressed at them.[33] Dick Martin adopted the persona of the successful, swinging bachelor celebrated in *Playboy*. In one "cocktail party" sequence, an attractive brunette's query if Martin was "involved in a lot of action in the war?" was answered by, "Yes, up until I got drafted!" While the comediennes were prominently featured, it was to supply stereotypes of women. Ruth Buzzi's "Gladys" persona was a tightly-wound, sexually-frustrated old maid; in the above-mentioned cocktail party segment, Gladys groused, "I tried to join the Sexual Revolution, but I couldn't pass the physical!" Goldie Hawn confined her talents to a "dumb blonde" routine, and Chelsea Brown embodied the sexy and sassy "black chick" stereotype-fantasy. Jo Anne Worley was the blathering socialite who seemed incapable of forming an opinion of her own, but rather parroted her husband ("Boris says ... Isn't Boris smart?!"). *Laugh-In* certainly did not offer any feminist counterpoint to the male-orientated comedy, although in retrospect it is surprising *Laugh-In* did not feature more "bra-burning" jokes, considering the show's predilection for one-liners about the bosoms of Raquel Welch and Sophia Loren as much as the politics of Ho Chi Mihn or George Wallace.

Despite its early and phenomenal popularity, *Laugh-In*'s drastic decline in the ratings by the early 1970s, and its eventual cancellation in 1973 after only five seasons, can be attributed to the show's inevitable overuse and exhaustion of the very components that made the show innovate for network television. As Peter Bürger noted:

> A further difficulty inheres in the aesthetics of shock, and that is the impossibility to make permanent this kind of effect. Nothing loses its effectiveness more quickly than shock.... *As a result of repetition, it changes fundamentally; there is such a thing as expected shock*.... [A] nearly institutionalized shock probably has little effect on the way the recipients run their lives. The shock is "consumed." What remains is the enigmatic quality of the forms, their resistance to the attempt to wrest meaning from them.[34]

Ostensibly "experimental" TV quickly became numbing predictability once the initial "shock effect" wore off, and *Laugh-In*'s avant-garde became "institutionalized shock effect" entirely reduced to "enigmatic forms [and] their resistance to wrest meaning from them." When Buñuel claimed that "nothing symbolized anything" in *Un Chien andalou*, the lack of fixed meaning allows the audience to make multiple, conflicting interpretations. When a perplexed Goldie Hawn periodically informed viewers, "I don't get it," it was less of an ironic, internal commentary than simply informing the viewer that if a *Laugh-In* regular didn't "get it," there was really nothing to "get" on the show on the first place. To be less charitable, Johnson's catchphrase "Very interesting ... but stupid!" became not only one of the show's best-remembered lines, but a definition of *Laugh-In*'s approach to topical comedy as a "style over substance" circulation of pop-culture references it both appropriated (celebrity images) and created (stock characters and catchphrases).

While *Laugh-In* borrowed its idiosyncratic "antiform" from Ernie Kovacs, it was ultimately rooted in the philosophy of Andy Warhol: the "avant-garde" as mass-producible, mass-marketable, and mass-consumable pop-culture iconography. Ironically, Warhol once stated his favorite TV show of the era was the quite formally traditional and apolitical *Carol Burnett Show*, which he championed for being impervious to "repetitive novelties."[35] Indeed, *Laugh-In* functioned through an endless series of "repetitive novelties" where episodes did not simply resemble each other, but became completely indistinguishable from the previous one and the following one. *Laugh-In* embodied the television show as a cultural commodity ideally suited to the needs and demands of the Culture Industry in the 1960s — an avant-garde comedy show that potentially could be inexhaustibly produced and easily consumed *because* of the superficial weirdness and *through* a pop-culture vocabulary (*Family Guy* being the epitome of this approach). In short, *Laugh-In* was the first postmodern television comedy show — postmodernism, as Fredric Jameson put it, as "blank parody."

For all of its oppositional politics, *The Smothers Brothers Comedy Hour* remained a standardized variety show. For all of its pseudo-experimentalism, *Laugh-In* was "avant-garde" firmly in the sway of the Culture Industry. Arguably, *The Smothers Brothers Comedy Hour* and *Laugh-In* were not the most "politically subversive" variety shows of the era. In 1969, Jean-Luc Comolli and Jean Narboni defended the work of Hollywood directors such as John Ford over the more concretely political filmmakers of the era because of the *overdetermination* of ideology that appeared in their ostensibly affirmative texts versus an explicitly oppositional text:

> Films which seem at first sight to belong firmly within the ideology and to be completely under its sway, but which turn out to be so only in an ambiguous manner.... Looking at the framework, one can see two moments in it: one holding it back within certain limits, one transgressing them. An internal criticism is taking place which cracks the film apart at the seams. If one looks at the film obliquely, looking for symptoms; if one looks beyond its apparent formal coherence, one can see it is riddled with cracks.[36]

Perhaps the variety shows that showed an America "cracking at the seams" in the late 1960s were the non-political variety shows that *imploded* under the weight of ideological contradictions rather than *exploding* the variety show genre with overt political commentary or flashy, unconventional style. In the wake of the Smothers Brothers' abrupt termination by CBS, the network determined that the logical replacement in the vacated timeslot was *Hee Haw*—a bizarre combination of *Laugh-In*'s formal approach to the comedy-variety show, country music, community theater, antiquated vaudeville and "farmer's daughter" jokes, and *Li'l Abner*–like rural caricatures. As if the Cabaret Voltaire and the Grand Ole Opry grotesquely merged, *Hee Haw,* in all of its incomprehensible glory, became a bizarre spectacle of rural Americana reduced to its tackiest clichés, reflecting a vision of Middle America as stupefying as the absurdist horrors of *Green Acres*. *The Ed Sullivan Show* desperately tried to unite America as a great cultural melting pot precisely at the moment America was becoming a collection of irreconcilable subcultures with irreconcilable political visions. Conceivably, *The Lawrence Welk Show* became the most "subversive" variety show of the 1960s—a mélange of tap-dancing African Americans; whitebread couples singing patriotic and religious songs; sparkling champagne music; and inserts of an ashen, elderly, nearly catatonic studio audience. *The Lawrence Welk Show* (over)determinedly presented a hopelessly anachronistic image of a simpler and happier America while the country was falling apart, an ideological vision of America that today looks not completely naive and implausible, but utterly surreal—or absurd. In these ways, these variety shows encapsulated the crises in America much less overtly, but just as dynamically, as their more overtly political counterparts.

The Great CBS Purge and the Rise of the Political Sitcom: *All in the Family*

In 1971, CBS embarked on a new cultural and economic mission by summarily canceling many of its established sitcoms and comedy-variety shows. Albert Aus suggested, "These changes had less to do with any contempt for the rural idiocy of the 'barnyard comedies' than the need to appeal to a younger-urban audience with larger disposable incomes."[37] While the sweeping changes in CBS programming were certainly rooted in a conscious, even drastic, strategy to attract this new audience, the rural comedies were still popular when they were eliminated; the very idea of canceling a show that has strong ratings (read: turning a profit), let alone *actually doing so* is a combination of blasphemy and career suicide for a television executive. Culture Industry logic would be to maintain the existing audience while absorbing a new audience by providing *both* the established and economically-successful cultural products, as well as new, attractive cultural products for the potential new consumers. CBS realized this was an untenable strategy in the context of American society at the time.

The rural comedies had become something of a self-imposed national embarrassment to CBS. It was not so much that the network objected to depicting America infested by country bumpkins and poor white trash, but to the criticism the shows endured as being the pinnacle of television-as-moronic, meaningless entertainment. By the early 1970s, CBS was perceived as the network of Middle American anti-intellectualism and low-brow cultural taste, while NBC was becoming the network of hip, affluent liberals. This popular view was exacerbated by CBS disposing of *The Smothers Brothers Comedy Hour* in favor of *Hee Haw*, while *Laugh-In* was defining "counterculture television" across the dial and topping the ratings for NBC. In 1971, *The Beverly Hillbillies, Green Acres, Mayberry RFD*, and *Hee Haw* were all abruptly cancelled.[38] The venerable *Ed Sullivan Show* was also cancelled in the 1971 overhaul, and other networks followed the CBS lead in eliminating perceived television anachronisms: NBC picked up the still-popular *The Red Skelton Show* after its cancellation by CBS in 1970, only to cancel it in 1971; ABC cancelled the long-running *Lawrence Welk Show* in 1971 as well.[39]

Hogan's Heroes (1965–71) was also among the CBS casualties.[40] Considering the national disaster Vietnam had become for America, a show that took an irreverent and seemingly pro-military attitude about war proved awkward and even distasteful for CBS (however, to read *Hogan's Heroes* completely against the grain, it could be seen as a subversive satire on U.S. involvement in Vietnam, with the bumbling Germans representing U.S. military strategy and the American POWs representing the wily Viet Cong).[41] Instead, *M*A*S*H* (1972–83) was introduced to the airwaves, a sitcom based on Robert Altman's critically and commercially successful 1970 anti-war satire. *M*A*S*H* was a "military sitcom" very much in the mold of its predecessors *McHale's Navy* (ABC, 1962–6), *Gomer Pyle*, and *Hogan's Heroes* in depicting a conflict between amiable pragmatism (Lt. Commander McHale, Gomer Pyle, Colonel Hogan) and officious buffoonery (Colonel Binghamton, Sergeant Carter, Colonel Klink). However, *M*A*S*H* added the dimension of the non-conformist Hawkeye Pierce (Alan Alda) being a free-love, anti-war liberal, and the "by-the-book" Frank Burns (Larry Linville) being a sexually-uptight, pro-war conservative.[42] Not a Norman Lear sitcom, but clearly inspired by his approach, *M*A*S*H*'s post-counterculture political consciousness was perfectly suited to the new CBS, providing slick situation-comedy, liberal-humanist political sentiments (the show's early and frequent sexism notwithstanding), and forays into ham-fisted drama.

However, the show that redefined television comedy and the new breed of CBS's socially-conscious sitcoms was unquestionably *All in the Family*

(1971–83; retitled *Archie Bunker's Place* in 1979).[43] After being rejected by ABC, *All in the Family* premiered on CBS in January 1971 as a midseason replacement. By the end of its first full season (1971–2), and for the following *five* seasons, *All in the Family* was the top-rated show in America, routinely garnering Emmys and becoming the flagship show of the more serious and socially-conscious CBS. Direct or indirect *All in the Family* spin-offs produced by Lear became part of the seminal CBS political sitcom line-up in the 1970s: *Maude* (1972–8); *Good Times* (1974–9); *The Jeffersons* (1975–85).[44]

All in the Family used the recognizable sitcom family and cast them into political stereotypes.[45] The bumbling father, future pop-culture icon Archie Bunker (Carroll O'Connor), became a blue-collar bigot and petty tyrant of the home. The daft wife and mother, Edith Bunker (Jean Stapleton), was transformed into a brow-beaten domestic slave. The "precocious children" were Archie's daughter Gloria (Sally Struthers), a nascent feminist, and his "Polack meathead" son-in-law Mike Stivic (Rob Reiner), who was nothing short of Archie Bunker's worst nightmare: a long-haired intellectual unapologetically committed to liberal activism. Designed to satirize the Right by featuring Archie Bunker proclaiming the infinite wisdom of Richard Nixon and routinely denouncing minorities, feminists, and know-it-all liberals, *All in the Family*'s popularity, at least in part, was ultimately owed to viewers who watched the show to hear Archie Bunker rage against all things un–American. Rather than *laughing at* Archie Bunker and his ill-mannered politics, some viewers *laughed with* him as he "told it like it is," and subsequently *laughed at* his targets of scorn ("coloreds," "Hebes," "spics," "homos," etc.). While Pat Paulson was CBS's contribution to the 1968 election, in 1972 the rallying cry in American popular culture was "Archie Bunker for President!"

In this regard, *Laugh-In*'s relatively rapid decline in popularity can be attributed to the success of *All in the Family*. By the early 1970s, *Laugh-In* increasingly became more overtly liberal, while *All in the Family*'s satire allowed conservative audiences to embrace the literal message, and liberal audiences the ironic intent. Not only could Lear and CBS pioneer a new brand of socially-relevant television, but *All in the Family* had a textual safety valve to ensure both the Left and the Right could enjoy the comedy — and, above all, generate ratings. As Peter N. Carroll noted, "The televised fantasy of discontent became an electronic substitute for real life. In this way television appeased its loyal followers, while simultaneously accomplishing it commercial purpose."[46]

Moreover, *Laugh-In*'s fast-paced comedy-variety format and off-the-cuff style of political commentary quickly fell out of favor with mainstream audiences with the advent of Lear's sitcoms, which combined a much more conventional and accessible sitcom format with a more solemn tone of political comedy. Essentially, *All in the Family* was a weekly Golden Age teleplay done as a classic sitcom, constructing a pseudo-realistic world that absorbed audiences to teach moral and ideological lessons by having them relate to complex characters and narrative situations. One key production tactic Lear insisted on was that *All in the Family* be produced and filmed in the manner of the classic 1950s sitcoms (*I Love Lucy*, *The Honeymooners*): a three-camera, theatrical performance taped in front of a studio audience (studio film production methods and added laugh tracks being the dominant production practice at the time). This strategy also permitted the show to be performed, as much as possible, as a live teleplay. Moreover, Lear's sitcoms encouraged studio audience responses as part of the show — the antithesis of Ernie Kovacs, who rejected the involvement, or interference, of a live audience in his TV comedy. Indeed, *All in the Family*'s studio audience became the primary means to mediate the thorny nexus of comedy, drama, and satirical intent for the viewer (if not altogether successfully): hearty laugher at the jokes, supportive applause when a particularly cogent point was made, tense silence during the dramatic moments. While *All in the Family* and Lear's ensuing spin-offs are credited with synthesizing the two dialectical strains of television up to that point — amusing sitcoms versus socially-relevant television dramas — they actually *reinforced* the oppositions between television comedy and drama and their perceived social functions. Rarely, if ever, was comedy beyond the insults, domestic barbs, and ethnic slurs (as intended as they were as satire). As the messages became serious or poignant in a given episode, the shows simply dispensed with comedy and moved into the realm of serious drama as the tone and message of an episode warranted.

One of the more famous episodes of *All in the Family* remains "Archie Is Branded" (1973). The episode begins with the Bunker home mysteriously vandalized: a swastika has been painted on the front door. Initially, Archie dismisses it as a random act by neighborhood teens, but Mike fears the swastika has more ominous intent. Indeed, Mike's concerns are soon confirmed. The Bunkers' home was mistaken for a Jewish family recently moved into the neighborhood and who are being targeted for harassment in order to force them to move. Paul Benjamin (Gregory Sierra) arrives to offer the services and protection of his organization, the Hebrew Defense Association (a thinly-veiled reference to the Jewish Defense League). The sitcom becomes a platform for a dramatic debate over the ethics of political violence, with the stage being the Bunker TV living room. Archie is put in the position of being a target of bigotry, yet the vandals mirror his own anti–Semitism and desires for neighborhood purity. Archie also develops a quick respect for Paul, far more impressed by his hard-nosed political philosophy of direct action than Mike's politics of loud, moral indignation. In turn, while Mike and Paul share obvious disgust for Nazism, their divergent tactics make any alliance impossible. As Paul prepares to leave, he tells Mike, "Sometimes, you need this," holding up his clenched fist. Mike stares back and responds, "'This'... only leads to *this*"—and holds up his fist. An uneasy calm returns to the Bunker home, but only for a moment: an explosion is heard off-camera. The shot cuts to the swastika-adorned front door, and Archie flings it open, followed by Mike. They both stare in horror at an off-camera scene they describe for the viewer: Paul's car is engulfed in flames, the result of a bomb planted while he was inside the Bunker home. In what became a common trope on *All in the Family*, the episode ends with a close-up of Archie's confused and stunned expression as he must come to grips with the realization that his politics are fundamentally flawed. Paul's death is the end result of intolerance and violent reaction winning out over understanding and peaceful resolution. It provides the show's moral, ethical, and political lesson that "violence only begets violence," and that Mike Stivic, meathead that he is, was nevertheless correct. The credits follow, but with one important variation from other episodes of *All in the Family*. Instead of the customary studio audience applause heard over the credits, they are shown in silence, signifying that the show has indeed achieved a level of "stunned silence" and become "deadly serious."

Ultimately, *All and the Family* aspired to the artistic pretensions and ideological mission of the Golden Age of television—to become a site of quality entertainment that educated the American public on how to be better citizens. With Lear, the sitcom was converted into a space for dialogue-driven character studies in which said characters learned something about themselves, and, by extension, the audience learned something about itself through the characters. The condemnation of Western theater voiced by Artaud in the 1930s becomes almost prophetic of the ultimate failure of the liberal sitcoms and their social mission, exemplified by *M*A*S*H* and Hawkeye Pierce's alternations between glibly expressing moral outrage over war, effortlessly seducing the unit's nurses, and histrionically wrestling with a periodic psychological crisis:

> To look at theater as we see it here, one would think that there is nothing more to life than knowing if we will make love well, whether we will make war or will be cowardly enough to make peace, how we will learn to live with our little anxieties, and whether we will become aware of our "complexes" (to use technical language), or on the contrary, our "complexes" will do us in. It is rarely that the conflict rises to the social level or that our social and moral system is put on trial. Our theater never goes so far as to wonder whether by chance this social or moral system is unjust.[47]

Indeed, if American television became a site where "the conflict rises to a social level or that our social and moral system is put on trial," it was not through the teleplay portentousness of Lear's political sitcoms, but far more unlikely sources: *The Gong Show* and Andy Kaufman.

Part Four. Anti-Television: American Television Comedy, 1975–1983

Television is truly a two-edged sword. It can uplift, inform, delight, and inspire. By the same token, it can embarrass, offend, even debase.
— Lawrence Welk, "How TV Influences Our Lives" (1976)

Nothing is more delightful than to confuse and upset people.
— Tristan Tzara, "Lecture on Dada" (1922)

CHAPTER 7

Game Shows of Cruelty: Chuck Barris and *The Gong Show*

> If you can make something happen in the program that will stop their forks halfway between their plates and their mouths at least once each half hour, you'll have hit television.[1]
> — Chuck Barris

Disasters Waiting to Happen: *The Dating Game* and *The Newlywed Game*

Writing in 1978, Peter Andrews described Chuck Barris's game shows as "without exception ... unremittingly witless, tasteless, illiterate and stupid."[2] It is these very qualities that also made them possibilities for avant-garde television. Barris began his television career by creating and producing two long-running daytime game shows for ABC that offered cruel satires on American sexual life: *The Dating Game* (1965–73) and *The Newlywed Game* (1966–74). On these shows, Barris utilized, or rather *parodied*, the game show format to nationally televise what could possibly be the most traumatic and humiliating moments in any person's life: being rejected for a date or fighting with a spouse. In the process, the entire premise of the game show, the teleological drama of following a contestant's quest to win cash and prizes, was subverted.[3] Instead, *The Dating Game* and *The Newlywed Game* generated an absurd yet real-life romantic melodrama where winning the grand prize was mere addendum to what transpired beforehand. It was one thing to watch a stranger ponder trivia questions (*Jeopardy*), guess correct prices of products (*The Price Is Right*), or hurry about the stage to complete a task before time ran out (*Beat the Clock*). It was quite another to watch anxious contestants trying to impress potential suitors to win a dream-date weekend, or argue with their spouse in order to win a kitchen appliance or a piece of furniture.

A key aspect of Barris's game shows was the spontaneity, unpredictability, and even potential volatility of the shows. Segments were done in one take and entirely unscripted (save for the inane, innuendo-infused questions). While edited in post-production, mostly to trim the dull spots and insert the necessary bleeps, they aired "as they happened," and as close to live TV as possible. *The Dating Game* furthered the already distressing combination of competing on a game show and negotiating a romantic social contract by incorporating the variable of the dreaded "blind date." The white set was decorated by large, plastic Pop Art daisies of various lurid colors, and a partition separated the contestants so that they could hear but not see each other — in most cases, a young, attractive bachelorette who posed questions to three eligible bachelors. Based on the quality of their responses — and the word "quality" should not be equated with intelligence or taste — a date was selected. After a perfunctory meeting with the two dejected runner-ups, the bachelorette anxiously and finally greeted her new beau, who, as the board game "Mystery Date" promised, could either be "a dreamboat" or "a dud."[4] As Barris explained, "When boy met girl — in front of millions of coast to coast television viewers — she and he would suffer some sort of traumatic reaction, either one of extreme disappointment or ecstasy. *An indifferent response would be catastrophic.*"[5] As a grand prize, the couple won a chaperoned romantic weekend — at worst, in Burbank; at best in "Sunny Acapulco!" For the elated couple, this could be the start of a beautiful friendship; for the contestant less than enamored with their choice, abject misery would certainly ensue.

The Dating Game became the television equivalent of spending a half-hour in a tacky singles' bar watching leisure suit–clad Casanovas trying to win the bachelorette over with a plethora of clichéd compliments, pathetic pick-up lines, insipid banter, and an occasional lewd comment, sinking to ever-lower depths of romantic discourse to pitch woo at a woman who "doubles as the town moron and community punchboard."[6] In the process, *The Dating Game* cruelly mocked the emerging myths of the Sexual Revolution in America (*Playboy*, *Laugh-In*). The debonair, successful American bachelor and the sexy but wholesome girl-next-door were reduced to caricatures of horny losers groveling for a piece of ass, and dumb bimbos whose deepest romantic thoughts were generated by a pre-scripted index card. The idyllic excitement of pursuing modern romance could, and often *would*, become a demeaning nightmare: the very formula of *The Dating Game* meant that for every winner in the politics of romance, two losers were marched out and displayed first. The promises and potential of free love in the Sexual Revolution became exercises in self-debasement as contestants desperately tried to join the new order of American sexuality, or become tragically left behind, and *alone*, in its wake.[7]

Following the success of *The Dating Game*, Barris modified the formula slightly and devised *The Newlywed Game*. Four newly-married couples were asked questions about their spouses and awarded points if the spouse matched the answer, with the couple with the most points winning furniture or an appliance: "We couldn't make the prizes too luxurious; when we did, the program would turn violent."[8] Again, the final outcome was irrelevant compared to what transpired over the course of a given show. Ideally, one spouse provided a stupid answer, the other spouse provided an equally stupid but different reply, and a fight ensued when they failed to correspond. Moreover, *The Newlywed Game* could pursue the most explosive quality of relationships *The Dating Game* was forced to constrain: *sex*. The mild innuendo *The Dating Game* and its swinging singles hinted at was positively embraced by *The Newlywed Game* in its continual fascination with how young American married couples "made whoopee"—or failed to make whoopee to the other's satisfaction. If the Sexual Revolution became a mockery on *The Dating Game*, *The Newlywed Game* transformed American marriage into a bizarre nexus of *True Confessions* magazine, *The Kinsey Report*, and Ionesco's *The Bald Soprano*.

The Dating Game and *The Newlywed Game* premiered when marriage and sexual morality were undergoing a cultural transformation in America, and the power and prestige of matrimony and monogamy was evaporating. Free love, one-night stands, and swinging became national pastimes. Young couples did not "wait for marriage," or no longer pretended they waited for marriage as their parents claimed they did. Elaborate weddings were replaced by "living together," romantic nuptials increasingly ended in messy divorces, and divorce itself was losing its stigma as a betrayal of American family values. The struggles of singles on *The Dating Game* and couples on *The Newlywed Game* mirrored the audiences own insecurities and apprehensions negotiating American sexual politics in the 1960s and 1970s. Audiences were capable of *laughing with* the contestants attempting to resolve the public's own anxieties about sex and marriage in what Benjamin called a "therapeutic eruption of mass psychosis." However, they were also capable of *laughing at* them as they became objects of derision: pitiful casualties of the Sexual Revolution to be ridiculed through the "bourgeois sadism" of mass culture decried by Adorno. With *The Dating Game* and *The Newlywed Game*, Barris exposed the dialectical pleasures of a game show: not only supportively cheering on a contestant and their success, but seizing the opportunity to revel in the contestant's embarrassing failure on national television.[9] A critique of mass culture itself became the focus of Barris's most infamous creation, *The Gong Show* (NBC, 1976–8; syndicated 1976–80).

Two Minutes of Fame: *The Gong Show*

By 1975, Barris's television fortunes ebbed. Game shows he created in the wake of *The Dating Game* and *The Newlywed Game* (*The Family Game, The Parent Game, How's Your Mother-in-Law?*) failed to find an audience; *The Dating Game* and *The Newlywed Game* were both cancelled in the early 1970s. Inspired by the many street performers on the Sunset Strip, Barris envisioned a talent contest-game show, and the possibility that given the right exposure, any number of contestants could become stars. Production costs would be minimal; potentially exciting unknown performers would be drawn to the show just for the chance to showcase their unique talents; and audiences would be attracted to a show that might at any moment introduce the next Frank Sinatra or Great Houdini to the American public. For comic relief, a particularly terrible act could be tossed in as well. ABC was impressed and financed a pilot. As Barris recalled, things quickly went awry: "There weren't tons of exceptionally talented people roaming the streets. What were roaming the streets were tons of exceptionally *un*talented people: kooks, loons, horrible singers ... atrocious comedians, embarrassing acrobats."[10] Barris abandoned the ABC project altogether before he devised a simple solution: "If I couldn't do a talent show that had *more good acts than bad*, I could certainly do a talent show that had *more bad acts than good*."[11] Planned as a syndicated show, Barris also sold the project to NBC as a daytime game show, and *The Gong Show* premiered in 1976, built around Andy Warhol's maxim, "One day everyone will be famous for fifteen minutes"—to which Barris added the qualifier: "I thought fifteen minutes might be thirteen minutes too many."[12]

Contestants were allotted a minimum of forty-five seconds and a maximum of two minutes to be famous. If the act proved to be too excruciating after forty-five seconds, any or all of the three celebrity guest judges could end the performance by hitting a huge gong behind them; afterwards, the judge(s) gave an arbitrary explanation for why the act was gonged. If the act was allowed to finish, the judges rated the performers on a one-to-ten scale, and the performer awarded the most points received the standard grand prize: a trophy of a small gong and a check for $516.32 (later $712.05). These figures were not arbitrary; they were the standard minimum payments for a speaking appearance on television per union scale at the time. However, as with

The Dating Game and *The Newlywed Game*, the competition was purely secondary to the overall spectacle — not only the wealth of "talent" that appeared on the show, but, more importantly, the various reactions to the proceedings.

Contestants performed with élan. Those who survived were proud, or at least relieved; those gonged reacted variously with resignation, heartbreak, or outright indignation. The judges provided reactions ranging from hysterical laughter, jubilant encouragement, bemused smiles, condescending stares, or complete shock. One particularity memorable *Gong Show* moment occurred when African American comedian Scooey Mitchell appeared as a guest judge and watched the elderly "Bernie Jolson" perform a wretched version of "Mammy." Mitchell's incredulous expression, captured in a one-second reaction shot as Jolson belted out the minstrel-show standard on one knee ("Mammy — speak to me, Mammy!"), hilariously commented on racism in America as effectively as years of moralistic messages on Norman Lear sitcoms. In another show, contestant "Christy-Lou" performed a tuneless and overwrought version of Tammy Wynette's "Stand by Your Man." More important than Christy-Lou's performance was a guest judge, none other than Soupy Sales, who acted as a human shield by standing in front of the gong, arms outstretched, when mainstream comedian-actor Ronnie Schell attempted to gong her. Sales then wrestled Schell to the ground, while Christy-Lou, visibly confused and preoccupied by the events at the judges' table, completed her song and earned a respectable 23 points.

However, a last-minute crisis altered *The Gong Show*'s direction drastically. NBC chose John Barbour to host the daytime version: "The show was make-believe, camp, a put-on ... a caricature of all the other amateur shows.... The NBC daytime television network had selected a host who was convinced he was ... *discovering new stars for the show-biz firmament.*"[13] Barris pleaded with NBC to replace Barbour. The network brass finally agreed — on the condition that Barris host *The Gong Show* himself. Barris, who never appeared on television, reluctantly agreed. Barris understood that the demeanor of the host could be the linchpin of his game shows' success or failure, particularly given the large degree of built-in instability between competition and comedy. On *The Dating Game*, Jim Lange passively but effectively stood in the background in his garish tuxedos like a disinterested prom chaperone. *The Newlywed Game*'s Bob Eubanks demonstrated an uncanny skill at running the show by making bad situations worse without losing control: escalating tensions when there was a particular moment of contention over the answer; defusing tensions when they reached a point of becoming intolerable. He could adroitly guide a contestant into giving an especially inappropriate answer when stumped on a question, and could ask and acknowledge the most ludicrous questions and answers with deadpan demeanor: "Ladies, what vowel

Unidentified contestant and Chuck Barris (right) jump for joy on a typical evening on *The Gong Show* (NBC/Photofest).

does you husband most resemble when he sleeps?" (One contestant's response: "An R.") By staring directly into the camera with a perplexed look or a lascivious smile as the situation warranted, and avoiding the condescension such moments could easily afford, Eubanks became a commentator as well as intermediary between the show and TV audience.

In contrast, Barris's on-camera style owed much more to Pinky Lee's crazed enthusiasm than Ed Sullivan's stiff formality, the demeanor former *Laugh-In* announcer Garry Owens parodied as host of *The Gong Show*'s nighttime syndicated version the first season (Barris fired Owens and assumed his hosting duties in 1977).[14] Barris began each show in bedlam and continually escalated the anxiety and absurdity, none of which was dissipated until the meaningless grand prize was awarded and the credits began to roll. As host, Barris proved to be as amateurish, even inept, as many of the performers on the show (whether intentionally or not is less certain). Visibly nervous on-camera, Barris's upper lip was usually bathed in sweat. He constantly fidgeted, and compulsively clapped his hands to visually punctuate his sentences. Always avoiding eye contact with the camera, his trademark became wearing oversized, comical hats along with his tuxedo, so the huge brims obscured his eyes altogether. He routinely missed cues and mangled his hyperbolic introductions, and his congratulatory — or conciliatory — post-performance interviews with *The Gong Show* talent were steeped in sarcasm.

And what talent *The Gong Show* offered. Certainly, a gifted singer, skilled magician, or accomplished dancer occasionally appeared; however, they could easily be beaten for the grand prize by a teenage boy balancing a ladder on his chin or a woman twirling batons while riding a unicycle.[15] A certain number of performers survived the ordeal to gain two minutes of fame through achieving a "so bad, it's good" camp appeal with their earnest if abysmal attempts at crooning or comedy; others provided "novelty-act" charm. At its best, *The Gong Show* functioned as an "anti-talent show" bordering on television's equivalent of the Cabaret Voltaire, or at least its low-brow American cousin. While Barris did not necessarily envision *The Gong Show* as a subversive space for a televised anti-art spectacle, but rather a display of "untalented kooks and loons," many of the performances on *The Gong Show* paralleled Tzara's own conception of Dada:

> In art, Dada reduces everything to an initial simplicity, growing evermore relative. It mingles its caprices with the chaotic wind of creation and the barbaric dances of savage tribes. It wants logic reduced to a personal minimum.... Only the elasticity of our conventions creates a bond between disparate acts. The Beautiful and the True in art do not exist; what interests me is the intensity of a personality transposed directly, clearly into the work; the man and his vitality; the angle from which he regards the elements and in what manner he knows how to gather sensations, emotion, into a lacework of words and sentiments.[16]

In this sense, *The Gong Show* featured acts that reached the levels of Dada or what could now be termed "outsider art": avant-garde amateurs who somehow combined primitivism and poetics.[17] George "Bones" Gilmore, a balding, portly man sweating profusely in a white polyester suit and huge necktie, played castanets, flailed his arms, stomped his feet, and careened in circles to "Sweet Georgia Brown." Elderly woman Dorothy Ida Jones rendered her song completely unidentifiable, singing without any regard for tonality and destroying any meter by continually pausing to refer to her index cards containing the lyrics (guest judge Jamie Farr gave Jones a standing ovation and a score of two). Another elderly woman, Bertha Goodman, "the Scrub Woman," appeared on stage with a mop and an "Archie Bunker" t-shirt; she recited an incomprehensible, rambling song-poem which seemed to be a sort of feminist manifesto before being gonged. Gary Simpson appeared onstage dressed in a top hat, heavy mascara, a tight black leotard, and knee-high, leopard-skin boots. Combining Fred Astaire and Alice Cooper, he sang a harrowing version of "Mairzy Doats" while punctuating his performance with ballroom dancing maneuvers and assaulting a rubber chicken (Jaye P. Morgan gave him a nine for his boots). Valerie Ray Clark performed "Frankie and Johnny" as an atonal torch-song accompanied by a waist-high, inflatable clown (a popular toy designed for children to use as a punching bag). She quite suggestively caressed and stroked the plastic clown as she sang, and shot it with a squirt gun at the point in the lyrics the jilted Frankie murders her lover Johnny. Sadly, she was gonged, and when Barris did the customary post-gonging interview, Clark sighed, "They missed the death." Barris's reply: "Well, Valerie, commercial television is just not ready for social significance, I guess."

At times, *The Gong Show* featured performances that Hugo Ball or Tristan Tzara may have conceived. After a typical Barris introduction — enthusiastically claiming the contestant rushed over from a sold-out concert at Madison Square Garden, and then badly struggling to pronounce the contestant's name — Emilio Roucia came onstage in a multi-colored Alpine mountaineer's outfit holding a tightrope walker's balancing pole and stood motionless for the next two minutes, only slightly wavering from side to side, as if engaged in an onstage battle against gravity. Another contestant, Raphael Marcia, a young, handsome man in a blue tuxedo, calmly walked on stage and stood in front of the mike in front of the house band, a spot usually reserved for straight musical performances. Marcia proceeded to frantically meow, snort, and quack before the inevitable gonging: a Dada "sound-poem" as performed by Mel Blanc. Yet another performance featured a nondescript bald man in a suit. He stared directly into the camera, which captured him in tight close-up for the dubious benefit of the television audience; he proceeded to contort his eyes and mouth into various positions as he performed "a medley of faces." Of course, he was gonged almost immediately, but Barris insisted he be allowed to continue and complete the minimum forty-five seconds promised to each contestant, much to the vocal displeasure of the judges and studio audience.[18]

Admittedly, any aesthetic distinction between "avant-garde" and "outsider art" as opposed to "bad act," "joke act," or "novelty act" appearing on *The Gong Show* proved quite vague (especially, as will be discussed, the more "ringers" Barris began to use in the competition segments). Yet the destruction of these distinctions was also the essence of the show's strange and startling impact on television: a potential, daily dose of nationally televised Dada. However, Barris described *The Gong Show* as nothing short of a mass-media Roman Circus: "The Christians (the act and host) versus the lions (everybody else), right there on the boob tube for everyone to see."[19]

The Process of Elimination

As noted in Chapter Two, Horkheimer and Adorno in their critique of mass culture sadism in *Dialectic of Enlightenment*, described "Donald Duck in the cartoons and the unfortunate in real life [who] get their trashing so the audience can learn to take their own punishment." Barris suggested:

> *The Gong Show* gave the little person his or her moment in the spotlight — and the consequences thereof. *The rest of the world was given the opportunity to be jealous and kick shit in the little person's face* (a microcosm of life?).... When someone or something was 'gonged,' that person or thing *was deemed to be too awful to exist any longer....* To be gonged on *The Gong Show* was the lowest, the lamest: a pronouncement of despicable and indelible personal consequences. *Something like a concentration-camp tattoo. To some maybe even more demeaning.*[20]

The humiliation of being gonged on national television was itself a statement of rejection and condemnation, but occasionally an act received a universal denunciation when all three judges banged the gong simultaneously to end that person's performance. Known as a "gang-gonging" — or a "gang-banging" of the gong on the helpless contestant — it signified a televised gang-rape of the contestant's psyche. The most disturbing portions of *The Gong Show* were the occasional acts prompting a judge (or judges) to immediately stand by the gong, mallet in hand, and impatiently wait until the minimum allotted time passed before rending their thumbs-down with the gong. The contestant, reduced to pathetically staring wide-eyed at the panel as they gamely tried to salvage their two minutes of fame, knew all-too-well their impending fate.

At its most sinister, *The Gong Show* became the televised equivalent of the horrifying selection and extermination processes of the concentration camp — an aspect of the show Barris was quite aware of. In this respect, *The Gong Show* can certainly be compared with and contrasted to America's current reigning talent show, the deadly serious *American Idol* (Fox, 2002–). *American Idol*'s purpose is not just "discovering new stars for the show-biz firmament," but watching the numerous casualties accumulate along the way. For *American Idol*, each season's early emphasis on the "bad act" — the out-of-tempo, out-of-tune singer — is strictly included for the viewer to laugh *at* and manufacture some satisfaction in watching someone embarrass themselves as a failure, and have that failure clearly pointed out to them. Yet the bad act is not the *raison d'être* of *American Idol* as it was on *The Gong Show*, but quite the opposite. *American Idol*'s more abysmal contestants are designed to construct a strict and recognizable distinction between hopeless amateurism and the true talent the show features in the finals — talent defined as having the proper charisma and technical competence to deservingly become a star (or, as the *American Idol* promos for the 2007 season proclaimed, the difference between the "deluded wanna-bes" and the "talented gonna-bes"). By the time the finalists are designated, *American Idol*, if anything, becomes *more* ruthless, where each week the payoff is that someone failed in their attempt to find public adoration and success.[21] The process of selection and elimination is ritually acted out each week as host Ryan Seacreast designates whether each contestant survives the ordeal for another week by pronouncing them "safe" until one is eliminated from the competition and sent to the ovens of obscurity. In one particularly cryptic comment, Seacrest once encouraged call-in voters to "save your favorite singer from *industry extinction*."[22]

Furthermore, *The Gong Show* could never match the standards of bourgeois sadism constructed by the likes of *Survivor* (CBS, 2000–) and *Fear Factor* (NBC, 2001–6), Social-Darwinist game shows where any humor, or even comedy, is thoroughly replaced by cutthroat competition, grim determination, and a tolerance for mortification through Aryan challenges of physical fitness coupled with a willingness to eat shit — or the closet thing to it that network television will allow — in order to win money.[23] In a tense interview with Mike Wallace on *60 Minutes* during the peak of his "popularity" in the late 1970s, Barris almost prophetically expressed his idea for the definitive game show: "Greed," in which contestants would be offered increasing amounts of money until they agreed to perform some reprehensible act, such as kicking the crutches out from under an old man.[24] Obviously, Barris knew such a show could never be produced — not so much for being patently offensive and outrageously cruel, but for having all the potential hallmarks of "hit television" (fork-dropping shock and the opportunity to kick shit on the little person).

"The King of Schlock"

In 2006, *American Idol*'s Simon Cowell's own variety-show/talent-search competition, *America's Got Talent*, premiered on NBC. Essentially derived from *The Gong Show*, with *Star Search* aspirations, *AGT* can be seen as everything Barris did *not* want *The Gong Show* to become. *AGT*'s first season featured a compendium of various competent and undistinguished variety show acts, including singers, musicians, dancers, jugglers, acrobats, and cloying novelty acts (such as the "Rappin' Granny"). Regis Philbin hosted the proceedings as if a teenage boy playing "Sweet Home Alabama" on the harmonica had just been revealed as the next Van Cliburn.[25] The "other" as an object of mass culture contempt was supplied in the form of "Leonid the Magnificent"—a lanky, towering Russian who combined gymnastics and drag numbers set to such pop-hits as "I'm Coming Out" (so much for subtlety). After being voted off, Leonid returned to *AGT* as a "Wild Card" selection, presumably so viewers could have the opportunity to vote him off a second time. Of course, there were an assortment of feeble joke acts, several of which became stagy, of not outright staged, confrontations between indignant, self-indulgent contestants and the three judges (David Hasselhoff, Brandy, Piers Morgan). Borrowing almost directly from *The Gong Show*, each judge could hit a buzzer and "X" the performer; unanimously "X-ing" the performer ended the performance and the contestant's career aspirations immediately. Above all, *AGT*, like *American Idol*, established a strict binary between "kooks and loons" and "authentic talent"—the former to be reviled, the latter to be applauded. As Morgan pointedly informed one sweaty contestant balancing motorcycles and ovens on his chin, "This is a talent show, *not* a freak show."[26] *The Gong Show* obliterated any distinction between talent show and freak show, and their supposed distinct function as television entertainment.

The context of *AGT* becomes critical in discussing *The Gong Show*, as it briefly became a national phenomenon. Tzara realized that the potential dead-end for Dada was that once audiences expected to be shocked and annoyed, Dada was no longer confronting but satisfying audience expectations.[27] While Barris may have simply wearied of what he considered a seemingly infinite and ever-worsening supply of "kooks and loons," a talent show focusing on the untalented—even if they supplied unpredictable and potentially avant-garde performances—could, and would, become expected shock. The danger lay in *The Gong Show* quickly becoming self-parody; and whether it ultimately avoided that end result can, admittedly, be debated. Consequently, whether to institute "quality control" (for lack of a better term), or perhaps minimize the overtly sadistic overtones, Barris retooled *The Gong Show*. Rather than converting the show into a credible talent competition-variety show peppered with bad joke acts (what Barris originally conceived, and precisely what *America's Got Talent* became three decades later), Barris geared *The Gong Show* to a cult–TV audience who got the put-on—critics, mainstream viewers, dissenting voices in Barris's own production staff, and, above all, NBC be damned.[28]

The Gong Show quickly evolved from its origins as an "anti-talent show" into a consciously bad and often offensive "anti-variety show" (especially in its post–NBC syndicated years). The competition became increasingly incidental: several acts appeared without even being scored by the judges and were simply lead off-stage after (or during) their performance. In the event a contestant was judged, they were simply given points and some comments, but the contestant's name and cumulative score was not displayed on-screen after the judging. The awarding of the grand prize, which was *never* the actual goal of a Barris game show, became even more of a tangential coda. One immediate change was the stable of comedic regulars added to *The Gong Show*, limiting the time allotted to amateur performances. Most famous was "The Unknown Comic" (Murray Langston), a comedian in a cheap suit with a paper bag over his head who told exceedingly crude bathroom jokes, with Barris acting as straight-man.[29] Another comedy act was "Scarlet and Rhett," two men dressed as *Gone with the Wind*'s main characters. Rhett inevitably lost his temper, and the resulting, recurring onslaught of expletives were bleeped by a variety of sound effects and cartoon inserts parodying the fight scenes from the *Batman* TV show reading "OOOPS!" or some other interjection. Another change was Barris's use of comedians as "contestants" doing conceptual routines akin to Andy Kaufman or Steve Martin, further limiting the number of actual amateurs per show. The most famous was Paul Reubens, who appeared several times on *The Gong Show*. In one performance, Reubens appeared as "Jay Longtree" in a ridiculously gaudy Native American costume, replete with an oversized feathered headdress. He sang a Vegas-style lounge number, "It's Gonna Rain," accompanied by *The Gong Show* house band and Longtree's sidekick — a man dressed as the Lone Ranger playing bongos named "Whitey Walker." Longtree's "rain dance" was the same tip-toe dance Pee-Wee Herman famously did in the biker bar to "Tequila" in *Pee-Wee's Big Adventure*. Whether the judges got the joke or were prepped by Barris, Reubens received raves, a perfect score (30), and was co-awarded the grand prize for that show. (Barris can even be heard referring to Reubens as "Good Ol' Paul" at the conclusion of the show, indicating Barris and Reubens were well-acquainted.)

Another strategy Barris employed was using stagehands on the show, beginning with the rotund Gene Patton: "Gene Gene, the Dancing Machine." Barris began to periodically put him on the show to dance, usually before commercial breaks. If *The Pinky Lee Show* formula entailed something had to occur onscreen at all times to avoid dead air, Patton's appearances simply and pointlessly consumed TV time before messages from the sponsors. However, when Patton achieved some national notoriety, it also served as a testament to *The Gong Show*'s democratization of stardom: anyone could potentially become a star on *The Gong Show*. *The Gong Show* represented a negation and repudiation of the Culture Industry's continual and deliberate attempts to manufacture marketable stars (the mission of *American Idol*) which "preserves not the unique aura of the person but the 'spell of the personality,' *the phony spell of a commodity*."[30] In this respect, the biggest controversy involving *American Idol* has not been the accusations of racism or rigged voting, but mass audition reject William Hung, who was inadvertently catapulted to national fame (and a recording contract) by *American Idol* with his rousing version of Ricky Martin's "She-Bang," which Hung delivered with an unbridled and unapologetic enthusiasm devoid of vocal tonality or physical coordination.[31]

NBC responded to Patton's newfound popularity by ordering Barris to remove him from the show, citing union agreements forbidding stagehands from appearing on-camera. In retaliation, Barris not only featured Patton with more regularity but added additional stagehands to the show. Ed Holland became the rambling priest "Father Ed." Burly Red Rowe acted as *The Gong Show*'s bouncer and occasionally dragged contestants off-stage in mid-performance. Barris also used stagehands in skits or as incompetent contestants (they were among those not scored by the judges, as conflict of interest statutes prohibit television network employees or family from competing on any game shows on that network). The situation reached its inevitable conclusion, and Barris discontinued the practice when NBC issued an ultimatum that any and all stagehands appearing on-camera at any point in the future would immediately be fired.[32]

This feud became only one of many battles over *The Gong Show* between NBC and Barris. As *The Gong Show* evolved from "anti-talent show" to "anti-variety show," the "moral shock effect" of Dada's repudiation of art and culture was increasingly overshadowed by the more immediate, if ultimately limited, *shock value* of "bad taste," and Barris quickly ran afoul of NBC censors over content. In 1978, the Popsicle Twins garnered their two minutes of infamy. As the house band played "I'm in the Mood for Love," two wholesome looking young women simulated fellatio on their respective Popsicles. Everyone on the set was thoroughly astonished. The judges were too dumbfounded to even gong them, although in a not-too-subtle aside to the casting-couch tactics of Hollywood, Jaye P. Morgan exclaimed, "That's the way I started. I give the girls a ten!" However, the American public was less enthusiastic, having apparently dropped their forks and immediately picked up their phones. Inundated with complaints, NBC pulled the show's feed from the air before it could be seen anywhere besides the East Coast, and Barris was threatened with cancellation if *The Gong Show* continued on its current course.[33] Instead, the show veered further out of control. The final straw came weeks later when Jaye P. Morgan flashed the studio audience, which was captured by a cameraman, and well before the days of "wardrobe malfunctions" (contrary to public memory, the moment was edited from the original telecast). NBC barred her from *The Gong Show* and, amid rapidly deteriorating relations between Barris and NBC, *The Gong Show* was subsequently cancelled. It ultimately proved more infuriating than embarrassing for the network. On the final daytime show for NBC, Barris performed "Take This Job and Shove It." He was gonged.

Barris recounted during the late 1970s, "A little bad taste was in good taste. And, since it's easier to unleash vulgarity than keep it harnessed, my programs flourished in those years."[34] While *persona non gratis* in network television by 1978, Barris continued to produce *The Gong Show* as a syndicated nighttime show. Freed from network constraints, *The Gong Show* continued its assault on the sense and sensibility of the American public for another two years (Carol Connors, best known for appearing in *Deep Throat*, was added as *The Gong Show*'s requisite game show model). In the wake of *The Gong Show*'s success, Barris produced several other syndicated game shows, all of which seemingly attempted to outdo the other in bad taste. *The $1.98 Beauty Show* (1978–80), hosted by campy, manic comedian Rip Taylor, was a vicious satire of beauty contests. Young women with varying degrees of attractiveness competed in the requisite interview, talent, and swimsuit competitions, occasionally against such ringers as buxom Russ Meyer discovery Kitten Natividad and a then-unknown Sandra Bernhard. The winner was awarded $1.98, a plastic tiara, and a basket of spoiled fruit and vegetables. The short-lived *3's a Crowd* (1978), a game show modeled on *The Newlywed Game*, pitted a man's wife and his secretary against each other to match answers to embarrassing questions about his sexual interests, with the obvious hope the secretary would score more points than the spouse ("Would your husband rather see your bust on his secretary, or his secretary's bust on you?"). *The Dating Game* and *The Newlywed Game* returned, running in syndication from 1977 to 1980. Most questions were specifically designed to produce obscene answers, and even the most general of questions could, and often would, accomplish that goal. On one episode of *The Newlywed Game*, the answer to the query, "Before I met my husband, I never knew a man could ... blank?" became a long, rambling monologue by the contestant extolling her husband's incredible staying power and copious ejaculations. For another question asking, "Most of the electricity in our house runs from the blank to the blank?" the wife emphatically responded: "From the plug-in to the vibrator." Undoubtedly, the most infamous *Newlywed Game* moment occurred in 1977, when Eubanks posed the question, "Where's the *weeer-dest* place ... you've ever had the urge to make whoopee?" The husband answered "the car." When asked the same question, his wife thoughtfully considered her reply and then responded, absolutely deadpan: "Is it 'in the ass?'" Needless to say, the response was bleeped.[35]

The ABC incarnation of *The Dating Game* is remembered as a space that gave brief national television exposure to struggling actors; future stars such as Farrah Fawcett, Steve Martin, John Ritter, and Tom Selleck all appeared as contestants.[36] On the revised *Dating Game*, Barris implemented his *Gong Show* strategy and included comedians posing as bachelors. Paul Reubens,

Michael Richards, and Phil Hartman took turns as "bachelors," and none other than Andy Kaufman appeared as a contestant in the fall of 1978 as his "Foreign Man" persona, introduced as "Baji Kimran." Kaufman single-handedly turned the show into magnificent chaos, misunderstanding questions and then answering in fragmented *non sequiturs*— to the complete bewilderment of the contestant and the howls of the audience (one suspects many in the studio audience recognized Kaufman, who by that point had appeared frequently on *Saturday Night Live* and recently became a regular on *Taxi* as "Latka Gravas"). Even the usually stoic Jim Lange could not maintain his composure. However, the bachelorette, who tried to be sympathetic, and the other two bachelors, quite intent on winning the date, could scarcely contain their disdain and obviously were *not* aware of the joke. Fittingly concluding the disaster, Kaufman rose from his seat when another bachelor was selected; informed he lost, he blurted, "No, I won the date — I answered all of the questions correctly!"

As TV critics heaped vitriol on Barris's shows, in 1979 Barris embarked on *The Gong Show Movie* (Barris wrote, directed, and starred in the film). While *The Gong Show Movie* included *The Gong Show* regulars, and the show's infamous moments (the footage of Morgan exposing her breasts, and excerpts of the Popsicle Twins performance), Barris decided against doing an R-rated version of *The Gong Show*.[37] Instead, he used *The Gong Show* as a platform to make a semi-autobiographical "message film" on the foibles of celebrity and show business. A gang-gonging by the critics was a given, but *The Gong Show Movie* was emphatically gang-gonged by the public as well. Thoroughly disillusioned with TV, and his film debut a box-office disaster, Barris retired from show business. Chuck Barris Productions ceased operations in 1980.[38]

Clifton Fadiman, in one of many denunciations of Barris in the 1970s, stated, "There is no way of reconciling the vision offered by Shakespeare and Newton with the vision of life offered on *The Gong Show*."[39] It could also be said that "there is no way of reconciling the vision offered by *The Gong Show* with the vision of life offered by Shakespeare and Newton." Certainly, there was no reconciling the vision offered by Chuck Barris with the vision of life offered by Norman Lear. Lear combined sitcom wit and teleplay weightiness to depict a world that can be changed by compassion and understanding. Barris depicted television and life as equally barbaric, humiliating, ignoble, stupid, ugly, and vulgar. Indeed, if television's purpose was to provide quality entertainment and productively educate the American public, Chuck Barris was certainly the anti–Norman Lear of 1970s. With Barris, the game show was converted into monstrous spectacles of equal parts absurdity and cruelty. Commercial television and the Culture Industry became the contestants — and were gonged mercilessly.

CHAPTER 8

Situationist Comedy: Andy Kaufman

> They say, "Oh, wow, Andy Kaufman, he's a really funny guy." But I'm not trying to be funny. I just want to play with their heads.[1]
> — Andy Kaufman

That's Entertainment: The World of Andy Kaufman

As a child, Andy Kaufman was preparing for a career in television: "I used to stay in my room and imagine that there was a camera in my wall. And I used to really believe that I was putting on a television show.... I had about four hours of programming every day."[2] By age nine, Kaufman was the designated neighborhood entertainer at local birthday parties; in his teens, they became his first paying performances. Childhood friend, and Kaufman's musical director, Gregg Sutton estimated that *80 percent* of the material Kaufman eventually performed in his stand-up routines originated in these birthday party shows.[3] Moreover, aspects of popular culture informing Kaufman's artistic sensibilities during his formative years were not merely influences but became life-long obsessions. They were not appropriated with the conceited irony of postmodernism or the elitist amusement of camp, but reverently embraced — in particular, three 1950s American pop-culture phenomenon: Howdy Doody, Elvis Presley, and professional wrestling.

Kaufman venerated Howdy Doody throughout his life, and children's TV was a key influence on his stand-up routines, as well as his TV specials

Andy's Funhouse (broadcast by ABC as *The Andy Kaufman Special*) and the PBS *Soundstage* "Andy Kaufman Show." At age 10, a concert at his elementary school by African percussionist Babatunde Olatunji inspired Kaufman to learn the congas, which he used in a number of his stand-up routines. Exposure to rock and roll records spurred his life-long fascination with Elvis Presley, and Kaufman's "Foreign Man to Elvis" transformation became a staple of his stand-up act. Appearing onstage in his endearing but exasperating "Foreign Man" persona, Kaufman told antiquated vaudeville jokes and performed abysmal celebrity impersonations (or "eeemitations") in a heavy accent, no change in vocal inflection, and a deliberate lack of conventional comedic timing. As an abstract punchline to end the routine, usually as the audience's patience waned, he closed with an extraordinary Elvis impersonation. If not inventing "Elvis impersonation" proper, Kaufman certainly popularized it, and Kaufman's rendition earned the approval of Presley himself.[4]

However, from a formal standpoint, as well as content, the most important influence on Kaufman's comedy was professional wrestling. Growing up in the heyday of televised pro-wrestling in the 1950s, a thirteen-year-old Kaufman attended his first live wrestling event at Madison Square Garden in 1963, with a headline match of two pro-wrestling legends, "Nature Boy" Buddy Rogers and Bruno Sammartino. Kaufman permanently fell under wrestling's dynamic spell, especially its overpowering effect on the audience, which he vividly recalled as "frenzy."[5] As Roland Bathes suggested in his essay "The World of Wrestling" (ca. 1957), wrestling's inherent power was not athletic competition but a theater of simplified and exaggerated passions combining action, comedy, melodrama, and sport: "Wrestling is a sum of spectacles, of which no single one is a function: each moment imposes the total knowledge of a passion which rises erect and alone, without ever extending to the crowning moment of a result."[6] Beyond his notorious wrestling matches with women and his legendary, highly-public "feud" with pro-wrestler Jerry "the King" Lawler, Kaufman utilized a fundamental principle of pro-wrestling dramatics throughout his comedy career: the ability to create and exacerbate "a sum of spectacles" where "passions" became mutually intertwined as an escalating series of "moments." In other words, comedy became a series of *provocations* by the performer to stir visceral *reactions* by the audience—the similar strategy of Dada and the Situationists. As Kaufman adamantly stated:

> I am *not* a comic. I've never told a joke.... The comedian's promise is that he will go out there and *make you laugh with him*. I've never done that in my life. My only promise is that I will *entertain* you as best I can. *I can manipulate people's reaction* ... I just want real reactions. I want people to laugh from the gut, be sad from the gut—*or be angry from the gut*.[7]

In the early 1970s, while attending Grahm Junior College in Boston, Kaufman hosted his own children's show, *Uncle Andy's Funhouse*, on the campus closed-circuit station, and began refining the material performed throughout the years as a children's entertainer into stand-up comedy routines, which might include a straight educational segment or leading the audience in sing-alongs. Other routines involved playing congas while singing, shirking, and vivid storytelling in an invented, primitive-sounding language. Akin to "outsider music," Kaufman periodically offered enthusiastic if atonal versions of Broadway numbers, such as "Oklahoma." More notorious routines were his exercises in monotony and audience endurance; as Man Ray once stated, a goal of Dada was to "try the audience's patience."[8] As "Foreign Man," Kaufman occasionally spent the entire set floundering onstage (as will be discussed shortly regarding Foreign Man's first appearance on *Saturday Night Live* in 1975). In what became one of his more famous (or infamous) routines, he attempted to read *The Great Gatsby* in an affected British accent from cover to cover while asking the audience to refrain from the inevitable laughter that ensured. Performed in a hilarious, truncated version on *SNL* in March 1978, the "Great Gatsby" routine frequently became a contentious endurance contest between Kaufman and the audience when performed onstage for an entire set; on occasion, Kaufman eventually emptied the venue.[9]

Contemporary comedians of the era recognized the avant-garde qualities of his work; Richard Lewis described Kaufman as "Ionesco doing stand-up," and Richard Belzer suggested, "He was a performance artist before the term existed."[10] While Kaufman's brand of Dada may have owed as much to "Nature Boy" Buddy Rogers and Soupy Sales as to Hugo Ball and Tristan Tzara, it is also comparable to Walter Benjamin's assessment of Dada. Kaufman negated the comedian's role as an object of comedic *contemplation* (telling jokes and providing laughs) by making the comedian a target of humorous *distraction* (creating situations and provoking reactions).[11] Kaufman abhorred and determinedly avoided this standardized comedian-audience relationship — to increasingly detrimental effects on his career — as he consciously tried the audience's patience *offstage* as well as *onstage* (performance spaces that became indistinguishable over the course of his career).

"I Don't Know if You're Laughing with Me or at Me": *Saturday Night Live*, 1975

In 1975, Kaufman's work drew the interest of NBC executive Dick Ebersol, who, intentionally or not, eventually became to Kaufman what CBS president Robert D. Wood was to the Smothers Brothers. Ebersol recommended

Kaufman to Lorne Michaels, creator and producer of a late-night comedy show in development, *Saturday Night Live*. While Kaufman was not added to the roster of "The Not Quite Ready for Prime Time Players" (perhaps *SNL* realized even then that Kaufman operated best as a "loose cannon"), Kaufman performed solo on three of the first four *SNL* broadcasts in 1975, beginning with his legendary "Mighty Mouse" routine on the premiere telecast of *SNL* (October 11, 1975). As Ebersol recalled, "When the show was over, the commercial parodies and Andy were the only thing people talked about."[12]

Introduced by NBC house announcer Don Pardo, Kaufman stood onstage motionless for several seconds, looking preoccupied and overwhelmed, prompting concern he had missed his cue to begin — or, even worse, was experiencing severe stage fright on live TV. Finally, Kaufman reached over to a portable record player and put the stylus on the record; a very scratchy recording of the theme from the *Mighty Mouse* television show began. As the song played, Kaufman remained still, his non-performance so far in direct violation of the cardinal rule of broadcasting, creating dead air where nothing occurs, and motivating the audience to find more exciting fare to watch on another channel.[13] Suddenly, Kaufman struck a confident posture. Left arm raised, and with the bravado of an opera singer, he lip-synched the line where Mighty Mouse proclaims: "Here I come to save the day!" Much to the audience's relief, a joke (of sorts) had been delivered, and generated a burst of laughter. Finishing the line, Kaufman immediately returned to his initial state of detachment. He simply repeated the process for the second verse, and during the song's instrumental break, Kaufman's only action was taking a sip of water to sooth parched vocal cords. After the third verse, with Kaufman once more joining in with Mighty Mouse's exclamation, he returned to his disengaged state. The song finished, and Kaufman bowed enthusiastically a few times to conclude the routine.

Kaufman returned to *SNL* two weeks later (October 25, 1975) to perform an even stranger treatment of a recording of "Pop Goes the Weasel." Beginning almost identically to "Mighty Mouse," Kaufman walked onstage to a phonograph, put the needle on the record, and simply lip-synched to a scratchy recording of the song. Midway through, a young girl's voice appeared as the singer's daughter, alternating between discussing and singing the song with her father. With precise timing, Kaufman lip-synched the father's dialogue, with the daughter's on-stage role assumed by the record player, which Kaufman treated as though he were interacting with an on-stage partner — possibly the first time the verbal sparring of an onstage comedy team was between a human being and a mechanical object.[14] Indeed, these stand-up routines can be read as modernist studies on the "man-machine" relationship as much as *Ballet mécanique* or *Modern Times*.

Two weeks later (November 8, 1975), in a vastly different appearance, Kaufman introduced Foreign Man to a national audience on *SNL*. Kaufman used the performance to create the first of many uncomfortable national television performances that questioned the social function of comedy. Foreign Man bounced onstage, paused for several seconds while he nervously surveyed the room, and then told a long, incomprehensible joke about three children and a cannon. After concluding with no discernable punchline, Foreign Man offered an equally baffling explanation of *why* the joke was funny. Next was an "eeemitation" of Archie Bunker — without any change in his voice but reciting Bunker's catchphrases: "You're stuup-peed ... Get out of my chair, meathead ... Is de dingbat cooking de food?" However, things took an ominous turn when a long, uncomfortable pause followed and it became painfully apparent that Foreign Man forgot his material. Clearly violating the fundamental rule of television by creating dead air, and *knowing it*, Foreign Man blurted in desperation, "Do you want to see me dance?" As the audience roared its approval, he flapped his arms and legs in uncoordinated tap dancing moves for a few seconds. He added, "I can sing too," and yelped some gibberish, then yelled "Opera!" and yodeled in a falsetto.

After quickly exhausting that strategy of amusing the audience and filling dead air by any means necessary, Foreign Man again frantically darted his eyes and stumbled over unfinished sentences, creating *another* disconcerting moment of dead air. As Foreign Man struggled onstage, the audience's laughter was noticeably different than the typical chorus of guffaws accompanying the steady streams of the comedian's quips; sporadic loud chortles and nervous titters punctuated the otherwise awkward silence. Visibly demoralized, Foreign Man looked offstage and pleaded, "I tink we should shut off de tape"— a comment that only clarified that Foreign Man was bombing on a live, nationally-televised broadcast, and his failure was being witnesses by millions as it happened. Seemingly on the verge of tears, Foreign Man gazed at the stage and pondered the fundamental paradox of comedy: "I tink we should turn off de TV ... You're laughing, *but I don't know if you're laughing with me or at me*" (emphasis added). Finally, for the "punchline," Foreign Man broke into exaggerating sobbing and pounded the conga onstage next to him in frustration; he burst into a brief song combining rhythmic conga playing and singing-sobbing before dancing off stage as the house band joined in, returning for a bow to clarify it had indeed been a put-on.

Foreign Man was not an ethnic stereotype that could be specifically categorized (German, Irish, Mexican).[15] As "Latka Gravas" on *Taxi*, he might be of Slavic origin; as "Baji Kimran" on *The Dating Game*, he could be Middle Eastern or East Indian; on one *Tonight Show* appearance, Foreign Man told Johnny Carson he was from "Caspiar," an island in the Mediterranean Sea.

Any specific ethnicity of Foreign Man was the product of the name only. Rather, Foreign Man was an all-purpose stereotype of "the foreigner," in which the only thing that was certain was what he was *not*: an American (hence, the significance of imitating America's favorite bigot, Archie Bunker, in the routines). Kaufman's Foreign Man served as *an other*, the personification of difference in society Kaufman utilized and even mobilized to test the audiences' patience and compassion as he often miserably struggled onstage — making the *audience reaction* the focus of the performance. Like *The Gong Show*, the performance became a determination if the oddball-other would be warmly embraced, politely spared, or callously crucified in their moment in the spotlight.

While watching Foreign Man bomb on his *SNL* premiere was obviously a routine, it exemplified what long-time friend and frequent co-conspirator Bob Zmuda called Kaufman's fascination with "magnificent failures."[16] Foreign Man's ineptitude provided an uncomfortable mixture of hilarity, aggravation, and pathos which Kaufman usually, but not always, diffused with his dead-on Elvis impersonation or other comedic solution (as in the aforementioned *SNL* performance). As his career progressed, Kaufman adopted new personas of magnificent failure rooted in arrogance as much as incompetence, and generated hostility rather than sympathy: new *others* who provoked gut reactions that increasingly became stunned and furious responses rather than confused laughter.

"Maybe I Went Too Far": Pushing the Boundaries of Television

From 1975 to 1978, Kaufman, frequently but not always as Foreign Man, performed several times on *Saturday Night Live,* appeared on miscellaneous talk shows and game shows, and was a regular on Dick Van Dyke's short-lived comedy-variety show, *Van Dyke and Co.* (NBC, 1976). In 1978, Kaufman — or, more correctly, his Foreign Man persona — attained stardom as garage mechanic "Latka Gravas" on the sitcom *Taxi* (ABC, 1978–82; NBC 1982–3). Highly reluctant to commit to a sitcom, a format he detested, Kaufman and the *Taxi* producers agreed to a part-time contract: rehearsal and filming two days per week and appearing on half of the shows. Foreign Man was quickly absorbed, or co-opted, into mass culture via *Taxi*; his signature line, "Dank you, vedy much," became a pop-culture catchphrase (itself referenced from Elvis's trademark "Thank you very much"). In fact, by this time Kaufman began to replace Foreign Man with a new primary persona, although "alter-ego" would be more accurate, and with emphasis on the *ego*: "Tony

"I am *not* Andy Kaufman!" Tony Clifton (left, played by Michael Kaufman) and Andy Kaufman perform at Carnegie Hall (Photofest).

Clifton." If Foreign Man was a critique of stardom as the magnificent failure desperately seeking the approval of the audience, Tony Clifton was an even greater affront as the magnificent failure who is a star because he says so — and demands to be treated as such.

Originally a persona Kaufman developed in his stand-up routines (then simply Kaufman in a cheap suit jacket, fake moustache, and sunglasses), Tony Clifton was an abhorrent, arrogant nightclub entertainer specializing in dreadful singing, dancing, and stand-up comedy performances — alternating with copious insults hurled at the audience. With Clifton's addition as a periodic guest star on *Taxi*— at Kaufman's insistence (which will be discussed shortly) — Clifton was developed into a bona fide personality. The amount of make-up and wardrobe required to complete the transformation to the Tony Clifton persona allowed not only Kaufman, but any number of people, to portray him in public. Kaufman and Clifton (played by Michael Kaufman) even appeared together when they performed a rousing version of "Carolina in the Morning" during the encore of Kaufman's legendary Carnegie Hall concert (April 26, 1979; an abridged version premiered on Showtime in June, 1980).

Clifton (played by Andy Kaufman) also opened the Carnegie Hall concert with a rendition of the National Anthem, stand-up, and a poetry reading before finally being told (several times) to leave the stage. The Kaufman-Clifton song and dance number became a metaphor for the "song and dance" Kaufman subsequently began with the Clifton persona. As a colossal in-joke, as much as satire, Bob Zmuda occasionally appeared as Clifton in concert appearances, as well as on talk shows like *Late Night with David Letterman* and *The Merv Griffin Show*, to vigorously claim he was *not* Andy Kaufman (which was technically true) and vehemently denounce Kaufman in the process. On a *Merv Griffin Show* appearance in the summer of 1981, Clifton (Zmuda) even announced his intention to sue Kaufman "for unauthorized use of his image."

Along with Kaufman's resolve to limit his participation as a regular on *Taxi*, one condition for joining the show required *Taxi*'s producers hiring Tony Clifton for four guest appearances per season. Clifton was cast as "Nicky DiPalma," brother of Danny DeVito's sleazy "Louie DiPalma" character. In September of 1978, Andy Kaufman transformed into Tony Clifton to make his first and last appearance on *Taxi* — or, more correctly, the *Taxi* set.[17] Arriving on the set late, intoxicated, and with two prostitutes in tow, Clifton mangled dialogue and ad-libbed jokes that were funny to no one but Clifton.[18] Tension mounted while Clifton insulted the cast and crew, and Clifton then committed the ultimate transgression: he began directing a fellow actor, *Taxi*'s star Judd Hirsch, who stormed off the set. Shortly after the disastrous rehearsal, and not quite sharing Kaufman's enthusiasm, *Taxi* producer Ed Weinberger informed Kaufman the Clifton experiment was over. Kaufman requested Weinberger set up the next rehearsal so Clifton would be fired on the set and escorted off the studio grounds by security: "I want Tony Clifton to be bodily removed from every major motion-picture studio in Hollywood."[19] The next day Clifton arrived, and immediately began a vulgar tirade on the set when informed he was fired. Still fuming over the previous day's rehearsal, Hirsch and Clifton had to be separated by studio security (the first of many such moments for Hirsch and Kaufman on the *Taxi* set), and a profanity-spewing Clifton was thrown off the set. For good measure, a reporter for *The Los Angeles Times* doing a story on Kaufman had been deliberately invited to the rehearsal, ensuring the on-set events would make the news.

Kaufman's manager, George Shapiro, recounted that Kaufman was exhilarated by the *Taxi* events as "a *theater of life*."[20] Bob Zmuda also noted, "Andy's plan turned out to be more *anarchistic than artistic*."[21] Clifton's "performance" on the *Taxi* set became a defining moment in Kaufman's career — a comedy routine that intensely dismantled the barrier between reality and performance, and sabotaged television at its core (studio production as much as audience reception). In effect, it heralded Kaufman's evolution from Dada to situationist. By way of contextualization, the Situationist International was formed in 1957 as an avant-garde art movement focusing on the use of *détournement*:

> The integration of present or past artistic production into a superior construction of a milieu. In this sense there can be *no situationist painting or music, but only situationist use of these means*.... [D]étournement within the old cultural spheres is ... a method which testifies to the wearing out and loss of importance of those spheres."[22]

In this sense, *détournement* is far beyond self-absorbed postmodern irony and referencing — the "neutral mimicry" of pastiche (e.g., Madonna or the Blue Man Group). Indeed, as SI leader Guy Debord emphatically stated, "*Détournement* is *the antithesis* of quotation."[23] *Détournement* is "serious parody," an appropriation and negation of existing artistic forms in which the originals are radically distorted to create new, potentially subversive forms. In the essay "The User's Guide to Détournement" (1956, co-authored with Gil J. Wolman), Debord suggested that simple if limited forms of *détournement* could include republishing canonical books under different titles for popular consumption (George Sand's *Consuelo* as "Life in the Suburbs") or screening *Birth of a Nation* with a new soundtrack denouncing its racist imagery.[24] Another example might be staging performances for unsuspecting audiences of Edward Albee's *The Zoo Story*, set in Central Park, *in* Central Park — or Amiri Baraka's *The Dutchman*, set on a NYC subway train, *in* a NYC subway train. At its most advanced, it attained a level of *ultradétournement*: "'The tendencies of *détournement* to operate in everyday social life' (e.g., password, disguises, belonging to the field of play)."[25] *Ultradétournement*, in this sense, is akin to the workings of secret societies, espionage, or revolutionary cells (secret codes, disguise, propaganda and disinformation campaigns); to this extent, the use of the Tony Clifton persona as a seditious "disguise" can be seen as an example of comedy as *ultradétournement*. Moreover, in the growing cultural chaos of the 1960s, the SI became less interested in how art could be applied to direct political action, but how direct action could itself be seen as a form of art. In *The Revolution of Everyday Life* (1967), SI leader Raoul Vaneigem proclaimed, "The only modern phenomenon comparable to Dada are the most savage outbreaks of juvenile delinquency."[26] Thus, Mark Balma's painting *Pietà* (2005, the Vatican Museum) can be seen as a postmodern quotation of Michelangelo's *Pietà*, substituting JKF and Jackie Kennedy in the presidential limo for Jesus and Mary in the tomb. A situationist *détournement* might have been Lazlo Toth's attack on Michelangelo's *Pietà* at St. Peter's Cathedral with a hammer in 1972.[27]

For Debord and Wolman, the failure of the Dada's *détournement*—

Duchamp's drawing a moustache on a postcard replication of the Mona Lisa — was simply scandalizing art and bourgeois culture versus everyday social life; the *détournement* of Brecht — whose methods were closer to the "revolutionary orientation" of situationist tactics — failed because of Brecht's fundamental faith in the cultural value of instructive theater (Golden Age teleplays were "instructive theater" as well) and not addressing representation and false consciousness beyond the theatrical stage.[28] Neither the *détournement* of Dada nor Brecht was sufficient to confront the modern situation Debord discussed in *The Society of the Spectacle* (1967):

> The spectacle is the acme of ideology ... it exposes and manifests the essence of all ideological forms: the impoverishment, enslavement, and negation of real life.... What ideology already was, society has become. A blocked practice and its corollary, an antidialectical false consciousness, are imposed at every moment on an everyday life in the thrall of the spectacle — an everyday life that should be understood as the systematic breakdown of the faculty of encounter, and the replacement of that faculty by a *social hallucination*: a false consciousness of encounter."[29]

The restoration of the "facility of the encounter" was through *situations*: "A moment of life, deliberately and concretely constructed by the collective organization of a unitary ambience and a game of events [*jeu d'événements*]."[30] The deliberately constructed situation became a possible means to demolish the social hallucination of everyday life in the spectacular society. If a goal of the avant-garde is to "defamiliarize social reality," the situation was potentially the most confrontational and dangerous method — the stage could be any space, it could potentially be extended indefinitely, and it could take any form: "Moments constructed into situations might be thought of as moments of rupture, accelerations, *revolutions in individual everyday life*."[31]

In this sense (the title of this chapter notwithstanding), it is more correct to say Kaufman's was not situationist comedy, but a situationist *use* of comedy — a *détournement* of a disparate variety of sources into a form of "anti-comedy" composed of stand-up, kiddie-TV, various genres of music, and the theory and practice of pro-wrestling. As Debord and Wolman noted, "Any elements, no matter where they are taken from, can serve in making new combinations.... [It] supersedes the original elements and produces a synthetic organization of greater efficacy."[32] For Kaufman, who was acutely aware of the key role television played in perpetuating the social hallucination, comedy increasingly became a series of situations: planned hoaxes devised by Kaufman and a select number of participants not at all limited to the actual set, stage, or TV screen.[33] Moreover, Kaufman often improvised or altered these "situations" as they transpired, so even those involved were not sure what direction it was taking and what could, or would, happen. Such situations were designed to disturb the production of the show and audience expectations by violently disrupting the pre-established, stable relationships between performers and audiences through obliterating the distinction between representation and reality. Or, as Kaufman simply put it, "What's real? What's *not*? That's what I want to do with my act, *test how other people deal with reality*."[34]

By the fall of 1979, Kaufman drastically and dangerously upped the ante, baffling and enraging the public as he seemingly embarked on a deliberate course of career suicide. In addition to Kaufman's infamous appearance as Tony Clifton on *Dinah!* (to be discussed shortly), Zmuda recounted that many "routines" took place in the public sphere and with an unsuspecting "audience": planting outrageous rumors about Kaufman that appeared in *The National Enquirer*, or staging a press conference at Harrah's before a concert engagement in which Zmuda, playing a reporter, harshly criticized Kaufman's comedy act.[35] In by far the most controversial career move, Kaufman inaugurated himself "Intergender Wrestling Champion of the World." While Kaufman incorporated challenging women to wrestling matches early in his stand-up act, offering a monetary prize if a woman could pin him, the "intergender wrestling" generated a storm of outrage — not only to the extent Kaufman convinced the public the matches were real, but for the outrageously sexist statements. The wrestling routines allowed Kaufman to both assume the persona of the villainous, audience-baiting pro-wrestling "heel" and also construct a political *other* to confuse and upset people — the misogynistic, anti-feminist macho man (an image of American masculinity decidedly out of fashion in the decade of Alan Alda and Phil Donahue).[36] In comparison, in his final two Letterman *Late Night* appearances (September and November of 1983), Kaufman was accompanied by three African American males who he proudly announced he adopted. In a theater of life parody of *Diff'rent Strokes* (NBC, 1978–88), Kaufman emerged as the dedicated "Big Brother," a new burgeoning persona (or *other*) appropriately incongruent to the early 1980s: the bleeding-heart, guilty white liberal whose politics had become nationally accepted as "well-intentioned failures," as once described by Ronald Reagan. Indeed, the new kinder, gentler Kaufman as the "magnificent failure" of the Great Society could have become a new object of derision for he American public, as the word "liberal" became infused with pejorative contempt.

Despite becoming synonymous with Kaufman's career, very few of his wrestling matches actually appeared on network television. Rather, as noted, much of the controversy came about due to the sexist statements made during the routines, as well as in the press and on TV, as to *why* he wrestled women. For someone who expressly sought to blur performance and reality, Kaufman's satire seems almost heavy-handed in retrospect, given the overdetermined lengths he went to insist the reason he wrestled women was because he was incapable of defeating most men (in effect, stating he only wrestled women because they were easier to bully, making it easier to prove his masculinity).[37] Nevertheless, the response to Kaufman's intergender wrestling was immediately and overwhelmingly negative, and the indignation both amused and bemused Kaufman. As Zmuda noted, "[Kaufman] assumed they would know, as in mainstream pro wrestling, that it was all for show and that the insults, violence, and animosity were merely theater. That seemingly hip crowds became so incensed over his ring antics was a shock to him."[38] Ironically, Lorne Michaels believed that Kaufman's "crossover" potential was his ability to bridge comedy nightclubs and avant-garde artistic circles, and saw an affinity between Kaufman's comedy with the avant-garde of Warhol and Brecht.[39] However, to "get" Kaufman, one also needed to have an understanding of the avant-garde of pro-wrestling as well as Pop Art, and Kaufman alienated even those who supposedly had the erudition to fully grasp the ironies, problematics and dynamics of Kaufman's work — and here "work" can be used in the pro-wrestling vernacular "to work the audience," as much as a body of comedic "work." With Kaufman, to paraphrase Malcolm X, one became "Either part of the situation or part of the problem."

In fact, Michaels became part of the problem in the situation constructed by Kaufman's second Intergender title defense on *SNL* on December 22, 1979.[40] After a match on Tom Snyder's *Tomorrow* in August, and *SNL* in October, Kaufman appeared on *SNL* in November, teeming with wrestling heel invective. He belligerently announced that no one in America could stop him from wrestling on TV until a woman beat him, and a woman could never defeat him because they "lacked the brains." He personally solicited women to apply to *SNL* to be his next on-air opponent, asking them to include, in order of importance: photos, their measurements, and a short reason why they wanted to wrestle. In addition to a $1,000 prize, Kaufman promised to have his head shaved live on the air if he lost.[41] Coincidentally (or perhaps not), Bea Arthur, who had become America's poplar symbol of liberal-feminism as Maude Findlay on *Maude*, hosted *SNL* that night. After Kaufman's tirade, she announced her hope that the eventual challenger "beats him badly!" Kaufman responded audibly off-camera by challenging *her* to a match.[42]

Eventually, *SNL* selected Dianna Peckham, an Amazonian woman accompanied by her father, a former Olympic wrestling coach. In contrast, Kaufman secured none other than boyhood idol "Nature Boy" Buddy Rogers to act as *his* corner man. Bob Zmuda, as with all of Kaufman's matches, acted as ring announcer and referee, and he recounted how the performance took an unexpected and decidedly acrimonious turn before the show. Michaels ordered a long, pre-match routine between Kaufman and Rodgers cut from the telecast to ensure air-time for a "Mr. Bill Christmas Special" film specifically made for that evening's telecast ("Mr. Bill" shorts were arguably *SNL*'s most popular segments at the time). Kaufman ignored the edict, and Michaels became incensed when they did the routine as rehearsed on live TV, forcing him to cut Mr. Bill from the telecast.[43] Kaufman and Zmuda always dealt with the variable of the potential *audience* reaction, but the routines-as-situations were well-orchestrated and well-rehearsed between the principals. In this case, Kaufman and Zmuda did not have *internal* control, let alone the many *external* factors. Kaufman was about to wrestle a woman who did not view the match as a put-on, and could quite possibly "beat him badly" on national television. He goaded the *SNL* studio audience into a frenzy over a match they eagerly hoped would conclude with Kaufman's sheared locks. Kaufman and Michaels were now furious at each other. Zmuda recalled that after Kaufman pinned Peckham, and then noticing a beaming Rogers, "I realized that the match had *not* been between Andy and the girl, but Buddy and dad: *real* wrestling versus *fake* wrestling."[44] Indeed, the match was also Kaufman versus *SNL* and, above all, *theater versus reality*. Comedy reached a level of danger perhaps only Artaud dreamed possible.

However, Kaufman's victory seriously damaged his most favored performer status with *SNL*; he was not invited back to the show for over two years, and only after Dick Ebersol assumed the reigns of *SNL*. While on "hiatus" from *SNL*, in January 1981 Kaufman starred on *The Midnight Special* (NBC, 1972–81) for a showcase concert performance aired in January 1981. While *The Midnight Special* usually featured several rock bands and occasional comedians over the course of a given show (Kaufman had performed several times on the show previously), the entire broadcast was devoted to Kaufman (Dick Ebersol was producing *The Midnight Special* at the time). Like his Carnegie Hall concert, it could be described as a Dada *détournement* of the traditional comedy-variety show. After opening with his trademark Foreign Man–Elvis routine, Kaufman followed with a lengthy and intentionally inept routine combining ventriloquism and puppet show. Using thrift store dolls of Howdy Doody and Little Red Riding Hood, the dialogue became indecipherable mewing and screeching as Kaufman tried to speak without moving his lips. He also performed a stirring version of the syrupy Disney ode to multiculturalism, "It's a Small World." Adorned in a Hawaiian shirt (garb of the stereotypical American tourist), Kaufman played congas, danced, and warbled the lyrics backed by the intimidating B Street Conga Band—an African American, New York City–based percussion quartet who looked more like musicians for an evening of Black Power poetry readings. In addition to providing a relentless beat, they joined in on backing vocals, singing the corny lyrics with stone-faced expressions.[45] Kaufman's special musical guests included 1950s rock star Freddie Cannon, who Kaufman accompanied on congas, and country legend Slim Whitman, who Kaufman simply watched perform with unabashed awe from the side of the stage. Of course, a sizable amount of time was devoted to "special guest star" Tony Clifton, who effortlessly hogged the stage while annoying and insulting the audience; at one point there is a wipe to bulk edit Clifton's performance and a disclaimer reading, "Now we're back on time!" Kaufman played Clifton, despite Kaufman being seen laughing in the crowd in one audience reaction shot. Bob Zmuda appeared as "Bob Gorsky," a volunteer from the audience who became the target of Clifton's weak Polack jokes and was ordered off the stage after Clifton poured water on his head. Interspersed with the concert were three short documentary segments. One was devoted to Kaufman's wrestling exploits; little actual match footage was shown, and instead focused on Kaufman's now-infamous pre-match diatribes. The second was on working on *Taxi*, with virtually no mention of *Taxi*; Kaufman mostly discussed his own early stand-up career and current solo projects at length as a satirical commentary on his own strained relationship with the show. The third was on Kaufman's actual part-time job — moonlighting as a busboy at Jimmy's Famous Deli while starring on *Taxi*.[46]

The Midnight Special was shortly followed by one of Kaufman's most notorious television appearances: February 20, 1981, as guest host of ABC's *Fridays*, "The West Coast answer to *Saturday Night Live*." Debuting in 1980, *Fridays* was widely panned for being a vastly inferior *SNL*. Certainly, the initial telecasts of *Fridays* left much to be desired, and the show was all but officially cancelled by ABC prior to Kaufman's appearance. While ingrained in public memory as the night an out-of-control Kaufman single-handedly turned *Fridays* into nationally televised chaos, producer John Moffitt and head writer Jack Burns approached Kaufman to guest host and "do the show with no restrictions. The only edict given him: Kick start this dog and give it some attention."[47] For *Fridays*, a final sketch where Kaufman broke character on live television was planned in advance. However, Kaufman would not start laughing at his own jokes and corpse the other performers (the often-overused tactic of Red Skeleton or Tim Conway on *The Carol Burnet Show*). Instead, he would criticize the weak material and refuse to complete the sketch, ending the show in disarray. At Kaufman's insistence, the cast and crew were *not* informed of the plan for the final skit or that Kaufman was given free reign by Moffitt and Burns for the evening's entire live telecast. Moffitt, fearing the situation could become *too* volatile, later admitted the key participants in the final sketch — Michael Richards, Melanie Chartoff, and Maryedith Burell — were warned only that Kaufman would break character in the final sketch and respond accordingly as events unfolded (with strict orders that Kaufman *not* know they had been alerted).[48]

A week of uneventful rehearsals and cast camaraderie were summarily sabotaged when Kaufman veered wildly from the rehearsed opening monologue and ran far over his allotted time, incessantly laughing at his own dismal routine while accomplices Moffitt and Burns impolitely yelled at Kaufman to get off the stage from off-camera. The extended and quite interminable monologue left the show's cast and crew desperately scrambling to drastically reconfigure a well-organized and rehearsed show while it was airing live, immediately creating turmoil behind the scenes. Matching the deficiency of his monologue, throughout the show Kaufman gave disinterested and unprofessional performances. To further exacerbate the building tensions, Kaufman began bullying the already-aggravated cast and crew backstage. Cast member Jim Roarke and Kaufman had a brief scuffle backstage prior to the infamous "restaurant sketch," which ended the live telecast on a level of unanticipated commotion and controversy — an outcome that no doubt delighted Kaufman.

Kaufman and *Fridays* regulars Burrell, Chartoff, and Richards played two couples at a restaurant where each person goes to the bathroom to smoke a joint and comes back to the table stoned. Kaufman's timing was (intentionally) terrible throughout the tedious sketch, which may have been written to be *intentionally* unfunny and tiresome as well. The reliance on a "let's get high" premise was all-too-typical of *Fridays*' constant pattern of cannabis and cocaine jokes, an aspect of the show particularly despised by critics and thus a perfect setting for Kaufman to denounce the material.[49] When he returned from the bathroom, Kaufman broke character and said, "I can't do this," claiming his holistic lifestyle could not condone gratuitous drug humor. Zmuda recounted, "Seconds of dead air time seemed like hours ... he reiterated he wouldn't continue."[50] Taking the lead, Richards angrily stormed offstage, grabbed a set of cue cards, threw them in a pile on the table, and spitefully told Kaufman to "read these." The audience burst into applause, perhaps releasing their own pent-up frustrations generated by Kaufman throughout the show. Richards's apparent anger with Kaufman escalated both the tensions and the comedy. Indignant, Kaufman doused Richards with a glass of water, and Chartoff retaliated by throwing a plate of butter on Kaufman's head. As Chartoff and Kaufman began to viciously argue, Richards turned to the studio audience and sarcastically snarled, "Hey, this is *funny*!" Jack Burns stormed onto the set, repeatedly screaming the classic TV cliché in times of crisis: "Cut to commercial!" Burns confronted Kaufman, and the two exchanged words. When Burns shoved Kaufman, they began to throw punches (none coming close to actually connecting). With the show's guest star and head writer resorting to fisticuffs live on national television, the entire crew of *Fridays* stormed the stage, all of whom thought the confrontation was real, and Kaufman was brusquely escorted off the set by stagehands as the show went to commercial. The cast was visibly shaken, and noticeably relieved, when *Fridays* returned for the customary sign-off.

The show made national headlines, and capitalizing on the notoriety, Kaufman appeared in a videotaped "apology" on the following week's telecast of *Fridays*— a routine Kaufman and Zmuda referred to as "the Viet Cong Confession."[51] Modeled on disturbing films of political hostages or POWs being forced to read confessions on-camera, a haggard and unshaven Kaufman began his prepared statement in a dazed monotone and appeared to be cold-reading from cue cards. After bursting into tears and refusing to read his pre-scripted apology, Kaufman claimed the *Fridays* incident had lead to his possible dismissal from *Taxi*, being blacklisted by other shows, and a separation from his wife. Sobbing, Kaufman closed by pleading: "We were just trying to have fun. Maybe I went too far."

Of course, the "Viet Cong Confession" was itself another hilarious hoax on the viewing audience. Kaufman was never married, nor was his status on *Taxi* ever threatened (one suspects ABC was thrilled *Fridays* received any critical attention beyond the uniform disparagement). As Moffitt stated, "I'm sure that single event got us picked up for the next year."[52] Perhaps as a gesture of thanks to Kaufman, as well as a move that certainly ensured ratings, Kaufman made a triumphant return to guest host *Fridays* on September 18, 1981— the premiere episode of the second season. Along with performing his best-loved routines for an appreciative audience (Foreign Man, Elvis, "Mighty Mouse"), Kaufman, a model of contrition, announced his conversion to Christianity and sang gospel numbers with his new "fiancée," Kathie Sullivan, a singer from *The Lawrence Welk Show*.[53] The *Fridays* appearances became another defining moment in the brief remainder of Kaufman's television career, which devolved into an ongoing series of false apologies alternating with controversial incidents which confused, infuriated, and eventually alienated both the television industry and his audience.

"I Was Just Teasing in Fun": Taking on the Talk Show

The talk show format became one of Kaufman's primary vehicles to sabotage television entertainment. Kaufman had early but brief success on *The Tonight Show*, and Johnny Carson was particularly intrigued because Kaufman did not break character after doing the act but continued the performance on the couch, during the commercial breaks, and backstage well after the taping ended. However, in an August 1977 appearance, perhaps anticipating that Carson was expecting another evening of Foreign Man chitchat, Kaufman "broke character" by doing a dull interview as Andy Kaufman that greatly annoyed Carson; except for a 1978 appearance with guest host Steve Martin, Kaufman was never invited back to *The Tonight Show*.[54] In this context, the rather acerbic references to *The Tonight Show* throughout "The Andy Kaufman Show" *Soundstage* special may stem from Kaufman's own experiences with *The Tonight Show* as the first television forum that unofficially banned him.

In contrast, the mundane daytime talk shows in the late 1970s became nothing short of time-intensive Dada and situationist spectacles. For his 1978 appearance on *The Mike Douglas Show*, Kaufman closed his appearance by belting out "You'll Never Walk Alone" without any regard for tonality while accompanying himself by pounding on a high-hat with drumsticks. It was as hilarious, and avant-garde, as any of his *SNL* performances. Crooner Robert Goulet watched Kaufman's performance with sheer open-mouth disbelief, and Carol Channing helplessly observed with a polite grin — mirroring the reactions of millions of American television watchers. However, Kaufman's shift from Dada to situationist can be seen in comparing his two *Dinah!* appearances.

As Zmuda noted, "Andy held little respect for sitcoms and even less for poor Dinah's show, which was solidly in his 'contempt' category, the ass end of television ... a homogenized effluent of mindless patter and less-than-trivial guests and features."[55] In 1977, Kaufman (as Foreign Man) treated the cream of the "show-biz firmament" to a song as they lined up along the piano: Shore, Sammy Davis, Jr., Bob Hope, and composer Marvin Hamlisch. Kaufman alternated between two chords and sang the line "I love you — Give me a keess, keess, keess, keess, keess" repeatedly in his Foreign Man accent as he punctuated the song with awkward pauses, an out-of-tune falsetto for the word "kiss," and slobbering kissing sounds into the microphone as he tinkled away on the piano. Hamlisch, the Academy Award–winning composer of pop standards such as "The Way We Were," could only manage an incredulous stare.

In September of 1979, Kaufman agreed to appear on *Dinah!*—but only as Tony Clifton. After consuming a substantial amount of Jack Daniels in the dressing room, Clifton wobbled onto the set for his opening number, a dreadful rendition of "On the Street Where You Live" from *My Fair Lady*—an immediate signal indicating how he would be treating the "fair lady" of daytime talk (and on her own show). The visibly drunk Clifton then sat down for the requisite interview, which began by Clifton curtly interrupting Shore to introduce "some very special people in the audience." With the studio and home audience expecting Clifton to introduce some family or close friends, he introduced three women dressed to resemble prostitutes (personal assistants of Kaufman and Zmuda who were participating in the situation). One by one, they stood up and waved to the studio audience and camera; they were hilariously given the customary round of polite applause. After an unsuccessful attempt to interview the drunk and belligerent Clifton, an exasperated Shore asked him to sing another number, which had originally been scheduled as a Shore-Clifton duet that Shore canceled that day due to illness. Under Clifton's relentless badgering and growing studio audience pressure, Shore relented and performed a duet with Clifton. Their tension-filled version of "Anything You Can Do" became all the more hilarious as Clifton and Shore regaled each other with the song's famous chorus — "No, you can't! Yes, I can!"—speaking volumes for the power struggle going on between Shore and Clifton over the disastrous direction Clifton was taking *Dinah!* After the acrimonious duet finished, Shore lead Clifton to an onstage kitchenette for *Dinah!*'s signature segment where guests cooked their favorite dishes. It ended with Clifton pouring a bowl of liquefied eggs and raw bacon over Shore's head; in the trademark Clifton exit, he was thrown off the premises while spewing profane insults.[56]

In the early 1980s, Kaufman became a fixture on *Late Night with David Letterman*; Kaufman appeared on *Late Night* ten times in the space of 18 months (February 1982–November 1983). Letterman, whose own talk show sensibilities owed as much to the Steve Allen and Ernie Kovacs versions of *The Tonight Show* as Johnny Carson, provided a forum for Kaufman's experiments on television, and the *only* space left on network television for Kaufman near the end of his career. Letterman noted, "Andy would orchestrate and rehearse each of his appearances for maximum impact. And when the impact worked, *good or bad*, he would savor it."[57] Undoubtedly the most famous *Late Night* appearance, which arguably even outdid *Fridays* in controversy, was the July 28, 1982, joint appearance by Kaufman and Jerry "the King" Lawler.

By 1982, Kaufman's controversial intergender matches allowed him to fulfill a life-long dream of entering the world of professional wrestling proper, and Kaufman started a public feud with Lawler and the entire city of Memphis, Tennessee (hilariously chronicled in the Kaufman documentary *I'm from Hollywood*). Kaufman sent a series of videotaped promos aired by the local Memphis promoters in their weekly wrestling broadcasts which insulted Lawler and the citizens of Memphis, including a notorious promo where Kaufman instructed the city on the use of a strange, modern invention called "toilet paper." Agreeing to settle the dispute in the ring, Kaufman announced an impending match with Lawler on *Late Night* on April 1, 1982 (most assumed Kaufman's announcement was an April Fools joke), and an actual match between Lawler and Kaufman took place in Memphis on April 5, 1982. It ended with Lawler mercilessly executing three pile-drivers on a helpless Kaufman, sending him to the hospital and making national news. As Zmuda vividly recounted:

> The crowd screamed in glee as the invading Hebrew from Hollywood got his comeuppance ... [and] cheered madly over the fact that if the arrogant Kaufman next addressed them, contritely admitting he had been wrong, it would be from the confines of a wheelchair. Or maybe they'd been really lucky and Jerry had done what they asked him to and killed the Jew.[58]

With the "Kaufman-Lawler" feud, Kaufman did not merely turn the TV studio or broadcast into a situationist "game of events," but an *entire city*. As Zmuda's description indicates, Kaufman did not simply cast himself as a conceited heel, but constructed a very specific ethnic stereotype the Memphis public could rally against — *an other* they could universally despise, scapegoat, and ultimately punish: the Jew. Kaufman embodied, exploited, and grotesquely exaggerated every Jewish stereotype that Hitler made central to Nazism — the haughty, wealthy Jewish outsider who was the cause of the common folks' misery. Conversely, Kaufman also served as "the Agitator" for the Memphis public — the rage-filled speaker hurling invective to ferment the public's hatred for the given society's designated "Other."[59] For Kaufman, the wrestling heel *combined* charismatic personality and public loathing, someone who could serve as *both* the Agitator and the Other, as Kaufman conducted an experiment in the dynamics of fascism by turning an American city into a microcosm of the Third Reich.

The match in Memphis reportedly left Kaufman with a serious neck injury; in fact, Kaufman was uninjured in the carefully choreographed match with Lawler, and the oversized neck brace Kaufman wore in public for months afterward was purely for theatrical and comical effect.[60] In a May *SNL* appearance, Kaufman ostensibly apologized to the American public for his wrestling shenanigans (to be discussed further), and two days later appeared on *Late Night*, now saying he "forgave" Lawler, who should now apologize to him. The stage was set for a highly publicized Kaufman-Lawler appearance on *Late Night*, their first face-to-face meeting since the match. However, people expecting Kaufman and Lawler to shake hands and make up were in for a rude awakening.

Prior to the interview, an excerpt of the match was shown — Lawler's pile-drivers on Kaufman which resulted in the alleged neck injury. The interview immediately began badly, with Kaufman walking out several steps behind Lawler: visibly nervous, apparently still in a great deal of physical discomfort, and still encumbered by his bulky neck brace. As the two sat down, Kaufman maneuvered his chair away from Lawler. Kaufman briefly explained his view of the match, and once he realized he could not beat Lawler, he would "just run away from him the whole time." Of course, Kaufman omitted that while he was running away during the match he was pointing at Lawler, scratching under his arms like a monkey, and luring Lawler to the edge of the ring and then placing a limb over the ropes and pointing to his temple with a forefinger (the gesture of pointing to his head borrowed from Buddy Rogers) — signifying Lawler (Memphis) was a "dumb ape" and Kaufman (the Jew) "had smarts" — actions that infuriated Memphis wrestling fans.

When asked to tell his side of the story, Lawler immediately adopted an aggressive and unrepentant stance: "Andy Kaufman, the way he is now — you know, Mr. Nice Guy — very lovable little Latka character and everything — is not the Andy Kaufman I saw." To prove his point, Lawler aired some of the highly insulting videos Lawler claimed were sent to his home over the course of the feud. A montage of the more insulting moments from the Memphis promos followed. When asked about the tapes by Letterman, Kaufman smiled sheepishly and issued a classic reply: "*I was just teasing in fun.*" As Letterman went to commercial, Kaufman interjected: "I can't see how you could be mad ... I was just kidding." Setting an increasingly tense tone for the interview to go to commercial, Kaufman's comment became a virtual guarantee the situation would worsen.

Indeed, when the show returned from the commercial break, Kaufman's tone had shifted from wary to hostile. Resentfully noting he'd already apologized about his wrestling routines and "all the abuse I've ever given the people *who didn't understand what I was doing*" (emphasis added; a reference to the May 1982 *SNL* "apology"), he reiterated his demand that Lawler apologize to him. Lawler not only refused, but when asked by Letterman if he wanted to "hurt" Kaufman, Lawler answered, "Well ... yeah. I thought I had to hurt him." The comment was the cue for Kaufman and Lawler to start insulting each other — and quite hilariously, despite the growing, palpable tension. While the mood and exchange was highly inappropriate for a celebrity-based talk show, even one as fairly unconventional as *Late Night* was at the time, the interview was a typical pro-wrestling promo (the mutually baiting on-camera interviews which provide back-story and teasers for feuds realized in the ring).

As Letterman tried to maintain a semblance of order, Lawler insisted that Kaufman was a publicity-seeking complainer who got more than he bargained for and everything he deserved with his antics: Lawler serving as the voice of many of Kaufman's critics who were saying precisely the same things about

Kaufman at this point in his career. ("Did you laugh after, when you were laying in the hospital? Was it a joke then?") Kaufman responded with a string of insults directed at Lawler's integrity and manhood while casting himself as the victim, culminating in Kaufman informing Lawler, "You're lucky I didn't sue you!" Within the space of a few minutes, Kaufman transformed from misunderstood artist to his "Hollywood (Jew) heel" wrestling persona. As the insults flew, Letterman tried "to pause here for station identification, and get the hose...." Kaufman muttered something under his breath which caused Lawler to get up. After hovering over Kaufman for a moment, Lawler slapped him in the head, sending Kaufman sprawling to the floor as the band began to play and the show quickly cut to commercial. The moment of actual physical violence guaranteed another "cliff-hanger," with the television audience by now completely confused as to whether they were watching a Kaufman-Lawler comedy routine or a genuine confrontation: the essence of Kaufman's theater of life.

In fact, after slapping Kaufman, Lawler was escorted off the set by security and sequestered in the guest waiting station for almost half an hour while Kaufman stormed through the corridors demanding Lawler be arrested for assault. Lawler later recounted that Kaufman's performance was so convincing that he was concerned he was actually going to be arrested.[61] After Lawler returned to the set and taping resumed, Letterman tentatively asked, "Andy, are you coming in here again or...." After a well-timed dramatic pause, Kaufman barged onto the set stage right, shielded behind Letterman's desk, and unleashed one of the most memorable monologues in television history: "I am sick of this bullshit!...I will sue your ass! You're a motherfucking asshole! ... You hear me?! A fucking asshole! Fuck you! I will sue you for this!" Of course, the television viewer heard nothing more than what amounted to a continuous bleep. Kaufman stormed off the stage again, leaving Letterman, Lawler and the audience in bewildered silence. However, after a timely pause, Kaufman returned to the stage, the audience wildly applauding — a reaction becoming increasingly rare for Kaufman. "I am sorry," Kaufman began. "I am sorry to use those words on television. I apologize to all my fans. I'm sorry!" By now, Kaufman was on his knees, seemingly on the verge of tears. Again, the entire mood of the scene shifted to a palpable and highly-uncomfortable silence, before Kaufman transformed the entire situation again. Standing up and again moving behind the safety of Letterman's desk and pounding on it with his palms, he glared at Lawler and screeched: "But you, you're a fucking asshole! You're a fucking asshole! You hear me?! A fucking asshole!" Then, to use a physical gesture as a visual exclamation point for the diatribe, Kaufman threw a cup of coffee into Lawler's face (which Lawler easily dodged and Kaufman aimed well to the right). As the studio audience responded with what might be called "frenzy," Kaufman promptly fled the stage. Like *Fridays*, the "confrontation" made national news.

The entire Kaufman-Lawler feud was a "work" meticulously planned and thoroughly rehearsed by Kaufman, Lawler, and various others involved in its planning and execution throughout its lengthy course. The *Late Night* appearance served as a nationally televised promo for Kaufman and Lawler to rekindle their wrestling feud for another year, with escalating absurdity in the ring and increasing fury from the public.[62] It also epitomized how Kaufman *détourned* the pro-wrestling formula into a situationist use of comedy; the more the performance could become provocative and even ridiculous, the greater potential for genuine tension, shock and outrage — anywhere and at any time.

"Andy Kaufman Is Not Funny Anymore!": Revenge of the Culture Industry

By 1982, it is not hyperbole to suggest that Andy Kaufman was not merely one of the most controversial figures in American popular culture, but one of its most despised. Kaufman's inexplicable wrestling career and (staged) blow-ups on *Fridays* and *Late Night* created the popular perception that Kaufman was, at best, mentally unstable and, at worst, a social menace. *Taxi*'s ratings were steadily plummeting, and many blamed Kaufman's indifference and unpredictable presence for making the production of a quality show impossible, and the often negative publicity he generated for alienating viewers. Bored with sitcom constraints and increasingly at odds with the rest of the cast, Kaufman quit attending rehearsals altogether, with the approval of the producers. To keep Kaufman interested in the show, the producers and writers resorted to giving Latka a multiple-personality disorder — a none-too-subtle in-joke about Kaufman's public image. In "Latka the Playboy" (1981), Latka became "Vic Ferrari," a sexist, obnoxious personification of the Disco era and "Me Decade" which essentially allowed Kaufman to do a more palatable version of Tony Clifton.[63] After a fight between Kaufman and Hirsch erupted when Kaufman refused to break out of the Ferrari character during one taping session, Latka's next personality promptly became "Alex Reiger," Hirsch's common-man-as-philosopher character on the show, with Kaufman doing a remarkably accurate and quite acerbic parody of Hirsch in the episode "Mr. Personalities" (1981).[64] Cancelled by ABC in 1982, *Taxi* was picked up by NBC for its final season. *Taxi* producers added comedy veteran Carol Kane as Latka's wife, "Simka Gravis." She became the comic focus of the couple, with Kaufman little more than an incidental straight man who occasionally appeared but had essentially been written out of *Taxi*.

Another particularly disconcerting performance occurred in August 1982 at a taping for *Catch a Rising Star Tenth Anniversary HBO Special*.[65] Kaufman began performing his Foreign Man routine until interrupted by Zmuda, playing a heckler in the audience, and it quickly became a disturbing confrontation (the 1979 staged press conference at Harrah's could be seen as the precursor). The stage and spotlight became a nightmarish version of the police interrogation room as Zmuda belittled Kaufman for several minutes, with Kaufman issuing ineffective defenses. It was character assassination as public spectacle, with Zmuda assailing Kaufman with criticism that could have been lifted verbatim from the negative press Kaufman was receiving at the time. When the audience began to turn against Zmuda, he produced a lapel mike and informed them that Kaufman planted him as a heckler just to create more controversy, turning audience discontent back toward Kaufman. A disheartened Elvis impersonation provided a decidedly mixed resolution to the situation, with Andy Kaufman bombing on HBO in 1982 being a far cry from Foreign Man bombing on *SNL* in 1975.

As Kaufman's TV career careened from one nationally televised disaster to another, perhaps it was inevitable that Kaufman received his expulsion from network television (*Late Night*, of course, notwithstanding). It occurred on *Saturday Night Live* on November 20, 1982. With Dick Ebersol now executive producer, Kaufman finally returned to *SNL* in January 1982 (the first appearance since the previously discussed "Intergender" wrestling match in December 1979). In the wake of Albert Goldman's scandalous biography *Elvis*, Kaufman's comeback *SNL* sketch began with his Elvis impersonation: a version of Presley's "Trouble," followed by lip-synching to a record of a chicken clucking opera while walking into the audience to acknowledge two swooning female fans. Zmuda, playing Elvis's assistant, Red West, brought the women to Elvis's dressing room where Elvis asked the women to wrestle in their panties while he watched. As the women began to strip, Kaufman stood up and removed the Elvis wig, and announced to the studio audience that the sketch was based on allegations in the Goldman biography, "And I disapprove of that book, and I disapprove of what I just did." For Kaufman, the sketch was a public defense of his idol he reiterated a month later on his first *Late Night* appearance by publicly challenging Goldman to a wrestling match over the authenticity of the book.[66] It also allowed Kaufman to put the audience in the uncomfortable position of laughing at a sketch where the punchline was Kaufman disavowing it.

Far different in tone was Kaufman's appearance on *SNL* for an interview with Brian Doyle-Murray telecast on May 15, 1982. It would be Kaufman's last in-person appearance on *SNL*. Recounting the previous month's Lawler-Kaufman match, Kaufman, sitting awkwardly in his mammoth neck brace, meekly provided on-air commentary over actual footage of the match. Kaufman ended the interview by retiring from wrestling, or, more correctly, *renouncing* his wrestling career and issuing a blanket apology to pro-wrestlers, women, and the American public. The live audience cheered and applauded, although it is uncertain whether this was a show of support and forgiveness, or an expression of relief Kaufman was discontinuing his perplexing obsession with pro-wrestling. While Kaufman sounded sincere and repentant — far from the "Viet Cong Confession" mode — Kaufman's demeanor suggested something sinister, a sense of annoyance underneath the contrition that fully revealed itself two months later on *Late Night* when he bitterly noted he already had to apologize to the public for "not understanding what I was doing." The seemingly sincere apology proved to be as big a prank as his acts of penitence on *Fridays*, and the apparent *SNL* "wrestling apology" was yet another comedic work — performed, and perceived, as absolutely serious.

Scheduled to appear on *SNL* on October 23, 1982, Kaufman planned on premiering a sideshow fakir routine. Due to the show running long and Ebersol unenthusiastic with Kaufman's planned act, he was cut from that evening's *SNL*.[67] Instead of a make-up appearance the next week, Kaufman devised a routine with Ebersol where he would be asked back, even altering his own schedule of concert performances, only to be bumped again, and engage in a heated argument with Ebersol — none of which would be televised but certainly reported in the press. On the November 13, 1982, *SNL* telecast, Ebersol appeared on-air to issue a statement informing *SNL* viewers that Kaufman's scheduled appearances had been cancelled at the last minute because they failed to meet *SNL* "standards." The studio audience issued a thunderous round of applause when Ebersol declared: "Andy Kaufman is not funny anymore!"

Kaufman's battle with *SNL* was intended as an extended merger of theater and reality where any difference became indistinguishable. Perhaps fittingly, accounts of what "really" occurred vary considerably, although what is generally agreed upon is that what began as a complex, constructed situation ended with Kaufman banished from the show and his career effectively over.[68] To set the stage, Kaufman was impressed with a highly popular April 1982 routine on *SNL* when Eddie Murphy interrupted a dreadful sketch involving a TV-chef about to boil a lobster; he informed the viewers they could call in to the show to determine the fate of "Larry the Lobster," and an actual call-in vote was held. Moreover, through his involvement in a series of fund-raising concerts as part of Jerry Brown's failed 1982 California U.S. Senate campaign, Kaufman became fascinated with the "theatre of life" inherent in political campaigning and elections (hardly surprising, given their emphasis on public image, speeches composed of dynamic performance and vague rhetoric, and, above all, the calculated process of mass audience manipulation). Furthermore, there was the ubiquitous pro-wrestling subtext as well, the vote very much along the lines of a "loser-leaves-town" match (usually implemented when a wrestler planned to retire or signed a contract with another wrestling promotion).

Kaufman conceived an intricate series of performance events, both on-camera and, especially, off-camera, with the *SNL* election envisioned as a pivotal moment in a new situation, a new installment in Kaufman's theater of life. However, the stage was not the city of Memphis, the audience not incensed Southerners, and the villain not an obnoxious Jew. Instead, the stage was national television, the audience was *SNL*'s viewers similarly out for blood, and the villain was Andy Kaufman. The off-camera arguments with Ebersol and his on-air condemnation were part of constructing the situation. Also adding fuel to the controversy was a *Late Night* appearance three days before the *SNL* vote in which Kaufman performed the routine Ebersol rejected for *SNL*: dressed as a fakir in a turban and a diaper, Kaufman actually swallowed a sword, belly-danced by adroitly rippling his abdominal muscles, and closed with a rendition of Slim Whitman's "Rose Marie." During his interview with Letterman, Kaufman blasted his critics.

On November 20, 1982, *SNL* began with an announcement that an actual call-in vote would be held for viewers to decide whether or not to permanently ban Kaufman from the show. Kaufman lost by over 20,000 votes, and the final tally was greeted with tumultuous applause from the studio audience. The nationally televised repudiation of Kaufman on *SNL* opened the floodgates for a long-simmering and sweeping backlash. After a taped segment from Kaufman thanking his fans aired during an *SNL* "Weekend Update"—to overwhelmingly negative reaction in January of 1983—Ebersol scrapped any plans for Kaufman's return to the show.[69] It was viewed as an utter betrayal by Kaufman and his associates; as Zmuda succinctly stated, "The joke was on Andy, and Andy wasn't laughing."[70] In his subsequent "Andy Kaufman Show" *Soundstage* special, Kaufman responded to the *SNL* vote with a vengeance.

Ultimately, the convoluted particulars of *what* happened with the Kaufman *SNL* vote are less important than *why* it happened. Perhaps it was a forgone conclusion that the final curtain on Kaufman's theater of life was his virtual expulsion from television. As Richard Leppert noted, "[The avant-garde] refuses to deliver the package the art consumer believes they have bought. Or to construct the metaphor a bit differently, when the package is opened what's there is notably not what was ordered."[71] Kaufman's steadfast refusal to "deliver the goods," which continually kept the art customer *un*satisfied, not only made his volatile mixture of mirth and mayhem avant-garde but *dangerous*—a critique and protest against the conformity, mediocrity, and predictability of television, the Culture Industry, and even its audiences. In this regard, Zmuda pointed to a conversation he had with a friend and psychology professor, who suggested:

> Andy had been flirting with being "shut down" for some time.... With Andy Kaufman on camera, [television's] precious connection to the American consumer was in danger of being interfered with ... pushed to its (and the viewers') limits, thus diminishing the possibility of selling, not entertaining.... Someone had to remove the madman from the controls. Andy underestimated his own impact, and when he was thrown off the stage of *Saturday Night Live* as Andy, not Tony, he was shocked.[72]

Requiem for a Comedian: "The Andy Kaufman Show," *Soundstage* (PBS, 1983)

For what amounted to his final major television appearance, Kaufman's special for PBS's *Soundstage* aired in July 1983, simply titled "The Andy Kaufman Show" (henceforth referred to as *Soundstage*). To provide a brief context, in the summer of 1977 Kaufman made a special for ABC, *Andy's Funhouse*. ABC rejected the show as too unorthodox and non-commercial, eventually airing it once in a late-night time slot in August 1979 as *The Andy Kaufman Special*, largely owing to Kaufman's growing mainstream popularity on *Taxi*. *Andy's Funhouse* was a *détournement* of the variety show, talk show, and children's show. Instead of a studio audience, Kaufman included an on-camera peanut gallery of adults—one of whom, presumably a plant, watches the show with what might be charitably described as incredulous boredom. Comedy routines (Foreign Man–Elvis, "It's a Small World" with the B Street Conga Band) alternated with children's show segments, such as a how-to demonstration on making chocolate milk and a sing-along about barn animals (his talk show desk had a built-in piano). *Andy's Funhouse* also featured an interview with *Laverne and Shirley* star Cindy Williams, with Kaufman parodying the indifferent host asking meaningless questions off an index card before badgering an unsuspecting and unprepared Williams to sing "Mack the Knife" (the unofficial signature song of Ernie Kovacs). Conversely, his long interview with "special guest" Howdy Doody was a touching tribute and recollection by Kaufman about the vital importance of the show in his childhood.

With *Soundstage*, Kaufman purged the overt comedy and his best-known routines (except for an obligatory Elvis impersonation and a cameo by Foreign Man that served as self-reflexive commentaries about his career). With then-undiagnosed lung cancer claiming his life a year later, Kaufman almost prophetically remade — or *détourned*—*Andy's Funhouse* into nothing short of an autobiographical eulogy on his career and life.

Technically, Kaufman and Clifton appear together, with a *marionette* of Tony Clifton serving as Kaufman's announcer-sidekick. Though this references *Howdy Doody* (with Kaufman the Buffalo Bob Smith to Clifton's Howdy Doody), *The Tonight Show* becomes the overt source of parody, with Kaufman the show's Johnny Carson and the marionette Clifton its Ed McMahon. While Clifton begins *Soundstage* by defiantly telling Kaufman he will not tolerate any "phony baloneys" on the show, including an altercation with Howdy Doody later in the show, his final segment on *Soundstage* is a puppet-show commercial for "Veggie-Dog" pet food with a wind-up toy poodle (a parody of Ed McMahon's Alpo commercials). Clifton himself becomes a "puppet" of the TV industry, no longer a subversive troublemaker but now a TV shill — on commercial-free PBS, no less. The talk show aspect of *Soundstage* also features the most blatantly comic bit: Kaufman's desk is elevated several feet in the air, a commentary on the spatial power structure of the talk show format, specifically Johnny Carson's slightly elevated desk on the set of *The Tonight Show* (where Carson's desk, situated slightly higher than the guests' chairs, placed him in a physical space where he looked down on the guests like a reigning king).[73] However, any comedy becomes less clear-cut with his first guest, comedienne and former girlfriend Elayne Boosler. The interview quickly digresses into a very uncomfortable passive-aggressive argument between Boosler and Kaufman over the particulars of their past relationship problems — who was to blame for the dissolution, and even a detour into the "No, I broke up with you" exchanges of contentious ex-couples — to the point it becomes difficult to determine whether or not the exchange has indeed become personal.

The children's show segments of *Soundstage* house caustic attacks on television. After *Soundstage* confusingly "begins" (which will be discussed shortly), Kaufman introduces the "Magic Screen" portion of the show. Asking the TV viewer to get some plastic wrap and a black crayon, with Kaufman specifically adding that only a *black* crayon will work, he gives the viewer a minute to acquire necessary materials from the kitchen, at which time the show grinds to a halt with a minute of dead air; Kaufman sits on the edge of the peanut gallery stand, his only action checking his watch as if to explicitly point out that "time" is being wasted. He finally directs the viewer back to the TV and walks over to an old portable television. It serves as an on-screen TV monitor depicting what the viewer is seeing on their own television at that moment, and Kaufman demonstrates how to place the clear plastic over the TV screen. The shot abruptly cuts to a black screen, and Kaufman enters from the left side of the frame, instructing the viewer to "trace the line" as a white jagged line resembling stairs is superimposed on the screen. Kaufman then runs up and down the "staircase," accompanied by a tinkling piano, an Ernie Kovacs–style sight gag where the humor is simply the visual effect and use of the medium. However, noticing some of the TV viewers did not participate, even addressing them by common first names (a device commonly used by children's show hosts), Kaufman again explains they must "trace the line" for the joke to work. With a strange menace and agitation growing in his voice, Kaufman again darts up and down the stairs: "Trace the line — see how much fun we have when you trace the line ... *and you do what you're supposed to do?*" (emphasis added). The performer and the viewer of television have fun by "following orders"— the viewer diligently "traces the line" while Kaufman *toes the line*, literalized by Kaufman frantically running up and down the white line of the stairs like a lab animal in a maze. In one respect, the Magic Screen segment becomes a satire on television's meaningless pseudoactivity. By insisting the viewer can only use a black crayon, tracing the line eliminates the white line on the screen, actually negating the sight-gag rather than making it work. Moreover, the viewer is instructed to leave the plastic wrap over the screen because the Magic Screen segment will be repeated later in the show; theoretically, by following orders, the viewer will watch the reminder of *Soundstage* with a jagged black line in the middle of the screen — or a crack in the TV screen. Conversely, the status of "tracing the line" by the viewer also becomes an important political gesture: it is only through viewer participation and awareness of the power of the "Magic Screen" that the line Kaufman has to "toe" on television can be erased.

During *Soundstage*'s "Going-Too-Far Corner," Kaufman introduces another guest, professional wrestler Stan "Plowboy" Frazier, whose sideshow-inspired performance consists of drinking a glass of two raw eggs, spitting the contents back into the glass, drinking it again, spitting it back into the glass, and repeating the process to a torrent of boos. The scene suddenly jump-cuts to an elderly couple watching television in their modest apartment; the man exclaims, "That's disgusting — he's gone too far!" and his wife interjects, "You can say that again!" The shot cuts back to Kaufman gleefully watching Frazier's performance when a police whistle blows and the shot abruptly cuts to a black screen. The shot fades in to Kaufman superimposed on a generic courtroom sketch. A voiceover for the cartoon judge proclaims, "This time you've really done it! You've gone too far! ...Mr. Kaufman, you've been banned from television! You are off the air!" Certainly, the courtroom scene is Kaufman's scathing commentary on the *Saturday Night Live* vote the previous year, with the judge being Dick Ebersol and the jury being *SNL*'s audience. However, the courtroom scene allows Kaufman the protest he could not lodge on being voted off *in absentia*. With the fury of an enraged wrestling heel, Kaufman snarls: "Wait a minute! You can't take me off the air! You can't cut me of just like that ... I *dare* you to take me off the air! I *DEFY* you —"

Kaufman's rebellious tirade abruptly cuts to another black screen lasting some ten seconds of dead air, signifying Kaufman can indeed be "cut off just like that." Finally, a sheepish Kaufman emerges from the side of the frame and into the black screen, informing the viewer that the show can continue as long as everyone behaves and stays quiet. Unfortunately, his next guest is Morris "Butch" Stewart, another "phony baloney": a James Brown *impersonator* who performs "Baby, Baby, Baby" against the black screen with the appropriate high-volume grunts and shrieks associated with the Godfather of Soul. Wincing, Kaufman implores Stewart to tone down his performance, but the police officers again enter and roughly escort Kaufman out of the shot. Cutting to another drawn background — a cartoon desert island — the superimposed Kaufman and "TV police" enter the frame. Kaufman is thrown on the beach, and one of the policemen barks, "All right, Kaufman, this oughta teach you a lesson ... you can keep your warped sense of humor here for a few years, you bum!" Kaufman again resorts to "Magic Screen" viewer intervention by asking the viewer to connect a set of rectangular dots on the screen; it will "magically" create a "boat" that Kaufman can use to escape from the island.[74] In the first "Magic Screen" segment, if the audience participates, they erase the line Kaufman has to toe on TV. Now, the stakes are raised: it is only active audience participation with the Magic Screen that can release Kaufman from TV exile. Kneeling in the boat (or, more correctly, in the middle of the unconnected dots), Kaufman happily waves and tells the audience he'll see them "back at the show." The scene cuts to the thoroughly confused elderly couple watching the show in their living room, the man complaining, "What's he doing now?" His wife answers, "Oh, he's playing with the medium." This cuts to another Kovacs-style sight-gag where Kaufman plays cards with a magician in a turban (also a reference to his fakir character that was integral to his *SNL* expulsion). The magician ("the medium") lays down his hand and triumphantly says, "Gin!" Kaufman shrugs, as a cartoon-style piano flourish accompanies Kaufman's defeat and the shot fades to black. When Kaufman "plays with the medium," it is the *medium* that wins.

In this respect, a key subtext in *Soundstage* is Kaufman's critique of stardom, and, eventually, his own career. *Soundstage*'s "The Has-Been Corner" is a routine recycled directly from *Andy's Funhouse*: Kaufman's essay and eulogy on the many casualties of show business who attained their 15 minutes of fame, were promptly shoved aside for the next batch of stars, and desperately sought one more moment in the spotlight.[75] It begins with Kaufman providing a short biographical introduction to one "Jim Brandy," a singer who scored "somewhat of a hit record" with the song "Wild, Wild Lovin'" in 1959 while Elvis was in the Army. Brandy achieved brief notoriety as a minor teen idol, and after Elvis returned to the world of pop-music, "[Brandy's] career," Kaufman deadpans, "fizzled into oblivion." After proudly introducing Brandy — an older, overweight man in an ill-fitting, polyester safari jacket and slacks — Kaufman, absolutely straight-faced, asks his first question: the clichéd talk show opening, "So, what have you been up to?" The joke becomes almost ghoulish in that Brandy has obviously been up to very little in the world of show business. Brandy awkwardly replies that he's been singing, taking whatever jobs he can get booked. As the interview continues, the uncomfortable comedy escalates when the stoic Kaufman asks, "So, how does it feel, now, when you look back and you think about all the success you had at one time and were supposedly going to have and you never had — how does it feel?" Brandy, smiling but taken aback by the question, stammers, "Lousy ... It feels lousy!"

After a morbid parody of *This Is Your Life*, with Brandy providing an overview of his life, accompanied by a number of unflattering photos, Brandy performs the lounge-standard "The Nearness of You." He fidgets from side to side, shuffling his feet in a vain attempt to keep time to the music, and nervously clutches the microphone in a two-handed death-grip as he stares blankly and sings in a dreary, flat monotone. Watching Brandy desperately attempting to return to his glory days, simultaneously becoming an object of pity and an object of ridicule, the viewer is placed in the position of actively deciding whether one should be *laughing with* the send-up of a typical lackluster talk show performance segment or *laughing at* the untalented fool embarrassing himself on television. Indeed, it becomes unclear if laughter is even an appropriate response to the Brandy spectacle: the reaction shots of the peanut gallery include baffled stares and uncomfortable snickering. When one woman bursts into laughter during Brandy's performance, she immediately and self-consciously covers her mouth, embarrassed at herself for laughing *at* Brandy.

Kaufman runs on stage, congratulating Brandy amid the peanut gallery applause; he calls for an encore in the form of "Wild, Wild Lovin'." Brandy hesitates, but as a fifties-style rock number begins, Brandy gamely launches into the song only to immediately forget the words. Kaufman hands him a lyric sheet, but Brandy has to don his glasses before he can resume. Again, comedy merges with tragedy as Brandy awkwardly sways to the music with a white-knuckle grip on the mike in one hand and the lyric sheet clutched in the other. Reaction shots of Kaufman enthusiastically dancing and clapping, and even the Tony Clifton marionette bouncing up and down to the music, are intercut with Brandy's stiff, uneasy performance. "A standing ovation —

that's for YOU!" Kaufman exclaims, and Brandy can scarcely contain his delight that for a brief moment in his life he has once again been "a star"— the moment of triumph *and* tragedy for the "magnificent failure" who has been given another few minutes of dubious fame, or at least public attention.

"The Has-Been Corner" provides a grim context for the final segments of *Soundstage* and the self-reflexive commentaries on Kaufman's own career. Standing next to the big desk with Clifton after his return from the desert island, Kaufman recounts a recent, horrifying incident involving his childhood idol, Howdy Doody. With a framed newspaper account featuring the headline "How *Dare* They Doody That?" Kaufman explains how a Howdy Doody marionette was horribly mangled by vandals who broke into the studio he was stored at and "mutilated" him by cutting off his head and an arm. With some relief, Kaufman explains that the assaulted marionette was "not the actual Howdy Doody but looks exactly like him," and was known as "Photo Doody"— Howdy Doody's stand-in for publicity photos and public appearances. The almost absurd explanation is based on fact. According to Zmuda, Kaufman became livid when two "Photo Doodys" were brought for *Andy's Funhouse*; Kaufman spotted the "phony baloneys" immediately and adamantly insisted an actual Howdy Doody marionette used on the show be brought in for the taping.[76] The cultic "star" does not even have to be a living (animate) object — a performer, a character, or even an animal (Lassie, Flipper, Mister Ed, Arnold Ziffel) — but an inanimate object that attains intense popular adoration simply by being endowed with a certain affective persona (hand puppet, marionette, ventriloquist dummy, cartoon character, Paris Hilton).

When Kaufman announces that Photo Doody will be called "Howdy Doody" in honor of making his first televised appearance since miraculously surviving the assault, the scene borders on the *Grand Guignol* as Photo Doody descends onto the Big Desk and stands next to Clifton — his head wrapped in bandages, his arm in a sling, his torso and limbs strangely gaunt and emaciated compared to a grotesquely oversized head. Vainly attempting to be the "real" Howdy Doody, Photo Doody pathetically tries to rally the peanut gallery with a feeble impersonation of Howdy Doody's voice reciting his signature lines. This aspect of Photo Doody's *Soundstage* appearance also stems from the Howdy Doody appearance on *Andy's Funhouse* and Kaufman's extreme disappointment in meeting Buffalo Bob Smith, who supplied Howdy Doody's voice in his many years on television, and who was specifically invited to provide Howdy Doody's authentic voice on *Andy's Funhouse* (given Kaufman's virulent reaction to the Photo Doodys, Smith's involvement amounted to a necessity). The antithesis of his sturdy, kindly *Howdy Doody* TV persona, Zmuda wryly recounted that Smith proved to be uncomfortably reminiscent

8. *Situationist Comedy: Andy Kaufman* 187

of Tony Clifton—a foul-mouthed, chain-smoking drunk whose only interest in *Andy's Funhouse* or even *Howdy Doody* was a paycheck.[77] Ironically, Howdy Doody's appearance on *Andy's Funhouse* came shortly after the syndicated revival of *Howdy Doody* failed miserably; and while Howdy Doody was given a poignant tribute, Smith could have easily been a real-life candidate for another *Andy's Funhouse* segment: "The Has-Been Corner."

In this respect, watching the mutilated Photo Doody performing as a lame substitute for Howdy Doody is both cruelly hilarious and oddly heartrending. Kaufman's beloved childhood idol is reduced to a (literally) deconstructed version of himself: a mangled Photo Doody posing as the real Howdy Doody on *Soundstage* versus the "authentic" Howdy Doody Kaufman insisted appear on *Andy's Funhouse*. Rather than a tribute, Photo Doody is given a humiliating and abrupt ejection by Kaufman's new "puppet"—his own alter-ego, Tony Clifton. Branding Photo Doody as a "phony baloney," Clifton begins sarcastically singing "It's Howdy Doody Time!" while swiftly and repeatedly kicking Photo Doody in the seat of his pants like a Punch and Judy routine. One final boot sends Photo Doody flying back into the rafters, signifying that there no longer is room for the anachronistic playfulness of Howdy Doody, himself now a "has-been" in the context of *Soundstage*.

After brutally disposing of Photo Doody, Clifton suggests Kaufman do something the audience might enjoy: his famed Elvis impersonation. After a hyperbolic introduction from Clifton, Kaufman launches into his Elvis impersonation, performing "Blue Moon over Kentucky" on the same stage Jim Brandy (another ersatz Elvis) performed. Indeed, there is something disconcerting in Kaufman's patented Elvis impersonation this time; it's more of a lackluster run-though of Elvis mannerisms than the reverent and almost shamanistic ability of Kaufman to capture the charismatic power of Elvis. Just as Kaufman's childhood idol Howdy Doody becomes obsolete, so too does his teenage idol, Elvis Presley. Presley's death in 1977 rendered the art of Elvis impersonation into a campy pop-culture phenomenon. Kaufman's perfunctory recreation of Elvis suggests less of his innovative Elvis impersonation in its humorous glory than a subtle parody of Elvis impersonation as a now-dead art—a pathetic exercise in sequined jumpsuits and hip gyrations.

After Clifton's aforementioned "Veggie-Dog" commercial, *Soundstage*'s final segment features Kaufman and Martin Harvey Friedberg, considered "the comedian's comedian" by his peers (Friedberg was an actual performer and teacher on the New York City comedy circuit and appeared in several films). After seeing a Friedberg performance at the Improv glowingly described as "the greatest comedy bit I've ever seen," Kaufman invited Friedberg on the show to perform the routine. Following a short interview and set-up, the exact moment Friedberg actually begins the "greatest comedy bit even seen" the sequence cuts back to the elderly couple planted in front of their television. The man remarks, "Oh, this is where we came in." The woman answers, "Well, we might as well sit and watch the ending," and the man snarls in response, "I don't care for this at all!" In fact, *Soundstage* begins with a voice-over announcing the show is being "joined already in progress." The opening shots of *Soundstage* are of Kaufman laughing hysterically at the antics of Friedberg running about the stage yelling and jumping into the show's peanut gallery. After Friedberg bounces off the stage, Kaufman thanks his guests (none of whom the viewer has yet seen), and then performs a cheerful farewell song in front of the peanut gallery while waving goodbye to the camera. He appreciatively thanks the television audience for watching as the credits began to roll and the screen fades out. The familiar PBS logo appears on the screen, followed by the WTTN logo (the Chicago PBS station that produced *Soundstage*). Immediately, it appears that a scheduling problem has occurred and the viewer has only caught the final few moments of the show, despite having tuned in on time. Only after an establishing shot of the set with the title "The Andy Kaufman Show" does the viewer realize *Soundstage* starts by showing the last two minutes of the show. The television audience is immediately "had" by Kaufman. Thus, the precise moment that the displeased elderly couple (the TV viewer) "came in" is the moment *Soundstage* was joined "already in progress," with Kaufman and the peanut gallery convulsing in laughter as Friedberg runs around screaming and diving into the audience—the classic style of immediate, manic physical comedy beloved by American audiences which Kaufman's idiosyncratic and conceptual brand of anti-comedy rejected. As Kaufman profusely thanks Friedberg, not only has the television viewer been cheated out of the opportunity to witness "the greatest comedy bit ever seen," they have been cheated out of the chance to see the bit *twice*.

Soundstage ostensibly ends as it began, with Kaufman copiously thanking the guests gathered around the towering desk (the viewer realizes a blond woman in a black dress did not appear on the show). However, as Kaufman waves goodbye to the viewer in front of the peanut gallery at the point the beginning of the show faded out, the camera now lingers on Kaufman as his smile becomes obviously forced, his waving transforms into a sarcastic gesture, and his sincere "thank you's" are replaced by a vicious diatribe: "The people out there in the public are a bunch of sheep.... They just sit in front of their television like *idiots*! *Sheep*! ...They follow along; they gotta find a leader.... Talk about stupidity and ignorance...." For his final on-camera tirade, Kaufman combines the persona of the megalomaniacal star and the fascist agitator. Kaufman, in no uncertain terms, expresses his dissatisfaction with the TV audience for their own participation in, as Adorno observed thirty years earlier, "a medium of undreamed of psychological control" where "ideas of conformity and conventionalism ... have been translated into rather clear-cut prescriptions of what to do and what not to do"— where the TV viewer's only role is to sit, watch, and passively "trace the line" or, like the elderly couple (a metaphor for the TV viewer), complain and continue watching. As Kaufman acerbically makes clear on *Soundstage*, the power and purpose of TV and mass culture lies in its potential to manipulate and indoctrinate as much as entertain and educate.

Having unleashed his anger on the audience, Kaufman then repeatedly asks the crew when the show is going to be over, demands a hamburger, and defiantly asks, "Who wants to wrestle?" The boorish, arrogant, obnoxious behavior suggests not only Kaufman's "Wrestling Heel" persona but "Vic Ferrari," the sanitized version of Clifton designed by *Taxi* (the "Photo Doody" or "phony baloney" of Tony Clifton). Going backstage, via a superimposed image, he encounters Foreign Man in Kaufman's famous "I Love Grandma" sweatshirt. Foreign Man confronts Kaufman: "Why are you so mean? ... You're not only hurting your career, but you're hurting *my* career." When Foreign Man suggests the reason Kaufman only does nasty things to the audience is because he is insecure, defensive, and afraid to be liked, Kaufman responds with exaggerated sobbing, confessing that that is the precise reason he tries to get people to react negatively rather than positively. Finishing the show for the emotionally devastated Kaufman, Foreign Man tells the audience he loves them and to be nice, and *he* then turns towards the off-frame crew and snarls, still in character: "Are we off de air? Where's my hamgbeerger? Who wants to wrestle?" As the shot fades out, the final punchline to the show is how Kaufman's own career underwent a process of *détournement*:

> [A] parodic-serious stage where the accumulation of the detourned elements, far from aiming at arousing our indignation or laughter by alluding to some original work, will express our indifference towards a meaningless and forgotten original, and concern itself with rendering a certain sublimity.[78]

Through the course of *Soundstage*, Howdy Doody becomes a mutilated reification; Elvis becomes a kitsch motif; Tony Clifton becomes a Culture Industry puppet; the Wrestling Heel and Vic Ferrari become clichés of the insecure bully; the star Andy Kaufman becomes the Agitator practicing mass manipulation. Most of all, Kaufman's Foreign Man, "the lovable little Latka character" who briefly became a darling of American pop-culture, is revealed as not so "lovable" after all. With his other personas exhausted and Foreign Man standing alone in the studio corridor challenging no one save the TV viewer, it becomes Kaufman's tacit admission that the next stop for Andy Kaufman could well be an interview with himself on "The Has-Been Corner."

"A Sum of Spectacles": The Legacy of Andy Kaufman

Many believed that Andy Kaufman's announcement he was terminally ill with lung cancer, his public appearances in a wheelchair, his increasingly gaunt appearance, and his undergoing faith-healing treatment in the Philippines were all part of a routine that had sunk to a new low in taste. Even after Kaufman's death in June of 1984, some believed it was still all a hoax and that Kaufman would one day reappear from the afterlife to have the last laugh. Given that Kaufman had been all but driven out of network television, there was a surprising amount of posthumous appreciation; Judd Hirsch, Kaufman's fellow cast member and frequent sparring partner on the *Taxi* set, even wrote an appreciative eulogy of Kaufman for *Rolling Stone*. Perhaps the ultimately irony is that in death Kaufman could be safely hailed as a misunderstood genius by the very same industry that effectively shut him down for the danger he posed.

One exception was actor-comedian Harry Shearer, who pointedly noted, "I never liked Andy's act.... What I've decided is that Andy Kaufman acted out the hostility for the audience that so many people in Hollywood feel but don't dare admit.... *It's the worst kind of behavior dressed up as performance art, then it's OK*."[79] What Shearer failed to recognize, or simply chose to ignore, was that Kaufman's "hostility for the audience" and "worst kind of behavior dressed up as performance art" was a direct challenge to the fundamental principles of being a comedian: the continual requirement for appropriate laughter to validate the act, the perpetual fear that the audience may reject the performance, and the indescribable horror of bombing. Typifying the traditional comedic approach, Conan O'Brien suggested:

> No matter how long you do it, or how much you get paid, or what you think your ranking is in the world of comedy, when it works, it feels *great*, and you have that feeling that you had when you were 15 and you were making everyone in the classroom laugh. When it doesn't work, I don't care if you're making 50 million dollars a year as a comedian, if it doesn't work, you —*you want to die*.[80]

For a Conan O'Brien, comedy "works" when the comedian and audience are in complete synch and everyone gets the joke: purely *associative* comedy where everyone can knowingly nod in unison and approvingly laugh *with* each other and laugh *at* the target of the joke (O'Brien's specious "self-deprecating" style notwithstanding). For Kaufman, the pinnacle of comedy was when it "worked" in the pro-wrestling sense of the term, and "didn't work" as comedy—and, more importantly, how long that uncomfortable, even unbearable relationship between the performer and audience could be sustained.

If there was hostility in Kaufman's work, it was not Kaufman's hostility for his audience, but the space Kaufman opened in his performances that freed "gut reactions" from the confined and proscribed relationships between the performer and audience, and the seemingly pathological willingness to be the *target* of audience hostility. Robin Williams provided an intriguing but flawed analysis by suggesting, "Andy made *himself the premise* and *the rest of the world was the punchline.*"[81] Williams still applies the traditional comedian-audience relationship to Kaufman: the comedian as the center of the comedic universe and everything else the object of the comedian's observations and antics. Kaufman, who repeatedly insisted he was "never a comedian" and "never told a joke in my life," created unsettling *situations.* Kaufman's performances, *onstage or offstage,* were designed as "moments of rupture ... revolutions in individual daily life" to provoke a wealth of gut reactions from the audience — laughter, pathos, bewilderment, impatience, and, more often than not, anger — usually directed at Kaufman himself: the hapless Foreign Man, the insufferable Tony Clifton, the big-mouthed Wrestling Heel, the Hollywood star having meltdowns on national television. Kaufman made *the rest of the world his premise* and *himself the punchline* in the comically cruel theater of life.

As Jim Carrey suggested, "[The audience] were the stars.... Andy was the director and the audience."[82] Moreover, by making the audience the stars and placing the onus of the performance on them, as Elayne Boosler noted, "He wanted to make the audience work, *to rethink the obvious.*"[83] Indeed, what the audience had to rethink, and think differently, was their very relationship to comedy — not just if they were getting the joke, but who the joke was on, and if anyone should be laughing in the first place. In this way, Marty Feldman best described the truly revolutionary aspect of Kaufman's *humor*: "In Andy, there is something underneath the playfulness, *a sense of danger, a kind of genial anger, as if the way we wearily come to see the world is simply insufficient.*"[84] Kaufman was the closest American television comedy came to approaching the ambitions of Artaud: "[The] anarchistic, dissociative power of comedy ... immediate and pernicious ... that spirit of profound anarchy that is all poetry ... *the total destruction of all reality in the mind.*" The moment the entire audience was confused and upset became the moment of final victory for Kaufman — the moment he pinned reality to the mat.

Part Five. Is Avant-Garde Television Comedy Still Possible?

If anything should be blown up, it is the foundations of most habits of modern thinking.
— Antonin Artaud, "The Alfred Jarry Theater" (1927)

We shall not have succeeded in demolishing everything unless we demolish the ruins as well. But the only way I can see of doing that is to use them to put up a lot of fine, well-designed buildings.
— Pere Ubu, *Ubu enchaîné* (1899)

CHAPTER 9

Damage Control: Comedy-Variety and Situation-Comedy After 1974

> My fellow Americans, our long national nightmare is over.
> — Gerald R. Ford, August 9, 1974

Now Ready for Prime Time Players: *Saturday Night Live*

When *Saturday Night Live* premiered on NBC in 1975, it initially appeared to be a progressive convergence of the comedy-variety show posited by *The Smothers Brothers Comedy Hour*'s anti–Establishment content and *Rowan and Martin's Laugh-In*'s unconventional form.[1] *SNL* was the first comedy-variety show where all the principals were rooted in the counterculture and allowed to express that attitude in a way that the Smothers Brothers were not permitted. A far cry from traditional vaudeville comics of the previous generation, the initial stable of *SNL* writers and "Not Quite Ready for Prime Time Players" honed their skills in improvisational comedy clubs and various *National Lampoon* projects in the early 1970s. John Belushi projected a counterculture swagger that Hollywood legends, let alone Richard Nixon, appearing on *Rowan and Martin's Laugh-In* could not generate; and the king of counterculture comedy, George Carlin, hosted the premiere *SNL* telecast (Carlin did not appear in any sketches, but instead acted as an informal MC and sporadically performed stand-up comedy routines throughout the show).

196   PART FIVE. Is Avant-Garde Television Still Possible?

The traditional comedy-variety show format largely died with the long-running *The Carol Burnett Show* leaving prime-time in 1979, the same period the comedy-variety show as a whole became an unintentional self-parody, exemplified by *The Brady Bunch Hour* (ABC, 1977) and the infamous *Pink Lady and Jeff* (NBC, 1980) — two shows which have since achieved a certain prestige as camp. In contrast, *SNL* in its 1975–80 glory days unquestionably redefined the comedy-variety show. While *SNL* maintained the comedy-variety show structure, the live sketches, the weakest element of *SNL* from its inception, freely alternated with musical performances, guest comedians, and pre-recorded segments. The early seasons offered musical performances ranging from Abba to Frank Zappa, short films by Albert Brooks, guest performers such as Andy Kaufman, and even puppet shows featuring bad-tempered monsters in a phantasmal, primal world, courtesy of Muppets creator Jim Henson. Comedy was topical, but largely confined to Gerald Ford's physical coordination and Jimmy Carter's hick Southern accent. The most controversial segment in the early seasons was a pre-filmed segment, "The Claudine Longet Invitational," which was a montage of stock footage of skiers tumbling down the slopes to the sound of overdubbed gunshots. At the time, Longet was under a criminal investigation after fatally shooting her boyfriend, pro-skier Spider Sabich, which she claimed was accidental. *SNL* issued an on-air apology the next week, reportedly to avoid a libel lawsuit by Longet.

Ultimately, television itself became a primary target, and *SNL* frequently parodied TV commercials, genres (the "Weekend Update" news segment, talk shows, game shows), and actual TV shows (most notably, Tom Snyder's *Tomorrow* and the classic "*Star Trek* cancellation" sketch). *SNL* also stressed a self-reflexive approach: producer Lorne Michaels storming through the studio to fire a drunk director midway through a sketch; the confused cast opening one show in the studio control room hovering over a director who suddenly died moments before the evening's live telecast. Dan Ackroyd claimed *SNL* differed from all previous comedy-variety shows because it was "not a joke machine, but a concept machine."[2] What he neglected to add was that many of the concepts were indirectly inspired or directly borrowed from Sid Caesar and especially Ernie Kovacs, who supplied similar self-reflexive and equally satirical studies of the medium of television two decades before *SNL*. In retrospect, the contemporary *SCTV* supplied a more consistently focused — and funnier — critique of television than *SNL*.

As Tony Hendra pointed out, *SNL*'s creator and executive producer, Lorne Michaels, began his television career writing for *Rowan and Martin's Laugh-In*, and the TV comedy lessons learned from *Laugh-In* were as essential in shaping *SNL* as any counterculture or early TV lineage. Despite the nostalgic remembrances of the first five years of *SNL* as subversive anti-television, Hendra contended:

> What "worked" on *SNL* were the continuing characters, the safe situations, the material that reminded the audience of what "worked" last time.... Nowhere was this more the case — and nowhere do Michaels' *Laugh-In* roots show more baldly — than in the ever-proliferating number of catchphrases. As "Never mind" and "But noooo..." rang around the nation, it became clear how little had changed since "Very interesting..." and "You bet your sweet bippy" had been all the rage, and "Sock it to me" had helped Nixon into the White House.[3]

Moreover, by the late 1970s, the president most frequently attacked on *SNL* was NBC president Fred Silverman, whose programming debacles had seriously damaged NBC's critical credibility and, much worse, its ratings: NBC was now the dreaded third network behind CBS's socially-conscious programming and ABC's jiggle-shows. By 1980, *SNL*'s original "The Not Quite Ready for Prime Time Players" had already defected or departed for Hollywood. Most of the key writers, and even Michaels, planned to leave the show at the conclusion of the fifth season, and the jokes directed at Silverman evolved into a highly personal and rancorous feud, exemplified by Al Franken, not entirely joking, calling for Silverman to resign or be fired by NBC in a 1980 "Weekend Update" editorial. The final episode of the fifth season was very much intended as the farewell telecast of *SNL*, as far as the original participants were concerned.

However, with NBC desperate for any proven programming, *SNL* returned for a sixth season with a new producer (Jean Doumanian), a new writing staff, and an entirely new cast. The result was an unmitigated disaster and a major embarrassment for NBC. The show became an abysmal and unintentional self-parody, with the nadir occurring on February 21, 1981— the very night after Andy Kaufman's headlines-making *Fridays* appearance. Whether an inadvertent mistake (as later claimed) or a desperate attempt to upstage the national attention given to the previous night's *Fridays* telecast, Charles Rocket committed the ultimate television transgression and used the word "fuck" unbleeped. The stunt backfired severely, and in early March *SNL* was placed on hiatus; cancellation seemed all but certain. Instead, Doumanian and much of the cast were fired, and Dick Ebersol took over the show's production. A single show appeared in April; the most memorable moment was Al Franken's guest editorial on "Weekend Update" asking fans of the show to write NBC and "put *SNL* to sleep." Far from any self-criticism, *SNL* had finally resorted to jokes about its own rapid decline.

A fortuitous writer's strike suspended production of the show until October 1981 and the beginning of the 1981–2 season. The only remnants from the previous season were two performers who generated some popularity: Eddie

Murphy and Joe Piscopo. Murphy's popularity can arguably be credited for single-handedly saving *SNL* in the early 1980s, as the show essentially became "Eddie Murphy Live" (so much so that a 1983 *SNL* began with some cast members dressed as Murphy's personas — Gumby, Buckwheat, Velvet Jones — in a desperate attempt to get some airtime). Indeed, under Ebersol's autocratic control, *SNL* institutionalized conventional comedy-variety show strategies: building ratings through developing stars, and doing so by featuring the most popular cast members and their recurring stock characters (comedic personas or celebrity impersonations). There was a strict adherence to traditional sketch comedy focusing on sex jokes and topical political commentary that made *Laugh-In* appear positively profound. The inclusion of ever-increasing pre-filmed segments seemed intended to simply limit the time allotted to the frequently labored live comedy. The real "comedy-variety" element of *SNL* became the constant purges and personal changes owing to the resignations and firings of numerous cast and crew members.

Of course, if any single event signified the final transformation of *SNL* into a standardized and standardizing comedy-variety show, it was the on-air banishment of Andy Kaufman in 1982, whose increasingly confrontational and confusing brand of comedy was indeed "not funny anymore" in the context of the new *SNL*. Yet an equally significant change came with Eddie Murphy leaving the show in 1984. Ebersol responded by loading the new *SNL* with established comedy stars as the featured performers: Billy Crystal, Christopher Guest, Harry Shearer, and Martin Short. After yet another season of well-publicized disputes (Shearer abruptly quit the show in mid-season, Jim Belushi was fired and rehired during the season), Ebersol left as executive producer in 1985 when NBC vetoed his plan to convert *SNL* into a pre-recorded comedy-variety program.[4] *SNL* (again) avoided cancellation when Lorne Michaels returned to helm the show. However, Ebersol's reign demarcated the course of *SNL* has since unwaveringly pursued, becoming a space to introduce and promote performers as marketable Hollywood and prime-time comedy commodities rather than creating controversial television.[5] As Hendra simply put it, "For the successive waves of *SNL* cast members, the most important thing was not dissent but celebrity."[6]

Happy Days Are Here Again

As discussed in Chapter Six, the crisis in American television comedy in the late-1960s culminated in 1971 with *All in the Family* taking the domestic sitcom and infusing it with contemporary political debate and the serious, message-laden drama of Golden Age teleplays. By 1975, Norman Lear spun-off three more highly-successful sitcoms from his CBS–*All in the Family* universe: *Maude*, *Good Times*, and *The Jeffersons*.[7] These shows offered very attractive but extremely idealistic liberal-humanist sentiments and solutions to politics: injustice, racism, poverty, and war could be overcome by fairness, tolerance, a belief in the American Dream, and a moral and ethical approach to international relations.

The America envisioned by Lear's sitcoms briefly became a political reality with Jimmy Carter's presidency in 1976. However, as Carter quickly became perceived as an abject failure in domestic and foreign policy, by the late–1970s the American sitcom family of choice was no longer the cantankerous Bunkers but the tranquil Cunninghams of *Happy Days* (ABC, 1974–84). *Happy Days* owed its origins to the 1950s nostalgia wave inspired by the success of George Lucas's *American Graffiti* (1973): *Happy Days* star Ron Howard was featured in *American Graffiti*; another *American Graffiti* cast member, Cindy Williams, later starred on *Happy Days*' spin-off, *Laverne and Shirley* (ABC, 1976–83). However, the premiere of *Happy Days* also coincided with the tacit admission that the U.S. lost in Vietnam despite achieving "peace with honor," as well as the rampant abuses of presidential power detailed in the Watergate hearings — seeming proof positive that the Smothers Brothers had been right all along. If the decade between JFK's assassination and Nixon's resignation had been "a long, national nightmare," *Happy Days*, as its very title suggested, became television's lullaby to assuage the bad dream. Not only was *Happy Days* a 1950s-style sitcom, with all its ideological affirmations, it was actually set in the idyllic 1950s. If *Saturday Night Live* targeted young, disenfranchised audiences whose outlook was cynically shaped by Vietnam and Nixon, *Happy Days* offered the disillusioned Silent Majority a nostalgic retreat from political turmoil by recreating the 1950s in all its idealized history, which itself became a political reality in the 1980s with Ronald Reagan and the advent of neo-conservatism. As Lear's CBS liberal sitcoms faded into political exhaustion during the Reagan administration, two NBC sitcoms defined the neo-conservative era. *Family Ties* (1982–9) turned *All in the Family* on its head by transforming the old-fashioned Bunkers into the ex–flower children Keatons — both couples equally behind their respective times, and the voice of political credibility going from hippie Mike Stivic to Young Republican Alex P. Keaton (Michael J. Fox). *The Cosby Show* (1984–92) presented an almost utopian world of upper middle-class affluence whose patriarch was a prosperous, white-collar, African American professional: the urbane, witty, all-knowing Dr. Cliff Huxtable (Bill Cosby) as the antithesis of Archie Bunker and George Jefferson. It is in this context that *The Simpsons* emerged to "revolutionize" the domestic sitcom in 1989.

CHAPTER 10

Fair and Balanced Satire: Against *The Simpsons*

> Postmodernism ... weird for the sake of weird.
> — Moe Szyslack, in "Homer the Mo"

A Franchise Is Born

In 1985, Rupert Murdoch's News Corporation bought 20th Century–Fox, and soon after obtained Metromedia, the media conglomerate formed out of the demise of the Dumont network in 1954, acquiring ownership of WNEW (now WNYW) in New York City and other Metromedia stations such as KTTW in Los Angeles and WFLD in Chicago. By purchasing a movie studio to produce shows and TV stations in key market cities to broadcast them, Murdoch laid the groundwork for FOX Broadcasting Corporation, the first attempt at a fourth TV network since the end of Dumont left CBS, NBC, and ABC as the triumvirate of network television. Numerous independent stations became FOX affiliates, and in 1986 *The Late Show Starring Joan Rivers*, a weeknight talk show, was the premiere show of the nascent network. On Sunday, April 5, 1987, FOX network began primetime broadcasts with two comedies. One was *Married with Children*, which, in retrospect, was arguably a more confrontational effort to demolish the sitcom than *The Simpsons*. It was also the show that put FOX on the TV map, the claims of FOX and *The Simpsons* to the contrary. By the time *The Simpsons* premiered in December 1989, *MWC* had garnered national attention for its censorship disputes with FOX, critical vilification as the epitome of "Trash TV," and become the target of a national campaign to have the show cancelled, lead by Michigan housewife Terry Rakolta, who was invited onto ABC's *Nightline* to denounce *MWC* in March 1989. Ratings for *MWC* soared.

The other inaugural show was *The Tracy Ullman Show* (1987–90), a sketch comedy show starring the British actress-singer. It included short, crudely-done animated segments featuring a family named "Simpson," and their popularity prompted FOX to spin-off "The Simpsons" into their own half-hour animated sitcom.[1] *The Simpsons* has since become the longest running sitcom in television history, and almost universally canonized by critics and audiences for redefining the genre through its abundant cultural references and sharp social commentary. In short, if *All in the Family* invented the *political sitcom*, *The Simpsons* invented the *postmodern sitcom*. When then–President George H.W. Bush singled out *The Simpsons* for criticism in 1992, complaining in a speech to religious broadcasters that American TV needed more families like the Waltons and not the Simpsons, the show could not have asked for better anti–Establishment credentials. However, it is less certain to what extent *The Simpsons* is—or ever was—anti–Establishment, let alone subversive.

Simpsons, Meet the Simpsons...

The Simpsons creator Matt Groening cited *Green Acres* as a key influence: "The bizarre web of ridiculousness just under the surface of normalcy is what *The Simpsons* and *Green Acres* have in common."[2] The problem with Groening's comparison is that his formula needs to be reversed to apply to *Green Acres*, which presents a bizarre web of normalcy just under the surface of ridiculousness. As discussed in Chapter Five, *Green Acres* depicts a fundamentally "always-already" absurd world that becomes even more humorous and horrifying because of the kernel of distorted and disturbing reality that lies underneath—a critique of America that satirized the Whole as a convoluted apparatus.[3] *The Simpsons* is a critique of Americans that satirizes the parts of the Whole—the silly inhabitants who are the ridiculous parts underneath the surface of normalcy and constructs of American life (specifically, work and family). In this way, despite its postmodern sheen of cultural literacy and ostensibly liberal social commentary, at its core *The Simpsons* is as ideologically consistent as it is contrary to any domestic sitcom.

The lineage of *The Simpsons* is not *Green Acres*, nor even another show Groening has cited as a major influence, *Rocky and Bullwinkle* (which routinely referenced pop-culture with as much, if not more, verve and wit than any postmodern comedy), but the seminal Hanna-Barbera cartoon sitcoms *The Flintstones* (ABC, 1960–6) and *The Jetsons* (ABC, 1962–4; CBS, 1964–5).

The Flintstones was itself a prehistoric parody of *The Honeymooners* (so much so that Jackie Gleason contemplated suing Hanna-Barbera Productions), with the *noir* angst and righteous anger of Ralph Kramden converted into colorful animation and the voluminous ignorance of Fred Flintstone (the American worker as a cartoon caveman in a prehistoric era). Conversely, *The Jetsons* was derived from Chick Young's *Blondie*; and "the pastoral world of primal innocence from which America had clearly graduated" that McLuhan abhorred in *Blondie* was still thriving in *The Jetsons'* middle-class future of gizmos and robots. The drudgery of work for George Jetson was simply showing up and sitting behind his desk until he could go home. It was not coincidental that Fred Flintstone's collar was *blue* and George Jeston's was *white*.

In this sense, Homer J. Simpson is the missing link in the evolution between Hanna-Barbera's working-class caveman of the outdated past and the corporate man of the whiz-bang future in present-day Springfield, U.S.A. (a parodic reference to the locale of *Father Knows Best*). Like Fred Flintstone, Homer personifies the stereotype of loud, working-class ignorance; like George Jetson, Homer's middle-class status is effortlessly attained in the miracle of the corporation and a desk job where the most exertion required to earn a living is eating a donut, taking a nap, and preventing the Springfield nuclear powerplant from exploding (frequently *despite* his efforts, not because of them). In this context, *The Simpsons* is not simply "a bona fide satire of middle-class family life,"[4] it is also a bona fide satire of the working-class, with Homer Simpson being the American middle-class "other" because he has yet to evolve from the proletariat-as-primate to Atomic Age (post)modern man.

Class and work becomes a central issue in "Last Exit to Springfield" (1993), when Homer is made leader of the powerplant union and a strike ensues. At the conclusion, the union members circle in solidarity and Lisa Simpson (of course) performs a protest folk-song. Mr. Burns watches from the balcony of his office and concedes defeat. Yet the victory of the workers is not conveyed by referencing a film such as Eisenstein's *Strike*, which, if nothing else, would have been an appropriate and even high-brow cultural reference. Instead, the ending is taken from Dr. Seuss's *How the Grinch Stole Christmas*, the only thing missing being the actual moment Mr. Burns' heart grew three sizes that day. Subsequently, when Mr. Burns gives in to union demands on the condition Homer resigns, Homer does the Curley Howard whirling dervish dance on the floor in celebration while Burns ruefully mutters he may have severely overestimated Homer as an adversary. The hidden message is that if Mr. Burns had not been overcome by sentimentality and successfully ascertained the true inferiority of his opponent, the strike could have successfully been squashed.[5] In this way, the episode does end with a backhanded homage to Eisenstein of sorts — an associative montage of Homer announcing they are going back to work, the lights in Springfield coming back on at the local strip clubs, and a company that manufactures "fake vomit" back in operation, with its product splattering onto the conveyor belt. The metaphorical reading: now the workers have ended the strike, Springfield's economy is back at work because the nudie-bars are up and running and "the pukes" have returned to the assembly line.

Whereas *The Honeymooners* was tragicomedy about the betrayal of the American Dream, *The Simpsons* concentrates on satirical jibes at consumerism, corporations, and the Protestant work ethic. The difficulty arises because a crucial element in the satire is employing the stereotype of the slothful, stupid American worker, and manifesting the hidden message that even the most inept of Americans — Homer Simpson — can effortlessly attain the American Dream despite himself. In "Homer's Enemy" (1997), the haughty "self-made man" Frank Grimes is quite effectively satirized, but only through his realization that Homer's endearing incompetence has become its own reward at home and at work. In addition to being a dreadful but adored husband and father, and being gainfully employed, in various episodes Homer has won a Grammy, voyaged into space with NASA, become a successful modern artist and talk show host, routinely traveled the world, and cavorted with numerous celebrities. If Arnold Ziffel's successes in the arts and sciences are absurd on *Green Acres* because he is, after all, a pig, Homer's achievements are equally absurd because they fall outside his working-class limitations — intelligence and motivation.

Beyond class structures, the sitcom family stereotypes are also defended as much as satirized on *The Simpsons*: the blundering but loveable dad, the haggard but dutiful mom, the precocious children. While Marge Simpson is well aware that she is not merely underappreciated but generally exploited in the nuclear family arrangement, she steadfastly accepts and even determinedly clings to her domestic sitcom role as selfless wife and mother. The laziness, immaturity, and self-centeredness of Bart Simpson (the popular school rebel) are celebrated, while the creativity, intellectualism, and social activism of Lisa Simpson (the unpopular school nerd) become an object of frequent scorn (which will be addressed further shortly). In these respects, there is a sense of wishful reading when Marc wrote in 1997: "If Marge is trapped in a life designated either by or for Phyllis Schlafly, there is at least hope that Lisa might be heir to Camilla Paglia."[6] Any such hopes were dashed by the episode "Bart to the Future" (2000), where, as adults, Bart becomes a slacker rock musician and Lisa "the first straight woman president" of the U.S., which is bankrupt and entirely dependent on foreign investors who are demanding payment. Lisa, having proved incapable of running the country thorough intellectual liberal-feminism, must call on her savvy-smart brother to save the day — and the country. Or, as Nelson Muntz might say: "A woman president — HA HA!"

Biting the FOX That Feeds It?

One reason *The Simpsons* is perceived as subversive comedy is the frequent ripostes directed at FOX. However, *The Simpsons* has certainly not experienced a relationship rivaling the contentiousness that developed between FOX and shows such as *MWC* and *Arrested Development*. *MWC*'s notorious "No Pod to Peas In" (1994) featured a "FOX viewing positions" gag where the Bundys pose like contortionists in the living room pointing foil and antennas in various directions to receive Fox on their local UHF channel. FOX was livid at the joke and initially refused to air the episode, although it can be assumed the network displeasure sprang from the fact that "No Pod to Peas In" was about FOX making a sitcom based on the Bundys — "Peas in a Pod" — that is cancelled after one episode because, as Peg Bundy (Katy Segal) explained, "Some housewife in Michigan didn't like it." Yet, in championing *The Simpsons* over *MWC*, Marc claimed the failure of *MWC* was not the highly problematic sexism and misogyny, but its inability to overcome "self-reflexive parody ... the *self-congratulatory, more irreverent-than-thou, tone* makes it difficult to enjoy."[7] The problem is not so much Marc's assessment of *MWC*, although *MWC*'s own abrasive and seemingly incompatible marriage of Brecht and burlesque was consciously intended to make the show difficult to enjoy as sitcom entrainment. Rather, this criticism of *MWC* is most applicable to *The Simpsons*, especially regarding *The Simpsons* and any "oppositional" relationship to FOX.

"Missionary: Impossible" (2000) ends with Betty White and FOX president Rupert Murdoch hosting a telethon to raise money for FOX (White did her own voice, Murdoch did not).[8] Accompanied by a *Family Guy* ad, White asks, "If you don't want to see crude, low-brow programming disappear from the air, call now!"[9] Murdoch answers the phone and elatedly proclaims, "Ten thousand dollars! We're saved!" The shot cuts to Bart Simpson hanging up the phone and proudly looking at the camera: "Wouldn't be the first time." However, Bart's aside is not a sardonic rejoinder against FOX programming, but the restating of a public perception FOX is more than happy to endorse: that rise of FOX as a viable fourth network was synonymous with the critically-acclaimed and financially profitable *The Simpsons*, and not the controversies and ratings initially generated by *MWC's* "trash–TV." Echoing these sentiments in 1996, Matthew P. McAllister argued:

> *The Simpsons* was a watershed program in the establishment of FOX.... The FOX program most consistently praised by critics ... [*The Simpsons*] signaled FOX's staying power to the rest of the industry, and for viewers was a powerful illustration of the innovative nature of FOX programming when compared to the conventional TV fare.[10]

In fact, the "watershed" that ultimately established FOX as the legitimate fourth network was its acquisition of NFL broadcasting rights in 1994. Nevertheless, *The Simpsons* served a vital function for FOX that *MWC* did not in the early–1990s. Not only providing critical respectability to FOX comedy as much as commercial viability and public attention, *The Simpsons* manufactured the public perception that FOX was the network of groundbreaking TV comedy, and even the network of subversive, anti–Establishment comedy (certainly, using "FOX" and "anti–Establishment" in the same sentence in 2006 amounts to being an absurdist *non sequitur*). In this respect, Bart's comment is also self-congratulatory to the extent it can maintain the idea *The Simpsons* single-handedly "saved" FOX from becoming a cultural wasteland with its singular, intellectually superior postmodern approach to comedy (versus the rest of FOX's programming history of "crude, low-brow comedy," from *MWC* to *Family Guy*).

As FOX's conservatism has become increasingly overt in the 21st century, along with *The Simpsons* becoming nothing short of an American cultural institution, the relationship between *The Simpsons* and FOX has proven more compatible than hostile. As Herbert Marcuse noted, one problem of cultural opposition is its tendency to be co-opted into cultural commodities: "[They] suffer the fate of being absorbed by what they refute. As modern classics, the avant-garde and the beatniks share in their function of *entertaining without endangering*."[11] As discussed earlier, Andy Kaufman's refusal to engage in "entertaining without endangering" is precisely what curtailed his TV career. On the other hand, *The Simpsons* has become to FOX what Bart Simpson has become to Principal Skinner: the designated nuisance who supplies periodic but manageable defiance, but will also work with his adversary when mutually advantageous for both parties. For instance, *The Simpsons* has done two football-themed episodes; despite their superficially sardonic overtones, they were specifically designed to compliment and coincide with FOX broadcasts of the Super Bowl (1999's "Sunday, Cruddy Sunday" and 2005's "Homer and Ned's Hail Mary Pass"). When Springfield Elementary staged a "Li'l Starmaker" contest in "A Star Is Torn" (2005), the episode amounted to a half-hour promotion — rather than satire — of *American Idol* (the reigning *AI* winner, Fantasia Barrino, was the guest star on the episode). "Don't Fear the Roofer" (2005), guest-starring Ray Romano, was blatant cross-promotion for CBS's *Everybody Loves Raymond* as it completed its final season (Mike Scully was a producer on both shows at the time). Even the jokes about the conservative bias of FOX News fall flat as criticism because they merely point out what FOX News is more than willing to concede. In short, *The Simpsons* might bark, but does not bite.

Parody, Pastiche, Politics

In 1996, David Kemp hailed *The Simpsons* as "the only consistently funny, *constantly smart* source of American political humor in American mainstream culture — the only one out there with ... *intellectual charge*."[12] However, especially in the decade since Kemp's lofty appraisal, *The Simpsons* offers two critical problems. One is that the "intellectual charge" Kemp championed in *The Simpsons* is the antithesis of the shock effect — be it Artaud's dissociative shock, Benjamin's shock of distraction, Brecht's estrangement effect, Kluge's theory of montage and *phantasie*, or even Eisenstein's associative shock. Rather, the intellectual charge of *The Simpsons* is the cat-and-mouse game of cultural literacy between the show and audience, where well-placed references to George Burns, George W. Bush, George Eliot, or *George of the Jungle* can appear with equal probability. If, as Jameson claimed, a key failing of postmodernism has been the conversion of parody into pastiche ("parody amputated of the satiric impulse"), the postmodern comedy approach pioneered by *The Simpsons* has made the cultural reference an *end*— the joke in and of itself.

As examples, one of the foremost practitioners of postmodern comedy, *Late Night with Conan O'Brien* (NBC, 1993–), featured a short, self-explanatory segment titled "Cactus Playing Billy Joel's 'We Didn't Start the Fire' on Flute." One can easily imagine a cactus playing flute for a few seconds as a typical Ernie Kovacs blackout sight-gag. With O'Brien, the surreal humor inherent in "Cactus Playing Flute" is reduced to postmodern comedy because what makes "Cactus Playing Flute" funny is that it is playing a Billy Joel tune, and any pop-song could have sufficed; the pop-culture reference is the punchline and gives it "meaning."[13] A cactus simply playing the flute is what becomes "weird for the sake of weird"— or stupid. The failure of another postmodern TV comedy, *Family Guy*, was expressed no better than in the *South Park* episode "Cartoon Wars" (2006). The *Family Guy* writing staff is depicted as manatees in an aquarium, and a FOX executive explains that the manatees take "'idea balls,' each with a noun, verb, or pop-culture reference, and put it in the 'joke combine'": a sorter where the randomly selected idea balls are arranged into the show's sketches. Tzara posited the way to write a Dadaist poem was to cut the words out of a newspaper, put them in a bag, and pull them out and copy them to paper: a demonstration of the uselessness of art, culture, and language. *Family Guy*'s merger of postmodern vanity and burlesque mentality posits that pulling incessant pop-culture references seemingly out of a bag (or from a "joke combine"), combined with a surplus of coarse comedy (mostly directed at women, gays, and minorities in general), not only produces consistently insightful comedy and social criticism, but can somehow achieve the "moral shock effect" of Dada.

The problem of pastiche is directly related to the problem of *The Simpsons* and its political humor. The plethora of references become infused with class, ethnic, racial, and sexual stereotypes which are perpetuated as much as satirized by depicting them as cute, cartoon caricatures and investing them with postmodern panache. Bart's ostensibly subversive put-down that closes "Missionary Impossible," along with the episode's numerous PBS references and Fox in-jokes, masks what can be seen as a fairly racist episode concerning Homer's comical adventures as a missionary enlightening stereotypical Third World savages who are even more ignorant than him. This ethnocentric attitude permeates *The Simpsons*, and is especially pronounced in its periodic "vacation" episodes: Australia, China, Japan, South America, Africa, India, and various European countries have been visited and mocked accordingly.[14] Marc argued that one aspect of *The Simpsons*' political satire is that "The middle-class Americans of Springfield are revealed as a population of 'dim sheep' who are prone to jingoism [and] xenophobia."[15] As noted, a problem with Marc's assessment of *The Simpsons* is that the middle-class Americans of Springfield are *working-class* stereotypes; Moe, Lenny, Carl, Barney, Marge's sisters, Groundskeeper Willie, and (obviously) Cletus, the Slack-Jawed Yokel are not the petit bourgeoisie, but the lumpenproletariot. Consequently, the erudite audience is given the luxury to indulge in jingoism and xenophobia while superficially mocking the "dim sheep" who express those ideas. In other words, the viewer can laugh at Homer's Ugly American stereotype, and also laugh at the non–American "others" and stereotypes of their tacky cultures: India as a collection of Bollywood references, Latin America a collection of Univision and Telemundo references, or Japan a collection of Godzilla and *manga* references.

Closer to home, Springfield's prominent African American, Dr. Julius Hibbard, is a parody of Bill Cosby's Cliff Huxtable character, added to the cast when *The Simpsons* moved to Thursdays in 1990 to compete head-to-head with *The Cosby Show*. While an unusually sardonic swipe at TV network relations, as far as any commentary on race relations, Hibbard owns a poodle named "Rosa Barks," and in various flashbacks has the "appropriate" hairdo of the era (an Afro, dreadlocks, a Mr. T. Mohawk). The East Indian convenience-store clerk Apu is a stereotype deemed satire because the learned audience member realizes it is referenced from Satyajit Ray's "Apu Trilogy." Waylon Smithers is Springfield's resident, stereotypical homosexual who loves musicals, collects "Malibu Stacy" dolls, and has quietly and unobjectionably stayed in the Springfield closet for almost two decades (although his sexual orientation is well-known to viewers). When *The Simpsons* tackled same-sex marriage in the episode "There's Something About Marrying" (2005, the only *Simpsons* episode given a "viewer discretion advised" disclaimer), the promos strongly hinted that Smithers might finally come out, or even that Lenny and Carl might be revealed to be more than just drinking buddies. Ultimately, it was Marge's mannish and man-hating sister Patti who revealed she was gay and was left at the altar when her future wife turned out to be a man posing as a woman so he could compete in the Ladies Professional Golf Association.[16] Rather than adding a same-sex couple, *The Simpsons* not only dodged the issue, but adroitly added a lesbian stereotype to its Springfield ranks in the process.

Most of all, if Lisa Sampson was once the show's heroic underdog and liberal conscience, she has increasingly become the character open to the most criticism. 1991's "Mr. Lisa Goes to Washington" was not so much a parody as homage to Frank Capra's *Mr. Smith Goes to Washington* (1939). Winning an essay writing contest extolling the American Way, she wins a trip to Washington DC, only to be dismayed by the workings of Congress. She instead presents an essay revealing the corrupt politicians, who are brought to justice and reaffirms her faith in America. The episode is ideologically consistent with Capra, whose Mr. Smith (Jimmy Stewart) arrives in Washington an idealistic liberal and through tenacious fighting proves the American political system can work. Lisa's activism is still equated with conscientious crusading. In "Lisa the Simpson" (1997), Lisa becomes despondent when she believes she has inherited the "Simpsons gene" that makes all Simpsons inevitably stupid, but becomes ecstatic when she learns the Simpson gene only affects men, and Simpson women have become successful professionals (doctors, lawyers, corporate executives). The feminist message notwithstanding, in one scene Lisa imagines her inevitable fate as becoming an ignorant, lazy, overweight housewife living in a trailer park (thus, even the antithesis of her mother — a common-sense, diligent, slim housewife in the suburbs). The overt message of gender equality is underscored by a hidden message of class inequality.

By 2006, Lisa's status on *The Simpsons* has become decidedly different. In "The Monkey Suit," Ned Flanders successfully pushes for creationism to be taught in Springfield Elementary, and Lisa files a lawsuit. However, the crux of the episode is not to debate the issue of "church vs. state" but a lengthy parody of *Inherit the Wind* (1960, dir. Stanly Kramer), a chronicle of the 1925 "Scopes Monkey Trial" when a teacher was prosecuted for teaching evolution in a public school. While Kramer's film was unabashedly liberal in its stance, *The Simpsons* is surreptitiously conservative in its parody. At the end of the episode, and despite her victory in court, Lisa — the know-it-all secular-progressive — realizes *she* has been the one being disrespectful and intolerant of Ned's sincere if strident fundamentalist Christianity. Ned graciously accepts her apology and treats her to a hot-fudge "fundae." "G.I

10. Fair and Balanced Satire: Against The Simpsons 209

(Annoyed Grunt)" was a satire on the ineffectiveness of the U.S. military in Iraq, although a "safe" satire which aired the weekend after the 2006 election — by which time American public opinion had decidedly soured on Iraq (in contrast to *South Park*'s treatment of the issue, as will be discussed next chapter, in the episode "I'm a Little Bit Country," which premiered mere weeks after the Iraq invasion and attacked the logic, or illogic, of *all* sides of the debate). The overt liberal slant notwithstanding, there is the obligatory moment of "Lisa-bashing" when the gung-ho military commander running roughshod over Springfield is tortured by Homer with an air horn until he surrenders. When Lisa begins pontificating on the historical lessons of Vietnam, the Army officer pleads with Homer for more air horn, who politely complies. Physical torture becomes more preferable to the torture of a liberal lecture.

In "Girls Just Want to Have Sums," Lisa is delighted to learn that the school will be divided into same-sex classrooms to make education more equitable for girls. However, she is bitterly disappointed when the boys are taught math the old-fashioned, nard-nosed way and the girls taught through progressive-feminist methods: "How does math make you *feel?*" Resorting to masquerading as a boy to gain access to their superior math class (with the help of Bart), Lisa learns boys, not girls, are really the ones who have it harder in the rough and tumble world of public school. When Lisa wins the math award at the end of the episode, she claims it is proof that girls are as smart as boys; Bart responds, quite non-ironically, that she won because she "learned to think like a boy." As Bart and Lisa argue, Principal Skinner announces there is another award: Martin Prince, the school's resident male intellectual powerhouse, has won the music award for "best flutist." Dressed in Shakespearean garb, his acceptance speech quotes lyrics from progressive-rock band Jethro Tull's "Thick as a Brick" (so the reference is not too obscure, the credits close over an excerpt from the song). The hidden message is manifest *through* the pop-culture reference. The progressive–rock genre was (and is) almost uniformly castigated by rock critics as effete and pretentious — in short, the musical domain of "art-fags." Jethro Tull, versus an equally well-known and hipper progressive-rock band such as King Crimson, is referenced because the flute was a staple of Jethro Tull's sound, and can incorporate the common stereotype of the flute as a girl's instrument.[17] While always a wimpy nerd (a particularly favored *Simpsons* stereotype), by excelling in math and science Martin maintained a semblance of masculinity and some social usefulness. Now a preening artiste instead of a scientific wunderkind, both his academic skills and any remnants of masculinity are sabotaged by progressive education and poisoned by the school's music and drama programs: the dubious triumph of a liberal arts education.

This is not to criticize *The Simpsons* simply on the basis of politics. It is to criticize *The Simpsons* for having much in common with FOX programming and politics while self-consciously (and, at times, condescendingly) separating itself from them to maintain subversive credibility. This was no more apparent than in "This Is Your Wife" (2006). The episode began with numerous in-jokes and commentary on the dearth of FOX programming. Homer and Marge participate in a FOX reality show, "Mother Flippers," with a British couple, Charles and Verity Heathbar. The hidden messages become positively overt over the course of the episode when Marge's docile, supportive approach to being a wife empowers the browbeaten, milquetoast Charles to seek a divorce from Verity, the dour, pompous, emasculating shrew of an intellectual woman now tormenting Homer. However, the issue becomes moot when Verity informs Charles she is leaving him because she found true love in Springfield — with local lesbian Patti.

In this context, the occasional jokes directed at specific conservative targets (Ned Flanders, Mr. Burns, the Bush administration, FOX News) conceal the fact that *The Simpsons* (unlike *Green Acres*, or, as will be discussed, *South Park*) does not critique the ideological tenets behind the specific political issues, but often reinforces them. On *The Simpsons*, the American Dream can be realized by any dullard, the traditional family and gender roles and stereotypes are routinely stabilized, and Springfield's "others" can be laughed at as offensively inoffensive cartoon stereotypes. Indeed, *The Simpsons* has developed an increasingly formulaic relationship with the audience who can *laugh with* the myriad cultural references and/or *laugh at* the dumb citizens of Springfield.[18] This formula becomes glaringly manifest with *Family Guy* and *American Dad* (FOX, 2005–), where any liberal satire can be completely negated by the capacity of the shows to be read as "comical" exercises in jingoism, racism, sexism, and homophobia that become obscured by the slew of pop-culture references.

The myth of satire and comedy is that it is inherently subversive, oppositional, or anti–Establishment. However, and intentionally or not, satire and comedy can very much work to support rather than oppose the *status quo*. As Adorno noted:

> He who has laughter on his side needs no proof. Historically, therefore, satire has for thousands of years, up to Voltaire's age, preferred to side with the party which could be relied on, with authority. Usually it acted on behalf of the older strata ... which sought to impose their traditionalism with enlightened means.... For this reason, what was once a deft rapier appears to later generations as a decidedly cumbersome cudgel.[19]

In short, the issue becomes the extent that *The Simpsons* now sides with authority (read: FOX), the extent it masks a traditional world-view with postmodern flair, and the extent its former rapier wit has become cudgel-like comedy. If *The Simpsons* has saved FOX more than once, its greatest coup has been repackaging the Golden Age domestic sitcoms and dominant ideology into the fair and balanced satire of postmodern sitcoms even liberal intellectuals can appreciate.

Chapter 11

Comedy Is Not Pretty: In Praise of *South Park*

> We must make reason shit.[1]
> —Antonin Artaud

A Sore Sight for Eyes

If there is any vestige of avant-garde comedy in current American television, it is *South Park* and its unholy convergence of *Peanuts*, the Marquis de Sade, and Jarry's *Ubu* plays. *South Park* is an intentionally vulgar comedy in *both* form and content, initially done with construction paper cut-outs and stop-motion animation — the technique used by Terry Gilliam for his Max Ernst collage-influenced animated segments on *Monty Python's Flying Circus* (*South Park* creators Trey Parker and Matt Stone cite *Monty Python* as a primary influence). The production schedule soon necessitated a changeover to computer animation, and while technological developments have smoothed out the rough edges since the show's debut on Comedy Central in 1997, *South Park* has strived to retain its original, primitive style. The characters and backgrounds are drawn at a grade-school level, appropriate in that the show revolves around the misadventures of elementary school students Stan Marsh and Kyle Broflovski (the Charlie Brown and Linus Van Pelt of the show); the town's resident "fat, little, foul-mouthed racist" Eric Cartman (Lucy Van Pelt by way of Archie Bunker — or Pere Ubu); and Kenny McKormick, who speaks in high-pitched gibberish that the characters effortlessly interpret (*South Park*'s idea of a running joke in the early seasons was Kenny being horribly killed at some point in an episode). One of the more sacred elements of art (and especially the sitcom) — the privileged point of view of the child — is immediately satirized. The boys of *South Park* do not live in innocent wonder and provide precocious observation; they are infused with world-weary cynicism and react with foul-mouthed candor.

As well as the rudimentary drawings and clunky animation, *South Park* exacerbates visual incongruities and distorts any pseudo-realism by incorporating photographs, stock footage, found footage, and news footage — either "as is" or modified. The sexually-knowledgeable Kenny has a *Sports Illustrated* swimsuit model poster in his bedroom; the mentally fragile Butters has a photographic reproduction of Munch's *The Scream*. Celebrities and historical figures are occasionally depicted by using cut-out photographs of their heads on cartoon bodies. In "Tom's Rhinoplasty" (1998), Mr. Garrison gets a nose job that makes him look like David Hasselhoff— courtesy of photographs of Hasselhoff's head. In "Cartoon Wars" (2006), following a fictitious *Family Guy* controversy for showing the image of Mohammed, news videotape of Osama bin Laden taken from Al-Jazeera with English subtitles translate: "[he] has a real problem with *Family Guy* ... the jokes never follow from the premise."

When other shows or genres are parodied, *South Park* replicates their visual style of animation as much as content (*The Simpsons* and *Family Guy* have themselves been satirized). "Osama bin Ladin Wears Farty Pants" (2001), which first aired less than a month after 9/11, featured an epic battle between Cartman and bin Laden directly parodying World War II–era Warner Brothers cartoons, and which contained enough textual ammunition to be read as vehemently pro-war and anti-war at the same time. "Good Times with Weapons" (2004), featuring misadventures with illegally bought martial arts weapons, contained extended sequences of the kids "playing ninjas," archly parodying Japanese animation (of course, Butters loses an eye). Video game technology is also used for purposes of parody. In "Red Hot Catholic Love" (2002), Father Maxi's *Raiders of the Lost Ark*–like dash through the forbidden recesses of the Vatican was depicted by animation identical to the 1980s video game *Pitfall*. "Make Love, Not Warcraft" (2006), which could also be read as either a defense or criticism of "stay the course" policies in Iraq, extensively replicated the internet fantasy game *World of Warcraft*.[2] CGI effects are also used — mostly to insert photographic images of explosions and flames over the course of frequent destruction of cartoon cities. Live-action segments have also been included; in "Quest for Ratings" (2004), the boys' school news program is routinely beaten by another student's show, "Animals Close-Up with a Wide-Angle Lens," which, of course, is montages of actual close-ups of dogs and cats with a wide-angle lens set to the signature music from *The Benny Hill Show*.

214   Part Five. Is Avant-Garde Television Still Possible?

"Hello children!" Chef, Kenny, Kyle, Stan, and Eric Cartman of *South Park*; note the "MILK IS YUMMY" lunchroom poster (Comedy Central/Photofest).

South Park has further incorporated jokes specifically designed to play on the medium of TV, such as live-action commercial parodies that sometimes initially seem quite authentic. In "Towelie" (2001), the title character is a pot-smoking, genetically engineered "smart towel" designed for super absorbency by the Military-Industrial Complex which Cartman referred to as "the worst character ever" at the end of the episode. Parodying K-Tel commercials from the 1970s, a Comedy Central "commercial" for Towelie T-shirts and a full-sized Towelie towel with a squeezable corner that uttered his catchphrase — "Wanna get high?" — appeared when the episode went to it its first advertising break (the "555" phone prefix and disclaimer "Towel not included" at the end were the only clues that the commercial was a put-on, although by 2007 Comedy Central began marketing actual "Towelie Spring Break" towels). When *South Park* entered syndicated markets in 2005, episodes necessarily had to be edited. In "Red Hot Catholic Love," the child molestation main plot is underscored, for good measure, by a subplot where Cartman devises a way to insert food anally and defecate out his mouth. In "Fat Camp" (2000), Kenny, after being bribed by his classmates to eat the heart of a manatee dissected in science class, becomes violently ill on the playground — and is paid by his classmates to eat his own vomit. In the syndicated versions, these sequences were replaced by disclaimers, accompanied by easy-listening jazz, informing the viewer that the scenes where "Cartman craps out of his mouth" or "Kenny eats his own puke" were "removed for your protection."[3]

"Friendly Faces Everywhere...."

By standards of network TV animation, *South Park*'s "anti-animation" appears absolutely amateurish yet outrageously experimental: the animated sitcom done through a *détournement* of children's drawings, collage, kitsch, photography, Pop Art, and underground comics. Between its disjointed, trashy form and deliberately tasteless content, *South Park* could be placed in the realm of Dada; however, the dehumanized characters and their ridiculous situations push the show into vile Absurdism. Much like Jarry specifically intended with *Ubu roi*, *South Park* strives to make its characters and their endeavors "wretched and repugnant." This is not to say that *South Park* is incapable of moments of pathos, but it generates them through absurd tragicomedy (especially in comparison to *The Simpsons*' frequent forays into traditional sitcom sentimentality in conflict resolution).[4] In "Kenny Dies" (2001), Stan is unable to come to terms with Kenny's impending death until Chef explains that bad things happen because God enjoys making and watching people suffer; he returns to Hell's Pass Hospital where Kenny has died during his absence. Dejectedly asking Kyle if Kenny had any last words, Kyle answers: "Yes: 'Where's Stan?'"[5]

Nevertheless, to describe *South Park*'s residents and frequent inclusions of actual people as cartoon caricatures is an understatement (as the show's opening disclaimer states, "All characters and events — even those based on real people — are entirely fictional"). For the most part, they are a parade of crude, and crudely-rendered, stereotypes and clichés: ineffective fathers, overprotective mothers, promiscuous spouses, sanctimonious Catholics, uptight Protestants, neurotic Jews, eternally-optimistic Mormons, hot-tempered rednecks, ignorant white-trash, the resentful working-class, the apathetic middle-class, the arrogant upper-class, the senile elderly, the misshapen handicapped, imbecile cops, incompetent educators, opportunistic politicians, judgmental activists, self-important journalists, and vacuous celebrities who are everything reported about them in the tabloids. In this sense, especially given the criticism directed at *The Simpsons* and *Family Guy* in the previous chapter, *South Park*'s own depiction of minorities and "others" need be addressed. At best, the term "politically incorrect" has been used in a non-pejorative way; at worst, *South Park* has been seen as patently racist and homophobic. While *South Park* undeniably features a wealth of offensive stereotypes, they are so blatantly exaggerated and grotesquely distorted that they become *overdetermined* stereotypes. In his study of *Li'l Abner*, Arthur Asa Berger, citing Orrin E. Klapp, suggests there is "personal mockery [and] type mockery ... 'the first punished a person for failure to live up to the norm but the second punishes a *norm* ... that is, throws into question an ideal, a role, or even an entire structure.'"[6] This distinction is crucial in comparing *The Simpsons* and especially *Family Guy*, which specialize in "personal mockery" of those outside the norm as stereotypical caricatures (as "an other"), to the "type mockery" of *South Park*, which mocks and exposes the reductive nature and social function of the stereotype by pushing it into the realm of the Grotesque (which is not to overlook *South Park*'s extremely personal attacks when satirizing actual people).[7]

Whereas *The Simpsons* has "Dr. Hibbard" and *Family Guy* offers "Cleveland Brown," the only African American child in *South Park* is named "Token Black," and his is the only affluent family on *South Park*: a parody of *The Cosby Show*'s ideological message of an America full of equal opportunity, and free of class and racial friction.[8] The only other African American citizen on *South Park* was Chef (voiced by Isaac Hayes from 1997 to 2006).[9] Despite his tendency to break into soul-funk songs about "sweet lovemaking" rather than offer homespun wisdom, Chef was frequently the individual the boys sought for advice, and the closest *South Park* had to a rural sitcom–style sensible pillar of the community. In contrast to *The Simpsons* and its "don't ask, don't tell" approach to homosexuality with Waylon Smithers, *South Park*'s openly gay characters have included Big Gay Al (the flaming homosexual stereotype) and Mr. Slave (the leather-clad homosexual stereotype). The virulently homophobic Mr. Garrison (also a racist and fundamentalist Christian) eventually acknowledged his homosexuality—to the surprise of absolutely no one in town. He subsequently had a sex-change operation and later became the town's loose woman and leading opponent of same-sex marriage before becoming a lesbian.

In *South Park*'s absurdist world, defined by its inhabitant's rampant narrow-mindedness, the vulgar stereotype logically becomes the *status quo*. However, this is not to argue that *South Park* becomes immune to the same problems of satire inherent in *All in the Family*, *The Simpsons*, *Family Guy*, and even Dave Chappelle's decision to scrap *Chappelle's Show* (Comedy Central, 2003–5). Chappelle quit the show, in part, due to his growing concern that the show was inadvertently reinforcing rather than satirizing racial stereotypes—that people were starting to laugh at the stereotype "as-is" rather than laughing with the satire.[10] Even the grotesque stereotype can be used for baldly reactionary purposes (the depiction of Jews in Nazi propaganda, or Asians in American World War II–era cartoons). In other words, *South Park*'s *type* mockery is not impervious to being read as *personal* mockery. As will be addressed further, *South Park* becomes even more problematic in its use of stereotypes for two reasons: one, because the show does not lend itself to easy interpretation based on an assumed underlying political philosophy (the assumed liberal slant of *All in the Family* or *The Simpsons*); two, because the show deliberately obscures the inherent binary of the literal versus the ironic message and meaning in satire altogether, and seeks to confuse and confront rather than elucidate and educate.

The narrative (for lack of a better term) of a typical episode of *South Park* is frequently informed by current events and parodies numerous (and often incongruent) literary, cinematic, and television sources. In "Two Days before the Day After Tomorrow" (2005), the Hurricane Katrina recovery debacle was combined with *The Day After Tomorrow* (2004). If the concept worked better in theory than in practice, meaning it was not the most successful *South Park* episode in terms of comedy, it was successful satire to the extent it pointed out how little difference there was between a tragic national disaster and a turgid disaster film; and the eerie similarities were far from funny. In this regard, the difference between *South Park*'s satirical parody and *The Simpsons*', and especially *Family Guy*'s, cultural pastiche also need be considered. *South Park* can certainly be capable of being more "self-congratulatory" and having a "more irreverent-than-thou tone" than any current postmodern TV comedy at its self-consumed worst, and the efficacy of the comedy often depends on the familiarity with the sources of parody. However, *South Park*'s barrage of cultural referencing is a *means*—a vehicle for satire—versus the reference as the *end*: the joke in and of itself.

By way of comparison, *The Simpsons*' episode "Beyond Blunderdome" (1999) featured genial Mel Gibson (lending his own voice as guest star) and Homer Simpson remaking Capra's *Mr. Smith Goes to Washington* so the common man–like Homer can relate to it better as slapstick: not by way of the Three Stooges, but Three Stooges routines referenced through Gibson in the *Lethal Weapon* film series. When enraged studio executives try to confiscate the film, a madcap chase through the studio lot ensues to reference Gibson's "Mad Max" films, assorted other movies, and other obligatory pop-culture references (the making of "Saving Irene Ryan"): the ultimate postmodern comedy logic of reference *ad infinitum*.[11] In *Family Guy*'s "North by North Quahog" (2005), Peter Griffin impersonates Mel Gibson to use his reserved hotel room and discovers a copy of *The Passion of the Christ 2: Crucify This*. When Peter steals it to prevent its release, Mel Gibson and his accomplices attempt to retrieve the film, allowing the episode to veer into a lengthy and self-indulgent parody of Hitchcock's *North by Northwest*—infused with the requisite *Family Guy* raunchy comedy.

In contrast, one can compare Mel Gibson's appearance (in both senses of the word) in "The Passion of the Jew" (2004). The release of Gibson's *The Passion of the Christ* inspires Cartman, *South Park*'s resident authoritarian personality, to lead a pogrom against the local Jews, stirring up the community by dressing in an SA uniform and delivering guttural, inflammatory speeches in German which his *Passion*-inspired followers believe is ancient Aramaic. Kyle, a stereotypical self-hating Jew, is plagued by guilt-ridden nightmares of the crucifixion of Christ: montages which include inserts of classical religious paintings, parodies of Christian educational cartoons, and a photo of Alan Alda. Later, Father Maxi explains to the distressed Kyle that the Bible has little account of the Crucifixion, but specifically points out "the Passion" which Gibson based his film on was a Middle Ages theatrical piece focusing on the Crucifixion designed to foment anti–Semitism. Meanwhile, Stan and Kenny travel to Hollywood to get their money back from Mel Gibson personally after sitting through his "snuff film" as "a matter of principle — like we did with *BASEketball*!" (a 1998 critical and commercial film fiasco starring *South Park* creators Parker and Stone). When Gibson finally appears, actual cut-out photos of Gibson's head are used over the cartoon body in his underwear. His psychotic behavior is a string of numerous references to Daffy Duck cartoons, culminating in Gibson inadvertently destroying the town's movie theater in a glorious CGI explosion and projectile farting in Cartman's face while Cartman grovels at Gibson's feet (or ass).

In this context, yet another controversial aspect of *South Park* is its gutter humor, with "sophomoric" and "scatological" being the two critical descriptions that have become synonymous with the show. *The Simpsons* is positively tame compared to many current network sitcoms, let alone *South Park*; the closest the show came to moral transgression was Homer and Marge's brief interest in "snuggling" in public places, and Bart using four-letter words like "crap" and "hell." *Family Guy*, while capable of being as crude and offensive as *South Park*, strictly confines itself to the level of nightclub sex and ethnic jokes. *South Park*, as much as cable TV permits, approaches the sheer, repulsive power of Sade. As Georges Bataille wrote:

> Nobody, unless they are totally deaf to it, can finish *Les Cent Vingt Journées de Sodom* [*The 120 Days of Sodom*] without feeling sick.... [T]here was nothing respectable he did not mock, nothing pure which he did not soil, nothing joyful which he did not frighten.... But what if he were to go further? Indeed, this book is the only one in which the mind of man is shown *as it really is*. This language of [*120 Days*] is that of *a universe which degrades gradually and systematically, which tortures and destroys the totality of the beings which it presents.*[12]

Besides the graphic particulars of *South Park*'s obsessions with anality, defecation, excrement, flatulence, and, of course, sodomy — with bestiality, cannibalism, coprophagy, dismemberment, ejaculation, masturbation, menstruation, murder, necrophilia, and pedophilia added on occasion for good measure (one self-explanatory episode: "Cartman Joins NAMBLA")—it is the destruction of respectability, purity, and joy, that Bataille found in Sade that *South Park* similarly manifests. The humor deliberately sickens, and becomes more sickening because the rampant horror and absurdity is rooted in the fact that *South Park*'s inhuman and inhumane characters routinely *do* what the moral and ethical viewer would shudder to think, let alone speak out loud. On *South Park*, Eric Cartman is the undisputed master of unconscionable actions based on pure self-interest. In "Hooked on Monkey Phonics" (1999), when the word "conscientious" is given to a contestant at a local spelling bee, Cartman instinctively blurts, "'Conscientious?' What the fuck does that mean?" In "Kenny Dies," Cartman telemarkets a batch of found fetuses for stem cell research originally intended to save Kenny ("Ok, you tell me where you're going to get aborted fetuses for 70 cents on the dollar?"), but ultimately uses the stem cells to clone his own Shakey's Pizza parlor rather than save Kenny's life. In "Toilet Paper" (2003), Cartman brings Kenny out to the center of Stark's Pond in a row boat and ineffectively attempts to murder him for "knowing too much" about an act of neighborhood vandalism—by repeatedly pummeling him with a wiffle ball bat (a parody of *The Godfather Part II*). In "Scott Tenorman Must Die!" (2001), Cartman purchases a bag of Scott Tenorman's pubic hair in an attempt to be the first boy in his circle to reach puberty; in revenge for the swindle, Cartman arranges the murder of Scott Tenorman's parents and feeds him their bodies in a bowl of chili (a parody of Shakespeare's *Titus Andronicus*).

Democracy Happens

> In the liberal system, the freedom of individuals is destroyed by mutual interference: one person's liberty begins where the other's ends.... The State is the bad conscience of the liberal, the instrument of a necessary repression for which deep in their hearts they deny responsibility.[13]
> — Raoul Vaneigem

While much of the attention given to *South Park* in the early seasons focused on the extent to which the show would go to push the boundaries of good taste, the current critical debate most frequently involving *South Park* is whether the show is liberal or conservative in its politics (a debate largely, and oddly, non-existent in critical discussions of *The Simpsons, American Dad*, and *Family Guy*). However, the *South Park* liberal-conservative debate has become eminently unproductive, not only because of the strict binary that now defines American liberalism versus American conservatism, and *South Park*'s potential to offend both sides in equal measure, but because of the use of the terms liberal and conservative. In a March 2006 interview with *Time* magazine, Trey Parker stated, "We still believe that *all people are born bad and are made good by society*, rather than the opposite," to which Matt Stone added, "Actually, I think that's where we're *conservative*."[14] In this sense, Parker and Stone's "conservatism" can be read against the classical liberal philosophy, from which American liberalism, American conservatism, and libertarianism are *all* derived. Classical liberalism posits that individuals enter the world as a *tabula rasa* with the natural right of freedom to fulfill their own destiny. By doing so, public good is produced by individuals pursuing competing self-interests and forming social contracts for their mutual benefit (John Locke, Adam Smith, John Stuart Mill, and even the hidden message of *Patterns*). *South Park*'s conservatism better compares to Thomas Hobbes's *Leviathan* (1651). Hobbes argued that the formation of civil society out of the "state of nature" is the result of mutual distrust between individuals and ultimately their fear of death; if all men are created equal, it is because each can take the others' lives. Without the civil society, as Hobbes famously claimed, life in the state of nature is "*war of every one against every one ... and the life of man, solitary, poor, nasty, brutish, and short.*"[15] In turn, individual liberty is not what the individual should be allowed to do in society, but to "be contented with so much liberty against other men, *as he would allow other men against himself.*"[16] Similarly, 18th century conservative philosopher Edmund Burke, a critic of classical liberalism, argued, "One of the first motives of civil society, and which becomes one of its fundamental rules, is that no man should be judge in his own cause.... *Men cannot enjoy the rights of a civil and uncivil state together.*"[17]

This is not at all to ignore *South Park*'s frequent opposition to political solutions dictated by paternalistic government policies (whether censorship or affirmative action), or activism based on imposing personal standards of moral conduct on others (animal-rights activists, environmentalists, and fundamentalists being the most recurrent targets).[18] For instance, "Cripple Fight" (2001) sided with the Mountain Scouts prohibiting Big Gay Al from joining their organization — not to favor discrimination, but to question the efficiency of legislating tolerance without addressing the underlying attitudes (when Big Gay Al drops his lawsuit after his court victory, deciding education rather than legislation is a more effective and long-term solution, his activist lawyer Gloria Allred brands him a "homophobe"). Conversely, "Follow that Egg!" (2006) sided in favor of same-sex marriage rights and ended with the town celebrating Big Gay Al and Mr. Slave's wedding (the obvious comparison being *The*

Simpsons and "There's Something about Marrying"). Beyond the fact that these episodes allowed *South Park* to take unpopular positions on the respective issues — and offend as many people as possible in the process — they are consistent with classical liberal ideology: the right of the individual to make decisions and form social contracts free from interference, and the credo "the government which governs best governs least."

While the overt messages lend to interpretations of *South Park* as endorsing a libertarian political viewpoint, the issue, as is often the case with *South Park*, becomes much more problematic.[19] In "Chickenlover" (1998), it is revealed that Officer Barbrady is illiterate and learns to read to solve a wave of sex crimes involving chickens. At the end of the episode, after tackling *Atlas Shrugged*, Ayn Rand's celebration of "objectivism" and rational individualism frequently hailed by libertarians as a canonical text, Barbrady announces, "I read every last word of this garbage, and because of this piece of shit I'm never reading again!" *South Park*'s fundamental skepticism of human nature — and the disturbing, Sadean depths humanity can sink to (read: Eric Cartman) — become a "hidden message" and the crux of *South Park*'s conservatism ("All people are born bad and made good by society"). More correctly, it is the *contradiction* between *South Park*'s classical liberal philosophy and classical conservative pessimism concerning the free, rational individual which becomes the fulcrum for political satire: the essential political problem of individual rights versus majority rule when the "mutual interference" between self-interested parties results in intolerant views, selective ethics, and uncivil behavior; the unreasonable expectation that a civil society will be the end product; and the State ultimately becoming the community's "bad conscience" to maintain life, liberty, and the pursuit of happiness. A typical episode of *South Park* depicts the daily breakdown and regression of the civil society into the uncivil "State of nature" where life is indeed nasty, brutish, and short (especially for Kenny). It satirizes the transition of the civil society in theory into the political practice of the State: what G.W.F. Hegel termed "the actuality of the ethical Idea" becomes "the *absurdity* of the ethical Idea."[20] In "Chef Goes Nanners" (2000), the controversy over the South Park city flag — white stick figures lynching a black stick figure — tears the town apart until the dispute is logically resolved in the confines of the *South Park* illogical universe by a new city flag with a multicultural group of white, black, red and yellow stick figures lynching a black stick figure. As Kyle enthusiastically explains, "It's people of all colors, and they added a black guy as one of the hangers so it's not racist!" In this respect, *South Park*'s acerbic critique of liberal-humanist tolerance (a frequent target of satire on the show) is not merely an attack on the excesses of "political correctness," but strongly echoes the ruminations of Adorno:

The familiar argument that tolerance, that all men are created equal, is a boomerang.... An emancipated society ... would not be a unitary state, but the realization of universality in the reconciliation of differences. Politics that are still seriously concerned with such a society ought not, therefore, propound the abstract equality of men even as an idea. *Instead they should point out the bad equality today ... and conceive the better state as one in which people could be different without fear.*[21]

South Park's consistent disdain for the dynamics of the crowd, be it Nietzsche's contempt for "herd mentality" or the Founding Fathers' fear of "majority tyranny," is not necessarily a celebration of the non-conformist individual. Rather, the danger lies in the simple fact that cruel, stupid individuals acting on personal self-interest form crueler, stupider groups acting on organized self-interest. As José Ortega y Gasset described: "[T]he triumph of hyperdemocracy in which the mass takes direction oblivious to the law, imposing its own desires and tastes by material pressure."[22] In "I'm a Little Bit Country" (2003), made and aired in less than two weeks after the U.S. invasion of Iraq, South Park, as usual, is bitterly divided into virulent pro-war and anti-war factions. After joining an anti-war protest so they can skip school, and embarrassing the school administration when they cannot answer basic questions on American history posed by a reporter, the boys are ordered by Mr. Garrison to write a book report on the Founding Fathers. Rather than study, Cartman attempts to have a sitcom-style flashback to 1776, culminating in electrocuting himself in a pool of water with a TV that has TIVOed fifty hours of the History Channel. During his resultant coma, Cartman imagines himself sitting in on the signing of the Declaration of Independence, which soon digresses into the same acrimonious pro-war and anti-war debate raging in present-day South Park, with the Founding Fathers screaming "Rabble! Rabble! Rabble!" at each other. Benjamin Frankin proposes the solution; in an inspired piece of casting, none other than Norman Lear, the founding father of American TV political comedy, supplied Franklin's voice. Franklin posits that America go to war with England while claiming to be opposed to going to war with England; and another Founding Father proudly adds, "Think of it ... an entire nation founded on doing one thing and saying another." Meanwhile, at South Park in the present, the two factions have organized competing concerts on the same stage between the country-singing pro-war group and the rock-singing anti-war group, which becomes a parody of the Donny and Marie Osmond chestnut, "I'm a Little Bit Country, I'm a Little Bit Rock and Roll." The concert soon turns into a rival chant worthy of Ionesco: "Support! Protest! Country! Rock and Roll!" The inevitable town riot erupts before a revived Cartman takes the mike and explains that both sides need each other to make democracy work: the pro-war side needs dissenters to present the image of America as "sane, caring individuals"; the anti-war side needs patriots to present an image of America not as "soft, pussy protestors."[23] After a community hug, the two factions unite for a musical reprise, ending with the lines: "Let the flag of hypocrisy fly from every pole/I'm a little bit country, I'm a little bit rock and roll." Stan and Kenny look on in pure astonishment, while Kyle nurses the beginnings of a severe headache and mutters, "I hate this town ... I really, really, do."

While *Green Acres* is an absurdist study of ideological contradictions, *South Park* is an absurdist denouncement of political double-standards. *South Park* subjects all ideas, ideologies, philosophies, politics, races, and religions to ridicule with an obscene ferocity—as if S. Clay Wilson had been on the staff of *Mad* magazine. As noted, this is to stress that *South Park* is not at all immune to the essential problem of satire—whether the reader selects the literal and satirical meaning or the ironic and intended message. Indeed, *South Park* exacerbates satire's inherent binary of literal versus ironic "double-meaning" to the point that no definitive interpretation of the message is even possible—a form of *dissociative satire* that continually offends and determinedly frustrates interpretation. Or, as one *South Park* episode concluded: "It's easy to perceive something some way, and then be wrong. So we all need to learn to be a little less perceptive."

While Adorno was in favor of Brecht's formal strategies, he did not support the overt political platform which eventually overshadowed the avant-garde elements: "What is artistically legitimate as alienating infantilism— Brecht's early plays came from the same milieu as Dada—becomes merely infantile when it starts to assume theoretical or social validity."[24] The difference between *South Park*'s Dadaist "alienating infantilism" versus *The Simpsons* and *Family Guy*'s postmodern "infantile theoretical and social validity" becomes crucial. *South Park* exhibits a juvenile rage versus the collegiate conceit of *The Simpsons* and the adolescent arrogance of *Family Guy* (which could be expressed by saying *South Park*'s academic domain is detention, *The Simpsons* the seminar, and *Family Guy* the frat house). While *South Park* can certainly be accused of pointing out all that is horribly wrong with the world and manifesting its own sense of absolute correctness in the process, *South Park* deliberately seeks to displease and offend all sides of the debate. It places any viewer in the uncomfortable position where they can be laughing at the jokes directed against the views they oppose, only to find that their own views can, and will, become the butt of the joke from one episode to the next, and frequently within the same episode (and "butt" should obviously be emphasized). While admittedly hyperbolic, if the problem of satire, as Adorno noted, is that it regresses from a rapier to a cudgel, *South Park* does not redeem the subtlety of satire but exacerbates it to its next level: it becomes a guillotine.

South Park's satire is a continual criticism of, and dismantling of confidence in, any and all political solutions; it denies not only a simplistic liberal or conservative reading, but the viewer's ability to *think* the show is within the liberal-conservative binary.[25] As Linda Hutcheon noted, "[I]rony can be provocative when it is conservative ... as easily when its politics are oppositional and subversive. It depends on who is using/attributing it *and at whose expense it is seen to be.*"[26] If *South Park* does reflect a "conservative" political agenda, it can be read as satire on the essential liberalist tenets of daily American political life: the natural rights of the individual license over societal obligation; the daily exploitation of the loopholes in the social contract; the idea that all men are created equal, but some are more equal than others; the Great Melting Pot as it reaches a boiling point; democracy and majority rule as it continually erupts into hyperdemocracy and mob rule; the illogical State as the expression of an irrational body-politic. Or, if *South Park* need be consigned to a liberal-conservative debate, it is not a squabble between Al Frankin and Rush Limbaugh, but a philosophical battle between Locke and Hobbes rendered through the brutality of Sade and the absurdity of Jarry. In this way, *South Park* is not only the most avant-garde, but the most "retro" of current TV comedy shows.

Chapter Notes

Introduction

1. See "The Culture Industry: Enlightenment as Mass Deception" in Max Horkheimer and Theodor W. Adorno, *Dialectic of Enlightenment*, trans. John Cumming (New York: Continuum, 1997). See also Theodor W. Adorno, *The Culture Industry: Selected Essays on Mass Culture*, ed. J. M. Bernstein (London: Routledge, 1991).

2. As quoted from Adorno's *Aesthetic Theory* in Theodor W. Adorno, *Adorno on Music*, ed. Richard Leppert, trans. Susan H. Gillespie (Berkeley: University of California Press, 2002), 71. Emphasis added.

3. Theodor W. Adorno, "Commitment," in *The Essential Frankfurt School Reader*, ed. Andrew Arato and Eike Gebhardt (New York: Continuum, 1994), 318.

4. Fredric Jameson, *Postmodernism, or, the Cultural Logic of Late Capitalism* (Durham, NC: Duke University Press, 1990), 17.

5. As quoted in Colin MacCabe, *Godard: Images, Sounds, Politics* (Bloomington: Indiana University Press, 1980), 19. Emphasis original.

6. Antonin Artaud, "For the Theater and Its Double," in *Selected Writings*, ed. Susan Sontag, trans. Helen Weaver (Berkeley: University of California Press, 1988), 240–1. Emphasis added.

Chapter 1

1. As quoted in John Baxter, *Buñuel* (New York: Carroll and Graf, 1994), 83. Emphasis added.

2. The *Ubu* cycle was written ca. 1891–1900. *Ubu roi*, as noted, premiered in 1896; *Ubu enchaîné* premiered in 1899. *Ubu cocu* was first published posthumously in 1944. Jarry also wrote *Ubu sur a Butte* (*Ubu on the Mound*), a condensed musical version of *Ubu Roi* specifically for marionettes (premiered in 1901, published in 1906). *Ubu roi* has itself been staged numerous times as a puppet show, beginning in 1898 in Paris.

3. As quoted in RoseLee Goldberg, *Performance Art: From Futurism to the Present*, revised and expanded edition (London: Thames and Hudson, 2001), 12.

4. As quoted in Goldberg, 12.

5. As quoted in Irene Hoffman, "Documents of Dada and Surrealism: Dada and Surrealist Journals in the Mary Reynolds Collection," page 3 of 10. Archived at: www.aetic.edu/reynolds/essays/hoffman.php. Accessed: 1/25/2005.

6. In 1918, German Dadaists held a "Pan-Germanic Poetry Contest" in which participants competed to finish reading poems aloud the fastest; it was refereed by painter George Grosz.

7. As quoted in Goldberg, 60.

8. See Goldberg, 74.

9. "The Work of Art in the Age of Mechanical Reproduction," *Illuminations*, trans. Harry Zohn (New York: Schocken Books, 1968), 237–8. Emphasis added.

10. In this sense, Adorno posits a different theory of contemplation. While agreeing contemplation's danger is its equivalence to adoration, contemplation must therefore be strengthened to critical awareness. True culture in its aesthetic and intellectual difficulty heightens contemplation, versus the mere commodity relationship between artist and audience in mass culture, which reduces distraction to diversion. "Contemplation, as a reside of fetish worship, is at the same time a stage of overcoming it." Theodor W. Adorno, *Minima Moralia: Reflection from Damaged Life*, trans. E.F.N. Jephcott (New York: Verso, 1997), 224. (See also Chapter Two.)

11. Duhamel as quoted in "The Work of Art...," 239. See also 237–41. Duhamel's crit-

icisms of cinema as a medium where "thought have been replaced by moving pictures" (238) mirrors Adorno's later critique of cinema.

12. "The Work of Art...," 240–1. Emphasis added.

13. "The Work of Art...," 237–8. Emphasis added.

14. "The Work of Art...," 250.

15. As quoted in Baxter, *Buñuel*, 42. Emphasis added. However, it is less clear if Breton embraced Feuillade for achieving a kind of "unintentional surrealism" despite being intended as commercial films for the public at large (the effect of Japanese *Godzilla* films or Mexican *lucha libre* films), or if he hailed these films for a tacky "so bad, they're good" appeal Susan Sontag later developed into the aesthetic of camp: inferior art-objects which "because in their relative unpretentiousness and vulgarity ... are much more extreme and irresponsible in their fantasy — and therefore quite touching and enjoyable" ("Notes on Camp," in *Against Interpretation* [New York: Doubleday Books, 1967], 283). It is this appreciation of "bad films" for their tacky vulgarity as camp amusement which has minimized the possibility of reading "bad films" as a potential form of confrontational avant-garde cinema which violates all standards of cinematic convention, an argument elaborated on in my own *Mexploitation Cinema: A Critical History of Mexican Vampire, Wrestler, Ape-man and Other Similar Films, 1957–1977* (Jefferson, NC: McFarland, 2005), especially Chapter 2.

16. As quoted in Rudolf E. Kuenzli, ed., *Dada and Surrealist Film* (New York: Willis Locker and Owens, 1987), 8.

17. See Amos Vogel, *Film as a Subversive Art* (New York: Random House, 1976), 50–2.

18. As quoted in René Clair, *A Nous La Liberté/Entr'acte* (London: Lorrimer, 1970), 112.

19. See *Dada and Surrealist Film*, 5–10.

20. *Performance Art*, 95. See also *Dada and Surrealist Film*, 4–6, 19–20.

21. See also *Dada and Surrealist Film*, 1.

22. *Buñuel*, 86. See also 84–6. From 1928 to 1931, Surrealist patron Charles de Noailles commissioned a yearly film project as a birthday present for his wife Marie-Laure. *Le Mystère du château de dé* was the 1929 project, which starred the de Noailles and their circle of friends and was filmed at their vacation villa.

23. See *Dada and Surrealist Film*, 100, 107.

24. *Buñuel*, 42. Emphasis added.

25. See *Dada and Surrealist Film*, 8.

26. See Baxter, 94–5.

27. In 1926, before his allegiance to Surrealism, Buñuel organized a screening of avant-garde films in Madrid; *Entr'acte* was the lone selection (loosely) affiliated with Surrealism. Instead, Buñuel included Albert Cavalcanti's experimental documentary about Parisian workers, *Rien que les heures* (*Nothing But the Hours*, 1926; often translated as *Nothing But Time*), the dream-sequence from Jean Renoir's *La Fille de l'eau* (*The Water Nymph*, 1925), and early cinematic motion studies (given Buñuel's penchant for violence and black comedy, one film was a slow-motion study of a bullet being fired by a rifle). See Baxter, 54.

28. Buñuel once famously described *Un Chien andalou* as "a desperate, passionate call to murder" (as quoted in *Dada and Surrealist Film*, 9).

29. In this respect, Stuart Lieberman suggested that *Un Chien andalou* can be considered in keeping with the dissenting Surrealist movement lead by George Battaille, the architect of the philosophy of transgression; see *Dada and Surrealist Film*, 155. Indeed, Breton abhorred homosexuality and the scatological, and despite his vilification of bourgeois morality, his own sexual views were, for lack of a better word, uptight.

30. Buñuel as quoted in Donald M. Lowe, *History of Bourgeois Perception* (Chicago: University of Chicago Press, 1982), 132.

31. *Dada and Surrealist Film*, 10. Emphasis added.

32. *Cinema 1: The Movement-Image*, trans. Hugh Tomlinson and Barbara Habberjam (Minneapolis: University of Minnesota Press, 1986), 175–6. Walter Benjamin would not have agreed with Deleuze's distinction between Dada and Surrealism as their view of the machine; Benjamin saw Surrealism as quite consistent with Dada and Futurism's fascination with the machine, and specifically took Surrealism to task for "the movement's over precipitous embrace of the uncomprehended miracle of the machine": "Surrealism," in *Reflections*, ed. Peter Demetz, trans. Edmund Jephcott (New York: Schocken Books, 1978), 185.

33. Tobis, the French company that produced *A Nous a liberté*, pursued a legal action against United Artists over *Modern Times*. Clair adamantly refused to be part of any litigation, stating he and cinema owed much more to Chaplin than *Modern Times* might owe to *A Nous a liberté*.

34. See also Benjamin, "The Work of Art...," 241–2. Benjamin argued Fascism entailed making politics an aesthetic practice (war as an art form); Marxism required the politicization of art.

35. Artaud wrote a number of unmade screenplays, such as *Dix-Huit secondes* (*18 Seconds*), an account of a man's racing thoughts in

the final eighteen seconds of his life before he commits suicide.

36. *Selected Writings*, 152. Emphasis added.
37. *Selected Writings*, 235. Emphasis added.
38. See "A Dialectical Approach to Film Form," in *Film Form*, ed. and trans. Jay Ledya (San Diego: Harcourt Brace, 1977), 48–50.
39. Giles Deleuze, *Cinema 2: The Time-Image*, trans. Hugh Tomlinson and Robert Galeta (Minneapolis: University of Minnesota Press, 1989), 167. Emphasis original. A highly recommended analysis of Deleuze in this respect is D. N. Rodowick, *Gilles Deleuze's Time Machine* (Durham: Duke University Press, 1997), Ch. 7.
40. See Susan Sontag, "Introduction," in Antonin Artaud, *Selected Writings*, xxxiv. In this respect, Artaud held the non-symbolic images of Buñuel and the highly-symbolic images of Cocteau in equal disdain, chastising *both* filmmakers for what he contended was using Surrealism at its most superficial — assemblages of provocative abstract images — and not going far enough in their surrealism to produce a "poetry of the unconscious" (*Selected Writings*, 280).
41. "Introduction," in Antonin Artaud, *Selected Writings*, xxxvii.
42. It does bear mentioning that Breton was specifically a supporter of Leon Trotsky and his vision of world socialist revolution. Shortly after Surrealism's allegiance to the Communist Parry, Trotsky was expelled from the Soviet Union by Stalin. Surrealism's unintended allegiance with Stalinism proved to be a key factor in the movement's gradual disintegration by the advent of World War II.
43. See *Selected Writings*, 141.
44. *Selected Writings*, 142–3.
45. *Selected Writings*, 240. Emphasis added. Given the time frame of *The Theater and Its Double* and the Marx Brothers work, Artaud probably wrote "The Marx Brothers" for *The Theater and Its Double* after *Monkey Business*, but before *Horsefeathers* and *Duck Soup*, which are most conspicuous by their absence.
46. See B. Donald Grose and O. Franklin Kenworthy, *A Mirror of Life: A History of Western Theater* (New York: Holt, Rinehart, and Winston, 1985), 613.
47. As quoted in Leonard Cabell Pronko, *Avant-Garde: The Experimental Theater in France* (Berkeley: University of California Press, 1966), 63.
48. In Ionesco's original ending and early productions of the play, the ending was the blackout, and then returning to the Smiths. It was only after numerous performances that Ionesco rewrote the ending to have the Martins replace the Smiths.

49. From 1952 to 1953 Abbott and Costello appeared in a weekly television show appropriately titled *The Abbott and Costello Show* (CBS). A variation on the sitcom, Abbott and Costello appeared at the beginning, intermission, and end of the show on a theatrical stage commenting on the "sitcom" portions of the show and occasionally performing unconnected routines. The sitcom element of the show was itself a threadbare narrative, or more often a simple premise, connecting independent comedy routines in various locations (streets, apartments, restaurants, etc.), including recycling the more popular routines which appeared in their films of the 1940s.
50. In this sense, while Laurel and Hardy can be seen as a homoerotic couple battling women, Abbott and Costello were defined by an abusive father-son relationship. The premiere post–World War II comedy team, Dean Martin and Jerry Lewis, can be seen as a metaphor of the atom itself: Dean Martin as the stable nucleus and Jerry Lewis as the whirling electron.
51. Despite his strenuous objections to cinema, one film Adorno specifically cited as a success was Antonioni's *La Notte* (*The Night*, 1961), largely for its paradoxical utilization and denial of the concept of *motion* in motion pictures. See "Transparencies of Film," in *The Culture Industry*, 180.
52. Jacques Lacan, "The Mirror Stage as Formative of the Function of the I as Revealed in Psychoanalytic Experience," *Ecrits*, trans. Alan Sheridan (New York: W. W. Norton, 1977), 5. Deleuze reads *Film* as a study of perception but strongly eschews a psychoanalytic reading; see *Cinema 1: The Movement-Image*, 66–8.
53. Peter Burger, *Theory of the Avant-Garde*, trans. Michael Shaw (Minneapolis: University of Minnesota Press, 1984), 81. Emphasis added.
54. See Nancy Franklin, "American Idiots," *The New Yorker* (January 16, 2006).

Chapter 2

1. Benjamin, "The Work of Art...," 220, 236. Emphasis added.
2. See Raymond Williams, *The Politics of Modernism* (New York: Verso, 1989), 107.
3. "A Dialectical Approach to Film Form," in *Film Form*, 63. Emphasis original.
4. See *Dialectic of Enlightenment*, 17–8.
5. Benjamin, "The Work of Art...," 236. Emphasis added.
6. "Only when in technology body and image so interpenetrate that all revolutionary

tension becomes bodily collective innervation, and all the collective bodily innervations become revolutionary discharge, has reality transcended itself to the extent demanded by *The Communist Manifesto*. For the moment, only the Surrealists have understood its present demands" ("Surrealism" [1929], *Reflections*, 192).

7. See The Work of Art...," 141–2.

8. *Selected Writings*, 313.

9. *Selected Writings*, 312–3. Emphasis added.

10. Miriam Hansen, "Mass Culture as Hieroglyphic Writing: Adorno, Derrida, and Kracauer," *New German Critique* 56 (Summer 1992): 56.

11. "On the Fetish-Character of Music and the Regression of Listening," in *The Culture Industry*, 40.

12. "The Schema of Mass Culture," in *The Culture Industry*, 63.

13. "Culture Industry Reconsidered," in *The Culture Industry*, 100–1. Emphasis added.

14. See Adorno, "Culture Industry Reconsidered," in *The Culture Industry*, 98–9.

15. "On the Fetish-Character of Music and the Regression of Listening," in *The Culture Industry*, 53. One can only imagine what Adorno would have made of disco, slam-dancing, mosh pits, and raves.

16. "Culture Industry Reconsidered," in *The Culture Industry*, 100.

17. "How to Look at Television," in *The Culture Industry*, 160, 163.

18. "How to Look at Television," in *The Culture Industry*, 166–7. Emphasis added. Adorno only describes the show as "extremely light comedy," but is certainly referring to *Our Miss Brooks*, based on his description.

19. "How to Look at Television," in *The Culture Industry*, 170–1. From a practical standpoint, genres and stock characters also expedited producing shows, given the rigorous deadlines and hectic pace of television production (see "How to Look at Television," 171).

20. As well as "Patterns," among the more famous teleplays were "Marty" *(Philco Television Theater*, 1953), "Requiem for a Heavyweight" *(Playhouse 90*, 1956), and "The Days of Wine and Roses" *(Playhouse 90*, 1958). All were subsequently made into feature films.

21. Coe as quoted in Anna Everett, "'Golden Age' of Television." Archived at: www.museum.tv/archieves/etv/G/goldenage/goldenage.htm, page 1 of 4. Accessed: 11/3/2004. A short but highly informative and interesting essay, my discussion of this era of television drama owes greatly to Everett.

22. "'Golden Age' of Television," page 1 of 4.

23. In 1956, Rod Serling wrote "Noon at Doomsday" *for U.S. Steel Hour* and, in 1958, "A Town Has Turned to Dust," for *Playhouse 90* (CBS, 1956–61). Both the teleplays explicitly dealt with racism in the South, and in both cases were heavily modified and censored by the sponsors and networks. Serling, already known for his opinionated temperament, grew incensed at the demands to avoid controversial issues and the forced alterations to his scripts; he became well-known for his frequent and public criticism of the networks. These incidents were a key factor in Serling developing *The Twilight Zone*, where the overtly liberal political messages could be hidden in science-fiction allegories, or aliens and future dystopias versus dramas set in everyday locations.

24. "'Golden Age of Television," page 1 of 4. Emphasis added.

25. Gould's enthusiastic review appeared in *The New York Times*, January 17, 1955. Archived at www.rdserling.com/NYTpatterns.htm. Accessed: 1/18/2005.

26. "How to Look at Television," in *The Culture Industry*, 173. Adorno's specific comments were directed at an unspecified teleplay depicting the final days of a dictator and his collapsing regime.

27. "How to Look at Television," in *The Culture Industry*, 165–6.

28. "Variety Shows," page 1 of 3. Archived at: www.museum.tv/archieves/etv/V/htmlV/varietyprogr/varietyprogr.htm. Accessed: 1/19/2005. Emphasis added.

29. David Marc, *Comic Visions: Television Comedy and American Culture*, 2nd ed. (Malden, MA: Blackwell, 1997), 73. In this respect, Marc's argument can be applied to the transition of TV drama from self-contained teleplay to dramatic genre series. Especially given the controversies surrounding Rod Serling's TV plays, a preexisting genre framework and stock characters required scripts and messages to fit into their show's format, or required the writer to effectively disguise them (as Serling did with *The Twilight Zone*, at times quite unsubtly).

30. John Ellis, *Visible Fictions: Cinema, Television, Video*, rev. ed. (London: Routledge, 1992), 129. Emphasis added.

31. *The Life of Riley* ran for one season (1949–50) on NBC, starring Jackie Gleason. The second version starred William Bendix.

32. See also Marc, *Comic Visions*, 76–7. On *The Jack Benny Show* (CBS, 1950–1964; NBC, 1964–65), Jack Benny played himself (a TV star) as well as his public persona (a thrifty bachelor). Like *The Abbot and Costello Show*, it was a loosely organized sitcom scenario designed to feature old and new Benny routines.

33. A far less successful implementation of

direct address is employed by *The War at Home* (FOX, 2005-7), in which periodic inserts of characters against a white screen (versus breaking character to address the camera) do not so much comment on representation but provide additional one-liners while manufacturing some insight into the character's concerns, motivations, or "inner psyche."

34. Robin Wood argued that the primary fiction of genres is ideological: "They represent *different* strategies for dealing with the *same* ideological tensions." "Ideology, Genre, Auteur," in *Film Theory and Criticism: Introductory Readings*, 4th ed, Gerald Mast, Marshall Cohen, and Leo Braudy, eds. (New York: Oxford University Press, 1992), 479. Emphasis added. In this regard, the domestic sitcom's rise on television was paralleled by, and an antidote to, the emphasis on the far less affirmative family melodrama genre in post–World War II Hollywood, such as Nicholas Ray's *Rebel Without a Cause* (1955) and the magnificent work of Douglas Sirk. See Thomas Elsaesser, "Tales of Sound in Fury: Observations on the Family Melodrama," in Mast, Cohen, and Braudy, eds., especially 519–27.

35. Marc, *Comic Visions*, 44.

36. As quoted in Miriam Hansen, "Of Mice and Ducks," *The South Atlantic Quarterly* 92:1 (Winter 1993): 32. Emphasis added. Benjamin eventually omitted all references to Mickey Mouse in "The Work of Art...," and largely avoided specific examples altogether, save for brief mentions of Charlie Chaplin, one of the few filmmakers Adorno respected.

37. As quoted in Hansen, "Of Mice and Ducks": 32. Emphasis added.

38. Horkheimer and Adorno, 138; see also 141. See also Hansen: 32; she quite perceptively noted that Adorno perhaps substituted Donald Duck for Mickey Mouse in that Donald Duck much better fit the model of the "Authoritarian Personality."

39. Ball insisted Arnez play her husband, despite network and sponsor fears that Arnez's Latin American ethnicity and heavy accent would be unappealing to mainstream viewers.

40. Marc, *Comic Visions*, 77. Emphasis added.

41. Horkheimer and Adorno, 183.

42. Gleason returned to CBS for *Jackie Gleason's American Scene Magazine* (1962–6) and a revamped version of *The Jackie Gleason Show* (1966–70).

43. See *Comic Visions*, 20. Marc suggested Gleason's motivation to do a 30-minute sitcom version of *The Honeymooners* for one season may have been financial as much as artistic. Gleason correctly perceived that filmed sitcoms would become the preferred mode of TV comedy preservation in syndicated reruns, where *The Honeymooners* thrived in subsequent decades. Reruns of comedy-variety shows have largely been non-existent in syndication. See also David Marc, "Jackie Gleason," page 3 of 4. Available at www.museum.tv/archives/etv/G/htmlG/gleasonjack/gleasonjack.htm.

44. See Marc, "Jackie Gleason," page 3 of 4.

Chapter 3

1. Kovacs as quoted in "The Lively Arts," Canadian Broadcasting Cooperation television interview conducted by Bill Bellman, aired on 10-31-61, page 2 of 7. Transcript archived at: http://usuers.rcn.com/manaben/Kovacs/CBC.html. Accessed: 11/21/2004.

2. As quoted in Diana Rico, *Kovacsland: A Biography of Ernie Kovacs* (San Diego: Harcourt Brace Jovanovich, 1990), 145.

3. *The Ernie Kovacs Show* filling in for *Caesar's Hour* is also appropriate. Sid Caesar's work can be seen as an influence on Kovacs, and *Your Show of Shows* routines, such as the lampoon of Italian Neo-Realist cinema or the famous mechanical statues on a huge Bavarian clock (the clock figures quite possibly the inspiration for the Nairobi Trio), compare much better to Kovacs than Milton Berle or Red Skelton.

4. Cross as quoted in Rico, 185.

5. Today "Exotica" is hailed as a kind of avant-garde popular music. In the 1950s and 1960s "exotica" records were promoted by record companies primarily for their state-of-the-art use of stereophonic sound and ideal background music for cocktail parties.

6. See Rico, 196–205.

7. Mogulescu as quoted in Rico, 261. Emphasis added.

8. See Rico, 278–9. *Silents Please* ran the previous year (1960) as a summer replacement show as well, minus a host. Kovacs was well aware he was added not for his hosting duties, but for Dutch Masters commercials.

9. This reluctance of Kovacs to be the "star" proved to be a source of contention between Kovacs and his sponsor, Dutch Masters Cigars. "They have had one complaint, which is becoming rather profound, and that is that they feel I should be seen more on camera on the show. ... But I just don't feel that it is the nature of the show for me to be *in front of the camera*. It is more of its nature to be—I keep telling them—that I'm representing myself *back of the camera*" (as quoted in "The Lively Arts" interview, page 4–5 of 7). Emphasis added.

10. "The Silent Show" was Kovacs's only

color broadcast, and he took full advantage of the opportunity by clothing the performers in gaudy color combinations against equally striking and clashing one-color backdrops (see Rico, 208).

11. As quoted in Lindsy E. Pak, "The Ernie Kovacs Show (Various)." Archived at: www.museum.tv/archieves/etv/E/htmlE/ErnieKovacsShow/erkovacshow.htm. Date accessed: 11/21/2004. Emphasis added.

12. As quoted in Rico, 203–4.

13. "The Work of Art...," 228–9. Emphasis added. Benjamin, who died in 1940, did not see the advent of television.

14. As quoted in "The Lively Arts" interview, page 2 of 7. Emphasis added.

15. *Visible Fictions*, 137. Emphasis added.

16. As quoted in Rico, 177. Emphasis added.

17. In America, the song also became strongly identified with Bobby Darin, whose version was number one on the pop-charts in 1958.

18. Roland Barthes, *Mythologies*, trans. Annette Wang (New York: Hill and Wang, 1997), 84.

19. Frank J. Chorba, "Ernie Kovacs," page 1 of 3. Available at www.museum.tv/archieves/etv/K/htmlK/KovacsErnie/kovacsErnie.htm.

20. As quoted in "The Lively Arts" interview, page 2 of 7.

21. Bertolt Brecht, *Brecht on Theater: The Development of an Aesthetic*, ed. and trans. John Willet (New York: Hill and Wang, 1992), 126. Emphasis added. Kovacs himself admired Brecht's work. Edie Adams recounted that Kovacs detested sponsors, who he viewed as antithetical to artistic creativity given their demands for high ratings and concern for production budgets. While Kovacs was hired as host of *Take a Good Look*, sponsored by Consolidated Cigar Company and its Dutch Masters line, Adams was hired by Consolidated Cigar to promote another product line, Muriel Cigars. By chance, Kovacs saw a man carrying some volumes of Brecht on the set while Adams was filming her first commercial. "My God, who's the guy with the Brecht?" he exclaimed to Adams. The "guy with the Brecht" was Consolidated Cigar vice-president Jack Mogulescu, who became Kovacs's chief liaison with Consolidated Cigar. Dutch Masters remained Kovacs's sponsor until his death (see Rico, 260).

22. See *Visible Fictions*, 137–40.

23. See Adorno, "How to Look at Television," in *The Culture Industry*, 171; one can easily assume Adorno would have taken great exception to Percy Dovetonsils.

24. As quoted in "The Lively Arts" interview, page 6 of 7.

25. The Nairobi Trio debuted on *Kovacs Unlimited* in 1954, and became a staple of Kovacs's shows. For the posthumous ABC show, Dutch Masters substituted their scheduled commercials with Nairobi Trio sketches.

26. The song became so identified with Kovacs that Maxwell's label, MGM Records, eventually changed the song's title from "Solfeggio" to "Song of the Nairobi Trio (Solfeggio)."

27. *Kovacsland*, 155.

28. As quoted in Rico, 279. Emphasis added. Kovacs's introduction and comments regarding "the money" becomes quite mordant. At this point in his career, Kovacs' return to television was largely motivated by his financial situation, due to owing the IRS considerable amounts of back taxes. Moreover, given Kovacs' notorious reputation for going over budget on his shows, the ABC contract required him to make up the difference for any budget overruns, which inevitably resulted in Kovacs paying ABC for each special.

29. See "Methods of Montage," in *Film Form*, 72–83.

30. Michele Langford, "Alexander Kluge." Emphasis added. Her highly informative discussion of Kluge's life and work can be found at www.sensesofcinema.com/contents/directors/03/kluge.html. Accessed: 10/6/2006.

31. As quoted from Kluge's essay "The Significance of Phantasy" in Langford. Emphasis added.

32. *Cinema 2*, 245.

33. A similar theme can be seen in D.W. Griffith's Biograph short *A Corner in Wheat* (1908), the story of a struggling farmer and the ruthless businessman who monopolizes the wheat market. The businessman's world is signified by constant motion and action, be it at the office or ritzy parties. In contrast, the farmer, for whom capitalism does not work, must eventually find support in a bread line, captured in a long take devoid of movement — essentially a freeze-frame of destitute farmers waiting for their stipend of bread. My thanks to Linda Mokdad for these observations on *A Corner in Wheat*.

34. "Culture Industry Reconsidered," in *The Culture Industry*, 101.

35. As quoted in Rico, 209; see also 205–10. The reviews Rico cited suggest that the immense critical disappointment with the Lewis special may have fueled the lavish praise bestowed on "The Silent Show." This is not to disparage Lewis, who is frequently a brilliant avant-garde comedian in his own right, exemplified by his 1970 film *Which Way to the Front?*

36. As quoted in "The Lively Arts" television interview. Emphasis added.

37. Again, this is not to deny that Kovacs could be considered Dada versus my view he is Surrealist, or even that Soupy Sales, who I categorize as Dada, could potentially be read as Surrealist (see Chapter Four).

38. According to Rico, *The Medicine Man* was little more than a Western parody sitcom, motivated for financial reasons on both the part of Kovacs and Keaton (299).

39. As quoted in Rico, 203.

40. *Kovacsland*, 203. *Eugene* is very comparable to Tati's own hilarious meditations on mechanized modern life, *Mon Oncle* (*My Uncle*, 1958) and *Playtime* (1967). While Tati is often stylistically compared to Chaplin, a comparison of Keaton to Chaplin in terms of Tati's own relationship to the machine bears future investigation.

41. In this respect, while Eugene's adventures might be described as a modernistic *Alice in Wonderland*, another children's story is also applicable: *Harold and the Purple Crayon*, in which a mischievous boy creates his own world by drawing objects which come to life with a magic crayon.

42. In this first portion of *Eugene*, the discerning viewer can notice subtle changes in Eugene's wardrobe. At one point the black vest beneath his black jacket is replaced by a white vest; later, Eugene wears a white jacket with a black vest; finally, after the first Dutch Masters commercial break, Eugene wears a plaid jacket and light colored pants, and a necktie instead of a bow tie. The variations are effective and humorous in that they both provide intended continuity lapses and essay the medium of black and white television — arguably, a color broadcast would have called *too much* attention to Eugene's wardrobe shifts.

43. "The Work of Art...," 238.

44. One is also reminded of Duchamp's definitive moment in art history when he drew a moustache on a reproduction of the Mona Lisa and titled it "*L.H.O.O.Q.*," which some suggested was a pun on "*Elle a un chaud cul*" ("She has a hot ass"). If Duchamp's gesture became the avant-garde's unconditional repudiation of the "artistic masterpiece," Kovacs could be seen championing the power of cinema over painting with a similar irreverence.

45. As noted in Chapter One, Benjamin saw — and criticized — Surrealism as not opposed to, but sharing the avant-garde's fascination with the machine ("Surrealism," in *Reflections*, 185).

46. In *Duck Amuck*, Daffy Duck becomes trapped in the animation process as it continually undermines his efforts to adjust to the world: backgrounds continually change and his body can be erased and redrawn as a hideous amalgam of animals, plants, and inanimate objects. Particularly relevant to Kovacs and *Eugene*'s sequence of events in the study, objects and the sounds are rendered completely incongruent in *Duck Amuck*. In one scene, Daffy Duck is erased and redrawn as a guitar-slinging cowboy; when he strums the guitar, machine-gun fire erupts, and when he smashes the guitar the shattering wood corresponds to a braying donkey. During one of his many diatribes directed at the animator torturing him, Daffy Duck's voice is suddenly replaced by recorded animal noises: a monkey, a tropical bird, and a cat. In this sense, *Duck Amuck* represents the animated character's descent into an existential hell of the technological process itself (the very cartoon animation process that gives Daffy Duck "life"): a process whose brutal manipulations of sight and sound deny rationality and existence becomes perceptual and cognitive torture inflicted by the petulant whims of the sadistic animator (revealed to be none other than arch-nemesis Bugs Bunny).

47. Erwin Panofsky, "Style in Medium in Motion Pictures," in *Film Theory and Criticism: Introductory Readings*, 4th ed., 229. Emphasis added.

48. *Kovacsland*, 208.

Chapter 4

1. As quoted in "The Soupy Sales Show," page 2 of 7. Archived at: www.tvparty.com/soupy.html. Accessed: 12/08/2004.

2. Children's TV remains one of the more potentially avant-garde TV genres, specifically a show such as the mind-boggling *Teletubbies* (BBC, 1997–2001), which can be viewed very much in relation to early experimental cinema.

3. See also Suzanne Rautiolla-Williams. "Howdy Doody." Archived at: www.museum tv/archives/etv/H/htmlH/howdydoodys/howdy doodys.htm. Accessed: 12/19/2004. I would depart from this essay to the extent my own view is that *Howdy Doody*'s use of the Native American stereotypes and celebration of technology have a hidden ideological function.

4. Winchell was greatly influenced by Edgar Bergen, and his dummies were essentially variations on Bergen's Charlie McCarthy (Mahoney) and Mortimer Snerd (Smiff).

5. Dick Shawn, a well-known comedian with the sensibilities of Andy Kaufman or Jonathan Winters, literally died onstage during a performance at UCSD in 1987. Shawn suffered a fatal heart attack, and unfortunately

everyone assumed it was part of his unconventional brand of stand-up comedy and patiently waited for him to resume the act.

6. *Late Night with Conan O'Brien* took this bit as the basis for O'Brien's "Desk Drive" routine, in which he sits behind his desk with a prop steering wheel while various changing backgrounds are rear-projected behind him on a green screen while O'Brien states the obvious scenery changes, or, more correctly, directs the scenery changes. In one show, a "desk drive" through Chicago featured O'Brien stating things like, "Hey, let's go to Wrigley Field," followed by stock footage of the exterior of Wrigley Field. In short, O'Brien played pop-culture tour guide versus Lee's reactor to surreal changes in time and space.

7. See Henry Jenkins, "Bob Keeshan." Archived at: www.museum.tv/archieves/etv/K/htmlK/keeshanbob/keeshanbob.htm. Assessed: 12/15/20004.

8. Numerous stars appeared on *The Electric Company*; cast regulars included Rita Moreno and a then-unknown Morgan Freeman. Bill Cosby appeared on occasion as a guest star, and Mel Brooks, Joan Rivers, and Gene Wilder did voices for animated segments.

9. In contrast, Reubens's breakout feature, *Pee-Wee's Big Adventure* (1984, dir. Tom Burton), tends to fall victim to the pastiche approach of postmodernism—a parody of Vittorio di Sica's *The Bicycle Thief* as a road comedy that houses references to everything from country singer Red Sovine to Godzilla movies.

10. *The Pee-Wee Herman Show*, the stage version of what evolved into *Pee-Wee's Playhouse*, was a hit on the LA club circuit and a concert special shown on HBO in 1981. Herman's avant-garde homage to children's TV worked much more effectively as *Playhouse* precisely because it was done as a Saturday morning kid's show. *The Pee-Wee Herman Show*, done on a theatrical stage with much more overt sexual jokes, had a much stronger affinity for burlesque.

11. Sales also did a short-lived, primetime comedy-variety program for ABC in 1962, *The Soupy Sales Show*.

12. See Soupy Sales with Charles Salzberg, *Soupy Sez!: My Zany Life and Times* (New York: M. Evans, 2001), 140–2. Sales noted that audio tracks of many of his shows were recorded for reference; given the almost mythic notoriety in popular culture of Sales's alleged statements, they would have inevitably surfaced in some recorded form. An infamous prank pulled on *Lunch with Soupy Sales!* revealed a naked woman behind the stage when Sales opened a door at the back of the set; it has appeared on several "blooper" shows.

13. The WNEW *Soupy Sales Show* was considered lost for many years, save for bootleg kinescope footage. However, *Soupy Sales: In Living Black and White*, a DVD compilation of material from the WNEW shows, was released in 2006 by Morada Vision.

14. Comedian Chuck McCann hosted a series of popular local "kidult shows" in New York City in the 1960s, including a *Chuck McCann Show* that aired on WNEW from 1965 to 1966. It was a similar deconstruction of TV taken to Dada levels (whether driving around the studio smashing into props on a scooter while lip-synching a song, or doing a lengthy impersonation of Jack Benny playing screeching violin worthy of Stockhausen). One hilarious segment of a *Chuck McCann Show* featured a late-night movie parody featuring his persona "Sid Dump." The segment alternated between endless commercial parodies, Dump's verbose monologues, and an occasional second or two of public domain footage from a low-budget movie—a representation of late-night TV not only satirically hilarious, but absolutely accurate in its depiction of late-night TV being a "dump" to consume air-time. Sandy Becker was another well-known NYC TV figure who hosted the "kidult" *The Sandy Becker Show* for WNEW from 1961 to 1968, which featured numerous Becker personas, a stable of puppets, and numerous genre satires.

15. Nastasi contended that the word "bippy" was one of several elements *Rowan and Martin's Laugh-In* appropriated from *The Soupy Sales Show*. See *Soupy Sez*, 125.

16. The News Year's Day controversy is recounted by Sales and Nastasi in *Soupy Sez!*, 135–41. According to Sales, he received $80,000, virtually all of it in Monopoly money; the few pieces of actual U.S. currency were donated to Jerry Lewis's MD fund through WNEW.

17. As quoted in "The Soupy Sales Show," page 1 of 7.

18. Mrs. Miller was a popular novelty act in the mid–1960s, and her version of "Downtown" was a hit single off her album *Mrs. Miller's Greatest Hits* (1966). She has since been championed as an example of "outsider music": unintentionally avant-garde popular music often combining earnest enthusiasm and difficult listening.

19. WNEW cancelled *The Chuck McCann Show* in 1966 and *The Sandy Becker Show* in 1968.

20. *Soupy Sez!*, 138; see also 120–3. Sales also did a short-lived, syndicated revival of *The Soupy Sales Show* format in 1979 as *The New*

Soupy Sales Show. Sales' post–WNEW work on TV was as a regular panelist on *What's My Line* from 1968 to 1974; hosting a Saturday teen game show *Junior Almost Anything Goes!* (ABC, 1976–7); and as a regular on *Sha-Na-Na!* (syndicated, 1976–81), a comedy-variety show starring the 1950s retro rock band Sha-Na-Na. He also made guest appearances on various game shows, talk shows, and variety shows. From 1985 to 1988, Sales worked on WNBC radio in New York City; his timeslot was between Howard Stern and Don Imus.

21. *Film Form*, 234.

22. See Rick Altman, "*The Lonely Villa* and Griffith's Paradigmatic Style," *Quarterly Review of Film Studies* 6, no. 2 (1981): 123–34.

23. As quoted in "The Soupy Sales Show," page 2 of 7.

24. The other exception would be "Peaches," who appeared on the WNEW shows as Sales's girlfriend. On camera, Peaches was played by Sales in drag in pre-recorded segments. Nastasi also played Peaches in "Nut at the Door"–style segments, with Sales conversing with her gesturing hands in the doorway.

25. See *Soupy Sez!*, 140. As well as doing the puppetry and being the mocking voice(s) of the off-camera crew, Nastasi played "the hands" and occasionally appeared as recurring characters, such as "Onions Oregano" in the gangster film parody "Philo Kvetch" skits. Clyde Adler was the head puppeteer on the Detroit shows, *Lunch with Soupy Sales!*, and *The New Soupy Sales Show*.

26. *Dada and Surrealist Films*, 19.

27. *Dada and Surrealist Film*, 19–20. Elsaesser argued that Picabia was disappointed by *Entr'acte*'s reception when it premiered as the intermission segment for his Dada ballet *Relâache* (a term used in theater to mean "no performance today" for sudden cancellations of a scheduled show). According to Elsaesser's account, Picabia was annoyed that the audience simply sat and passively watched the film rather than doing their normal intermission activities: talking, impatiently waiting for the second half of the show, or going to the lobby. While the film was Dada, it was unable to become a Dada performance. However, Clair recounted the premiere differently, and the film indeed provoked the intended audience response. See "Picabia, Satie, and the First Night of *Entr'acte*" in *A Nous la liberté/Entr'acte*, 111.

28. However, Sales noted that the show, despite its chaotic appearance, was written by him in advance, and the shows were much more organized and planned-out than they appeared to be on-camera. Daily production meetings consisted of coordinating the technical details with the producers and crew, a staff meeting over the script, and a run-through of the show before airtime. Nevertheless, the telecast was often subject to a great deal of improvisation, especially when the plan went awry due to a technical gaffe. See *Soupy Sez!*, 58–60, 122–3.

29. Sales began his entertainment career as a radio disc jockey, and began his TV career in 1950, hosting a weekday afternoon teen-dance show in WKRC in Cincinnati, *Soupy's Soda Shop* (1950–1). While the show featured big-band music instead of rock, Sales does note *Soupy's Soda Shop* prefigured future teen dance shows such as *American Bandstand*. See *Soupy Sez!*, 42–6.

Chapter 5

1. As quoted in Kenneth M. Dolbeare, *American Political Thought* (Monterey: Duxbury Press, 1981), 192.

2. *Gomer Pyle, USMC* borrowed its central premise from *No Time for Sergeants*, which was a hit play on Broadway in 1955, followed by a successful 1958 teleplay version that appeared on *The U.S. Steel Hour*, and soon after a Hollywood film directed by Mervyn LeRoy. Andy Griffith starred in all three versions, and constructed his popular persona as the "backwoods scholar" modeled after the myth of Abraham Lincoln (a persona Griffith also cultivated on his legal drama series *Matlock*).

3. Marshall McLuhan, *Understanding Media* (Cambridge: MIT Press, 1994), 167.

4. *Understanding Media*, 165–6. Emphasis added.

5. See also Paul Cullum, "Paul Henning," page 1 of 3. Archived at: www.museum.tv/scrchieves/etv/H/henningpaul/henningpaul.htm. Accessed: 11/5/2004.

6. Paul Cullum, "The Beverly Hillbillies," page 1 of 2. Archived at: www.museum.tv/archives/etv/B/beverlyhillb/beverlyhillb.htm. Accessed: 11/8/2004.

7. Jed's family members were, in effect, taken from *Li'l Abner*: Granny from Mammy Yokum, Elly May from Daisy May, and Jethro from Li'l Abner.

8. "The Beverly Hillbillies," page 1 of 2. Cullum noted that in 1966, the peak of *The Beverly Hillbillies*' popularity, Ebsen wrote and starred as Abraham Lincoln in the play *The Champagne Generation*.

9. The ideological construction of Lincoln in American cinema appears early on and is highly problematic. In Griffith's *Birth of a Nation* (1915), the valorization of the American South as victim of Northern tyranny is tem-

pered, or contradicted, by its valorization of Lincoln as the embodiment of Jeffersonian Democracy rather than the leader of Northern imperialist forces.

10. *The Communist Manifesto,* trans. Samuel Moore (New York: Pocket Books, 1964), 65.

11. Cullum, "The Beverly Hillbillies," page 2 of 2. Emphasis added.

12. However, *Petticoat Junction* can be seen as a parody of *My Three Sons* (ABC, 1960–5; CBS, 1965–72) or even *Bonanza,* which focused on widowed fathers raising sons in an all-male, patriarchal order. Norman Lear is often credited with introducing television's first single-mom-raising-daughters household with *One Day at a Time* (CBS, 1975–84). *One Day at a Time* did feature the first *divorced* single mother on network TV, but *Petticoat Junction* featured a "mother and daughters" family unit a decade earlier.

13. Shortly after *Green Acres* premiered to some surprisingly positive reviews, Henning took out a full page ad in *Variety* to thank the critics, but pointed out that Jay Sommers deserved the critical kudos. See Steve Cox, *The Hooterville Handbook: A Viewer's Guide to Green Acres* (New York: St. Martin's Press, 1993), xii.

14. However, David Marc noted that *Green Acres* can be read as a kind of conservative satire directed at the 1960s counterculture ethos to "drop out of the rat race and go organic" (*Comic Visions,* 117).

15. For instance, the early seasons of *The Beverly Hillbillies* and *Gilligan's Island* were done in black and white for budgetary reasons. *The Addams Family* (ABC, 1964–6) was filmed in black and white to parody the Gothic horror look.

16. As quoted in Grose and Kenworthy, 616. Emphasis original.

17. Slavoj Žižek, *The Sublime Object of Ideology* (New York: Verso, 1989), 131–2. Emphasis added.

18. Paul Cullum, "Paul Henning," page 1 of 3.

19. See also Paul Cullum, "Green Acres," page 1 of 2. Archived at: www.museum.tv/archives/etv/G/htmlG/greenacres/greenacres.htm. Accessed: 11/08/2004.

20. See also Marc, *Comic Visions,* 117.

21. In this respect, I borrow from Jacques Lacan's "Seminar on 'The Purloined Letter,'" reprinted in *The Purloined Poe: Lacan, Derrida, and Psychoanalytic Reading,* ed. John P. Muller and William J. Richardson (Baltimore: John Hopkins University Press, 1988), 28–54. Lacan uses Poe's story as a case study of the workings of the Symbolic Order. The letter, in both sense of the term, must be continually circulated, empowering the owner only to symbolically castrate them when they relinquish it: "The letter can only be *held,* not *possessed*" (*The Purloined Poe,* 42). However, in Jacques Derrida, "The Purveyor of Truth" (*The Purloined Poe,* 173–212), one of Derrida's criticism of Lacan is that the circulation of the signifier is not psychoanalytic (castration) but economic (exchange): "a circle of restricted economy" (*The Purloined Poe,* 184). On *Green Acres,* the emphasis is on the distribution and circulation of signifiers and its effect on integrating its victim — Oliver Douglas — into the workings of this "restricted economy."

22. *Green Acres* is remembered for the wealth of self-reflexive commentaries in the show, exemplified by the opening credits — which frequently appeared on props in the show, with characters commenting on them (for instance, names appear on Oliver's clothes while Lisa hangs the laundry, prompting her to ask: "Who's Paul Henning? ... And why do you have his shirt?").

23. Slavoj Žižek, "The Obscene Object of Postmodernity," in *A Žežik Reader,* ed. Elizabeth Wright and Edmond Wright (London: Blackwell, 1999), 48.

24. The Editors of *Cahiers du cinema,* "*Young Mr. Lincoln,*" trans. Helen Lacker and Diane Matais, reprinted in *Narrative, Ideology, Apparatus: A Film Theory Reader,* ed. Phillip Rosen (New York: Columbia University Press, 1986), 444–82.

25. Bill Nichols, *Ideology and the Image* (Bloomington: Indiana University Press, 1981), 107.

26. "Function and Field of Speech and Language," in *Ecrits,* 66.

27. Lacan, "Function and Field of Speech and Language," in *Ecrits,* 67.

28. "*Young Mr. Lincoln,*" 480–1.

29. *Comic Visions,* 118.

30. *Green Acres* did not have an official series finale episode. The final two episodes of *Green Acres,* "Hawaiian Honeymoon" and "The Ex-Secretary" (both 1971), were thinly-disguised pilots for other shows. Neither became a series.

31. William James, "What Pragmatism Means," in *Pragmatism* (New York: Barnes and Noble Books, 2003), 23.

32. Raymond Williams, *Marxism and Literature* (New York: Oxford University Press, 1977), 83; see also 83–87. Williams contended that Marx's determinism is often simplified as a sort of fixed, inexorable "natural law" based on "scientific" principles (economics); determinism must also be understood as variable historical "social processes" (culture, politics)

responding to *both* the "setting of limits" and "exertion of pressures" of capitalism. "Overdetermination" becomes "a *complex and interrelated process of limits and pressures ... in the whole social process itself and nowhere else*—not in an abstracted mode of production nor in an abstracted psychology" (87, emphasis added).

33. Louis Althusser, *For Marx*, trans. Ben Brewster (New York: Verso, 1991), 111. Emphasis original.

34. *For Marx*, 231. Emphasis added. While Althusser is addressing capitalism, ideology can certainly be seen as functioning the same way in the Soviet Union or Nazi Germany.

35. *For Marx*, 233. Emphasis original.

36. While Marx's work appeared decades before Freud, Althusser contended that Marx's conception of "false consciousness," the adoption of bourgeois ideology by the masses that was contradictory to their own interests, "is exactly like the theoretical status of the dream among writers before Freud." See Louis Althusser, "Ideology and Ideological State Apparatuses," in *Lenin and Philosophy and Other Essays*, trans. Ben Brewster (New York: Monthly Review Press, 1971), 159.

37. A highly-recommended summary of Althusser and the role of Lacan is Terry Eagleton, *Literary Theory: An Introduction* (Minneapolis: University of Minnesota, 1983), 171–3.

38. *For Marx*, 233–4. Emphasis added.

39. See "Ideology and Ideological State Apparatuses," 176. Perhaps the most succinct expression of the Althusserian formula of capitalist existence was the Godfathers' 1980s punk-anthem, "Birth, School, Work, Death."

40. *For Marx*, 100–1. Emphasis original. In this regard, Althusser points to Germany in 1849, and France in 1871, where overdetermination inhibited revolutionary action against capitalism; and Russia in 1917, where overdetermination exacerbated revolution. In this respect, determination cannot be seen as inevitably producing the end of capitalism (see 104–5).

41. *Pragmatism*, 114.

42. As quoted in Žižek, 28.

43. *Avant-Garde: The Experimental Theater in France*, 110–1.

Chapter 6

1. As quoted in "The Smothers Brothers Show," page 1 of 5. Archived at: www.tvparty.com/smothers.html. Accessed: 11/24/2004.

2. As quoted in Peter N. Carroll, *It Seems Like Nothing Happened: The Tragedy and Promise of America in the 1970s* (New York: Holt, Rinehart, and Winston, 1982), 62. Emphasis original.

3. Stephen Stills was among the finalists, but was not chosen. Contrary to pop-culture myth, aspiring musician Charles Manson did not audition to be a Monkee.

4. This was not an uncommon practice in the era. For instance, the Beach Boys frequently employed session musicians in place of band members on recordings.

5. In 1968, CBS began a Saturday morning cartoon version of the long-running Archie Comics (which began publication ca. 1940). Kirshner became the musical supervisor for the show, and a studio band supplied songs for "the Archies," the rock band composed of Archie Andrews and the other main characters of the show (Kirshner reportedly once commented that the advantage of working in animation was that characters could be erased if they talked back). The execrable single "Sugar Sugar" sold a million copies in 1969. In 1970, ABC successfully developed its own TV-music industry hybrid, the Partridge Family.

6. CBS bought *The Monkees* shows and aired them on Saturday afternoons from 1969 to 1973; ABC followed suit in 1973–4. MTV also added reruns of *The Monkees* to its programming schedule in the mid-1980s.

7. "Mijacogeo" is also known as "The Forbis Caper." It was written and directed by Dolenz, who also insisted on Buckley as a guest star. While "Song of the Siren" is not explicitly about drug addiction, the vivid, metaphorical link between the lure of the deadly sirens to drugs in the song can certainly be made. Buckley, who appears to be in a state of narcotics intoxication while performing the song on *The Monkees*, tragically died of a heroin overdose in 1975. ("Song of the Siren" eventually appeared on Buckley's 1971 album *Starsailor*, his most ambitious effort to combine folk and free-jazz.)

8. Largely due to a resurgence of interest when MTV added reruns of *The Monkees* to its schedule for a period in the 1980s, Dolenz, Jones, Tork, and occasionally Nesmith collaborated on occasional reunion tours and albums in the 1980s and 1990s.

9. See Marc, *Comic Visions*, 118–9.

10. As quoted in Tony Hendra, *Going Too Far* (New York: Dolphin/Doubleday, 1987), 208.

11. Aniko Bodroghkozy, "The Smothers Brothers Comedy Hour," page 1 of 4. Archived at: www.museum.tv/archieves/etv/S/html/S/smothersbrot/smothersbrot.htm. Emphasis added. Accessed: 11/06/04.

12. As quoted in Tony Hendra, *Going Too*

Far (New York: Dolphin/Doubleday, 1987), 207.

13. *Comic Visions*, 120. Emphasis added. See also 123.

14. Einstein's most famous comic persona is the hapless, self-destructive daredevil "Super Dave Osborne," a parody of Evil Kinevil.

15. *Going Too Far*, 222.

16. As quoted in Hendra, 219.

17. As quoted in "The Smothers Brothers Show," page 4 of 5.

18. The exception was *TV Guide*, which published an anonymous editorial supporting CBS.

19. As quoted in Christopher Arnott, "Turn in, Turn on, Laugh-In," *The New Haven Advocate.com*. (October 16, 2006). Archived at: www.ctnow.com/custom./nmm/newhavenadvocate/hcc-nha-1019-nh431aughin43artoct19,0,5829275,story. Accessed: 10/22/06.

20. ABC embarked on a disastrous attempt at counterculture comedy with the infamous *Turn-On*, a project from Schlatter which exacerbated the sex jokes and the jump-cut editing pace of *Laugh-In*. It was cancelled after a single episode aired on February 5, 1969. Contrary to public memory, *Turn-On* was not terminated by ABC in mid-broadcast; the myth owes to the fact that several local ABC affiliates did pull the show during the broadcast. (Note: Chuck McCann was hired as a regular on *Turn-On*.)

21. Henry Jenkins, "Rowan and Martin's Laugh-In," page 1 of 2. Archived at: www.museum.tv/archieves/etv/R/htmlR/rowananddmar/rowanandmar.htm. Accessed: 11/20/2004.

22. See also Aniko Bodroghkzy, "Laugh-In," page 1 of 3. Published in *The St. James Encyclopedia of Pop Culture* (2002). Also archived at: www.findarticles.com/p/articles/mi_glepc/is_t ov/ai_2419100698/print. Accessed: 11/25/2004.

23. The weekly *Laugh-In* segments were analogous to the various "departments" of a given issue of *Mad* magazine and its various satirical studies of current events and political figures on both the Left and the Right, such as artist Dave Berg's monthly "Lighter Side of..." comic scripts on life in America. Interspersed between the topical material was the equivalent of the *Laugh-In* "sight-gags": the slapstick of Antonio Prohias's legendary "Spy vs. Spy" or the surrealism of Don Martin in their comic strips. The numerous "marginals" by Sergio Aragonés, the barely visible comics that appeared on the margins of *Mad*'s pages, were not unlike the onscreen announcements that ran at the bottom of the screen in conjunction to the onscreen activities. See also McLuhan, *Understanding Media*, 164–9, for a discussion of *Mad* Magazine. (Note: *Mad* magazine entered into a licensing agreement with Fox in 1995 for the network to create *MADtv*, a sketch comedy show that kept *Mad*'s title, logo, the image of *Mad* poster boy Alfred E. Neumann in the credits, and brief "Spy vs. Spy" or Don Martin animated segments — and absolutely nothing else from the magazine. Save the logo, all references to *Mad* magazine on *MADtv* have since been eliminated in the show.)

24. The *Laugh-In* party segment was one of many Culture Industry staples archly parodied in Russ Meyer's *Beyond the Valley of the Dolls* (1970). *Laugh-In*'s "roaming bachelor" Dick Martin later married *BVD* star Dolly Read.

25. In fact, *Laugh-In* creator George Schlatter is married to Jolene Brand, a regular on the ABC *Ernie Kovacs Show* who appeared as the woman in the bathtub. Another Kovacs routine, in which a Native American stereotype fumbles with a bow and arrow in a variety of varied sight-gags, was recycled on *Laugh-In*, with Tom Conway playing Robin Hood — a change owing to the political climate and Native American rights movements.

26. Bodroghkozy, "Laugh-In," page 2 of 3.

27. As quoted in Arnott, *op. cit.*

28. In my screening of several episodes from the first two seasons, *one* joke referred to Nixon, remarking that his campaign plane was having problems because the right wing was out of balance with the left.

29. A pivotal aspect of Nixon's 1968 presidential campaign was his "Southern Strategy," and gaining the support of conservative white voters in the South who were traditionally Democrats. Nixon realized that the shrill Northern liberal Hubert H. Humphrey and his pro–Civil Rights record made him a particularly unattractive candidate, and thus a voting demographic to which Nixon could appeal. However, Nixon also realized correctly that a sizable number of Southern Democrats disenchanted with Humphrey could opt for Wallace rather than him, and that Wallace rather than Humphrey was his chief obstacle in securing key electoral votes in the South. Thus, Wallace's candidacy could not be dismissed as a minor third-party inconvenience, and Nixon had to run two campaigns — one against Humphrey and one separating himself from Wallace.

30. Bodroghkozy, "Laugh-In," page 2 of 3.

31. Jenkins, "Rowan and Martin's Laugh-In." page 1 of 2.

32. See Michel Foucault, *The History of Sexuality, Vol. I: An Introduction*, trans. Robert Hurley (New York: Vintage, 1990), especially Part Two and pgs. 150–152.

33. For all their platitudes of justice and equality, the New Left, Civil Rights movement, and counterculture were fraught with sexism and chauvinism, and many leading feminists in the 1970s actually emerged from that experience. A recommended history is Sara Evans, *Personal Politics: The Roots of Women's Liberation in the Civil Rights Movement and the New Left* (New York: Vintage, 1980).

34. *Theory of the Avant-Garde*, 80–1. Emphasis added.

35. As quoted in Marc, *Comic Visions*, 184.

36. Jean-Luc Comolli and Jean Narboni, "Cinema/Ideology/Criticism" in *Film Theory and Criticism: Introductory Readings*, 4th ed., 687. Comolli and Narboni were also among the *Cahiers* editors who wrote "*Young Mr. Lincoln.*"

37. Albert Aus, "Columbia Broadcasting Network," page 1 of 3. Archived at: www.museum.tv/archieves/etv/C/htmlC/columbiabroa/columbiabroa.htm. Accessed: 11/6/2004.

38. *Petticoat Junction* was cancelled in 1970. Bea Benaderet died of cancer in 1968, and the show faltered in the ratings when it attempted to continue in her absence. However, had *Petticoat Junction* still been on the CBS roster, one can speculate, with some degree of certainty, that it would have been cancelled.

39. After their respective cancellations, *The Lawrence Welk Show* and *Hee Haw* continued production as syndicated shows: *The Lawrence Welk Show* running until 1983; *Hee Haw* until 1993.

40. *Gomer Pyle* was cancelled in 1969 when Jim Nabors decided to leave the sitcom for comedy-variety. *The Jim Nabors Hour* ran on CBS from 1969 until (not surprisingly) 1971.

41. What was lost on critics was the fact that Werner Klemperer, who hilariously played the bungling, neurotic Colonel Klink, was Jewish, and his father, noted classical musician and conductor Otto Klemperer, was forced to flee Nazi Germany with his family. John Banner, who played the portly, idiotic Sergeant Schultz, and Robert Clary, who played the intrepid POW LeBeau, were also Jewish and had been interred in concentration camps during World War II. Klemperer and Banner both stated they relished the opportunity to play Nazis as objects of comic ridicule, such as in the films of Mel Brooks. Adorno found any attempts to critique fascism through comedy eminently unsuccessful — be it Chaplin's *The Great Dictator* or Brecht's *Arturo Ui* (see "Commitment," 305–6). One could assume his reaction to *Hogan's Heroes* or Roberto Benigni's Holocaust "comedy" *Life Is Beautiful* (1997) would have been similar.

42. See also, Marc, *Comic Visions*, 161–2.

43. The change in the title was not only motivated by major cast changes (Rob Reiner and Sally Struthers left in 1978, Jean Stapleton in 1980), but Archie's own socially mobility. In 1977 he quit his jobs as dock worker and part-time taxi driver to buy Kelsey's Bar, and re-christened it Archie Bunker's Place. The show's final years shifted the focus from Bunker's working-class resentment to his struggles as a middle-class entrepreneur. See also Marc, *Comic Visions*, 153–4.

44. *Good Times* was a spin-off of *Maude*.

45. See also Carroll, 61–62.

46. *It Seemed Like Nothing Happened*, 63.

47. "For *The Theater and Its Double*," in *Selected Writings*, 234–5.

Chapter 7

1. Chuck Barris, *Confessions of a Dangerous Mind: An Unauthorized Autobiography* (New York: Hyperion, 2002), 99. Barris's surreal autobiography alternates between his TV career and his claims he was working as a CIA assassin; it was made into a film in 2002, directed by George Clooney. In this respect, Barris's recollections on the particulars of his TV career may admittedly be somewhat suspect as well. My own reliance on *Confessions of a Dangerous Mind* is Barris's discussion of the "philosophy" behind the shows.

2. As quoted in Barris, 180.

3. For completely difference reasons, *Deal or No Deal* (NBC, 2006–) performs a similar operation. On *Deal or No Deal*, the drama and goal of the game show is not generated by the amount of money won, but the success or failure of the deal made by the contestant. A contestant can be considered a winner if they sell a suitcase containing a penny for a few thousand dollars, and a loser if they sell their suitcase in the low six figures if it contained the million dollar grand prize.

4. A popular board-game marketed to teenage girls, "Mystery Date" had players maneuver around the board and prepare for their rendezvous (planning and dressing appropriately) until they could uncover the identity of their mystery date: a photo behind a small plastic door on the game board. Any number of photos might be revealed, ranging from tuxedo-clad gentlemen and hunky male models to nerds and working-class slobs. Commercials for the product featured girls in pajamas, presumably during a slumber-party, playing the game. and each girl opening the little door while a male announcer thundered how the date might be a "dreamboat" (a photo of a handsome well-

dressed suitor) or a "dud" (a photo of the class geek or a construction worker).
  5. *Confessions of a Dangerous Mind*, 56. Emphasis added.
  6. Peter Andrews as quoted in Barris, 180.
  7. It was also the tension of *The Dating Game*'s absurd tragicomedy and malicious subtext that transcended the dearth of subsequent "reality dating shows" *The Dating Game* is blamed for spawning: the numbing banality of *The Love Connection* (syndicated, 1983–94), the ruthless soap operas *The Bachelor* (ABC, 2002–) and *The Bachelorette* (ABC, 2003–5), and the unremitting sadism of *Blind Date* (syndicated, 1999–2006), *ElimiDATE* (syndicated, 2001–6), *The Fifth Wheel* (syndicated, 2001–4); and *EX-treme Dating* (syndicated, 2002). *ElimiDATE* is particularly "noteworthy" in that many times it is a *male* contestant who four *women* vie over through a combination of brazen flirtation directed towards him and bitchy cattiness directed towards each other as he eliminates them one by one.
  8. *Confessions of a Dangerous Mind*, 97.
  9. The public outcry over the "quiz-show" scandals of the 1950s when contestants were given answers in advance may have stemmed not from the fact that the contestants "cheated," but that the American public had been "cheated" out of the ability to mock contestants who missed questions. Also, I refer back to "The $99,000 Answer" episode of *The Honeymooners*, in which Ralph Kramden's disastrous appearance on a game show, a site of public failure and humiliation, is typical of the many tragic-comic moments of his life where the American Dream has utterly betrayed him (see Chapter Two).
  10. *Confessions of a Dangerous Mind*, 155. Emphasis original.
  11. *Confessions of a Dangerous Mind*, 155. Emphasis added.
  12. *Confessions of a Dangerous Mind*, 161.
  13. *Confessions of a Dangerous Mind*, 161. Emphasis added. Barbour is not mentioned by name in the book, but is clearly the person Barris refers to only as "the Putz." Barbour is best remembered for hosting the "reality-variety show" *Real People* (NBC, 1979–84), which showcased the odd side of American life.
  14. *The Gong Show* was the joint creation of Barris and Chris Bearde, a former *Laugh-In* writer. *Laugh-In*'s occasional "New Talent Time," featuring strange novelty acts (Tiny Tim was once showcased) or comedians performing intentionally inept routines (Paul Winchell as inept ventriloquist "Lucky Pierre"), can certainly be seen as a precursor to *The Gong Show*. Around the time Barris took over the sole hosting duties, Barris also assumed sole creative control of the show as well. Neither Bearde nor Owens is mentioned in *Confessions of a Dangerous Mind*.
  15. The lone success story of *The Gong Show* was Cheryl Lynn, a young singer who landed a recording contract after her appearance and had a top 20 hit, "Got to be Real."
  16. Tristan Tzara, "Lecture on Dada" (1922), reprinted in *The Dada Painters and Poets*, 2nd ed., ed. and trans. Robert Motherwell (Cambridge: Belknap Press of the Harvard University Press, 1981), 248.
  17. For instance, Wesley Willis, a 300-pound diagnosed schizophrenic, gave new meaning to the term "minimalism" with his singular musical style, which used the same Casio keyboard program for every song, with various lyrics about his friends, favorite artists, or his battles with his weight and schizophrenia. Willis gained a large cult following in the punk and avant-garde musical community, and released a number of albums before dying of leukemia in 2003. Far closer to "primitive poetics" than the "joke act" he was sometimes considered, Willis would have been an ideal contestant-performer on *The Gong Show*.
  18. This particular performance is recounted from a personal memory of watching *The Gong Show* in the 1970s; my research was unable to ascertain this man's name.
  19. *Confessions of a Dangerous Mind*, 161.
  20. *Confessions of a Dangerous Mind*, 159–61. Emphasis added.
  21. This is not to ignore the affirmative nature of *American Idol*, namely the nationally televised "rags-to-riches" story of the eventual winner. Or, as fifth season *AI* winner Taylor Hicks proclaimed during his victory song, "I'm living the American Dream!" However, while Hicks won the popular vote, three other *AI* fifth season contestants also became winners by subsequently signing contracts with Simon Cowell's 19 Entertainment management agency: runner-up Catherine McPhee, country singer Kelli Pickler, and Alternative singer Chris Daughtry, whose unexpected vote-off seemed to stir more controversy in the press than the disputed 2000 Presidential elections.
  22. *American Idol*, 3/15/05 telecast. Emphasis added.
  23. In particular, *Survivor* replicates the "state of nature" as a "war of each against all" to, quite unintentionally, reveal the "nature" of liberal ideology: competing interests do not lead to mutual cooperation and civil society, but temporary and shifting alliances to achieve immediate goals until one person emerges victorious (see also Chapter 11).

24. This concept should not be confused with the actual game show *Greed* (Fox, 1999). Hosted by the unassuming Chuck Wollery (*The Love Connection*), Fox's *Greed* was a standard quiz-show, with the added dimension of team play which allowed for some cutthroat competition between two teams and within the teams.

25. Bianca Ryan, a talented teenage singer, won the first season *AGT* million dollar prize, and, of course, was quickly signed to Cowell's SYCO record label.

26. *America's Got Talent,* 7/5/06 telecast.

27. See *Performance Art*, 74.

28. See *Confessions of a Dangerous Mind*, 177.

29. Langston was a well-known comedian who appeared as a regular on *The Sonny and Cher Comedy Hour* (CBS, 1971–4) and *The Hudson Brothers Razzle Dazzle Show* (CBS, 1974–5). While the Unknown Comic was an inspired gimmick — a bad comic so ashamed of his himself and his material that he wore a paper bag over his head — Langston had recently filed for bankruptcy after a comedy-club venture failed and needed the work; he reportedly concealed his identity so the public would not recognize him and get the impression that he had resorted to working on the much-reviled *Gong Show*.

30. Walter Benjamin, "The Work of Art…," 231. Emphasis added.

31. The early auditions of *American Idol*'s fourth season were very much designed to prevent another William Hung "fluke" by insuring the most untalented performers in the early auditions were also depicted as belligerent, egotistical, and unsympathetic.

32. The NBC stagehand controversy is recounted in *Confessions of a Dangerous Mind*, 190–1. *The Late Show with David Letterman* has since used this strategy, with Letterman's stable of comedic regulars being his stagehands, interns, and nearby business owners rather than professional comedians and actors.

33. For a hilarious account of the Popsicle Twins incident, see *Confessions of a Dangerous Mind*, 178–9.

34. *Confessions of a Dangerous Mind*, 63.

35. Eubanks claimed for decades that this incident never occurred, but eventually recanted when the infamous segment appeared on a 2002 NBC special, *Outrageous Game Show Moments*, which was hosted by Eubanks.

36. Tom Selleck appeared twice, and lost to another bachelor both times. One can only imagine the lifetime of bragging rights for the contestant who scored a date with Farrah Fawcett or the men who beat Tom Selleck's time — or the embarrassment endured by the contestants who knew they once turned down a romantic evening and potential rendezvous with Tom Selleck.

37. Had Barris created *The Gong Show* after the proliferation of cable and satellite TV, hypothetical *Gong Show: Too Hot for TV!* pay-per-views might have been an ideal outlet rather than a feature film.

38. For Barris's own account of *The Gong Show Movie* and its aftermath, see *Confessions of a Dangerous Mind*, 198–204. Barris eventually returned to television with new versions of *The Dating Game* and *The Newlywed Game* that ran in syndicated markets in the late 1980s.

39. As quoted in *Confessions of a Dangerous Mind*, 139.

Chapter 8

1. As quoted in "The Kaufman Chronicles." Achieved at: http://andykaufman.jvinet.com/kaufchro.htm. Accessed: 12/5/2004.

2. As quoted in *The Midnight Special* (Sony Music Video, 1981).

3. As recounted in *Biography: Andy Kaufman* (Arts and Entertainment network, 1999).

4. See Bob Zmuda, with Matthew Scott Hansen, *Andy Kaufman Revealed!: Best Friend Tells All* (Boston: Little, Brown, 1999), 96–9. I gratefully acknowledge my reliance on Zmuda's book beyond his eyewitness accounts in two respects: one, Zmuda's discussion of many Kaufman routines which were never seen on national TV but were perhaps even more strange and confrontational than his best-remembered work; two, his "behind the scenes" accounts of Kaufman's most famous TV appearances — details which are essential in that Kaufman's "performance" backstage was often as entertaining and provocative as the "performance" in front of the audience.

5. As quoted in *Biography: Andy Kaufman*.

6. Roland Barthes, "The World of Wrestling," in *Mythologies*, 16.

7. As quoted in "The Kaufman Chronicles."

8. As quoted in *Dada and Surrealist Film*, 32.

9. Zmuda recounted that Lorne Michaels only agreed to let Kaufman do "The Great Gatsby" on *SNL* provided he limit it to five minutes and devise a satisfactory resolution for the routine — a punchline. For *SNL*, Zmuda came up with the ending: After five minutes, Kaufman offered the audience a choice between a continued reading of Fitzgerald or lip-synching to a record. Of course, the audience demanded the record, and Kaufman placed the needle on the record: a recording of him

reading *The Great Gatsby*. See *Andy Kaufman Revealed!*, 89; see also 104.

10. As quoted in Bill Zehme, *Lost in the Funhouse: The Life and Mind of Andy Kaufman* (New York: Delta/ Random House, 1999), 139. I also acknowledge my reliance on Zehme's biography; however, I depart from Zehme's interpretation of Kaufman's career. Zehme applauds Kaufman's on-stage work (the avant-garde stand-up and TV specials), but is decidedly not impressed with Kaufman's off-screen "theater of life" performances, such as the *SNL* vote fiasco and especially his pro-wrestling career. In short, Zehme appreciates Kaufman the Dadaist, and *not* Kaufman the Situationist. It should also be noted that Zehme's accounts vary, sometimes considerably, from Zmuda's in *Andy Kaufman Revealed!* In discussing the more infamous moments of Kaufman's career — Tony Clifton's *Taxi* and *Dinah!* appearances; Kaufman's final "intergender" wrestling match on *SNL*, the *SNL* vote — the major discrepancies between Zmuda and Zehme will be noted as appropriate to qualify my own analysis.

11. In the 1970s NYC comedians unionized against club owners in order to receive better, or even any, payment for their appearances. Despite being among the more left-leaning comedians, Kaufman did not join the comedians union, arguing that guaranteed payments for performances placed an exchange value on the evening between performer, club, and audience: it would inevitably require the performer to satisfy audience and club demands over unrestricted and, if necessary, confrontational creativity. See Zmuda, 102–3.

12. As quoted in Zehme, 161. However, Kaufman appeared "uncredited" in the show's opening skit between Michael O'Donoghue and John Belushi. O'Donoghue played a stuffy professor teaching absurd English phrases about "eating wolverines and badgers" which Belushi repeated dead-pan, his character obviously derived from Kaufman's "Foreign Man" persona, even replicating the accent.

13. The use of silence is a frequently neglected element of comedy, which has often emphasized a surplus of frenetic action, both physically and verbally: vaudeville, Jerry Lewis, Robin Williams, Jim Carrey. Jack Benny and especially Bob Newhart have been the exceptions in privileging silence, where the comedy occurs in the spaces where nothing is said. Indeed, Kaufman's use of silence by actively and consciously creating "dead air" can be compared to the avant-garde music of John Cage as much as stand-up comedy, and the extensive use of silence over excessive use of noise to create uncomfortable tension between the performer and audience (Cage's *4'33"*—in which the performer sits at the piano four and a half minutes without playing).

14. This routine originated as one of Kaufman's birthday party staples; see Zmuda, 59–60.

15. This is precisely why comparisons between Kaufman and Sacha Baron Cohen's "Borat" become untenable beyond the fact Cohen does a nebbish foreigner persona and does the performance in the public sphere. While defended by liberals as a satirical exposé of American jingoism, Borat is both an acknowledged put-on and a specific Arab stereotype. Thus, rather than becoming a target of public outrage like Kaufman, Borat allows space to *laugh with* him as a put-on, and/or *laugh at* "the Arab," a stereotype and "an other" ideally suited for derision in a post–9/11, post–Iraq America. The better comparison is Yakov Smirnoff, whose popularity in the 1980s owed greatly to resurgent Cold War sentiment.

16. *Andy Kaufman Reveled!*, 180.

17. For detailed and somewhat divergent accounts of the Clifton *Taxi* "performance," see Zmuda, 132–36; Zehme, 223–31.

18. Kaufman's holistic lifestyle forbade the use of cigarettes and tobacco; he consciously avoided profanity in his routines. As Clifton, Kaufman chain-smoked, guzzled booze, and unleashed streams of curse words.

19. Kaufman as quoted in Zmuda, 136. Zehme's account suggests that Clifton being thrown off the set by security was *not* part of the on-set firing agreement with Weinberger (229).

20. As quoted in *Biography: Andy Kaufman*. Emphasis added.

21. *Andy Kaufman Revealed!*, 132. Emphasis added.

22. The Situationist International (SI), "Definitions," *Situationist International* 1 (1959). Authorship attributed to the SI. Reprinted in Ken Knabb, ed. and trans., *The Situationist International Anthology* (Berkeley: Bureau of Public Secrets, 2001), 45. Emphasis added. All SI texts are also available at the Bureau of Public Secrets website: www.bopsecrets.org.SI.

23. Guy Debord, *The Society of the Spectacle*, trans. Donald Nicholson-Smith (New York: Zone Books, 1995), 145.

24. Guy Debord and Gil J. Wolman, "A User's Guide to Détournement," 9–10. Originally published in *Les Lèvres Neus* 8 (May 1956). Reprinted in *The Situationist International Anthology*, 8–13, as "Methods of Détournement."

25. The Situationist International, "Détournement as Negation and Prelude," *Situationist International* 3 (1959). Reprinted in Knabb, 55. See also Debord and Wolman, 13.

26. Raoul Vaneigem, "Spurious Opposition," in *The Revolution of Everyday Life*. Translated by Gord Hall and Donald Nicholson-Smith. London: Rebel Books, 2001. Also available online at: http://librarry.nothingness.org/articles/SI/en/pub_contents/5. In 1965, Debord hailed the Watts riots as a situation *par excellance*; see "The Decline and Fall of the Spectacular Commodity Society," *Situationist International* 10 (1966). Reprinted in Knabb, 153–9.

27. Toth was not a situationist, but claimed to be Christ resurrected. His actions and involuntary psychiatric commitment without legal process became a *cause célèbre* with the European left in the early 1970s (Toth was released and deported to Australia in 1975). Don Novello, best known as "Father Guido Sarducci" on *SNL*, subsequently wrote numerous satirical letters — sometimes inflammatory, sometimes nonsensical — to public and corporate figures under the penname Lazlo Toth; the letters, as well as the serious responses, have since been collected and published in several books, such as *The Lazlo Letters*. Novello's tactics here can also be seen as a situationist use of comedy.

28. See Debord and Wolman, 9.

29. Debord, *The Society of the Spectacle*, 151–2. Emphasis original.

30. SI, "Definitions," 45 (Knabb). *Jeu d'événements* is sometimes translated as "play of events." However, "play," in this sense, does not refer to a theatrical play (*pièce du théâtre*) but the play of games or children. In this same essay, while "situations" and "situationist" are defined (a "situationist," in short, is someone who participates in "situations"), "Situationism" is defined as "a meaningless term," in that a unified theory of Situationism is opposed to the very nature of constructing and executing situations and being a situationist. For this reason, I have avoided the use of the term "Situationism" in discussing Kaufman.

31. "The Theory of Moments and the Construction of Situations," *Situationist International* 4 (1960). Emphasis original. No authorship attributed, but it is believed to be written by Debord. Archived at: www.notbored.org/moments.html. Accessed: 4/7/2005.

32. "Methods of Détournement," 9–10.

33. Contemporaneous to Kaufman, a situationist use of music occurred with the "great rock and roll swindle" of the Sex Pistols under the direction of their manager, Malcolm McLaren, who had been active in the English Situationist group King's Mob in the early 1970s and a successful entrepreneur of détourned fashion. Between late 1976 and their demise in January 1978, the Sex Pistols signed to EMI and A&M, only to be booted for controversial public behavior — and keeping sizable advances totaling approximately $250,000. After being dropped by A&M, rumors of dubious credibility (possibly even planted by McLaren) soon appeared in the music press claiming that key A&M recording artists, specifically Rick Wakeman, pressured the label to drop the band. Whether true or not (Wakeman has vigorously denied the charges for decades), the very idea that Wakeman, the cape-wearing keyboardist and purveyor of classical-rock bombast, was involved in the firing made perfect fodder to fuel further controversy. Next signing with Virgin Records, best known as the bastion for English avant-garde rock artists (Henry Cow, Robert Wyatt), the Sex Pistols released the inflammatory "God Save the Queen" single during Queen Elizabeth's Silver Jubilee celebrations. By the end of 1977, and amid all the situationist hoopla, the band managed to release a rather powerful album, *Never Mind the Bullocks, Here's the Sex Pistols*. Of course, use of the verboten word "bullocks" (the British equivalent of "bullshit") guaranteed more controversy, and many stores refused to carry the album, which nonetheless immediately topped the British charts. However, the American tour to support *Bullocks* in January 1978 both imploded and exploded the increasingly volatile situation. True to his situationist roots, McLaren booked most of the concerts in Southern cities, such as Atlanta, San Antonio, and Tulsa, where the band was guaranteed to be less-than-warmly received. Onstage and off-stage chaos culminated in what became the final Sex Pistols concert in San Francisco, which singer Johnny Rotten closed with the rhetorical question: "Ever had the feeling you've been cheated?" Unfortunately, when the Sex Pistols' original line-up reunited for the 1996 "Filthy Lucre" tour, their remaining achievement was finally gaining golden-oldies status.

34. As quoted in "The Kaufman Chronicles." Emphasis added.

35. See *Andy Kaufman Revealed!*, 153–5. See also 175–7.

36. David Marc noted that Alan Alda consciously toned down the womanizing aspects of Hawkeye's early years, describing him as "a sexual Archie Bunker," to conform to his quite different public and political image (Alda as quoted in *Comic Visions*, 163).

37. However, while Kaufman may have been doing a satire on male chauvinism, the wrestling routines served a more immediate purpose: they were shameless exercises in public sexual gratification for Kaufman, a well-known womanizer who became verbally and physically aroused sexually during the matches — which occasionally ended in one-night stands with his "opponents." See Zmuda, 164–6.

38. *Andy Kaufman Revealed!*, 166.

39. See Zmuda, 61, 99, and especially 146, where Michaels discusses Kaufman's comedy in relation to Warhol and Brecht.

40. Zmuda's detailed account of this performance can be found in *Andy Kaufman Revealed!*, 181–4. Zehme recounts this performance far more briefly and quite differently, suggesting the excitement generated by the promos resulted in a highly anti-climatic match that ended in a draw, which was overall quite "boring" (*Lost in the Funhouse*, 274, 277).

41. The loser suffering the public indignity of having his head forcibly shaved is a common angle in professional wrestling, especially in *lucha libre* (Mexican professional wrestling) where "hair vs. hair" and "hair vs. mask" matches are frequently staged.

42. See Zehme, 274.

43. See *Andy Kaufman Revealed*, 182–3.

44. *Andy Kaufman Revealed!*, 183. Emphasis original.

45. Kaufman originally performed "It's a Small World" on *Andy's Funhouse*, and did the routine in a modified form on *Saturday Night Live* in 1979, in which Kaufman performed the song "I Go Mad When I Hear the Yodel" rather than "It's a Small World."

46. While starring on *Taxi*, Kaufman began his second career as a busboy at The Posh Bagel. After The Post Bagel closed, Kaufman then worked at Jimmy's Famous Deli. Zmuda noted that Kaufman's decision to start busing tables was motivated by two factors. One was that Kaufman's politics were socialist, and his job was a kind of performance art gesture indicating that he preferred the company of the working class to Hollywood and the avant-garde elite (sentiments Kaufman directly expressed in *The Midnight Special* segment). It also served a more practical purpose: Kaufman genuinely believed he needed a back-up career in case his comedy career ended. See *Andy Kaufman Revealed!*, 200–3. See also Zehme, 297.

47. Zmuda, 203–4. See also Zehme, 292–4. The "*Fridays*" listing at TV Party website offers an informative account of the Kaufman appearances on *Fridays*, archived at: www.tvparty.com/80fridays4.html. Accessed: 12/05/2004. Jack Burns was already a veteran in American television comedy before becoming *Fridays'* head writer. After teaming with George Carlin as "Burns and Carlin" in the early 1960s on the night club circuit, Burns replaced Don Knotts on *The Andy Griffith Show* as "Deputy Warren Ferguson" from 1965 to 1968. In the 1970s, Burns partnered with Avery Schreiber as "Burns and Schreiber," and appeared frequently on variety shows and talk shows. They became famous for their "Yeah? Right! Yeah? Right! Yeah? Right!" exchanges.

48. Richards, who later achieved stardom as Cosmo Kramer on *Seinfeld* (and infamy for an on-stage, racial epithet–filled tirade in late 2006), had been informed of the Kaufman situation the day before, perhaps giving him time to plan his adroit "reaction"; Burrell had also been warned of the planned chaos by Moffitt (see Zmuda, 208). According to the "Fridays" TV Party website, Moffitt informed Chartoff of the plan as well, because of concern the explosive situation might cause her to "freak out" on-air (Chartoff and Kaufman dated during the week of rehearsals).

49. Due to the well-organized and inflexible schedule, a common internal complaint on *Fridays* was that the cast was in the unenviable situation of going on live TV with material they knew would bomb. As a result, *Fridays* quickly began to emphasize sex and drug humor that, if not particularly cerebral or even witty, at least generated some immediate laughs and whoops by the studio audience.

50. *Andy Kaufman Revealed!*, 204.

51. See *Andy Kaufman Revealed!*, 94, 205. A far less intentional but equally hilarious "Viet Cong Confession" could be seen in Janet Jackson's videotaped apology issued to the news media in the wake of her infamous 2004 Super Bowl halftime show "wardrobe malfunction."

52. As quoted in "Fridays," page 3 of 10.

53. See *Andy Kaufman Revealed!*, 206–7. The routine originally called for Kaufman and Sullivan to be married live on *Fridays*, a parody of the Tiny Tim–Miss Vickie wedding on *The Tonight Show*; Sullivan initially agreed to the marriage stunt, but declined when Kaufman arranged for an official civil ceremony on the air which would have been annulled after the telecast, which ran against Sullivan's religious beliefs.

54. See *Andy Kaufman Revealed!*, 63–4; and Zehme, 191–2.

55. *Andy Kaufman Revealed!*, 168.

56. For full accounts of the Clifton *Dinah!* performance, see Zmuda, 168–73; and Zehme, 258–60. Zehme contended that the egg pouring never occurred, but that when Clifton

pressed broken egg shells into Shore's palms producers and security immediately intervened. Zmuda adamantly insisted that Clifton indeed poured the eggs over Shore's head (see also *Biography: Andy Kaufman*).

57. *Rolling Stone* interview with Bill Zehme (February 18, 1993). Emphasis added.

58. *Andy Kaufman Revealed!*, 234–5.

59. See Theodor W. Adorno, "Freudian Theory and the Pattern of Fascist Propaganda," in *The Culture Industry*, 132–57, especially 133. See also Horkheimer and Adorno, "Elements of Anti-Semitism: The Limits of Enlightenment," in *Dialectic of Enlightenment* (168–208).

60. See Zmuda, 237–8.

61. See Zehme, 317.

62. Kaufman subsequently teamed with Jimmy Hart, a famous wrestling manager, after the Kaufman-Lawler feud was rekindled on *Late Night*. (In his 2004 autobiography *Mouth of the South*, Hart also claimed substantial credit for masterminding the Kaufman-Lawler work.) Kaufman offered a $5,000 "bounty" to any wrestler that put Lawler in a pile-driver, and Kaufman and Hart later staged an on-camera disagreement which looked identical to the fighting style of two infants and was effortlessly broken up by slender, middle-aged announcer Lance Russell. Kaufman then offered Lawler $10,000 to be his tag-team partner; Lawler agreed to team up with Kaufman in a match against Hart and a tag-team known as the Assassins on the condition Kaufman guarantee he'd *never* wrestle again. Kaufman double-crossed Lawler during the match by throwing powder in his face, temporarily "blinding" him so that the Assassins could deliver a series of pile-drivers on Lawler, giving Kaufman the last laugh over the Memphis populace. In *I'm from Hollywood*, a reaction shot depicts a frail, elderly woman clearly mouthing the words "Son-of-a Bitch!" in response to Kaufman's moment of heinous betrayal. See also *Andy Kaufman Revealed!*, 237–9.

63. Zmuda bitterly viewed Vic Ferrari as little more than a bastardized appropriation of Clifton by *Taxi*. Zmuda also noted that *SNL* adamantly refused to allow Tony Clifton to appear on the show, largely because *SNL* writers created their own imitation of Tony Clifton in the form of Bill Murray's character "Nick," an obnoxious, untalented lounge singer. See *Andy Kaufman Revealed!*, 218–9.

64. Certainly, by this stage of *Taxi* Hirsch was the entertainment industry consummate professional, as opposed to its eccentric malcontent. While Kaufman was being thrown off the set of Dinah Shore's show and cussing out Jerry Lawler on national television, Hirsch snared an Academy Award nomination for his role as a sympathetic psychiatrist in *Ordinary People* (1980).

65. For detailed accounts, see Zmuda, 241–4; and Zehme, 323–7.

66. Zmuda noted that Kaufman actually relished the sordid biography, and particularly the possibility that he and the King shared a sexual fetish for wrestling women (*Andy Kaufman Revealed!*, 220).

67. Perhaps as testament to Kaufman's growing career difficulties, amid the flurry of last-minute cuts for *SNL*'s 1975 premiere, including a scheduled stand-up routine by Billy Crystal, Kaufman's "Mighty Mouse" was considered untouchable. Kaufman's *SNL* "comeback" performance in January 1982 was consigned to the final half-hour of the show.

68. For Zmuda's account of the *SNL* vote, see *Andy Kaufman Revealed!*, 242–51. See Zehme, 328–35, for his quite different account of the *SNL* vote. Zmuda clearly placed the blame on Ebersol for the disastrous aftermath; Zehme placed much of it on Kaufman.

69. See Zehme, 334; his account contended that these segments were devised *after* the full impact of the vote became clear. Zmuda contended that Ebersol and Kaufman agreed to future appearances regardless of the outcome, including a scenario where Tony Clifton would appear on *SNL* (see *Andy Kaufman Revealed!*, 249–50).

70. *Andy Kaufman Revealed!*, 250.

71. *Adorno on Music*, 95.

72. *Andy Kaufman Revealed!*, 251. See also 104.

73. Carson's elevated desk was not at all a subliminal device but a well-known and often joked about part of the show. When Carson appeared on one of then–*heir apparent* David Letterman's *Late Night* shows, he brought his own folding desk on the set, explaining he could only talk from behind a desk. Letterman responded by noting that Carson had brought out a desk which was indeed slightly taller than his as well.

74. This "Magic Screen" segment was later used as a weekly routine by Pee-Wee Herman on *Pee-Wee's Playhouse*. In *Andy Kaufman Revealed!*, Zmuda has decidedly mixed feelings about *Pee-Wee's Playhouse* (see 219).

75. On *Andy's Funhouse*, "The Has-Been Corner" is played much more overtly comical than *Soundstage*, and Zmuda noted that "has-been" Gail Slobodkin, a child star who appeared on Broadway in *The Sound of Music* (not the film, as Kaufman implied on *Andy's Funhouse*), was part of the routine (*Andy Kaufman Revealed!*, 78). My research was unable to

ascertain Brandy's "authenticity;" but my own suspicion is that Brandy is also a "real" person and in on the routine.

76. See *Andy Kaufman Revealed!*, 81–2. The Photo Doodys were virtually indistinguishable from the TV Howdy Doody except for minor cosmetic alterations made for the purposes of appearing in flash photography rather than before TV cameras. It is a testament to Kaufman's devotion that he could even spot the imposters, let alone do so immediately.

77. See *Andy Kaufman Revealed!*, 82–3.

78. The Situationist International, "Détournement as Negation and Prelude," 55 (Knapp).

79. As quoted in "The Kaufman Chronicles." Emphasis added.

80. *Saturday Night Live: The Eighties* NBC special (2005). Emphasis original.

81. As quoted in "The Kaufman Chronicles." Emphasis added. In this sense, Williams's approach to taking performance beyond the stage is simply transplanting his incessant highstrung ramblings, cultural references, and quirky ethnic voices to the on-camera documentary interview, the talk-show couch, or awards-show podium.

82. "Backward from Jim Carrey," in *Andy Kaufman Revealed!* The "Backward" is printed backwards, and the reader is instructed to hold the book to a mirror to read it — in effect looking at themselves while they read.

83. As quoted in "The Kaufman Chronicles." Emphasis added.

84. As quoted in *Lost in the Funhouse*, 259. Emphasis added.

Chapter 9

1. *Saturday Night Live* was initially titled *NBC's Saturday Night*, due to *Saturday Night Live with Howard Cosell* (ABC, 1975–6), a live primetime variety-show hosted by the legendary (or infamous) ABC sports announcer, premiering some weeks previously. After ABC cancelled the Cosell show in 1976, the show was retitled *Saturday Night Live*, and is commonly referred to as *SNL*.

2. As quoted in *Saturday Night Live: The First Five Years* documentary (NBC, 2005).

3. *Going Too Far*, 441. Certainly Hendra's stance needs to be qualified, especially given the extent his personal feuds and critical assessments are inherently linked. Hendra was an editor with *National Lampoon* in the 1970s, and a bitter rivalry developed between *National Lampoon* and *SNL*, with *Lampoon* stalwarts such as Hendra arguing that *SNL* variously diluted, sold out, and stole much of *National Lampoon*'s concept as *SNL* became the popular torch-bearers of post-counterculture comedy. In turn, Michaels, rather disingenuously, claimed that beyond *SNL*'s early connections, *National Lampoon* had no influence on *SNL*.

4. Recounted by Ebersol in *Saturday Night Live: The Eighties* documentary (NBC, 2005).

5. The most controversial moments for *SNL* in recent history occurred when musical guest Sinéad O'Conner ripped a photo of the Pope in half during a song in 1992, and guest host Martin Lawrence provided an impromptu and highly insulting discussion of women's hygiene in his opening monologue in 1994. *SNL* explicitly disowned the incidents as unrehearsed and unsanctioned actions solely the responsibility of the performers. Lawrence was officially banned for life from *SNL*. For O'Conner, the incident effectively destroyed her already controversial career in America, making any retaliation by *SNL* moot.

6. *Going Too Far*, 404.

7. Lear also created *Sanford and Son* (NBC, 1972–7) during the era. While a ratings success, it also prompted accusations that Lear was promoting stereotypes of African Americans rather than satirizing them. *Good Times*, despite the overtly liberal politics, received the same accusations — from its own cast. As the show began to increasingly rely on the stereotypical slapstick antics of J.J. Evans (Jimmie Walker), stars John Amos and, later, Ester Rolle both quit the show, voicing their complaints to the press. Rolle eventually rejoined the show after Lear guaranteed changes in the show; Amos, who had publicly pointed out the contradictions of a show about the African American experience being mostly written by Caucasian-Americans, was killed off.

Chapter 10

1. Dan Castalleneta and Julie Kavner, the voices of Homer and Marge Simpson, were regular cast members of *The Tracy Ullman Show* as well.

2. Groening as quoted in *The Hooterville Handbook*, xvi.

3. In this respect, while *Green Acres* is live action and *The Simpsons* cartoon animation, *Green Acres* is far less pseudo-realistic than *The Simpsons*. A much-publicized live-action version of the opening credit sequence of *The Simpsons* was done in 2005, which unintentionally called attention to the ease with which *The Simpsons* could be converted into an idiosyncratic but nonetheless conventional live-action sitcom.

4. *Comic Vision*, 194.

5. In this respect, *The Simpsons* offers a comparison to *Patterns* (see Chapter 2). The tyrannical Mr. Burns has his sycophantic assistant Mr. Smithers. The Master-Slave structure of the office is comically justified around a homosexual crush. Moreover, whereas Staples challenges the system through ethical tenacity, Homer Simpson, the caricature of the American worker, challenges the system through incompetence and ignorance

6. *Comic Vision*, 194.

7. *Comic Visions*, 194, 196. Emphasis added.

8. However, Murdoch did appear as himself and lent his voice to the 1999 Super Bowl promotional episode "Sunday, Cruddy Sunday."

9. *The Simpsons* and *Family Guy* have had a rather acrimonious relationship throughout their runs. *The Simpsons*' "Treehouse of Horror XIII," the season premiere for the 2002–3 season, featured a story involving a magic hammock that clones countless Homers; as well as *The Tracy Ullman Show*–era Homer, Peter Griffith could be seen among the Homer clones (adding insult to injury, *Family Guy* had been cancelled for the 2002–3 Fox season). The shows have since traded barbs, most obviously the *Family Guy* episode "Mother Trucker" (2006), which featured a "How about that time..." cutaway where Stewie "sold out" and did a Butterfingers commercial, referring to the Butterfinger commercials starring Bart.

10. Matthew P. McAllister, "The Simpsons, page 3 of 3. Achieved at: www.museumtv/archieves/etv/S/htmlS/simpsonsthe/simpsonsthe.htm. Accessed: 10/15/06.

11. Herbert Marcuse, *One Dimensional Man* (Boston: Beacon Press, 1964), 70. Emphasis added.

12. As quoted in *Comic Visions*, 192–3. Emphasis added.

13. Ironically, Joel's song is a jingoistic defense of American interventionist foreign policy done as a lyrical pastiche of political catchphrases and buzz-words.

14. See also Chris Turner, "The Ugly Springfieldite," in *Planet Springfield: How a Cartoon Masterpiece Defined a Generation* (New York: Da Capo, 2005), 317–55. Despite the book's laudatory title, Turner is highly critical of *The Simpsons* in its frequent ethnocentric subtext. However, by way of a defense, Turner argues that the primary targets of satire on *The Simpsons* are Americans. Again, the problem is that *The Simpsons* satirizes Americans with ethnocentric views, but not the views themselves.

15. *Comic Visions*, 193.

16. Examples I personally recall from the 1970s include the LPGA being referred to as the Lesbian Professional Golf Association, and the Dinah Shore Invitational termed "America's first national lesbian convention."

17. King Crimson was among the few progressive-rock bands that made the successful transition to a post–punk rock world in the 1980s. Jethro Tull was among the more notable "dinosaurs" of rock rendered effectively extinct after punk.

18. Indeed, the occasional critiques of modern art and postmodernism — "Mom and Pop Art" (1999), "Homer the Moe" (2001), or "The Seven-Year Snitch" (2005) — best typify *The Simpsons*' success regarding its ability to manufacture satire that can be read both ways by the audience(s): on the one hand, the viewer who can knowingly laugh with the cameos by painter Jasper Johns or architect Frank Gehry; on the other hand, the viewer who can laugh at the put-down of pretentious, artistic eggheads.

19. *Minima Moralia*, 210. See also Linda Hutcheon, *Irony's Edge: The Theory and Politics of Irony*, (London: Routledge, 1994), 29–30.

Chapter 11

1. As quoted in *Dada and Surrealist Film*, 171.

2. Blizzard Entertainment, makers of *World of Warcraft*, assisted on the animation of the episode, and certainly benefited from the product promotion as much as being the target of satire.

3. In this respect, the use of music on *South Park* is done to exaggerate the parody through blatantly clichéd musical motifs: driving music during actions sequences, swelling music during introspective monologues, stirring music during inspirational speeches, and, of course, the "I learned something today..." moral message — sometimes sincere, more often satirical — set to a turgid, tinkling piano that ends many episodes. Rock anthem parodies have been used (Paul Stanly of Kiss wrote "Live to Win ('Til You Die)" for "Make Love, not Warcraft"), as well as actual rock hits used for satirical effect (such as when Ike Broflovski is seduced by his kindergarten teacher to the REO Speedwagon power-ballad "I Can't Fight This Feelin' Anymore").

4. The obvious comparison is *The Simpsons*' "Alone Again, Natra-Diddly" (2000), in which Maude Flanders (a parody of Maude Findlay) was killed off (largely because actress Maggie Roswell, who voiced Maude and other

ancillary characters, was involved in a contract dispute with the show's producers). The episode's not-so-hidden message is that Ned Flanders has a crisis in faith after the death of his wife, with his faith restored when he decides to go to church and meets the attractive singer in a Christian rock band. Even the earlier "'Round Springfield" (1995), in which Lisa's mentor, jazz musician "'Bleeding Gums' Murphy" dies, ends with a miracle when the local, low-wattage jazz station where Lisa is playing Murphy's records in his memory is hit by a lightning blot, allowing the station to be heard throughout the town for the duration of her tribute.

5. Kenny was killed off in "Kenny Dies" because Parker and Stone tired of figuring out new ways to kill him in each episode. Several episodes afterward did revolve around him being dead, and when he returned to the show alive a year later in "Red Sleigh Down" (2002), he was simply asked where he'd been. Of course, his reply was unintelligible.

6. Arthur Asa Berger, *Li'l Abner: A Study in American Satire* (Jackson, MS: University Press of Mississippi, 1994), 154. Emphasis original.

7. See also Berger, *Li'l Abner*, 144–8.

8. In "Here Comes the Neighborhood" (2001), Token's family originally had the last name "Williams." In subsequent episodes, the last name was changed to "Black." In "Here Comes the Neighborhood," wealthy African American celebrities who speak in stodgy British accents join the Blacks in South Park. Lead by Mr. Garrison, the white citizens respond to the influx of "richers" and "cash chuckers" by burning "a lower case t" in Kobe Bryant's front lawn (for "Time to leave"). After a "Million Millionaire March" in protest for equal rights for rich people, the citizens dress up as ghosts (KKK outfits) to scare the richers out of town in an absurd parody of *Birth of a Nation*'s racist finale.

9. Hayes, a Scientologist, acrimoniously left the show in early 2006 amid the well-publicized controversies surrounding the anti-Scientology episode "Trapped in the Closet" (2005). He was killed off, quite graphically, later that year in the ironically-titled "The Return of Chef." During his eulogy, Stan reflects that they shouldn't be mad at Chef, "But we should be mad at that fruity little club that scrambled his brains."

10. In discussing his decision to quit *Chappelle's Show* on *The Oprah Winfrey Show* in 2006, Chappelle explicitly discussed the issue of stereotypes and satire as a motivating factor — in short, his fear the show was beginning to appeal to racism rather than attack it. What Chappelle rejected (to the tune of a fifty-million-dollar contract) was precisely what Lear's sitcoms, *The Simpsons*, and *Family Guy* underestimate or ignore: satire does not mean the stereotypes won't be taken literally versus ironically, and ultimately reinforced and *laughed at*. In fact, Comedy Central's replacement for *Chappelle's Show*, the virtual copy *Mind of Mencia* (2005–), is far more comfortable perpetuating stereotypes in the guise of satirizing them. In other words, *Mind of Mencia* is focused on "personal mockery," *Chappelle's Show* was focused on "type mockery."

11. The finale of "Beyond Blunderdome" is itself referenced from *Pee-Wee's Big* Adventure, which was itself referenced from the Martin-Lewis comedy *Hollywood or Bust* (1951, dir. Frank Tashlin).

12. Georges Bataille, *Literature and Evil*, trans. Alistair Hamilton (New York: Marion Boyars, 1985), 121–2. Second emphasis added.

13. "Spurious Opposition," in *The Revolution of Everyday Life, op. cit.* Again, it should be emphatically stressed that in using the term "liberal," Vaneigem is referring to classical liberalism.

14. "Ten Questions with Matt Stone and Trey Parker," *Time* (March 16, 2006). Emphasis added.

15. Thomas Hobbes, *Leviathan* (Touchstone/Simon & Schuster, 1962), 100 (Pt. I, Ch. 13). Emphasis original.

16. *Leviathan*, 104 (Pt I, Ch. 14).

17. Edmund Burke, "Reflections on the Revolution in France," in *From Modernism to Postmodernism: An Anthology*, ed. Lawrence Calhoone (Malden, MA: Blackwell, 1996), 68. Emphasis original.

18. Certainly, *South Park* would not endorse Hobbes's solution to the problem of liberty, which is essentially a "scientific" defense of monarchy: the establishment of a sovereign figure given all authority by the body-politic, not by Divine Right, but practical necessity to maintain social order.

19. In fact, Parker has described his own political leanings as libertarian in past interviews. However, it is also the inherent problems with libertarian philosophy that equally informs *South Park*.

20. Hegel as quoted in Michael Hardt, "The Withering of Civil Society," in *Deleuze and Guattari: New Mappings in Politics, Philosophy, and Culture*, ed. Eleanor Kaufman and Kevin Jon Heller (Minneapolis: University of Minnesota Press, 1998), 25.

21. *Minima Moralia*, 102–3. Emphasis added.

22. José Ortega y Gasset, "The Crowd Phenomenon," in *From Modernism to Postmodernism*, 224.

23. In this respect, Parker and Stone's *Team America: World Police* (2004) need be addressed. Much of the debate over *Team America* revolved around whether the film expressed a liberal or conservative political stance. This is to discuss *Team America* at its most superficial; like *South Park*, *Team America* attacks both liberal and conservative political stances. Rather, *Team America* can be seen as the descendant of Kubrick's *Dr. Strangelove* (1964), which is remembered for its hilarious satire on the military and U.S. Cold War foreign policy (the title character is clearly a parody of Henry Kissinger). What is overlooked is that the ineffective President Merkin in *Dr. Strangelove* is a satire of Cold War liberalism and a parody of Adlai E. Stevenson. Ultimately, the strength of *Team America* was in parodying the TV show *Thunderbirds* and the entire cast being marionettes. At the level of satirizing Hollywood films such as *Top Gun*, there was a surplus of execrable "wooden" dialogue, and acting done by "plastic" stars literally made of wood and plastic. As a political satire, the message was that all participants on the stage of world politics are simply and quite literally "puppets."

24. "Commitment," in *The Essential Frankfurt School Reader*, 306–7.

25. In 2001, Parker and Stone did a short-lived sitcom for Comedy Central: *That's My Bush!* While a highly unflattering depiction of George W. Bush, replete with grotesque black comedy (in one episode, Bush goes to Texas to personally execute a prison inmate to impress his college buddies, using Drano for the lethal injection), the show was devised and scheduled *before* the 2000 election; it would have been titled *Absolutely Al!* and featured the Gore family had Al Gore won the election. The contentious and protracted 2000 election put the show severely behind its production schedule, and cost factors doomed *That's My Bush!* after eight episodes. Although it was primarily a satire of 1970s-style sitcoms, and in particular Norman Lear's shows, conservative critics vilified *That's My Bush!* before the show even aired. This becomes quite ironic to the extent that *South Park* has since become something of a critical darling in certain conservative quarters, specifically Brian C. Anderson's *South Park Conservatives* (2005). When asked about *South Park Conservatives* in the *Time* interview, Stone responded that there was some truth that the show has an anti-liberal element, "But you could easily write a book about South Park Liberals, because we've attacked all the funny stuff conservative people and institutions do in America." In a 2006 *CBS Sunday Morning* interview, Parker and Stone also noted that liberals tend to receive the brunt of criticism because liberals *react* more vociferously and, as a result, make for more rewarding satire.

26. *Irony's Edge*, 15.

Bibliography

Adorno, Theodor W. *The Culture Industry: Selected Essays on Mass Culture.* Edited by J. M. Bernstein. London: Routledge, 1991.
———. "Commitment," in *The Essential Frankfurt School Reader*, 300–318. Edited by Andrew Arato and Eike Gebhardt. New York: Continuum, 1994.
———. *Minima Moralia: Reflection from Damaged Life.* Translated by E.F.N. Jephcott. New York: Verso, 1997.
———. *Adorno on Music.* Edited by Richard Leppert. Translated by Susan H. Gillespie. Berkeley: University of California Press, 2002.
Althusser, Louis. *Lenin and Philosophy and Other Essays.* Translated by Ben Brewster. New York: Monthly Review Press, 1971.
———. *For Marx.* Translated by Ben Brewster. New York: Verso, 1991.
Altman, Rick. "*The Lonely Villa* and Griffith's Paradigmatic Style." *Quarterly Review of Film Studies* 6, no. 2 (1981): 123–34.
Arnott, Christopher. "Turn in, Turn on, Laugh-In." *The New Haven Advocate.com.* (October 16, 2006). Archived at: *www.ctnow.com/custom./nmm/newhavenadvocate/hcc-nha-1019-nh43laughin43artoct19,0,5829275,story.*
Artaud, Antonin. *The Theater and Its Double.* Translated by Mary Caroline Richards. New York: Grove Press, 1958.
———. *Selected Writings.* Edited by Susan Sontag. Translated by Helen Weaver. Berkeley: University of California Press, 1988.
Barris, Chuck. *Confessions of a Dangerous Mind: An Unauthorized Autobiography.* New York: Hyperion, 2002.
Barthes, Roland. *Mythologies.* Translated by Annette Wang. New York: Hill and Wang, 1997.
Bataille, Georges. *Literature and Evil.* Translated by Alistair Hamilton. New York: Marion Boyars, 1985.
Baxter, John. *Buñuel.* New York: Carroll and Graf, 1994.
Beckett, Samuel. *Waiting for Godot.* New York: Grove Press, 1956.
Benjamin, Walter. *Illuminations.* Edited by Hannah Arendt. Translated by Harry Zohn. New York: Schocken Books, 1968.
Berger, Arthur Asa. *Li'l Abner: A Study in American Satire.* Jackson, MS: University Press of Mississippi, 1994.
———. *Reflections.* Edited by Peter Demetz. Translated by Edmund Jephcott. New York: Schocken Books, 1978.
Biography: Andy Kaufman. Arts and Entertainment network (1999).
Bodroghkozy, Aniko. "Laugh-In." Archived at: *www.findarticles.com/p/articles/mi_glepc/is_tov/ai_2419100698/print.*
Brecht, Bertolt. *Brecht on Theater: The Development of an Aesthetic.* Edited and translated by John Willet. New York: Hill and Wang, 1992.

Breton, André. *Manifestos of Surrealism*. Translated by Richard Seaver and Helen R. Lane. Ann Arbor: University of Michigan Press, 1972.

Bürger, Peter. *Theory of the Avant-Garde*. Translated by Michael Shaw. Minneapolis: University of Minnesota Press, 1984.

Burke, Edmund. "Reflections on the Revolution in France," in *From Modernism to Postmodernism: An Anthology*, 58–71. Edited by Lawrence Calhoone. Malden, MA: Blackwell, 1997.

Carroll, Peter N. *It Seems Like Nothing Happened: The Tragedy and Promise of America in the 1970s*. New York: Holt, Rinehart, and Winston, 1982.

Clair, René. *A Nous La Liberté/Entr'acte*. London: Lorrimer, 1970.

Comolli, Jean-Luc, and Jean Narboni. "Cinema/Ideology/Criticism" reprinted in *Film Theory and Criticism: Introductory Readings*, 4th edition, 682–689. Edited by Gerald Mast, Marshall Chen, and Leo Braudy. New York: Oxford University Press, 1992.

Cox, Steve. *The Hooterville Handbook: A Viewer's Guide to Green Acres*. New York: St. Martin's Press, 1993.

Debord, Guy. "The Decline and Fall of the Spectacular Commodity Society." *Situationist International* 10 (1966). Reprinted in Knabb, 153–9.

_____. *The Society of the Spectacle*. Translated by Donald Nicholson-Smith. New York: Zone Books, 1995.

_____, and Gil J. Wolman. "The User's Guide to Détournement." Originally published in *Les Lèvres Neus* 8 (May 1956). Reprinted in Knabb, 8–13 (as "Methods of Détournement").

Deleuze, Gilles. *Cinema 1: The Movement-Image*. Translated by Hugh Tomlinson and Barbara Habberjam. Minneapolis: University of Minnesota Press, 1986.

_____. *Cinema 2: The Time-Image*. Translated by Hugh Tomlinson and Robert Galeta. Minneapolis: University of Minnesota Press, 1989.

Derrida, Jacques. "The Purveyor of Truth" in *The Purloined Poe: Lacan, Derrida, and Psychoanalytic Reading*, 173–212. Edited by John P. Muller and William J. Richardson. Baltimore: John Hopkins University Press, 1988.

Dolbeare, Kenneth M. *American Political Thought*. Monterey: Duxbury Press, 1981.

Eagleton, Terry. *Literary Theory: An Introduction*. Minneapolis: University of Minnesota, 1983.

Editors of *Cahiers du cinema*, The. "*Young Mr. Lincoln*." Translated by Helen Lacker and Diane Matais. Reprinted in *Narrative, Ideology, Apparatus: A Film Theory Reader*, 444–482. Edited by Phillip Rosen. New York: Columbia University Press, 1986.

Eisenstein, Sergei. *Film Form*. Edited and translated by Jay Ledya. San Diego: Harcourt Brace, 1977.

Ellis, John. *Visible Fictions: Cinema, Television, Video*, revised edition. London: Routledge, 1992.

Elsaesser, Thomas. "Tales of Sound in Fury: Observations on the Family Melodrama," in *Film Theory and Criticism: Introductory Readings*, 4th edition, 512–535. Edited by Gerald Mast, Marshall Cohen, and Leo Braudy. New York: Oxford University Press, 1992.

Esslin, Martin. *The Theater of the Absurd*, 3rd edition. New York: Vintage, 2004.

Evans, Sara. *Personal Politics: The Roots of Women's Liberation in the Civil Rights Movement and the New Left*. New York: Vintage, 1980.

Foucault, Michel. *The History of Sexuality, Vol. I: An Introduction*. Translated by Robert Hurley. New York: Vintage, 1990.

Franklin, Nancy. "American Idiots." *The New Yorker*. January 16, 2006.

"*Fridays*." Archived at *www.tvparty.com/80fridays4.html*.

Goldberg, RoseLee. *Performance Art: From Futurism to the Present*, revised and expanded edition. London: Thames and Hudson, 2001.

Gould, Jack. "*Patterns* Is Hailed as a Notable Triumph." *The New York Times*, January 17, 1955. Archived at *www.rdserling.com/NYTpatterns.htm*.

Greene, Doyle. *Mexploitation Cinema: A Critical History of Mexican Vampire, Wrestler, Ape-man and Other Similar Films, 1957–1977.* Jefferson, NC: McFarland, 2005.
Grose, B. Donald, and O. Franklin Kenworthy. *A Mirror of Life: A History of Western Theater.* New York: Holt, Rinehart, and Winston, 1985.
Hansen, Miriam. "Mass Culture as Hieroglyphic Writing: Adorno, Derrida, and Kracauer," *New German Critique* 56 (Summer 1992).
_____. "Of Mice and Ducks," *The South Atlantic Quarterly* 92:1 (Winter 1993).
Hardt, Michael. "The Withering of Civil Society," in *Deleuze and Guattari: New Mappings in Politics, Philosophy, and Culture,* 23–39. Edited by Eleanor Kaufman and Kevin Jon Heller. Minneapolis: University of Minnesota Press, 1998.
Hassan, Ihab. "POSTmodernISM: A Paracritical Bibliography." In *From Modernism to Postmodernism: An Anthology,* 382–400. Edited by Lawrence Cahoone. Malden, MA: Blackwell, 1997.
Hendra, Tony. *Going Too Far.* New York: Dolphin/Doubleday, 1987.
Hobbes, Thomas. *Leviathan.* Touchstone/Simon & Schuster, 1962.
Hoffman, Irene E. "Documents of Dada and Surrealism: Dada and Surrealist Journals in the Mary Reynolds Collection." Available at *www.aetic.edu/reynolds/essays/hoffman.php.*
Horkheimer, Max, and Theodor W. Adorno. *Dialectic of Enlightenment.* Translated by John Cumming. New York: Continuum, 1997.
Hutcheon, Linda. *Irony's Edge: The Theory and Politics of Irony.* London: Routledge, 1995.
Ionesco, Eugène. *Four Plays.* New York: Evergreen/Grove Weidenfeld, 1982. [Includes *The Bald Soprano*; *The Lesson*; *Jack, of the Submission*; *The Chairs.*]
James, William. *Pragmatism.* New York: Barnes and Noble Books, 2003.
Jameson, Fredric. *Postmodernism, or, the Cultural Logic of Late Capitalism.* Durham, NC: Duke University Press, 1990.
Jarry, Alfred. *The Ubu Plays.* New York: Grove Weidenfeld, 1968. [Includes *Ubu roi, Ubu cluckoid,* and *Ubu enchaîné*]
"Kaufman Chronicles, The." Archived at: *http://andykaufman.jvinet.com/kaufchro.htm.*
Kovacs, Ernie. "The Lively Arts." Interview conducted by Bill Bellman, aired on Canadian Broadcasting Cooperation, 10-31-61. Transcript archived at: *http://usuers.rcn.com/manaben/Kovacs/CBC.html* .
Knabb, Ken, ed. and trans. *The Situationist International Anthology.* Berkeley: Bureau of Public Secrets, 2001. Also available at the Bureau of Public Secrets website: *www.bopsecrtes.org.SI.*
Kuenzli, Rudolf E., ed. *Dada and Surrealist Film.* New York: Willis Locker and Owens, 1987.
Lacan, Jacques. *Ecrits: A Selection.* Translated by Alan Sheridan. New York: W. W. Norton, 1977.
_____. "Seminar on 'The Purloined Letter,'" in *The Purloined Poe: Lacan, Derrida, and Psychoanalytic Reading,* 28–54. Edited by John P. Muller and William J. Richardson. Baltimore: John Hopkins University Press, 1988.
Langford, Michelle. "Alexander Kluge." Archived at: *www.sensesofcinema.com/contents/directors/03/kluge.html*
Lowe, Donald M. *History of Bourgeois Perception.* Chicago: University of Chicago Press, 1982.
MacCabe, Colin. *Godard: Images, Sounds, Politics.* Bloomington: Indiana University Press, 1980.
Marc, David. *Comic Visions: Television Comedy and American Culture,* 2nd edition. Malden, MA: Blackwell, 1997.
Marcuse, Herbert. *One Dimensional Man: Studies in the Ideology of Advanced Industrial Society.* Boston: Beacon Press, 1964.
Marx, Karl, and Friedrich Engels. *The Communist Manifesto.* Translated by Samuel Moore. New York: Pocket Books, 1964.

McLuhan, Marshall. *Understanding Media.* Cambridge: MIT Press, 1994.
Motherwell, Robert, ed. *The Dada Painters and Poets,* 2nd edition. Cambridge: Belknap Press of the Harvard University Press, 1981.
Nichols, Bill. *Ideology and the Image.* Bloomington: Indiana University Press, 1981.
Ortega y Gasset, José. "The Crowd Phenomenon." In *From Modernism to Postmodernism: An Anthology,* 219–225. Edited by Lawrence Cahoone. Malden, MA: Blackwell, 1997.
Panofsky, Erwin. "Style in Medium in Motion Pictures," in *Film Theory and Criticism: Introductory Readings,* 4th edition, 233–248. Edited by Gerald Mast, Marshall Cohen, and Leo Braudy. New York: Oxford University Press, 1992.
Pronko, Leonard Cabell. *Avant-Garde: The Experimental Theater in France.* Berkeley: University of California Press, 1966.
Rico, Diana. *Kovacsland: A Biography of Ernie Kovacs.* San Diego: Harcourt Brace Jovanovich, 1990.
Sales, Soupy. *Soupy Sez!: My Zany Life and Times.* New York: M. Evans, 2001.
Situationist International, The. "Definitions." *Situationist International* 1 (1958). Reprinted in Knabb, 45.
_____. "Détournement as Negation and Prelude." *Situationist International* 3 (1959). Reprinted in Knabb, 55.
_____. "The Theory of Moments and the Construction of Situations." *Situationist International* 4 (June 1960). Authorship unattributed in *SI*. Archived at *www.notbored.org/moments.html.*
"Smothers Brothers Show, The." Archived at *www.tvparty.com/smothers.html.*
Sontag, Susan. *Against Interpretation.* New York: Doubleday Books, 1967.
"Soupy Sales Show, The." Archived at *www.tvparty.com/soupy.html.*
"Ten Questions with Matt Stone and Trey Parker." *Time* (March 16, 2006).
Turner, Chris. *Planet Springfield: How a Cartoon Masterpiece Defined a Generation.* New York: Da Capo, 2005.
Vaneigem, Raoul. *The Revolution of Everyday Life.* Translated by Gord Hall and Donald Nicholson-Smith. London: Rebel Books, 2001. Also available online at: *http://librarry.nothingness.org/articles/SI/en/pub_contents/5.*
Vogel, Amos. *Film as a Subversive Art.* New York: Random House, 1976.
Welk, Lawrence. "How Television Influences Our Lives." Reprinted in *Believing.* Edited by Myron Floren and Roger Elwood. Cincinnati: Standard Publishing, 1980.
Williams, Raymond. *Marxism and Literature.* New York: Oxford University Press, 1977.
_____. *The Politics of Modernism.* New York: Verso, 1989.
Wood, Robin. "Ideology, Genre, Auteur," in *Film Theory and Criticism: Introductory Readings,* 4th edition, 474–485. Edited by Gerald Mast, Marshall Cohen, and Leo Braudy. New York: Oxford University Press, 1992.
Zehme, Bill. *Lost in the Funhouse: The Life and Mind of Andy Kaufman.* New York: Delta/Random House, 1999.
Žižek, Slavoj. *The Sublime Object of Ideology.* New York: Verso, 1989.
_____. *A Žižek Reader.* Edited by Elizabeth Wright and Edmond Wright. London: Blackwell, 1999.
Zmuda, Bob, with Matthew Scott Hansen. *Andy Kaufman Revealed!: Best Friend Tells All.* Boston: Little, Brown, 1999.

The Museum of Broadcast Communications sources:

The MBC has published two editions of the *Encyclopedia of Television.* MBC has graciously made the first edition available on-line for research purposes and is archived at: *www.museum.tv/archieves/etv/index/html.* The following articles were cited:

Aus, Albert. "Columbia Broadcasting Network." Archived at: *www.museum.tv/archieves/etv/ C/htmlC/columbiabroa/columbiabroa.htm.*
Bodroghkozy, Aniko. "The Smothers Brothers Comedy Hour." Archived at *www.museum. tv/archieves/etv/S/html/S/smothersbrot/smothersbrot.htm.*
Chorba, Frank J. "Ernie Kovacs." Archived at *www.museum.tv/archieves/etv/K/htmlK/Kovacs Ernie/kovacsErnie.htm.*
Cullum, Paul. "The Beverly Hillbillies." Archived at: *www.museum.tv/archives/etv/B/bev erlyhillb/beverlyhillb.htm.*
____. "Paul Henning." Archived at *www.museum.tv/scrchieves/etv/H/henningpaul/henning paul.htm.*
____. "Green Acres." Archived at: *www.museum.tv/archieves/etv/G/htmlG/greenacres/green acres.htm.*
Desjardi, Mary. "Variety Shows." Archived at *www.museum.tv/archieves/etv/V/htmlV/vari etyprogr/varietyprogr.htm*
Everett, Anna. "'Golden Age' of Television." Archived at *www.museum.tv/archieves/etv/G/ goldenage/goldenage.htm.*
Jenkins, Henry. "Rowan and Martin's Laugh-In." Archived at: *www.museum.tv/archieves/ etv/R/htmlR/rowananddmar/rowanandmar.htm*
____. "Bob Keeshan." Archived at: *www.museum.tv/archieves/etv/K/htmlK/keeshanbob/kee shanbob.htm*
Marc, David. "Jackie Gleason." Archived at: *www.museum.tv/archieves/etv/G/htmlG/glea sonjack/gleasonjack.htm.*
McAllister, Matthew P. "The Simpsons." Archived at: *www.museumtv/archieves/etv/S/ htmlS/simpsonsthe/simpsonsthe.htm.*
Pak, Lindsy E. "The Ernie Kovacs Show (Various)." Archived at: *www.museum.tv/archieves/ etv/E/htmlE/ErnieKovacsShow/erkovacshow.htm*
Rautiolla-Williams, Suzanne. "Howdy Doody." Archived at: *www.museumtv/archieves/etv/ H/htmlH/howdydoodys/howdydoodys.htm.*

Index

Numbers in ***bold italics*** indicate pages with illustrations.

A Nous la liberté (*Freedom for Us*) 18, 226c1n33
Abba 196
Abbott, Bud 23–4, 106
Abbott and Costello 23–4, 83, 227c1n49–50
Abbott and Costello Show (CBS, 1952–3) 227c1n49
Absurdism 1–2, 4, 22–3, 27, 57, 83, 100–1, 133; *Green Acres* and 105–8, 115–6, 201, 223; *South Park* and 215–6, 219, 221–4; *see also* Theater of the Absurd
Adamov, Arthur 22
Addams Family (ABC, 1964–6) 234c5n15
Adorno, Theodor W. 2–3, 31–33, 36, 41–43, 46, 65, 97, 143, 149, 188–9, 210, 221–3, 225c1n10, 237c6n41
Adventures of Ozzie and Harriet (ABC, 1952–66) 40–1
L'Âge d'or (*The Age of Gold*) 16
The Agitator 174, 188–9
Albee, Edward 22, 164
Albert, Eddie 103–4, ***105***
Alda, Alan 134, 166, 218, 241c8n36
All in the Family (CBS, 1971–83) 1, 3, 117, 124, 134–7, 198–9, 201, 216–7
Allen, Gracie 40–1
Allen, Steve 50, 173
Althusser, Louis 112–5
Altman, Rick 89
American Bandstand (ABC, 1957–87) 92
American Dad (FOX, 2005–) 4, 210, 219
The American Dream 44, 101, 199, 203, 210, 238c7n9, 238c7n11
American Gothic (Wood) 104
American Graffiti (Lucas) 199
American Idol (FOX, 2002–) 149–153, 205, 238c7n21
America's Got Talent (NBC, 2006–) 150–1, 239c7n25
Anarchism 18
Anarchy 13, 19, 21, 30, 83, 163, 191

Andrews, Peter 141
Andy Griffith Show (CBS, 1960–8) 99–100, 103, 107, 111–2
"Andy Kaufman Show" see *Soundstage* ("The Andy Kaufman Show," 1983)
Andy Kaufman Special see *Andy's Funhouse*
Andy's Funhouse (ABC special: produced 1977; broadcast 1979) 81, 157, 181–2, 184, 186–7, 243–4c8n75
Anémic Cinema (*Anemic Cinema*) 15
Animal Crackers 5, ***21***, 22, 31
Anti-Semitism 136, 174, 216, 218
Antonioni, Michelangelo 24
Apu Trilogy (Ray) 207
Archie Bunker's Place (CBS, 1979–83) 135, 237c6n43
Archies 118, 235c6n5
Arnez, Desi 41, 43
Arp, Jean 10
Arrabal, Fernando 22, 27
Arrested Development (FOX, 2003–6) 2, 204
Art-Science dichotomy 30, 54
Artaud, Antonin 2, 4–5, 10, 16, 19–22, 29–31, 47, 64, 67, 76–7, 89, 106, 137, 168, 191, 193, 206, 212, 226–7c1n35, 227c1n40
Arthur, Bea 167
Atlas Shrugged 221
Atom Bomb/Atomic Age 29, 64, 79, 202
Audience: camera and 54; Dada and role of 10–2, 91–2; Kovacs' distain for studio audience 54, 58–9, 136; Lear's use of studio audience 136; role of in Kaufman's work 91–2, 157–8, 161, 183–4, 188–91; Sales' production crew as 91–2
Aura of art 11–12, 70
Aus, Albert 133
Authenticity 118, 186–7
Authoritarian personality 99, 122, 218
Avery, Tex 49
Aykroyd, Dan 196

255

B Street Conga Band 168–9
Bachelor (ABC, 2002–) 238c7n7
Bachelorette (ABC, 2003–5) 238c7n7
Baer, Max, Jr. 102
Baez, Joan 122–3
Bailey, Raymond 101
Ball, Hugo 10–1, 148, 158
Ball, Lucille 40, 42
Ballet mécanique (*Mechanical Ballet*) 14–6, 63–4, 159
Barbour, John 145, 238c7n13
Bare, Richard L. 103
Barnum, P.T. 106
Barrino, Fantasia 205
Barris, Chuck 1, 37, 141–5, *146*, 147–55, 237c7n1
Barthes, Roland 57–8, 157
Bartók, Béla 53
BASEketball 218
Bataille, Georges 218–9, 226c1n29
Batcheff, Pierre 16
Baxter, John 15
Bearde, Chris 238c7n14
Beatles 117–118, 125
Beaumont, Hugh 41
Beckett, Samuel 3, 22, 24–6, 57, 115
Begley, Ed 35
Belafonte, Harry 123
Belushi, Jim 198
Belushi, John 195
Belzer, Richard 158
Ben Casey (ABC, 1961–66) 34
Benaderet, Bea 101, 103
Benjamin, Walter 2, 11–3, 15, 29–31, 42, 47, 54–5, 64–6, 69–73, 76–7, 91, 143, 158, 206, 226c1n32, 226c1n34, 227–8c2n6
Benny, Jack 228c2n32, 240c8n13
Benny Hill Show (ITV, 1969–89) 57, 213
Berger, Arthur Asa 216
Berkeley, Busby 65
Berle, Milton 36–8, *39*, 43, 49, 81, 125, 128
Bernhard, Sandra 154
Betz, Carl 41
Beverly Hillbillies (CBS, 1962–71) 1, 100–3, 109–11, 134, 234c5n15
Bin Ladin, Osama 213
Birth of a Nation 89, 164, 233–4c5n9, 246c11n8
Black and white: use of in TV production 52–3, 104, 231c3n42, 234c5n15
Blackout sketches 23, 37, 53, 94, 125, 127, 130
Blanc, Mel 148
Blind Date (syndicated, 1999–2006) 238c7n7
Blondie 100, 202
Blue Boy (Gainsborough) 61
Blue Man Group 164
Bodroghkozy, Aniko 120, 127, 130
Bonanza (NBC, 1959–73) 34, 120, 122
Boosler, Elayne 182, 191
Boyle, Peter 32
Brady Bunch Hour (ABC, 1977) 196

Brand, Jolene 70, 76, 236c6n25
Brandy 151
Brandy, Jim 184–6
Breaking character 41, 169–72
Brecht, Bertolt 2–3, 12, 22, 29–30, 35–6, 59, 91, 165, 167, 204, 206, 223, 230c3n21
Breton, André 13–6, 18, 20, 27, 226c1n15, 226n1c29, 227c1n42
Broadway 34, 158
Brooks, Albert 196
Brown, Chelsea 130–1
Brown, James 184
Brown, Jerry 179
Brown, Maggi 69, 72
Bruce, Lenny 125
Buchanan, Edgar 103, 107
Buck Privates 23
Buckley, Tim 119, 235c6n7
Buckley, William F. 129
Buick-Berle Show (NBC, 1952–3) 38, 49
Bullwinkle Show (NBC, 1961–4; ABC, 1964–73) see *Rocky and Bullwinkle*
Buñuel, Luis 9, 14, 16–8, 22–3, 27, 58, 61, 131, 226c1n27–9
Burell, Maryedith 169–70, 241c8n48
Bürger, Peter 27, 131
Burke, Edmund 220
Burlesque 28, 37–8, 56–7, 84, 127–9, 204, 206
Burns, George 40–1, 122, 206
Burns, Jack 169–71, 242c8n47
Bush, George H.W. 201
Bush, George W. 206, 210
Buttram, Pat 106
Buzzi, Ruth 127, 131
Byner, John 129

Cabaret Voltaire 10, 133, 147
Cady, Frank 107
Caesar, Sid 37–8, 196, 229c3n3
Caesar's Hour (NBC, 1954–7) 38, 50
Cage, John 50, 240c8n13
Camera 12–3, 24–7, 31, 52–4, 59, 67–9, 77
The Cameraman 12–3, 18, 66
Camille (Dumas) 71–2
Camp 83, 145, 147, 156, 187, 196, 225c1n15
Canfield, Mary Grace 108
Cannon, Freddie 169
La Cantratrice chauve (*The Bald Soprano*) 22–3, 143, 227c1n48
Capitalism 2, 35–6, 65, 102, 107, 111–4
Capp, Al 100–101
Capra, Frank 41, 208, 217
Captain Kangaroo (CBS, 1955–84; PBS, 1987–93) 82–3
Carlin, George 130, 195
Carlo, Johann 84
Carmichael, Stokely 130
Carne, Judy 127
Carney, Art 45
Carol Burnett Show (CBS, 1967–79) 125, 132, 169, 196

Index

Carrey, Jim 20, 191
Carroll, Peter N. 135
Carson, Johnny 81, 128, 160, 171–3, 182, 243c8n73
Carter, Jimmy 196, 199
Cartoon animation 42, 49, 70, 73, 212, 216
Cartoon Network 1
Catch a Rising Star Tenth Anniversary HBO Special (HBO, 1982) 178
Catchphrases 125, 127–8, 131–2, 161, 197, 214
CBS Evening News (CBS, 1948–) 108, 124
Censorship 122–4, 127, 153, 200; *see also* self-censorship
Les Cent Vingt Journées de Sodom (*The 120 Days of Sodom*) 218
Channing, Carol 172
Chaplin, Charlie 9, 12, 15–9, 30–1, 42–3, 49, 61, 65–7, 73, 75
Chappelle, Dave 216, 246c11n10
Chappelle's Show (Comedy Central, 2003–5) 216
Chartoff, Melanie 169–70, 241c8n48
Chevillat, Dick 103
Un Chien andaloun (*An Andalusan Dog*) 14, 16, *17*, 76, 94, 131, 226c1n28–9
Child perspective of 42, 88, 212–3
Children's shows 4, 38, 78–88, 92, 94, 156, 158, 165, 181–3
Chorba, Frank J. 58
Christy-Lou 145
Chuck McCann Show (WNEW, 1965–6) 86, 232c4n14
Cinema 2, 11–7, 20, 26, 29–31, 37, 40, 42, 52, 70–1, 73, 77, 88–9, 91, 94, 118, 125; watching TV versus 55, 59–60, 82
Cinematic apparatus 18, 27, 91
Civil society 220–1
Clair, René 7, 12–4, 16, 18, 22, 52, 226c1n33, 233c4n27
Clark, Valerie Ray 148
Class structures 44–5, 101–3, 106, 202–3, 207–8, 216
"Clifton, Tony" (Kaufman persona) 161, **162**, 163–4, 166, 169, 172–3, 177, 181–2, 185–7, 189, 191, 243c8n63
Cocteau, Jean 15–6, 27
Coe, Fred 34
Cohen, Sacha Baron ("Borat") 240c8n15
Cold War 64, 79
Collage 212, 215
Columbia Pictures 50, 117, 119
Columbia Records 117–8
Comedy Central 1, 212, 214
Comedy-variety shows 3–4, 36–40, 78, 120, 122, 125, 127, 132–3, 135, 168, 181, 195–6, 198
Comic books 38
Commercials 51, 69, 82, 214
Commodities: culture as 11, 31–2, 180–1, 205; performers as 32, 145, 149–50, 152, 184, 198, 240c8n11; TV shows as 3, 34, 46, 59, 132–4
Comolli, Jean-Luc 132

Connors, Carol 154
Consciousness: changing of 3, 5, 19–21, 30–1, 63–4, 76–7, 88–9
Conservative/Conservatism 1, 79, 129, 134–5, 199, 205, 208, 210, 219, 221, 224; American 220; Classical 220–1, 224
Constructivism 15
Consuelo (Sand) 164
Contemplation 11–2, 55, 70–2, 75, 158, 225c1n10
Conway, Tim 169, 236c6n25
La Coquille et le clergyman (*The Seashell and the Clergyman*) 16, 19
Cosby, Bill 199, 207
Cosby Show (NBC, 1984–92) 199, 207, 216
Costello, Lou 24
Counterculture 83, 88, 100, 117–20, 123–5, 127, 134, 195–6, 234c5n14, 237c6n33
Cowell, Simon 150
Cronkite, Walter 124
Crosby, John 66
Cross, Perry 50
Crystal, Billy 198, 243c8n43
Cubism 15
Cullum, Paul 102
Culture Industry 3–5, 28, 31–3, 60, 117–9, 132–3, 152, 155, 181, 189

Dada 2, 4, 10–8, 20, 22, 27–30, 49, 66, 70, 73, 82–3, 86, 151, 153, 164–5, 206, 233c4n27; *The Gong Show* and 37, 147–8; Kaufman and 157–8, 168; 172; Kovacs and 56, 62–3, 91; Sales and 88–94; *South Park* and 215, 223
Dalí, Salvador 13–4, 16
Danny Thomas Show (CBS, 1957–64) 40–1
Dating Game (ABC, 1965–73; syndicated, 1977–80) 1, 141–5, 154–5, 160, 238c7n7
Davis, Sammy, Jr. 86, 93, 172
The Day After Tomorrow 217
Dead air 55, 57, 82, 152, 159–60, 170, 182, 184, 240c8n13
Deal or No Deal (NBC, 2006–) 237c7n3
Dean Martin Show (NBC, 1965–74) 125
Debord, Guy 164–5
Deep Throat 154
Deleuze, Gilles 18–20, 64, 66, 226c1n32, 227c1n39, 227c1n52
DeLugg, Milton 80
Democratic National Convention (1968) 123
De Noailles, Marie-Laure 52
Derrida, Jacques 234c5n21
Desjardi, Mary 37
Desnos, Robert 13, 16
Détournement 164–5, 168, 181–2, 189, 215
DeVito, Danny 163
Diff'rent Strokes (NBC, 1978–88) 166
Dinah! (syndicated, 1974–80) 166, 172–3, 242–3c8n56
Direct address (to audience) 37, 41, 59–60, 91, 118, 127–8

Dissociative power 19–21, 28, 31, 63, 106, 191, 206, 223
Distraction 11–3, 54–6, 66, 71–2, 75, 77, 158, 206
Dr. Kildare (NBC, 1961–6) 34
Dr. Strangelove (Kubrick) 247c11n23
Dolenz, Micky 117
$1.98 Beauty Show (syndicated, 1978–80) 154
Domestic sitcoms *see* sitcoms
Donna Reed Show (ABC, 1958–66) 41–2, 100
Donohue, Phil 166
"Don't Stop the Carnival" 123
Douglas, Donna 102
Douglas, Stephen 109
Doumanian, Jean 197
Doyle-Murray, Brian 178
Drag routines 38, 43, 151
Dragnet (NBC, 1951–9; 1967–70) 34
Drama versus comedy distinction 34, 136
Drug use (as topic of comedy) 118, 122, 170
Duchamp Marcel 14–5, 165, 231c3n44
Duck Amuck 73, 231c2n46
Duck Soup 22
Duhamel, Georges 11
Dulac, Germaine 16
Dutch Masters Cigar Company 51–2, 69–70, 75–6, 229c3n8–9
The Dutchman (Baraka) 164

Easy Rider 119
Ebersol, Dick 158–9, 168, 178–80, 183, 197–8
Ebsen, Buddy 101
Ed Sullivan Show (CBS, 1955–71) 37, 50, 62, 82, 120, 133–4
"1812 Overture" 63–64, 74
Einstein, Bob 122, 236c6n14
Eisenstein, Sergei 19–20, 30, 63, 89, 202, 206; *see also* Montage
Electric Company (PBS, 1970–7) 83, 92, 232c4n8
The Electric House 18
ElimiDATE (syndicated, 2001–2006) 238c7n7
Eliot, George 206
Elliot, "Mama" Cass 122
Ellis, John 40, 55, 59, 82
Elsaesser, Thomas 91, 233c4n27
Elvis impersonation 157, 161, 178, 181, 187
Emak Bakia 14–6, 63
Entr'acte (*Intermission*) 13–4, 16, 18, 52, 94, 226c1n27
Ernie in Kovacsland (NBC, 1951) 49
Ernie Kovacs Show (ABC, 1961–2) 49, 52, 57, 59–61, 63–4, 66, 229c3n9, 236c6n25
Ernie Kovacs Show (CBS, 1952–3) 49–50
Ernie Kovacs Show (NBC, 1955–6) 50
Ernst, Max 14, 212
Esquivel (Juan Garcia Esquivel) 64
Esslin, Martin 22
Estrangement effect (Brecht) 12, 22, 59, 91, 165, 206
Ethnocentrism 207

L'Etoile de la mer (*Star of the Sea*) 16
Eubanks, Bob 145–6, 154, 239c7n35
"Eugene" (*The Ernie Kovacs Show*, November 1961) 50, 55–6, 66–76
Everett, Anna 34
Everybody Loves Raymond (CBS, 1996–2005) 32, 205
Exotica music 50, 62, 64, 229c3n5
Expressionism 53, 60, 65, 80
EX-treme Dating (syndicated, 2002) 238c7n7

Fadiman, Clifton 155
False consciousness 113, 165, 235c5n36
Family 108, 203, 210
Family Guy (FOX, 1999–2002, 2005–) 4, 27–28, 132, 204–6, 210, 213, 215–9, 223, 245c10n9
Family Ties (NBC, 1982–9) 199
Farr, Jamie 147
Fascism 18, 29, 137, 149, 174, 216, 218, 226c1n34
Father Knows Best (CBS, 1955–56, 1958–63; NBC, 1955–58) 40–2, 100, 202
Fawcett, Farrah 154
Fear Factor (NBC, 2001–6) 150
Feldman, Marty 191
Feminism 103, 131, 135, 147, 166–7, 203, 208–9, 237c6n33
Ferrante and Teicher 50
Feuillade, Louis 13
Fifth Wheel (syndicated, 2001–4) 238c7n7
Film (1965) 24, **25**, 26–7, 227c1n52
Film noir 44, 53
Fishburne, Laurence 84
Five Easy Pieces 119
Flintstones (ABC, 1960–6) 201–2
Folk music 117, 120, 122, 202
Fonda, Henry 101–2
Fonda, Jane 123
Ford, Gerald R. 195–6
Ford, John 101–2, 109, 132
Ford Television Theater (CBS, 1948–52; NBC, 1952–6; ABC 1956–7) 34
Foreign Man (Kaufman persona) 155, 157–8, 160–1, 172, 178, 181, 189, 191
Form and Content 3–4, 27–8, 116, 120, 122, 125, 131–3, 212, 215
Foucault, Michel 130–131
Founding Father(s) 71, 109–110, 221–2
Fourier, Charles 42
FOX Broadcasting Company (FOX) 200–1, 204–6, 210–1
Fox, Michael J. 199
Frankin, Al 197, 224
Franklin, Benjamin 222
Frazier, Stan "Plowboy" 183
French, Leigh 122
Freudian psychoanalysis 13
Freund, Karl 39
Fridays (ABC, 1980–2) 169–71, 173, 177, 197, 242c8n49

Friedberg, Martin Harvey 187–8
Fritz the Cat 49
Futurism 15, 18

Gabor, Eva 103–4, **105**
Game shows 141–4, 150, 155
Garner, James 129–30
Gehry, Frank 245c10n18
Gender 38, 84, 110, 166, 203, 208–10
General Electric Playhouse (CBS, 1953–62) 34
Generation Gap 120, 122
Genêt, Jean 22
George Burns and Gracie Allen Show (CBS, 1950–8) 40–41, 106
George of the Jungle 206
Get a Life (FOX, 1990–1992) 2
Gibson, Henry 127–8
Gibson, Mel 217–8
Gilliam, Terry 212
Gilligan's Island (CBS, 1962–5) 2, 234c5n15
Gilmore, George "Bones" 147
Gimbel, Roger 54
Gleason, Jackie 36–7, 44, 202, 229c2n42–3
Godard, Jean-Luc 1, 4, 119
Goldberg, RoseLee 14
Golden Age of Television 34–6, 100, 136–7, 165, 198, 211
Goldman, Albert 178
Gomer Pyle, USMC (CBS, 1965–9) 100, 134, 233c5n2, 237c6n40
Gong Show (NBC, 1976–8; syndicated, 1976–80) 1, 4, 27, 37, 44, 80, 82, 92, 138, 144–5, **146**, 147–55, 161
The Gong Show Movie 155
Good Times (CBS, 1974–9) 135, 199, 244c9n7
Goodman, Bertha ("the Scrub Woman") 147
Goodyear Playhouse (NBC, 1948–1955) 34
Gould, Jack 36
Goulet, Robert 172
Grand Ole Opry 133
Grant, Cary 128
The Grapes of Wrath 101–2
Great Depression (economic collapse of the 1930s) 29, 104
The Great Gatsby 158; Kaufman's stand-up routing using 239–40c8n9
"Greed" (Barris' hypothetical game show) 150
Greed (FOX, 1999) 239c7n24
Green Acres (CBS, 1965–71) 1, 4, 22, 95, 100, 102–4, **105**, 106–16, 133–4, 201, 203, 210, 223, 234c5n13, 244c10n3
"Green, Green Grass of Home" 123
Grier, Rosey 122
Griffith, Andy 99, 233c5n2
Griffith, D.W. 13, 19, 26, 88–9, 230c2n33
Groening, Matt 201
Grosz, George 225c1n6
The Grotesque 216
Guest, Christopher 198
Gunsmoke (CBS, 1955–75) 34

Hamlisch, Marvin 172
Hanna-Barbera 201–2
Hansen, Miriam 31, 42
Happy Days (ABC, 1974–84) 199
A Hard Day's Night 117, 119
Hart, Jimmy 243c8n62
Hartman, Phil 84, 155
Hasselhoff, David 151, 213
Hawn, Goldie 128, 131
Hayes, Isaac 216, 246c11n9
HBO 1, 178
Head 119
Hee Haw (CBS, 1969–71; syndicated, 1971–93) 100, 133–4
Hefner, Hugh 130
Hegel, G.W.F. 35, 221
Help! 117
Hendra, Tony 120, 122–3, 196–8, 244c9n3
Henning, Paul 1, 99–101, 103, 106
Hennings, Emmy 10–1
Henson, Jim 196
Herman's Hermits 122
Hirsch, Judd 163, 177, 190, 243c8n64
Hitler, Adolf 30, 174
Ho Chi Minh 129–31
Hobbes, Thomas 220, 224, 246c11n18
Hogan's Heroes (CBS, 1965–71) 134, 237c6n41
Holland, Ed 153
Hollywood 13, 22, 24, 31–2, 128, 132, 153, 163, 174, 176, 191, 195, 197–8, 218
Hollywood or Bust (Tashlin) 246c11n11
Holmes, Oliver Wendell, Jr. 108
Holocaust 29
Homosexuality 61, 84, 127–8, 151, 203, 207–8, 210, 216, 220
Honeymooners (CBS, 1955–6) 41–42, 44–46, 136, 202–3, 238c7n9
Hootenanny (ABC, 1963–4) 120
Hoover, Herbert 104
Hope, Bob 172
Horkheimer, Max 32, 42, 149
Horsefeathers 22
How the Grinch Stole Christmas (Dr. Seuss) 202
Howard, Curley 202
Howard, Moe 20
Howard, Ron 199
Howdy Doody (marionette/TV star) 79, 156, 168, 181–2, 186–7, 189, 244c8n76
Howdy Doody (NBC, 1947–60; syndicated, 1976–7) 38, 78–79, 81, 83, 86, 182, 186–7
Humphrey, Hubert H. 129, 236c6n29
Hung, William 152–3
Hurricane Katrina 217
Huselbeck, Richard 10–1
Hutcheon, Linda 224
Hyperdemocracy 222

I Love Lucy (CBS, 1951–7) 39–44, 46, 136
Ideology 3–4, 18, 20, 30–1, 33, 41, 43, 46, 79, 89, 101–2, 106–7, 109, 111–6, 125, 132–3, 136–7, 165, 201, 210–1, 216, 223

"I'm a Little Bit Country, I'm a Little Bit Rock and Roll" 222
I'm from Hollywood 173
Individualism 220–2
Inherit the Wind (Kramer) 208
"Intellectual charge" 206
Intolerance 89
Ionesco, Eugène 7, 22–4, 27, 83, 105–7, 115, 143, 158, 222
Iraq 209, 213, 222–3
"It's a Small World" 168
It's a Wonderful Life 41
It's Garry Shandling's Show (Showtime, 1986–8; FOX, 1988–1990) 2, 41

Jack Benny Show (CBS, 1950–1964; NBC, 1964–65) 228c2n32
Jackie Gleason Show (CBS, 1952–55, 1956–9) 44
"Jalousie/Sentimental Journey" 64
James, William 111–2, 115
Jameson, Fredric 2, 4, 132, 206
Janco, Marcel 10–1
Jarry, Alfred 9–10, 193, 212, 215, 224
Jazz Age 29, 32
Jefferson, Thomas 99, 111, 115
Jeffersonian Democracy 102–3, 106, 111, 113, 115
Jeffersons (CBS, 1975–85) 101, 135, 199
Jenkins, Henry 125, 130
Jerry Springer Show (syndicated, 1991–) 2
Jetsons (ABC, 1962–4; CBS, 1964–5) 201–2
Jimmy's Famous Deli 169, 242c8n46
Johns, Jasper 245c10n18
Johnson, Arte 127, 129, 132
Johnson, Lyndon Baines 103, 123–4, 129–30
Johnson, Van 128
Jolson, Bernie 145
Jones, Chuck 49, 73
Jones, Davy 117
Jones, Dorothy Ida 147

Kafka, Franz 3, 24, 46, 72
Kane, Carol 177
Karloff, Boris 50
Kaufman, Andy 1–2, 4, 44, 81–2, 91–2, 138, 152, 155–161, **162**, 163–191, 196–8, 205, 240c8n11
Kaufman, Michael **162**
Keaton, Buster 9, 12–3, 16–9, 24, **25**, 26–7, 31, 49, 62, 65–7, 73, 75, 88
Keeshan, Bob (a.k.a. "Captain Kangaroo") 82
Kemp, David 206
Kennedy, Jacqueline 104, 164
Kennedy, John F. 103, 164, 199
Kennedy, Robert F. 123, 129
Keyes, Paul 129–30
Keystone Cops 13
Kiely, Richard 35
King, Martin Luther, Jr. 123
The Kinsey Report 143
Kirshner, Don 117–8, 235c6n5
The Kiss (Rodin) 70

Kitsch 38, 83, 104, 189, 215
Klapp, Orrin E. 216
Kluge, Alexander 63–4, 206
Knotts, Don 99
Kovacs, Ernie 1, 4, 15, 18, 22, 46, 49–50, **51**, 52–78, 86, 91, 93–4, 100, 127, 132, 136, 173, 181, 183–4, 196, 206, 229c3n9, 230c3n21
Kovacs Unlimited (WCBS, 1952–4) 49
Kraft Television Theater (NBC, 1947–1958; concurrent on ABC, 1953–5) 34–5
Ku Klux Klan 128, 130, 246c11n8
Kuenzli, Rudolf E. 17, 94

Lacan, Jacques 23–4, 26, 105, 107, 109–10, 113, 234c5n21
Landis, Monty 118
Langdon, Harry 9
Lange, Jim 145, 155
Langston, Murray 37, 152, 239c7n29
Language 10, 22–3, 30, 69, 83, 89, 92, 105, 109, 112, 116, 206; *see also* Symbolic Order
Late Night with Conan O'Brien (NBC, 1993–) 206, 232c4n6
Late Night with David Letterman (NBC, 1982–93) 163, 166, 173–80
Late Show Starring Joan Rivers (FOX, 1986–8) 200
Late Show with David Letterman (CBS, 1993–) 239c7n32
Laugh-In see *Rowan and Martin's Laugh-In*
Laugh tracks 58–9, 61, 91, 136
Laughter: laughing with versus laughing at 42–5, 135, 143, 149, 160, 178, 185, 191, 207, 210, 216, 223–4, 240c8n15, 245c10n18
Lauher, Bobby 58, 65
Laurel and Hardy 40, 45, 227c1n50
Laverne and Shirley (ABC, 1976–83) 181, 199
The Law 109–11, 115; *see also* Symbolic Order
Lawler, Jerry "The King" 157, 173–8, 243c8n62
Lawrence, Martin 244c8n5
Lawrence Welk Show (ABC, 1955–71; syndicated, 1971–82) 37, 125, 133–4, 171
Lear, Norman 4, 134–8, 145, 155, 198–9, 222, 244c9n7
Leave It to Beaver (CBS, 1957–8; ABC, 1958–63) 41, 88, 100
La Leçon (*The Lesson*) 23–24
LeCornec, Bill 78
Lee, Pinky 81–3, 86–7, 146
Léger, Fernand 14
Leonid the Magnificent 150–1
Leppert, Richard 180
Lester, Richard 117, 119
Lester, Tom 107
Lethal Weapon films 217
Letterman, David 173, 175–6, 180
Lewis, Jerry 66, 230c3n35
Lewis, Richard 158
L.H.O.O.Q. (Duchamp) 165, 231c3n44
Liberal democracy 219
Liberal-humanism 4, 83, 134, 199, 221

Index

Liberal/Liberalism 1, 3, 130, 134–5, 137, 166–7, 199, 201, 203, 208–11, 217, 219, 224; American 220; Classical 220–1, 224, 246c11n13
Libertarianism 220–1, 246c11n19
Life of Riley (NBC, 1953–8) 40
Li'l Abner 100, 115, 133, 216, 233c5n7
Limbaugh Rush 224
Lincoln, Abraham 102, 109–11, 233–4c5n8–9
Linville, Larry 134
Live-action 83, 213–4
Lloyd, Harold 9, 62
Locke, John 220, 224
Longet, Claudine 196
Lopez, Trini 86
Loren, Sophia 131
Love Connection (syndicated, 1983–94) 238c7n7
Lumière brothers 88
Lunch with Soupy (WXYZ, 1953–60) 84
Lunch with Soupy Sales! (ABC, 1959–61) **85**, 232c4n12
Lynde, Paul 84

Macbeth 9
Machines: man-machine relationship 15, 18, 62–5, 73–4, 159, 226c1n32
"Mack the Knife" 57, 73, 181
Mad (magazine) 125, 223, 236c6n23
Mad Love 39
Madison, James 99
Madonna 164
MADtv (FOX, 1995–) 236c6n23
Magritte, René 14, 57
Make Room for Daddy (ABC, 1953–57) 40; see also *Danny Thomas Show*
Man with a Camera 64–5
Manifest Destiny 79
Marc, David 38, 42–43, 111, 122, 203–4, 207
Marcia, Raphael 148
Marcuse, Herbert 205
Mareuil, Simone 16
Marinetti, F.T 18, 20
Marionettes 10, 78–9, 81, 182, 186–7, 225c1n2, 247c11n23
Marmer, Mike 56, 67
Marquis de Sade *see* Sade
Marriage 143
Married with Children (FOX, 1987–97) 2, 200–1, 204–5
Martin, Dean 66, 93, 128, 154
Martin, Dick 125, **126**, 131, 236c6n24
Martin, Steve 152, 154, 172
Martin and Lewis 227c1n50, 246c11n11
Marx, Harpo 22
Marx, Karl 112–3, 115
Marx Brothers 4–5, **21**, 22, 24, 30–1, 118
Marxism 3, 13, 16, 18, 20–1, 30, 102, 112–5, 226c1n34
*M*A*S*H* (CBS, 1972–83) 3, 134, 137
Mass culture 30–33, 42–3, 72, 143–4, 161, 189
Master-Slave dialectic (Hegel) 35, 245c10n5

Maude (CBS, 1972–8) 135, 167, 199
Mayberry RFD (CBS, 1968–71) 100, 134
McAllister, Mathew P. 204
McCann, Chuck 86, 232c4n14, 236c6n20
McCarthy, Eugene 129
McGowran, Jack 24
McHale's Navy (ABC, 1962–6) 134
McLuhan, Marshall 100, 115, 128, 202
McMahon, Ed 182
Me, Myself, and Irene (Farrelly Brothers) 20
Meadows, Audrey 44
Medicine Man (Kovacs/Keaton sitcom pilot, 1961) 67, 231c3n38
Méliès, Georges 14, 52, 88
Melton, Sid 108
Merkenson, S. Eptaha 84
Merv Griffin Show (syndicated, 1972–86) 163
Messages: overt versus hidden 33–36, 41, 43, 46, 79, 202–3, 208–10, 221
Metromedia 86, 200
Metropolis (Lang) 13
Meyer, Russ 154, 236c6n24
Michaels, Lorne 159, 167–8, 196–8
Mickey Mouse 42
The Midnight Special (NBC, 1972–81) 168–9
"Mighty Mouse" 159
Mike Douglas Show (syndicated, 1962–82) 172
Mikolas, Joe 61, 69–70, 72–3, 76
Mill, John Stuart 220
Milton Berle Show (NBC, 1953–9) 38
Mind of Mencia (Comedy Central, 2005–) 246c11n10
Mirror-stage (Lacan) 26–7, 113
Mr. Bill 168
Mr. Mike's Mondo Video (NBC special, 1979 [unaired]) 2
Mr. Rogers' Neighborhood (PBS, 1968–2001) 83, 88
Mr. Smith Goes to Washington 208, 217
Mitchell, Scooey 145
Mockery: personal verses type 216–7
Modern Times 18, 42–43, 159, 226c1n33
Modernity/modern world 3, 10, 13, 15, 19, 29–30, 42, 52, 64–7, 77, 79, 102–3, 130, 165
Moffitt, John 169–71
Mogulescu, Jack 51–2, 230c3n21
Mona Lisa (da Vinci) 71
Monkees 117–120
Monkees (NBC, 1966–8) 1, 56, 92, 117–119, 125
Monkey Business 21
Monotony 22, 24, 158
Montage: Eisenstein's theory of 19–20, 30, 63, 88–9, 206; Kluge's theory of 63–4, 206; Sales' use of 90, 94
Monty Python's Flying Circus (BBC, 1969–74) 1, 22, 212
Moore, Alvy 107
Morgan, Jaye P. 148, 153, 155
Morgan, Piers 151
Mostel, Zero 24

Index

"The Mouse" 88, 92–3
Mrs. Miller 87, 232c4n18
MTV 1
Multiculturalism 168, 221
The Mummy 39
Muppets 83, 196
Murdoch, Rupert 200, 204
Murphy, Eddie 179, 197–8
Murrow, Edward R. 83
Muybridge, Eadweard 88
My Favorite Husband 40
My Three Sons (ABC 1960–65; CBS, 1965–72) 234c5n12
Le Mystère du château de dé (*The Mystery in the House of Dice*) 15, 52–3, 226c1n22
"Mystery Date" (board game) 142, 237–8c7n4
Mystery Science Theater 3000 (Comedy Central, 1988–96; Sci-Fi Channel, 1997–9) 2

Nabors, Jim 100
Narboni, Jean 132
Nastasi, Frank 91–2, 233c4n24–5
National Lampoon 195, 244c9n3
Natividad, Kitten 154
The Navigator 18
Nazism *see* Fascism
NBC Television Playhouse (1948–55) 34
Nelson, Ozzie 41
Neo-Realism 53
Nesmith, Mike 117–20
Neuss, Wolfgang 57, 73
New Soupy Sales Show (syndicated, 1979) 232–3c4n20
Newhart, Bob 240c8n40
Newlywed Game (ABC, 1966–74; syndicated, 1977–80) 1, 141, 143–5, 154
News Corporation *see* FOX Broadcasting Company
Newton, Sir Isaac/Newtonian physics 53, 105, 155
Nicholson, Jack 119
Nietzsche, Friedrich 222
1968 presidential election 111, 122, 128–30, 135, 236c6n29
Nixon, Richard M. 123–4, 128–30, 135, 195, 197, 199, 236c6n28–9
"No Dialogue" (Ernie Kovacs Special, 1957) *see* "Silent Show"
No Time for Sergeants 233c5n2
North by Northwest (Hitchcock) 217
North to Alaska 50
La Notte (*The Night*) 227c1n51
Novello, Don 241c8n27
Novelty acts 147–8, 150

O'Brien, Conan 190, 206
O'Conner, Carroll 135
O'Conner, Sinéad 244c8n5
O'Donoghue, Michael 2
Olatunji, Babatunde 157
The Old Man and the Sea (Hemingway) 72

One Day at a Time (CBS, 1975–84) 234c5n12
$1.98 Beauty Show (syndicated, 1978–80) 154
"Oriental Blues" (Tony deSimone Trio) 76
Orphans in the Storm 89
Ortega y Gasset, José 222
The Other 38, 43–4, 84, 151, 161, 166, 174, 202, 207, 210, 215–6
Our Man from Havana 50
Our Miss Brooks (CBS, 1952–6) 33, 43
Outsider art 147–8
Overdetermination 82, 109, 112–5, 132, 216, 234c5n40
Owens, Garry 146, 238c7n14

Paglia, Camilla 203
Painting 2, 11, 14–5, 29, 54–5, 61–2, 68, 70–1
Panofsky, Erwin 73
Paragon, John 84
Pardo, Don 159
Paris qui dort (*Paris Sleeps*) 16
Parker, Trey 212, 218, 220
Partridge Family (ABC, 1970–4) 235c6n5
The Passion of the Christ 217–8
Pastiche 4, 84, 164, 206–7, 217
Patriarchy 41–2, 87–8, 106, 203
Patterns (1955 teleplay, *Kraft Television Theater*) 33, 35–6, 65, 220, 245c10n5
Patterson, Hank **105**
Patton Gene (a.k.a. "Gene Gene, the Dancing Machine") 152–3
Paul Winchell and Jerry Mahoney Show (NBC, 1954–6) 79, **80**, 81–2
Paul Winchell Show (ABC, 1957–60) *see* *Paul Winchell and Jerry Mahoney Show*
Paulson, Pat 122, 135
Peanuts 212
Peckham, Dianna 167
Pee-Wee Herman *see* Reubens, Paul
Pee-Wee's Big Adventure (Burton) 152, 232c4n9, 246c11n11
Pee-Wee's Playhouse (CBS, 1986–91) 83–4, 232c4n10, 243c8n74
Pepper, Barbara **105**
Performance art 158, 190
Perry Mason (CBS, 1957–66) 34
Personas 37–8, 82–3, 87; Kaufman's use of 44, 155, 161–4, 166, 174; *see also* stereotypes
Petticoat Junction (CBS, 1963–70) 100, 103, 107, 111, 234c5n12, 237c6n38
Phantasie (Kluge's theory of) 63–4, 206
Philbin, Regis 150
Philco Television Playhouse (NBC, 1948–55) 34
Photo Doody *see* Howdy Doody
Photography 31, 213, 215, 218; *see also* the Camera
Picabia, Francis 13–4, 52, 233c4n27
Pietà (Balma painting) 164
Pietà (Michelangelo sculpture) 164
Pink Lady and Jeff (NBC, 1980) 196
Pinky Lee Show (NBC, 1954–6) 38, 79, 81–2, 152

Pinter, Harold 22
Piscopo, Joe 198
Pitfall (video game) 213
Playboy 38, 125, 130–1, 142
Poetry 5, 9–10, 19, 21, 30–1, 62, 206; verbal 61–2, 127
"Polka (op. 30)" (Shostakovich) 67–8
Pop Art 125, 142, 167, 215
"Pop Goes the Weasel" 159
Pope Paul VI 128
Popsicle Twins 153, 155
Popular culture 4, 33, 38, 78, 122, 128, 132, 135, 156, 161, 177, 187, 189, 201, 206, 217
Postmodernism 1–2, 4, 28, 83, 128, 132, 156, 164, 200–2, 205–11, 217, 223, 245c10n18
Potemkin 19
Pragmatism 99, 102, 104, 108, 111–2, 115, 134
Presley, Elvis 156–7, 161, 178, 185, 187, 189
Pronko, Leonard Cabell 115
Propaganda 164, 216
Protestant work ethic 101, 103, 106, 112, 203
Pryor, Richard 130
Pseudo-activity 32, 82, 183
Pseudo-individuals 32
Pseudo-realism 30–1, 33, 35, 40–1, 44, 88–90, 95, 136, 213
Public access 1
Puppets/Puppet shows 9–10, 78, 85, 87, 89, 168, 196; *see also* Marionettes

Race relations 84, 101, 118, 122, 125, 129–30, 145, 166, 168, 186, 199, 207, 216, 221, 246c11n8
Radio 2, 37, 40
Rafelson, Bob 117, 119
Rakolta, Terry 201
Rand, Ayn 221
Ray, Man 9, 12–6, 19, 52–3, 62, 158
Reagan, Ronald 166, 199
Real McCoys (ABC, 1957–62; CBS, 1962–3) 99
Reality: destabilization of 5, 16–9, 21–2, 28, 30–31, 46, 56, 67, 74–5, 77, 89, 94–5, 97, 163–6, 168, 179, 191
Red Skelton Show (NBC, 1951–3, 1970–1; CBS, 1953–70) 38, 134
Reed, Donna 41
Reference (cultural) 4, 60, 132, 164, 201, 205–10, 217–8; *see also* Postmodernism
Reiner, Rob 135
Reubens, Paul 82–3, 152, 154
Richard Pryor Show (NBC, 1977) 2
Richards, Michael 155, 169–70, 242c8n48
Rico, Diane 63, 67, 75
Ritter, John 154
Roarke, John 170
Roberts, Doris 32
Rock music 38, 120, 157
Rocket, Charles 197
Rockwell, Norman 83, 104
Rocky and Bullwinkle (various, 1959–73) 2, 201

Rocky and His Friends (ABC, 1959–61) see *Rocky and Bullwinkle*
Rodriguez, Roland 84
Rogers, Fred 83
Rogers, "Nature Boy" Buddy 157–8, 167–8, 175
Romano, Ray 205
Roucia, Emilio 148
Rowan, Dan 125, **126**, 130
Rowan and Martin's Laugh-In (NBC, 1968–72) 1, 4, 38, 56–7, 92, 100, 118, 120, 122, 124–5, **126**, 127–35, 142, 146, 195–8, 232c4n15, 236c6n23, 238c7n14
Rowe, Red 153
Rural comedy (TV genre) 100, 133–4; *see also* rural sitcom
Rural sitcom 99–103, 105, 108, 111, 115, 216
Russian Revolution 19, 29
Ryan, Irene 102, 217

Sábado gigante (*Giant Saturday*, Univision, 1986–) 1
Sade 72, 212, 218–9, 221, 224
Sadism: role of in mass culture 42, 143, 148–51; *see also* laughter: laughing with versus laughing at
Sahl, Mort 130
Sales, Soupy 1, 4, 22, 46, 57, 77–8, 84, **85**, 86–95, 145, 158
Sammartino, Bruno 157
Sandy Becker Show (WNEW, 1961–8) 86
Sanford and Son (NBC, 1972–7) 244c9n7
La Sang d'un poète (*Blood of a Poet*) 15
Satire: problematics of 135, 166–7, 207, 210, 216–7, 223–4
Saturday Night Live (NBC, 1975–) 155, 158–61, 167–9, 174–5, 178–81, 183–4, 195–9
"Scarlet and Rhett" (*Gong Show* cast) 152
Schell, Ronnie 145
Schlafly, Phyllis 203
Schlatter, George 125, 129, 236c6n25
Schneider, Alan 24–25
Schneider, Bert 117, 119
The Scream (Munch) 213
Screwball comedy 40
SCTV (syndicated, 1976–80; NBC, 1981–3) 2, 196
Scully, Mike 205
Sculpture 70
Seacrest, Ryan 150
Seeger, Pete 120, 122–3
Segal, Katy 204
Seinfeld (NBC, 1990–8) 2
Self-censorship 34–5, 79, 127, 214–5
Self-reference *see* self-reflexivity
Self-reflexivity 41, 58–9, 87, 92–4, 127–8, 181, 186–7, 196, 204, 234c5n22
Selleck, Tom 154, 239c7n36
Sennett, Mack 13–5, 40, 118
Serials 13, 15, 76
Serling, Rod 33, 35, 228c2n23, 228c2n29
Sesame Street (PBS, 1969–) 83–84, 88

Sex Pistols 241c8n33
Sexual Revolution 38, 103, 125, 129–31, 142–3
Sexuality 38, 84, 130–1, 141–3
Shakespeare, William 9, 120, 155, 209, 219
Shandling, Gary 41
Shapiro, George 163
Shearer, Harry 190, 198
Sherlock, Jr. 18, 26–27
Shock effect 12, 14, 20, 27, 54–56, 58, 63–4, 71, 81, 206; expected shock and 131, 151; shock value versus 153, 206, 218–9
Shore, Dinah 172–3
Short, Martin 198
Sid Caesar Invites You (ABC, 1958) 38
Sierra, Gregory 136
Sight-gags 24, 40; Kovacs' use of 51–58, 66–76; *Laugh-In*'s use of 125–7
Silence 136, 159–60, 240c8n13
Silent Majority 125, 199
"Silent Show" (Ernie Kovacs special, 1957) 50, *51*, 65–6, 75, 229–30c3n10
Silents Please (ABC, 1960–1) 52, 229c3n8
Silverman, Fred 197
Simpson, Gary 147–8
Simpsons (FOX, 1989–) 1, 4, 33, 199–211, 213, 215–21, 223, 245c10n9, 245–6c11n4
Sinatra, Frank 86, 94, 125, 144
Sitcoms 2–4, 38–46, 55, 60, 87–8, 91, 94–5, 100, 106, 116, 133–8, 155, 198–201, 203–4, 211, 213, 215, 229c2n34; Kaufman's view of 161, 172; *see also* rural sitcoms
Situation-comedy (genre) *see* sitcoms
Situationist 2, 4, 157, 164–5, 172, 174, 177, 241c8n30; Kaufman as 166–81, 191; *see also* situations
Situations 165, 191, 179–80
60 Minutes (CBS, 1968–) 150
Skelton, Red 37–8, 122, 169
Sketch comedy 2, 4, 37, 53–5, 57, 68–9, 83, 94, 198, 201
Sloane, Everett 35–6
Smirnoff, Yakov 240c8n15
Smith, Adam 220
Smith, Buffalo Bob 78, 182, 186–7
Smith, Kate 122
Smothers, Dick *121*
Smothers, Tom 117, 120, *121*, 122–4
Smothers Brothers 120, *121*, 122–5, 129–30, 133, 158, 195, 199
Smothers Brothers Comedy Hour (CBS, 1967–9) 1, 3, 46, 100, 118, 120, *121*, 122–5, 129, 132, 134, 195
Smothers Brothers Show (CBS, 1965–6) 120
Snyder, Tom 167, 196
Social Darwinism 150
"Solfeggio" (Maxwell) 62, 230c3n26
Sommers, Jay 103
"Song of the Siren" 119
Sontag, Susan 20, 77
Sound: role in television of 40, 55, 59–60; Kovacs' use of 53–5, 66, 68–74

Sound-poems 10, 148
Soundstage ("The Andy Kaufman Show," 1983) 81, 157, 172, 180–9
Soupy Sales! (ABC, 1955) 85
Soupy Sales Show (ABC, 1962) 232c4n11
Soupy Sales Show (WNEW, 1964–6; syndicated, 1965–6) 27, 83–95
Soupy's Soda Shop (WKRC, 1950–1) 233c4n29
South Park (Comedy Central, 1997–) 1, 206, 209–10, 212–3, *214*, 215–24
Soviet Cinema 21, 29–30, 49, 89
Sponsors 34–5, 38, 50–2, 79, 86, 152
Sports Illustrated 213
Stalinism 29
Stand-up comedy 2, 37, 54, 86, 195; Kaufman's use of 156–62, 165, 168–9, 172
Stapleton, Jean 135
State of nature (Hobbes) 220–1, 238c7n23
Steinberg, David 124
Stendhal 100
Stereotypes 33, 35–8, 41, 61, 78, 84, 87, 126–7, 131, 135, 152, 160–1, 168, 174, 202–3, 207–10, 215–8, 246c11n10; *see also* mockery: personal versus type
Stewart, Jimmy 41, 208
Stewart, Marie Lynne 84
Stewart, Morris "Butch" 184
Stockhausen, Karlheinz 64
Stoler, Shirley 84
Stone, Matt 212, 218, 220
Strike 202
Struthers, Sally 135
Studio production 32, 39, 136, 163, 166; Kovacs' method of 52–3, 58–9, 91; Sales' method of 91, 233c4n28
Suburbia 42–4, 83, 87–8, 90–1, 94, 130
Sullivan, Ed 37, 93, 146
Sullivan, Kathie 171, 242c8n53
Sumac, Yma 50
Supremes 86
Surrealism 2, 4, 9–10, 12–22, 27, 29–30, 42, 47, 49, 127, 133, 206; Kovacs and 52, 56–8; 62–6, 70, 77, 91, 94; Sales and 89, 94
Survivor (CBS, 2000–) 150, 238c7n23
Sutton, Gregg 156
Swan Lake 62
Symbolic Order 18, 22, 24, 83, 92, 105–7, 109–112

Take a Good Look (ABC, 1959–61) 50–2, 57
Talk shows 61, 80–1, 122, 171–3, 181–2
Tati, Jacques 67, 231c3n40
Taxi (ABC, 1978–82; NBC 1982–3) 155, 160–3, 169, 171, 177, 181, 189, 243c8n63–4
Taylor, Rip 119, 154
Tchaikovsky, Pyotr 62–64, 74
Team America: World Police 247c11n23
Teleplays 34–6, 100, 136, 138, 155, 165, 198
Teletubbies (BBC, 1997–2001) 231c4n2
Texaco Star Theater (NBC, 1948–52) 38
That 70s Show (FOX, 1998–2006)

That's My Bush! (Comedy Central, 2001) 247c11n25
Theater 29, 37, 52, 54–5, 59–60, 179
Theater of Cruelty 4, 19–20, 77
Theater of the Absurd 10, 22, 24, 116
"Thick as a Brick" (Jethro Tull) 209
The Thinker (Rodin) 70
33 and 1/3 Revolutions per Monkees (NBC special, 1969) 119–20
Thomas, Danny 40–1
Thoreau, Henry David 111, 114
Three Stooges 40, 217
The Threepenny Opera (Weill-Brecht) 57
3's a Crowd (syndicated, 1978) 154
Toast of the Town (CBS, 1948–55) see *Ed Sullivan Show*
Tolerance 83–4, 92, 137, 199, 221–2
Tom Green Show (MTV, 1999–2000) 2
Tomorrow (NBC, 1973–82) 167, 196
Tonight Show (NBC, 1954–) 50, 54, 66, 81, 160, 171–3, 182
Tork, Peter 117, 119–20
Toth, Lazlo 164, 241c8n27
Tracy Ullman Show (FOX, 1987–90) 201
Trotsky, Leon 227c1n42
True Confessions (magazine) 143
Turn-On (ABC, 1969) 236c6n20
20th Century Fox 200
Twilight Zone (CBS, 1959–64) 34, 60, 228c2n23, 228c2n29
Two-reelers 13–6, 24, 39–40, 52, 66, 118
Tyler, Judy 78
Tzara, Tristan 10–1, 13, 16, 139, 147–8, 151, 158, 206

Ubu (Jarry play cycle) 9, 212, 225c1n2
Ubu cocu (*Ubu Cuckolded*) 9
Ubu enchaîné (*Ubu Enchained*) 9, 193
Ubu roi (*King Ubu*) 9–10, 22, 215
Ubu sur a Butte (*Ubu on the Mound*) 225c1n2
Ullman, Tracy 201
Ultradétournement 164
Underground comics 215
The Unknown Comic *see* Langston, Murray
Untouchables (CBS, 1959–63) 34
U.S. Steel Hour (ABC, 1953–5; CBS, 1955–63) 34

Les Vampires 13
Vance, Vivian 43
Van Dyke, Dick 161
Van Dyke and Co. (NBC, 1976) 161
Vaneigem, Raoul 164, 219, 246c11n13
Variety shows *see* comedy-variety shows
Vaudeville 23–4, 27, 37–8, 58, 81–3, 86, 89, 118, 122, 125, 133, 157, 195
Ventriloquism 79–80, 168
Verbal comedy 40, 49, 53, 55, 61–2, 80, 106, 159, 168; *Laugh-In*'s use of writing as 128–9
Vertov, Dziga 64–5, 89
Vietnam 86, 100, 118–9, 122–5, 129–30, 134, 199, 209

Voice: role of in television 40, 59–60
Voltaire 210

Wacky World of Jonathan Winters (syndicated, 1972–4) 2
"Waist Deep in the Big Muddy" 3
Waiting for Godot 24, 107
Wallace, George 129–31, 236c6n29
Wallace, Mike 150
Waltons (CBS, 1972–81) 201
War and Peace 72
War at Home (FOX, 2005–7) 228–9c2n33
Warhol, Andy 132, 144, 167
Warner Brothers cartoons 64, 213
Washington Crossing the Delaware (Luetze) 71
Watergate 199
Wayne, John 128–9
"We Didn't Start the Fire" (Billy Joel) 206, 245c10n13
Weber, Max 42, 107
Weinberger, Ed 163
Welch, Raquel 128, 131
Welk, Lawrence 139
Western (genre) 31, 34, 60–61, 69–70, 78–9, 122
Western Literature 31, 33, 55, 62, 71–2, 88
Western Theater 9–10, 19, 21, 24, 31, 35, 62, 88, 137
Westmoreland, William 130
Which Way to the Front? 230c3n35
Whistler's Mother 61
White, Betty 204
Whitman, Slim 169, 180
Williams, Cindy 181, 199
Williams, Raymond 112, 234–5c5n32
Williams, Robin 88, 191
Willis, Wesley 238c7n17
Wilson, Flip 130
Wilson, S. Clay 223
Winchell, Paul 79, **80**, 2231c4n4, 238c7n14
WNEW 85–8, 200
Wood, Robert D. 124, 158
World of Warcraft 213
World War I 10, 18, 29
World War II 18, 29, 123, 127, 213, 216
Worley, Jo Anne 128, 130–1
Wrestling 156–7, 165–9, 173–80, 189–1, 243c8n62; as theater 157, 167–8

Young, Chick 100, 202
Young, Robert 41
Young Mr. Lincoln 102, 109
Young Ones (BBC, 1982, 1984) 1
Youngman, Henny 86
Your Show of Shows (NBC, 1950–4) 2, 38

Zappa, Frank 119, 196
Zehme, Bill 240c8n10
Žežik, Slavoj 105, 109
Zmuda, Bob 161, 163, 166–74, 178, 180–1, 186–7, 239c8n4
The Zoo Story 164